iPhone
The Missing Manual

Tenth Edition

iPhone: The Missing Manual, Tenth Edition   BY DAVID POGUE

Published by O'Reilly Media, Inc., 1005 Gravenstein Highway North, Sebastopol, CA 95472.

O'Reilly books may be purchased for educational, business, or sales promotional use. Online editions are also available for most titles *(oreilly.com/safari)*. For more information, contact our corporate/institutional sales department: 800.998.9938 or *corporate@oreilly.com*.

Copy Editor: Julie Van Keuren

Indexers: David Pogue, Julie Van Keuren

Cover Designers: Monica Kamsvaag and Phil Simpson

Interior Designer: Phil Simpson (based on a design by Ron Bilodeau)

Print History:
      January 2017.   First Printing.

ISBN: 978-1-49-197924-2

Contents

Part Two: Pix, Flix & Apps

Part Five: Appendixes

The Missing Credits

 David Pogue (author, illustrator) is the tech columnist for Yahoo Finance (*yahoofinance.com*), the world's biggest business publication. He was groomed for that job by 13 years of writing the weekly tech column for *The New York Times*. He's also a monthly columnist for *Scientific American*, a four-time Emmy-winning correspondent for *CBS News Sunday Morning*, the host of 20 *NOVA* specials on PBS, and the creator of the Missing Manual series.

David has written or cowritten more than 100 books, including dozens in the Missing Manual series, six in the *For Dummies* line (including *Macs, Magic, Opera,* and *Classical Music*), two novels (one for middle-schoolers called *Abby Carnelia's One and Only Magical Power*), *The World According to Twitter,* and three books of essential tips and shortcuts: *Pogue's Basics: Tech, Pogue's Basics: Life,* and *Pogue's Basics: Money.*

In his other life, David is a former Broadway show conductor, a magician, and a funny public speaker. He lives in Connecticut with his wife, Nicki, and three awesome children.

Links to his columns and videos await at *www.davidpogue.com*. He welcomes feedback about his books by email at *david@pogueman.com*.

Julie Van Keuren (editor, indexer, layout) spent 14 years in print journalism before deciding to upend her life, move to Montana, and live the freelancing dream. She now works for a variety of clients who understand that skilled editing, writing, book layout, and indexing don't have to come from inside a cubicle. She and her husband, sci-fi writer M.H. Van Keuren, have two teenage sons. Email: *little_media@yahoo.com*.

Rich Koster (technical reviewer). The iPhone became Rich's first cellphone the very first evening it was sold. He began corresponding with David Pogue, sharing tips, tricks, and observations; eventually, David asked him to be the beta reader for the first edition of iPhone: The Missing Manual—and hired him as the tech editor of subsequent editions. For this edition of the book, Rich is glad to say all the work involved was accomplished on the iPhone 7 Plus. Rich is a husband, father, graphic artist, writer, and Disney fan (@DisneyEcho on Twitter).

Phil Simpson (original design) runs his graphic design business from Southbury, Connecticut. His work includes corporate branding, publication design, communications support, and advertising. He lives with his wife and some great felines. Email: *phil.simpson@pmsgraphics.com*.

Acknowledgments

The Missing Manual series is a joint venture between the dream team introduced on these pages and O'Reilly Media. I'm grateful to all of them, especially to the core of the iPhone Missing Manual team introduced here.

The work done on previous editions lives on in this one; for that, I'm grateful to Jude Biersdorfer, Matt Gibstein, Teresa Brewer, Brian Jepson, Apple's Trudy Muller, Philip Michaels, O'Reilly's Nan Barber, and my incredible assistant Jan Carpenter, who keeps me from falling apart like wet Kleenex. Thanks to David Rogelberg and Tim O'Reilly for believing in the idea; to Kellee Katagi for proofreading; and above all, to Nicki, Kell, Tia, and Jeffrey. They make these books—and everything else—possible.

—David Pogue

Also by David Pogue

- *macOS Sierra: The Missing Manual*
- *Windows 10: The Missing Manual*
- *Switching to the Mac: The Missing Manual, El Capitan Edition*
- *David Pogue's Digital Photography: The Missing Manual*
- *The World According to Twitter*
- *Pogue's Basics: Tech*
- *Pogue's Basics: Life*
- *Pogue's Basics: Money*

Introduction

How do you make the point that the iPhone has changed the world? The easy answer is "use statistics"—1 billion sold, 2 million apps available on the iPhone App Store, 140 billion downloads…. Trouble is, those statistics get stale almost before you've finished typing them.

Maybe it's better to talk about the aftermath. How since the iPhone came along, cell carriers (AT&T, Verizon, Sprint, and so on) have opened up the calcified, conservative way they used to consider new cellphone designs. How every phone and its brother now have a touchscreen. How Google (Android) phones, Windows phones, and even BlackBerry phones all have their own app stores. How, in essence, everybody wants to be the iPhone.

Apple introduces a new iPhone model every fall. In September 2016, for example, it introduced the tenth iPhone models, the iPhone 7 and 7 Plus, with more features and faster guts.

More importantly, there's a new, free version of the iPhone's software, called iOS 10. (Why not "iPhone OS" anymore? Because the same operating system runs on the iPad and the iPod Touch. It's not just for iPhones, and saying "the iPhone/iPad/iPod Touch OS" takes too long.)

You can run iOS 10 on *older* iPhone models without having to buy a new phone. This book covers all the phones that can run iOS 10: the iPhone 5, iPhone 5c, iPhone 5s, iPhone 6 and 6 Plus, iPhone 6s and 6s Plus, iPhone SE, and iPhone 7 and 7 Plus.

About the iPhone

So what is the iPhone? Really, the better question is what *isn't* the iPhone?

It's a cellphone, obviously. But it's also a full-blown iPod, complete with a dazzling screen for watching videos. And it's a sensational pocket Internet viewer. It shows fully formatted email (with attachments, thank you) and displays entire web pages with fonts and design intact. It's tricked out with a tilt sensor, a proximity sensor, a light sensor, Wi-Fi, Bluetooth, GPS, a gyroscope, a barometer, and that amazing multitouch screen.

For many people, the iPhone is primarily a camera and a camcorder—one that's getting better with every year's new model.

Furthermore, it's a calendar, address book, calculator, alarm clock, stopwatch, stock tracker, traffic reporter, RSS reader, and weather forecaster. It even stands in for a flashlight and, with the screen off, a pocket mirror.

TIP: If you want a *really* good pocket mirror, you can also use the Camera app in self-portrait mode. It's a brighter view (and you don't have to actually take a selfie).

And don't forget the App Store. Thanks to the 2 million add-on programs that await there, the iPhone is also a fast, wicked-fun pocket computer. All those free or cheap programs can turn it into a medical reference, a musical keyboard, a time tracker, a remote control, a sleep monitor, a tip calculator, an ebook reader, and more. Plus, the App Store is a portal to thousands of games, with smooth 3D graphics and tilt control.

All of this sends the iPhone's utility and power through the roof. Calling it a phone is practically an insult. (Apple probably should have called it an "iPod," but that name was taken.)

About This Book

You don't get a printed manual when you buy an iPhone. Online, you can find an electronic PDF manual that covers the basics well, but it's largely free of details, hacks, workarounds, tutorials, humor, and any acknowledgment of the iPhone's flaws. You can't easily mark your place, underline, or read it in the bathroom.

The purpose of this book, then, is to serve as the manual that should have accompanied the iPhone. (If you have an iPhone 4s or an earlier model, you really need one of this book's earlier editions. If you have an iPhone 5 or later model, this book assumes that you've installed iOS 10.2; see Appendix A.)

Writing a book about the iPhone is a study in exasperation, because the darned thing is a moving target. Apple updates the iPhone's software fairly often, piping in new features, bug fixes, speed-ups, and so on.

Therefore, you should think of this book the way you think of the first iPhone: as an excellent start. To keep in touch with updates we make to it as developments unfold, drop in to the book's Errata/Changes page. (Go to *www.missingmanuals.com*, click this book's name, and then click **View/Submit Errata**.)

> **TIP:** This book covers the iOS 10.2 software. There will surely be a 10.2.1, a 10.3, and so on. Check this book's page at *www.missingmanuals.com* to read about those updates when they occur.

About the Outline

iPhone: The Missing Manual is divided into five parts, each containing several chapters:

- Part 1, **The iPhone as Phone**, covers everything related to phone calls: dialing, answering, voice control, voicemail, conference calling, text messaging, iMessages, MMS, and the Contacts (address book) program. It's also where you can read about FaceTime, the iPhone's video-calling feature; Siri, the "virtual assistant"; and the surprisingly rich array of features for people with disabilities—some of which are useful even for people without them.

- Part 2, **Pix, Flix & Apps**, is dedicated to the iPhone's built-in software, with a special emphasis on its multimedia abilities: playing music, podcasts, movies, and TV shows; taking and displaying photos; capturing photos and videos; using the Maps app; reading ebooks; and so on. These chapters also cover some of the standard techniques that most apps share: installing, organizing, and quitting them; switching among them; and sharing material from within them using the Share sheet.

- Part 3, **The iPhone Online**, is a detailed exploration of the iPhone's third talent: its ability to get you onto the Internet, either over a Wi-Fi hotspot connection or via the cellular network. It's all here: email, web browsing, and tethering (that is, letting your phone serve as a sort of Internet antenna for your laptop).

- Part 4, **Connections**, describes the world beyond the iPhone itself—like the copy of iTunes on your Mac or PC that can fill up the iPhone with music, videos, and photos; and syncing the calendar, address book, and mail settings. These chapters also cover the iPhone's control panel, the Settings program; Continuity (the wireless integration of iPhone and Mac); and how the iPhone syncs wirelessly with corporate networks using Microsoft Exchange ActiveSync—or with your own computers using Apple's iCloud service.

- Part 5, **Appendixes**, contains two reference chapters. Appendix A walks you through the setup process; Appendix B is a master compendium of troubleshooting, maintenance, and battery information.

About→These→Arrows

Throughout this book, and throughout the Missing Manual series, you'll find sentences like this one: Tap **Settings→General→Keyboard**. That's shorthand for a much longer instruction that directs you to open three nested screens in sequence, like this: "Tap the **Settings** icon. On the next screen, tap **General**. On the screen after that, tap **Keyboard**." (In this book, tappable things on the screen are printed in **orange** to make them stand out.)

Similarly, this kind of arrow shorthand helps to simplify the business of choosing commands in menus on your Mac or PC, like **File→Print**.

About MissingManuals.com

Missing Manuals are witty, well-written guides to computer products that don't come with printed manuals (which is just about all of them). Each book features a handcrafted index; cross-references to specific page numbers (not just "see Chapter 14"); and an ironclad promise never to put an apostrophe in the possessive pronoun *its*.

To get the most out of this book, visit *www.missingmanuals.com*. Click the **Missing CDs** link, and then click this book's title to reveal a neat, organized list of the shareware, freeware, and bonus articles mentioned in this book.

The website also offers corrections and updates to the book; to see them, click the book's title, and then click **View/Submit Errata**. In fact, please submit corrections yourself! Each time we print more copies of this book, we'll make any confirmed corrections you've suggested. We'll also note such changes on the website, so you can mark important corrections into your own copy of the book, if you like. And we'll keep the book current as Apple releases more iPhone updates.

iPhone 7 and 7 Plus: What's New

Apple's usual routine is to introduce a new iPhone shape every other year (iPhone 3G, iPhone 4, iPhone 5, iPhone 6)—and then release a follow-up, upgraded "s" model in alternate years (iPhone 3GS, iPhone 4s, iPhone 5s, iPhone 6s). The 2016–2017 models fit right in. They're follow-up models that look exactly like the 6 and 6s but have a few enhancements:

- **No headphone jack.** Most people wouldn't call the removal of the headphone jack an enhancement; in fact, people shrieked and moaned. Now, to listen to audio privately, you have to use either (a) the adapter in the box (which accommodates existing headphones and plugs them into the Lightning charging jack), (b) the earbuds in the box (which also plug into the charging jack), or (c) wireless earbuds or headphones.

  So why did Apple get rid of the headphone jack? Because of size. The headphone jack may not seem very big—but on the *inside* of the phone, the corresponding receptacle occupies an unnerving amount of nonnegotiable space. Getting rid of it let Apple upgrade the speakers, battery, and camera, and helped make the iPhone 7 water- and dust-resistant.

- **Water resistance.** Yes, that's right: The iPhone is, at long last, water resistant. It can handle up to 30 minutes under a meter of water. Which means that rain and falls into the toilet can't hurt it.

  Apple's late to this ball game, but it's a really good ball game.

> **NOTE:** In addition to the standard metal colors (matte black, silver, gold, pink gold), there's a new finish available called Jet Black. It's glistening, shiny, deep piano black. It's gorgeous and sleek and smooth and you want to rub it like it's a worry stone. It's also incredibly fingerprinty. (Apple warns that "its high shine may show fine micro-abrasions with use," so it suggests that "you use one of the many cases available to protect your iPhone.")

- **Better battery.** The iPhone 7 battery is 14 percent larger than the previous model's—two hours more life per charge, says Apple—and you notice it. (The improvement in the larger Plus model is more modest: one extra hour per charge.)

- **Better, stabilized camera.** Apple makes a big deal of the iPhone 7's new camera. It's got more megapixels (12, up from 8), and the front camera has been goosed to 7 megapixels. Megapixels don't really mean very much, though; they have no effect on picture quality.

  Apple also raves about the camera's f/1.8 aperture (lets in a lot of light).

  The stabilized lens helps a lot—an internal assembly that acts as a shock absorber to counteract the typical tiny hand jiggles that often introduce blur into low-light photos.

  All of this makes a huge difference in low-light videos. The color is clearer, and the graininess much less pronounced. Low-light stills are enhanced to a lesser degree.

  The flash on the back is now made up of four LEDs instead of two, resulting in flashes (and flashlights) that are 50 percent brighter than before.

- **Two lenses.** On the iPhone 7 Plus, the camera enhancement is much bigger: Apple has installed *two* lenses, one wide-angle, one telephoto. With a tap on the screen, you can zoom in 2x. This is true optical zoom (rather than the simulated digital zoom on most phones, which impairs the photo quality). You can also dial up any amount of optical zoom between 1x and 2x.

  You can zoom before taking a still photo, or even while you're shooting video.

NOTE: Once you're at 2x zoom, the camera automatically switches to its regular digital zoom. That means the 7 Plus iPhone now offers up to 6x total zoom for video and *10x* for photos. That's twice what the previous models could manage.

The dual lenses also make possible a great feature Apple calls Portrait mode. It gives you the gorgeously soft-focused background that's common in professional photography.

- **Better screen.** Apple makes much of the iPhone 7's new screen with its "expanded color gamut," meaning that it can display more colors than previous screens, and its "25 percent brighter" display.

- **Stereo speakers.** The iPhone now has stereo speakers! They're at the top and bottom of the phone, so you don't get the stereo effect unless the phone is sitting sideways. Even then, there's very little left/right channel separation.

  But never mind that: The iPhone 7's audio system overall is definitely better than before. It may not be twice as loud, as Apple claims, but you'd definitely say that the 7 sounds fuller and stronger than previous models.

- **Faster processor.** This year's iPhone processor has four cores (brains), two of which are dedicated to lower-importance tasks (and consume less power—one of the reasons the phone gets better battery life).

- **More storage.** The pathetically small 16-gigabyte iPhone has finally gone to the great junk drawer in the sky. Now the three iPhone storage capacities are 32, 128, and 256 gigabytes (for $650, $750, and $850; installment and rental plans are available). For the larger 7 Plus model, the prices are $770, $870, and $970.

- **Immobile Home button.** The Home button, central to so many iPhone features—waking the phone, switching apps, commanding Siri, and so on—is no longer a moving, mechanical part. Now, when you press it, you *feel* a click, but it's actually a fakeout, a sharp internal vibration.

  The advantages of this setup: You can adjust how clicky the button is. There's no gap for water to get in. And this Home button is pressure-sensitive—it knows when you're pressing harder—which could someday permit some cool new features nobody's even thought of yet.

What's New in iOS 10

The design for iOS 10 doesn't look much different from iOS 9 before it (or iOS 8, or iOS 7); the improvements are focused on features and flexibility.

> **TIP:** If the fonts are too thin for your taste, you can fatten them up just enough by going to Settings→Display & Brightness and turning on Bold Text. While you're there, you can make text larger in most apps, too; tap the Text Size control.

You'd have to write an entire book to document everything that's new or changed in iOS 10; it's a *huge* upgrade. But here's a quick rundown.

Big-Ticket Items

First, there's been a colossal revamp of Messages, Apple's text-messaging app. Now you can dress up your messages with a wide range of hilarious new visual treats, animations, and effects, inspired by the ones in, for example, Snapchat and Facebook Messenger.

Second, Apple has rethought that moment when you pick up the phone—a hundred times a day. The iPhone now requires fewer steps to unlock itself, check the latest alerts, or fire up the camera.

A new option in Settings called "Raise to Wake" (available in the 6S, 7, and SE families) makes the screen turn on when you just pick up the phone.

Nips and Tucks

- **Mutlipage Control Center.** For years now, you've been able to swipe upward from the bottom of the screen—anytime, in any app—to see the Control Center. It's a single quick-access panel containing the most important switches, like airplane mode, Wi-Fi on/off, Bluetooth on/off, and the flashlight.

  In iOS 10, the audio-playback controls sit on a second Control Center screen, to the right of the first. (In the unlikely event that you have any HomeKit home-automation gadgets at your house, a third Control Center panel appears, so that you can control them.)

  Also, you can hard-press or long-press the buttons at the bottom of the Control Center to get shortcut menus of useful settings. For example, the flashlight button now offers Low, Medium, or High brightness!

- **Siri is more open.** Until now, only Apple decided what Siri, the voice-controlled assistant, could understand. Now, though, the creators of certain apps can teach Siri new vocabulary, too. Already, you can say, "Send Nicki a message with WeChat," "Pay Dad 20 dollars with Square Cash," and "Book a ride with Lyft."

- **Emergency Bypass.** This switch, new on each person's Contacts card, means "Let ringtones and vibrations play when this person calls, even when Do Not Disturb is turned on." A million parents will now get better sleep at night.

- **Recent searches.** When you tap Search in Notes, Mail, or Spotlight Suggestions, you see a list of suggested searches or previous searches you've conducted, to save you a little time.

- **Remember my parked car.** Maps automatically drops a pin at the spot when your phone disconnects from your car's Bluetooth system (or CarPlay system, if you have that). Later, it can guide you back.

- **More 3D Touch features.** If you have a phone whose screen responds to pressure (iPhone 6s and 7 families), you'll find more shortcut menus available in more places. For example, you can reply to a text-message notification, accept a Calendar invitation, or see where your Uber is on a map, all by hard-pressing. If you hard-press a Home-screen folder, there's now a Rename command. And if you hard-press in the Notification Center (the list that appears when you swipe down from the top of the screen) you get a Clear All Notifications command.

- **Delete the bloatware.** For the first time, you can hide Apple's starter apps on your Home screens (Watch, Home, Stocks, and so on), so you're not saddled with the icons you never use.

- **Donate your organs.** The Health app now offers you a chance to sign up for the Donate Life America registry, so that you can do some good even after your death.

- **Multilingual typing.** You can now type in two languages within the same text box without switching keyboard layouts. iOS figures out what language you've switched to and automatically changes the language for autocorrect entries and QuickType predictions.

- **Internet calls treated as phone calls.** Apps like Skype, Facebook Messenger, Slack, and WhatsApp let you place voice calls, phone to phone, over the Internet (instead of using the cellular network). For the first time, those calls are now treated by the iPhone exactly like regular phone calls. They appear in your Recents and Favorites list, they pop up the photo of the caller, and your Contacts list now has a place to save your friends' Internet calling handles.

- **Voicemail transcription.** The Voicemail list now includes approximate transcriptions of the messages people have left for you! They're very rough and filled with mistakes, but it's usually enough to get the gist of a message's topic and importance.

- **Bedtime-consistency management.** iOS 10's Clock app offers a new Bedtime tab. You answer a few questions about your sleep habits, and the app will attempt to keep your sleep regular—prompting you when it's time to get ready for bed, waking you at a consistent time, and keeping a graph of your sleep consistency.

- **Delete rarely played songs.** If you turn on Optimize Music Storage in Settings, then, as your phone begins to run out of storage space, iOS 10 automatically identifies music you haven't listened to recently. It removes those songs from your phone to save space. (Of course, you can always re-download them at no charge.)

- **Expanded lookup.** When you highlight a word and then tap Look Up, you now get a lot more than the dictionary definition. You get match-ing Wikipedia entries, movie names, book titles, websites, news headlines, maps, and so on. In essence, the Look Up button becomes an instantaneous reference feature that saves you a trip to Safari's search bar.

- **Music continues in Camera mode.** Opening the Camera app to take a still photo no longer pauses whatever music is playing. Fashion photographers who play rock music during photo shoots are celebrating.

- **More informative Wi-Fi listings.** Now, in Settings→Wi-Fi, you'll find out if the Wi-Fi network has no Internet connection ("No Internet Connection" appears in orange letters). And if you're connecting to an open network (no password), you get a "Security Recommendation" link. Tap it, and a message announces: "Open networks provide no security and expose all network traffic." In other words, take caution, because your Internet traffic is sniffable by the bad guys.

- **New magnifier.** The Accessibility settings offer a new magnifying screen that lets you control the zoom, color tint, and flashlight all at once—great when you're having trouble reading fine print in a dark restaurant or tiny black-on-gray print anywhere. You can set up your phone so that triple-clicking the Home button starts this mode.

- **Color-blindness filter.** Also in Accessibility: A feature called Display Accommodations, which adjusts the phone's screen to help color-blind people. It tells the iPhone's screen to substitute different, easier-to-see colors for the red and green tones that typically trip up color-blinders. If you're color blind, this feature may blow your mind.

App Upgrades

- **Apple Music.** Apple Music—the app, the $10-a-month service—was a hot mess. The newly redesigned app is far easier to navigate.

- **Photos.** The redesigned Photos can auto-generate lovely, musical videos, using your photos and videos as its raw material (from a recent time period, or a recent place you visited, or featuring a certain person). It comes with a selection of 80 soundtracks and plenty of customization controls.

  The Photos search box lets you find images according to what they show. You can search your photos for "dog," or "beach," or whatever.

  Perhaps more usefully, the editing mode now includes a markup feature: You can draw or type onto your photos, or add a circular magnified area.

  Finally, if you're a fan of Live Photos—Apple's name for the weird 3-second-video+photo feature available on the iPhone 6s and 7 families—you'll be happy to hear that iOS 10 brings image stabilization to them. You can also apply the usual Photos editing tools (tweak color, brightness, contrast, and so on) to the video.

- **Maps.** Apple's Maps app still doesn't know as much about the world as Google Maps, but Apple has put a lot of effort into slicking up the app itself. It looks great, and it now offers to reroute you if traffic will mar your planned commute. And now, app makers can add Maps Extensions—new features for Maps, like the ability to book a restaurant reservation with OpenTable or to call an Uber ride.

- **News.** The new app offers breaking-news alerts, subscriptions to certain publications, and a lovely new design.

- **New Home app.** This app lets you control your thermostat, electric drapes, lights, and other home-automation gadgets—assuming that they're compatible with Apple's HomeKit standard. (You probably don't own any.)

- **Notes.** You and another person can edit a page in Notes simultaneously. Great when you and your spouse are planning a party and brainstorming about guests and the dinner menu, for example.

- **Safari.** Website creators can now offer an Apple Pay button, meaning that you can pay for stuff without having to painstakingly type in your name, address, and credit card information 400 times a year. So cool: You can authenticate with your phone's fingerprint reader!

  Now Safari can fill in a secondary address for you in a web form (like your work address), or even someone else's address (grabbed from Contacts).

- **Calendar.** If you start to type a Calendar event that the app recognizes as something you've entered before, it proposes autocompleting it. Calendar also sometimes pre-fills in times and places as you create an appointment, based on information it spotted in an email or message.

- **Health.** You can now share your activity and calorie burn with your friends. It's fitness through humiliation.

- **Mail.** The Mail app occasionally offers an Unsubscribe button when it suspects that a message has come from a mailing list. Also in Mail, conversation view (where exchange messages are grouped) now places messages chronologically—no more scrolling to the bottom to see what everyone is talking about. You'll see. It's good.

What It All Means

Let's be honest: Apple is finding it harder to say "no" to new features these days. iOS has become a very dense operating system, with more features than you could master in years.

Then again, the public may not care about simplicity the way it once did. When smartphones were new, extreme simplicity was critical to helping them accept the concept.

Today's 10-year-olds weren't even alive before there were iPhones. And people who got their first smartphones as teenagers grew up along with iOS and Android—and evolved along with them—so the sheer complexity doesn't bother them much. It's usually only their parents who complain.

But never mind. iOS 10 is better, smarter, faster, clearer, and more refined than what came before. It takes hundreds of steps forward, and only a couple of tiny steps back.

That's a lot of tweaks, polishing, and finesse—and a lot to learn. Fortunately, 650 pages of instructions now await you.

PART ONE

The iPhone as Phone

1

The Guided Tour

You can't believe how much is hidden inside this sleek, thin slab. Microphone, speaker, cameras, battery. Processor, memory, power processing. Sensors for brightness, tilt, and proximity. Twenty wireless radio antennas. A gyroscope, accelerometer, and barometer.

For the rest of this book, and for the rest of your life with the iPhone, you'll be expected to know what's meant by, for example, "the Home button" and "the Sleep switch." A guided tour, therefore, is in order.

Home button

Silencer switch

Volume keys

Sleep Switch (On/Off)

You could argue that knowing how to turn on your phone might be a useful skill.

For that, you need the Sleep switch. It's a metal button shaped like a dash. On the iPhone 6 and later models, it's on the right edge; on the 5 family and SE, it's on the top edge.

Sleep switch

It has several functions:

- **Sleep/wake.** Tapping it once puts the iPhone into Sleep mode, ready for incoming calls but consuming very little power. Tapping it again turns on the screen so it's ready for action.

- **On/Off.** The same switch can also turn the iPhone off completely so it consumes no power at all; incoming calls get dumped into voicemail. You might turn the iPhone off whenever you're not going to use it for a few days.

  To turn the iPhone off, hold down the Sleep switch for 3 seconds. The screen changes to say **slide to power off**.

Confirm your decision by placing a fingertip on the ⏻ and sliding to the right. The device shuts off completely.

To turn the iPhone back on, press the switch again for 1 second. The Apple logo appears as the phone boots up.

- **Answer call/Dump to voicemail.** When a call comes in, you can tap the Sleep button *once* to silence the ringing or vibrating. After four rings, the call goes to voicemail.

  You can also tap it *twice* to dump the call to voicemail immediately. (Of course, because they didn't hear four rings, iPhone veterans will know you've blown them off. Bruised egos may result. Welcome to the world of iPhone etiquette.)

- **Force restart.** The Sleep switch has one more function. If your iPhone is frozen, and no buttons work, and you can't even turn the thing off, this button is also involved in force-restarting the whole machine. Steps for this last-ditch procedure are on page 624.

Sleep Mode

When you don't touch the screen for 1 minute (or another interval you choose), or when you press the Sleep switch, the phone goes to sleep. The screen is dark and doesn't respond to touch.

If you're on a call, the call continues; if music is playing, it keeps going; if you're recording audio, the recording proceeds. But when the phone is asleep, you don't have to worry about accidental button pushes. You wouldn't want to discover that your iPhone has been calling people or taking photos from the depths of your pocket or purse. Nor would you want it to dial a random number from your back pocket, a phenomenon that's earned the unfortunate name *butt dialing*.

The Lock Screen

In iOS 10, the iPhone has a newly expanded state of being that's somewhere between Sleep and on. It's the Lock screen. You can actually get a lot done here, without ever unlocking the phone and advancing to its Home screens.

You can wake the phone by pressing the Home button or the Sleep button. Or—if you have an iPhone SE, 6s family, or 7 family—you can do something new and game-changing: Just lift the phone to a vertical position.

The screen lights up, and you're looking at the Lock screen. Here—even before you've entered your password or used your fingerprint—you can check the time, read your missed messages, consult your calendar, take a photo, and more.

NOTE: You can turn off the new "wake when I lift you" feature. It's in **Settings→Display & Brightness**; turn off **Raise to Wake**. Now you have to press Sleep or Home to wake the phone, as before.

In iOS 10, this new netherworld of activity between Sleep and On—the Lock screen—is a complex, rich, busy universe; see Chapter 2.

Now then: If you want to proceed to the Home screens—to finish turning on the phone—then **click the Home button** at this point. That's a new habit to learn; you no longer do that by swiping across the screen, as you have on all iPhones since 2007.

TIP: iOS 10 offers a buried but powerful new option: Rest Finger to Open. (It's in **Settings→General→Accessibility→Home Button**.) When you turn this on, the second click—the one to get past the Lock screen—is no longer necessary.

If your phone is asleep, then just lifting it up (with your finger touching the Home button) wakes it and unlocks it; you never even see the Lock screen. Or, if the phone is asleep, you can click the Home button and just leave your finger on it. In each case, you save at least one Home-button click.

So what if you do want to visit the Lock screen? Just raise the phone, or click the Sleep button, without touching the Home button.

Home Button

Here it is: the one and only button on the front of the phone. Push it to summon the Home screen, your gateway to everything the iPhone can do.

The Home button is a wonderful thing. It means you can never get lost. No matter how deeply you burrow into the iPhone software, no matter how far off-track you find yourself, one push of the Home button takes you back to the beginning. (On the iPhone 7, it doesn't actually move, but it feels like it does; see page 7.)

On the iPhone 5s and later models, of course, the Home button is also a fingerprint scanner—the first one on a cellphone that actually *works*.

But, as time goes on, Apple keeps saddling the Home button with more functions. It's become Apple's only way to provide shortcuts for common

Home button

features; that's what you get when you design a phone that **has** only one button. In iPhone Land, you can press the Home button one, two, or three times for different functions—or even hold it down or touch it lightly for others. Here's the rundown.

Quick Press: Wake Up

Pressing the Home button once wakes the phone if it's asleep. That's sometimes easier than finding the Sleep switch on the top or edge. It opens the Lock screen, where you can check notifications or the time, hop into the camera, check your calendar, and more. See Chapter 2.

Momentary Touch: Unlock (iPhone 5s and Later)

Whenever you're looking at the Enter Passcode screen, just resting your finger on the Home button is enough to unlock the phone. (Teaching the iPhone to recognize your fingerprint is described on page 53.) You proceed to the Home screen. That convenience is brought to you by the Touch ID fingerprint reader that's built into the Home button.

Long Press: Siri

If you hold down the Home button for about 3 seconds, you wake up Siri, your virtual voice-controlled assistant. Details are in Chapter 5.

Two Quick Presses: App Switcher

If, once the phone is awake, you press the Home button **twice quickly**, the current image fades away—to reveal the app-switcher screen, the key to the iPhone's multitasking feature.

What you see here are **currently open screens** of the apps you've used most recently (older ones are to the left). They appear at nearly full size, overlapping like playing cards. Swipe horizontally to bring more apps into view; the Home screen is always at the far right.

With a single tap on a screen's "card," you jump right back into an app you had open, without waiting for it to start up, show its welcome screen, and so on—and without having to scroll through 11 Home screens trying to find its icon.

In short, the app switcher gives you a way to jump *directly* to another app, without a layover at the Home screen first.

> **TIP:** On this screen, you can also quit a program by flicking it upward. In fact, you can quit *several programs at once* that way, using two or three fingers. Fun for the whole family!

This app switcher is the only visible element of the iPhone's multitasking feature. Once you get used to it, that double-press of the Home button will become second nature—and your first choice for jumping among apps.

Two Touches: Reachability

Starting with the iPhone 6, the standard iPhone got bigger than previous models—and the Plus models are even *biggerer*. Their screens are so big, in fact, that your dinky human thumb may be too small to reach the top portion of the screen (if you're gripping the phone near the bottom).

For that reason, Apple has built a feature called Reachability into the iPhone 6 and later models. When you tap the Home button twice (don't click it—just *touch* it), the entire screen image slides halfway down the glass, so that you can reach the upper parts of it with your thumb!

As soon as you touch anything on the screen—a link, a button, an empty area, anything—the screen snaps back to its usual, full-height position. (The on/off switch for Reachability is in Settings→General→Accessibility.)

TIP: On the larger iPhones, the Home screen turns 90 degrees when you rotate them. The Dock jumps to the right edge, vertically. Try it!

Three Presses: Magnifier, VoiceOver, Zoom...

In Settings→General→Accessibility, you can set up a triple-press of the Home button to turn one of several accessibility features on or off. There's the *Magnifier*, new in iOS 10 (turns the iPhone into a giant electronic illuminated magnifying glass); *VoiceOver* (the phone speaks whatever you touch), **Invert Colors** (white-on-black type, which is sometimes easier to see), **Grayscale** (a mode that makes the whole iPhone black and white); **Zoom** (magnifies the screen), **Switch Control** (accommodates external gadgets like sip-and-puff straws), and **AssistiveTouch** (help for people who have trouble with physical switches).

All these features are described in Chapter 6.

Silencer Switch, Volume Keys

Praise be to the gods of technology—this phone has a silencer switch! This tiny flipper, on the left edge or at the top, means that no ringer or alert sound will humiliate you in a meeting, at a movie, or in church. To turn off the ringer, push the flipper toward the back of the phone (see the photo on page 16).

No menus, no holding down keys, just instant silence.

NOTE: Even when silenced, the iPhone still makes noise in certain circumstances: when an alarm goes off; when you're playing music; when you're using Find My iPhone (page 530); when you're using VoiceOver; or, sometimes, when a game is playing. Also, the phone still vibrates when the silencer is engaged, although you can turn this feature off in Settings→Sounds.

On the left edge are the volume controls. They work in five ways:

- On a call, these buttons adjust the speaker or earbud volume.

- When you're listening to music, they adjust the playback volume—even when the phone is locked and dark.

- When you're taking a picture, either one serves as a shutter button or as a camcorder start/stop button.

- At all other times, they adjust the volume of sound effects like the ringer, alarms, and Siri.

- When a call comes in, they silence the ringing or vibrating.

In each case, if the screen is on, a volume graphic appears to show you where you are on the volume scale.

Screen

The touchscreen is your mouse, keyboard, dialing pad, and notepad. You might expect it to get fingerprinty and streaky.

But the modern iPhone has an *oleophobic* screen. That may sound like an irrational fear of yodeling, but it's actually a coating that repels grease. A single light wipe on your clothes restores the screen to its right-out-of-the-box crystal sheen.

You can also use the screen as a mirror when the iPhone is off.

The iPhone's Retina screen has crazy high resolution (the number of tiny pixels per inch). It's really, really sharp, as you'll discover when you try to read text or make out the details of a map or a photo. The iPhone 5 and SE models manage 1136×640 pixels; the iPhone 6/6s/7 packs in 1334×750; the SE has 640×1136; and the Plus models have 1920×1080 (the same number of dots as a high-definition TV).

The front of the iPhone is made of a special formulation made by Corning, to Apple's specifications—even better than Gorilla Glass, Apple says. It's unbelievably resistant to scratching. (You can still shatter it if you drop it just the wrong way.)

NOTE: This is how Corning's website says this glass is made: "The glass is placed in a hot bath of molten salt at a temperature of approximately 400° C. Smaller sodium ions leave the glass, and larger potassium ions from the salt bath replace them. These larger ions take up more room and are pressed together when the glass cools, producing a layer of compressive stress on the surface of the glass."

But you probably guessed that.

If you're nervous about protecting your iPhone, you can always get a case for it (or a "bumper"—a silicone band that wraps the edges). But if you're worried about scratching the glass, you're probably worrying too much. Even many Apple employees carry the iPhone in their pockets without cases.

Screen Icons

Here's a roundup of the icons you may see in the status bar at the top of the iPhone screen, from left to right:

- **Cell signal (••ooo).** As on any cellphone, the number of bars—or dots, in iOS's case—indicates the strength of your cell signal, and thus the quality of your call audio and the likelihood of losing the connection. If there are no dots, then the dreaded words "No service" appear here.

- **Network name and type.** These days, different parts of the country—and even your street—are blanketed by cellular Internet signals of different speeds, types, and ages. Your status bar shows you the kind of network signal it has. From slowest to fastest:

E or **O** means your iPhone is connected to your carrier's slowest, oldest Internet system. You might be able to check email, but you'll lose your mind waiting for a web page to load.

If you see **3G**, you're in a city where your cell company has installed a 3G network—still slow compared to **4G**, which offers speed in between 3G and LTE.

And if you see **LTE** up there—well, get psyched. You have an iPhone 5 or later model, and you're in a city with a 4G LTE cellular network. And that means *very* fast Internet.

NOTE: You may also see a notation like "T-Mobile Wi-Fi" or "VZW Wi-Fi" up there. The iPhone 6/6s/7 models, it turns out, can make free phone calls over a Wi-Fi network—if your cellphone carrier has permitted it, and if you've turned the feature on (page 434). It's a great way to make calls indoors where the cell signal is terrible.

- **Airplane mode (✈).** If you see the airplane instead of signal and Wi-Fi bars, then the iPhone is in airplane mode (page 438).

- **Do Not Disturb (☾).** When the phone is in Do Not Disturb mode, nothing can make it ring, buzz, or light up except calls from the most important people. Details are on page 128.

- **Wi-Fi signal (📶).** When you're connected to a wireless Internet hotspot, this indicator appears. The more "sound waves," the stronger the signal.

- **9:41 AM.** When the iPhone is unlocked, a digital clock appears on the status bar.

- **Alarm (⏰).** You've got an alarm set. This reminder, too, can be valuable, especially when you intend to sleep late and don't want an alarm to go off.

- **Bluetooth (✱).** The iPhone is connected wirelessly to a Bluetooth earpiece, speaker, or car system. (If this symbol is gray, then it means Bluetooth is turned on but not connected to any other gear—and not sucking down battery power.)

- **TTY (▦).** You've turned on Teletype mode, meaning that the iPhone can communicate with a Teletype machine. (That's a special machine that lets deaf people make phone calls by typing and reading text. It hooks up to the iPhone with a special cable that Apple sells from its website.)

- **Call forwarding (↪).** You've told your iPhone to auto-forward any incoming calls to a different number. This icon is awfully handy— it explains at a glance why your iPhone never seems to get calls anymore.

- **VPN (▬).** You corporate stud, you! You've managed to connect to your corporate network over a secure Internet connection, proba- bly with the assistance of a systems administrator—or by consulting page 564.

- **Syncing (✲).** The iPhone is currently syncing with some Internet ser- vice—iCloud, for example (Chapter 16).

- **Battery meter (▬⚡).** When the iPhone is charging, the lightning bolt appears. Otherwise, the battery logo "empties out" from right to left to indicate how much charge remains. (You can even add a "% full" indicator to this gauge; see page 584.)

- **Navigation active (➤).** You're running a GPS navigation app, or some other app that's tracking your location, in the background (yay, multi- tasking!). Why is a special icon necessary? Because those GPS apps slurp down battery power like a thirsty golden retriever. Apple wants to make sure you don't forget you're running it.

- **Rotation lock (🔒).** This icon reminds you that you've deliberately turned off the screen-rotation feature, where the screen image turns 90 degrees when you rotate the phone. Why would you want to? And how do you turn the rotation lock on or off? See page 48.

Cameras and Flash

At the top of the phone, above the screen, there's a horizontal slot. That's the earpiece. Just above it or beside it, the tiny pinhole is the front-facing camera. It's more visible on the white-faced iPhones than on the black ones.

Its primary purpose is to let you take selfies and conduct video chats using the FaceTime feature, but it's also handy for checking for spinach in your teeth.

It's not nearly as good a camera as the one on the back, though. The front camera isn't as good in low light and takes much lower-resolution shots.

A tiny LED lamp appears next to this back lens—actually, it's two lamps on the 5s, 6, and 6s iPhones, and *four* on the 7 family. That's the flash for the camera, the video light when you're shooting movies, and a darned good flashlight for reading restaurant menus and theater programs in low light. (Swipe up from the bottom of the screen and tap the 🔦 icon to turn the light on and off.)

The tiny pinhole between the flash and the lens is a microphone. It's used for recording clearer sound with video, for better noise cancellation on phone calls, and for better directional sound pickup.

The iPhone 7 Plus actually has two lenses on the back—one wide-angle, one zoomed in. Details on this feature and everything else on the iPhone's cameras are in Chapter 9.

Sensors

Behind the glass, above or beside the earpiece, are two sensors. (On the black iPhones, you can't see them except with a flashlight.) First, there's an ambient-light sensor that brightens the display when you're in sunlight and dims it in darker places.

Second, there's a proximity sensor. When something (like your head) is close to the sensor, it shuts off the screen and touch sensitivity. It works only in the Phone app. You save power and avoid dialing with your cheekbone when you're on a call.

SIM Card Slot

On the right edge of the iPhone, there's a pinhole next to what looks like a very thin slot cover. If you push an unfolded paper clip straight into the hole, the *SIM card* tray pops out.

So what's a SIM card?

It turns out that there are two major cellphone network types: *CDMA*, used by Verizon and Sprint, and *GSM*, used by AT&T, T-Mobile, and most other countries around the world.

Every GSM phone stores your phone account info—things like your phone number and calling-plan details—on a tiny memory card known as a SIM (subscriber identity module) card.

What's cool is that, by removing the card and putting it into **another** GSM phone, you can transplant a GSM phone's brain. The other phone now knows your number and account details, which can be handy when your iPhone goes in for repair or battery replacement. For example, you can turn a Verizon iPhone 7 into a T-Mobile iPhone 7 just by swapping in a T-Mobile SIM card.

The World Phone

AT&T is a GSM network, so AT&T iPhones have always had SIM cards. But, intriguingly enough, every iPhone has a SIM card, too—even the Verizon and Sprint models. That's odd, because most CDMA cellphones don't have SIM cards.

These iPhones contain antennas for **both** GSM and CDMA. It's the same phone, no matter which cell company you buy it from. Only the SIM card teaches it which one it "belongs" to.

Even then, however, you can still use any company's phone in any country. (That's why the latest iPhones are said to be "world phones.") When you use the Verizon or Sprint iPhone in the United States, it uses only the CDMA network. But if you travel to Europe or another GSM part of the world, you can still use your Verizon or Sprint phone; it just hooks into that country's GSM network.

If you decide to try that, you have two ways to go. First, you can contact your phone carrier and ask to have international roaming turned on. You'll keep your same phone number overseas, but you'll pay through the nose for calls and, especially, Internet use. (One exception: On T-Mobile, international texting and Internet use are free.)

Second, you can rent a temporary SIM card when you get to the destination country. That's less expensive, but you'll have a different phone number while you're there.

The iPhone 4s used a card type known as a **micro-SIM** card. And for the iPhone 5 and later, Apple developed even tinier cards called **nano-**SIMs. (You can see all three at left.)

At this rate, you won't be able to see the iPhone 8's SIM card without an electron microscope.

Apple thinks SIM cards are geeky and intimidating and that they should be invisible. That's why, unlike most GSM phones, your iPhone came with the card preinstalled and ready to go. Most people never have any reason to open this tray.

If you were curious enough to open it up, you can close the tray simply by pushing it back into the phone until it clicks.

NOTE: Many countries offer LTE high-speed cellular Internet on all different radio frequencies. The iPhone 6/6s/7 can hop onto more of these networks than any other cellphone, but it still doesn't work in *every* country. Ask your carrier which countries your model works with.

Headphone Jack

Until the iPhone 7 came along, iPhones contained a standard jack for plugging in the white earbuds that came with it—or any other earbuds or headphones.

It's more than an ordinary 3.5-millimeter audio jack, however. It contains a secret fourth pin that conducts sound *into* the phone from the microphone on the earbuds' cord. You, too, can be one of those executives who walk down the street barking orders, apparently to nobody.

The iPhone can stay in your pocket as you walk or drive. You hear the other person through your earbuds, and the mike on the cord picks up your voice.

Next to the headphone jack, inside a perforated grille, a tiny second microphone lurks. It's the key to the iPhone's noise-cancellation feature. It listens to the sound of the world around you and pumps in the opposite sound waves to cancel out all that ambient noise. It doesn't do anything for *you*—the noise cancellation affects only what the *other* guy on the phone hears.

That's why there's also a third microphone at the top back (between the camera and flash); it's designed to supply noise cancellation for you so that the other guy sounds better when you're in a noisy place.

iPhone 7: No Headphone Jack

We, the people, may complain about how exhausting it is to keep up with the annual flood of new smartphones. But at least you don't have to create the annual set of new features. That's *their* problem.

Not just because it's increasingly difficult to think of new features, but also because the phone makers have pretty much run out of room for new components inside.

That, says Apple, is why it removed the headphone jack from the iPhone 7 and 7 Plus. The headphone jack may not seem very big—but on the *inside* of the phone, the corresponding receptacle occupies an unnerving amount of nonnegotiable space.

So how are you supposed to listen to music without a headphone jack? Apple offers three ways:

- **Using the adapter.** In the iPhone box, Apple includes a two-inch adapter cord that connects any headphones to the phone's Lightning jack.

- **Use the earbuds.** The phone also comes with new white earbuds that connect to the Lightning (charging) jack.

Of course, if your headphones are plugged into the Lightning jack, you can't charge your phone while listening over them. The only solution is an adapter like Belkin's $40 Lightning Audio + Charge RockStar, which lets you charge and plug in headphones simultaneously.

- **Use wireless headphones.** You can also use any Bluetooth wireless earbuds—from $17 plastic disposable ones to Apple's own, super-impressive AirPods. Page 142 has more on Bluetooth headsets.

In theory, those three approaches should pretty much cover you whenever you want to listen.

In practice, though, you'll still get zapped by the occasional inconvenience. You'll be on a flight, for example, listening to your laptop with headphones—and when you want to switch to the phone, you'll realize that your adapter cord is in the overhead bin. (Based on a true story.)

But this kind of hassle is the new reality. Motorola and LeEco (in China) have already ditched the headphone jack, and other phone makers will follow suit.

Microphone, Speakerphone

On the bottom of the iPhone, Apple has parked two important audio components: the speaker and the microphone.

Headphones   Microphone   Charge/sync   Speakerphone
(models before   (Lightning connector)
iPhone 7)

On the iPhone 7, in fact, there are two speakers, on the top and bottom of the phone. Stereo sound (and better sound) has finally come to the iPhone.

TIP: The speakerphone isn't super loud, because it's aimed straight out of the iPhone's edge, away from you. But if you cup your hand around the bottom, you can redirect the sound toward your face, for an immediate boost in volume and quality.

The Lightning Connector

Directly below the Home button, on the bottom edge of the phone, you'll find the connector that charges and syncs the iPhone with your computer.

30-pin connector
(iPhone 4S)

Lightning connector
(iPhone 5 and later)

For nearly 10 years, the charge/sync connector was identical on every iPhone, iPod, and iPad—the famous 30-pin connector. But starting on the iPhone 5, Apple replaced that inch-wide connector with a new, far-smaller one it calls Lightning.

The Lightning connector is a great design: It clicks nicely into place (you can even dangle the iPhone from it), yet you can yank it right out. You can insert the Lightning into the phone either way— there's no "right-side up" anymore. It's much sturdier than the old connector. And it's tiny, which was Apple's primary goal—only 0.3 inches wide (the old one was almost 0.9 inches wide).

Unfortunately, you may still occasionally encounter a car adapter or hotel-room alarm clock with the old kind of connector. (For $30, you can buy an adapter.)

In time, as the Lightning connectors come on all new iPhones, iPods, and iPads, a new ecosystem of accessories will arise. We'll arrive at a new era of standardization—until Apple changes jacks again in *another* 10 years.

Antenna Band

Radio signals can't pass through metal. That's why there are strips of glass on the back of the iPhone 5, 5s, and SE, strips of plastic on the iPhone 6/6s/7 models, and all plastic on the back of the 5c.

And there are a *lot* of radio signals in this phone. All told, there are *20* different radio transceivers inside the iPhone 6/6s/7. They tune in to the LTE and 3G (high-speed Internet) signals used in various countries around the world, plus the three CDMA signals used in the U.S.; and one each for Wi-Fi, Bluetooth, American GPS, and Russian GPS.

In the Box

Inside the minimalist box, you get the iPhone and these items:

- **The earbuds.** Every iPhone comes with a pair of the iconic white earbuds that announce to the world, "I have an iPhone!" These days, they're what Apple calls EarPods. They sound great, although their bulbous shape may get uncomfortable in smaller ears. A volume control/clicker is right there on the cord, so you can answer phone calls and pause the music without even taking the phone out of your pocket. (The EarPods that come with the new iPhone 7, of course, plug into the Lightning jack, since there's no headphone jack on that model.)

- **A Lightning cable.** When you connect your iPhone to your computer using this white USB cable, it simultaneously syncs and charges. See Chapter 15.

- **The AC adapter.** When you're traveling without a computer, you can plug the dock's USB cable into the included two-prong outlet adapter, so you can charge the iPhone directly from a wall socket.

- **Decals and info card.** iPhone essentials.

You don't need a copy of the iTunes software, or even a computer, to use the iPhone—but it makes loading up the phone a lot easier, as described in Chapter 15.

If you don't have iTunes on your computer, you can download it from *www.apple.com/itunes*.

Seven Basic Finger Techniques

On the iPhone, you do everything on the touchscreen instead of with physical buttons.

Tap

The iPhone's onscreen buttons are nice and big, giving your fleshy fingertip a fat target.

You can't use a fingernail or a pen tip; only skin contact works. (You can also buy an iPhone stylus. But a fingertip is cheaper and harder to misplace.)

Double-Tap

Double-tapping is pretty rare. It's generally reserved for two functions:

- In the Safari web browser, Photos, and Maps apps, double-tapping zooms in on whatever you tap, magnifying it. (At that point, double-tapping means "Restore to original size.") Double-tapping also zooms into formatted email messages, PDF files, Microsoft Office files, and other things.

- When you're watching a video (or recording one), double-tapping switches the aspect ratio (video screen shape).

Swipe

In some situations, you're asked to confirm an action by **swiping** your finger across the screen. That's how you confirm that you want to shut off the phone, for example. Swiping like this is also a great shortcut for deleting an email or a text message.

Drag

When you're zoomed into a map, web page, email, or photo, you scroll around by sliding your finger across the glass in any direction—like a flick (described next), but slower and more controlled. It's a huge improvement over scroll bars, especially when you want to scroll diagonally.

Flick

A **flick** is a faster, less-controlled **drag**. You flick vertically to scroll lists on the iPhone. The faster you flick, the faster the list spins downward or upward. But lists have a real-world sort of momentum; they slow down after a second or two, so you can see where you wound up.

At any point during the scrolling of a list, you can flick again (if you didn't go far enough) or tap to stop the scrolling (if you see the item you want to choose).

Pinch and Spread

In apps like Photos, Mail, Safari, and Maps, you can zoom in on a photo, message, web page, or map by **spreading**.

That's when you place two fingers (usually thumb and forefinger) on the glass and spread them. The image magically grows, as though it's printed on a sheet of rubber.

<table>
<tr><td>NOTE:</td><td>The English language has failed Apple here. Moving your thumb and forefinger closer together has a perfect verb: pinching. But there's no good word to describe moving them the opposite direction.

Apple uses the oxymoronic expression pinch out to describe that move (along with the redundant-sounding pinch in). In this book, the opposite of "pinching" is "spreading."</td></tr>
</table>

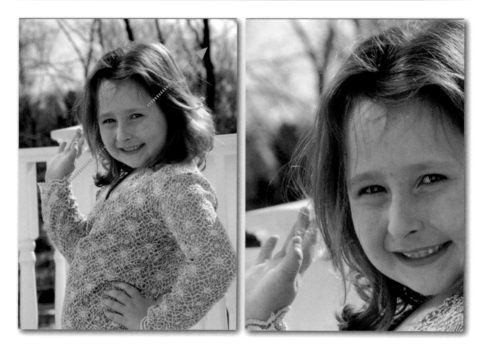

Once you've zoomed in like this, you can zoom out again by putting two fingers on the glass and pinching them together.

Edge Swipes

Swiping your finger inward from **outside** the screen has a few variations:

- **From the top edge.** Opens the Notification Center, which lists all your missed calls and texts, shows your appointments, and so on.

- **From the bottom edge.** Opens the Control Center, a unified miniature control panel for brightness, volume, Wi-Fi, and so on.

- **From the left edge.** In many apps, this means "Go back to the previous screen." It works in Mail, Settings, Notes, Messages, Safari,

Facebook, and some other apps. At the Home screen, it opens the Today screen (page 65).

It sometimes makes a big difference whether you begin your swipe *within* the screen or *outside* it. At the Home screen, for example, starting your downward swipe within the screen area doesn't open the Notification Center—it opens Spotlight, the iPhone's search function.

> **TIP:** If you have an iPhone 6s or 7, you can also hard-*swipe* from the left edge to open the app switcher described on page 19. Actually, all you have to do is hard-*press* the left margin of the screen, but hard-swiping might fit the metaphor better (pulling the app cards onto the screen).

Force Touch (iPhone 6s and 7)

The screen on the iPhone 6s and 7 (and their Plus siblings) doesn't just detect a finger touch. It also knows how *hard* your finger is pressing, thanks to a technology Apple calls Force Touch. This feature requires that you learn two more finger techniques.

Quick Actions

iOS 10 interprets the pressure of your touch in various ways. On the Home screens, you can make a shortcut menu of useful commands pop out of various app icons, like this:

Apple calls these commands *quick actions*, and each is designed to save you a couple of steps. There are more than ever in iOS 10. Some examples:

- **The Camera app** icon offers shortcut menus like Take Selfie, Record Video, Record Slo-mo, and Take Photo.

- **The Clock app** gives you direct access to its Set Alarm, Start Timer, and Start Stopwatch functions.

- **Notes** gives you New Note, New Photo, and New Sketch commands (a reference to the new finger-drawing features).

- **Maps** offers Directions Home (a great one), Mark My Location, Send My Location, and Search Nearby (for restaurants, bars, shops, and so on).

- **The Phone app** sprouts the names of people you've called recently, as well as a Create New Contact command.

- **Calendar** shows your next appointment, plus an Add Event command.

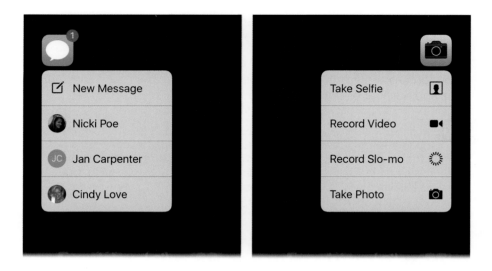

- **Reminders** lists your reminder categories, so you can create a new To Do directly inside one of them (for example, New in Family).

- **Mail and Messages** offer New Message commands. Mail also offers Search, Inbox (with a new-message counter), and VIPs (also with a counter).

- **Home-screen folders** sprout a Rename command at your fingertip.

- **The Notification Center** (the list that appears when you swipe down from the top of the screen) offers a Clear All Notifications command.

- **The Control Center icons** (page 47) offer some options. You can hard-press the Flashlight icon to choose Low, Medium, or High brightness. That's super cool, especially on the iPhone 7, whose much stronger LED flashlight is enough to light up a high-school football game at night. Meanwhile, the Timer button offers presets for 1 minute, 5 minutes, 20 minutes, or 1 hour. And the Camera button offers Take Photo, Record Slo-mo, Record Video, and Take Selfie. That kind of thing.

Similar quick actions also sprout from these Apple apps' icons: Photos, Video, Wallet, iTunes Store, App Store, iBooks, News, Safari, Music, FaceTime, Podcasts, Voice Memos, Contacts, and Find My Friends.

And, of course, in iOS 10, you can use hard presses to respond to notifications: reply to a text message, accept a Calendar invitation, or see where your Uber is on a map.

Other software companies can add shortcut menus to their apps, too. You'll find these shortcut menus on the Facebook, Fitbit, and Google Maps app icons, for example.

If you force-press an app that *doesn't* have quick actions, you just feel a buzz and nothing else happens.

NOTE: At the outset, this force-pressing business can really throw you when you're trying to rearrange icons on your Home screens. As described on page 335, that usually involves *long*-pressing an icon, which for most people is too similar to *hard*-pressing one. The trick is to long-press *very lightly*. You'll get used to it.

Peek and Pop

Hard to explain, but very cool: You hard-press something in a list—your email Inbox, for example (below, left). Or a link in a text message, or a photo thumbnail. You get a pop-up bubble showing you what's inside (middle):

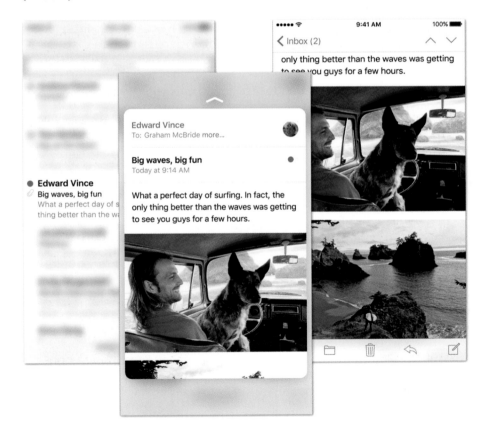

When you release your finger, the bubble disappears, and you're right back where you started.

Peeking is, in other words, exactly like the Quick Look feature on the Mac. It lets you see what's inside a link, icon, or list item without losing your place or changing apps.

Email is the killer app here. You can whip through your Inbox, hard-pressing one new message after another—"What's this one?" "Do I care?"—simply inspecting the first paragraph of each but not actually opening any message.

Then, if you find one that you do want to read fully, you can press harder *yet* to open the message normally (previous page, right). Apple calls that "popping."

Here are some places where you can peek in the basic iPhone apps: **Mail** (preview a message in a list), **Messages** (see recent exchanges with someone in the list of people), **Maps** (preview information about a push-pin), **Calendar** (see details of an event), **Photos** (preview a photo in a screenful of thumbnails), **Safari** (preview the page hiding behind a link), **Weather** (see weather details for a name in the list of cities), **Music** (see information about a song or album in a list), **Video** (read details about a video in a list), **Notes** (see the contents of a note's name in a list), **iBooks** (view a book-cover thumbnail larger), **News** (preview the body of an article in a list), and **Find My Friends** (see the map identifying the location of someone in your list).

But, for goodness' sake, at least get to know peek and pop in Mail and Messages. It's really kind of awesome.

And, again, app makers can add this feature to their own apps.

Charging the iPhone

The iPhone has a built-in, rechargeable battery that fills up most of its interior. How long a charge lasts depends on what you're doing—music playback saps the battery the least, GPS navigation saps it the most. But one thing is for sure: You'll have to recharge the iPhone regularly. For most people, it's every night.

NOTE: The iPhone's battery isn't user-replaceable. It's *rechargeable*, but after 400 or 500 charges, it starts to hold less juice. Eventually, you'll have to pay Apple to install a new battery. (Apple says the added bulk of a protective plastic battery compartment, a removable door and latch, and battery-retaining springs would have meant a much smaller battery—or a much thicker iPhone.)

You recharge the iPhone by connecting the white USB cable that came with it. You can plug the far end into either of two places to supply power:

- **Your computer's USB jack.** In general, the iPhone charges even if your computer is asleep. (If it's a laptop that itself is not plugged in, though, the phone charges only if the laptop is awake. Otherwise, you'd come home to a depleted laptop.)

- **The AC adapter.** The little white two-prong cube that came with the iPhone connects to the end of the cradle's USB cable.

Unless the charge is *really* low, you can use the iPhone while it charges. The battery icon in the upper-right corner displays a lightning bolt to let you know it's charging.

> **TIP:** If you have an iPhone 6, 6s, or 7 model, it'll charge much faster if you charge it with the 2.1-amp wall adapter that comes with an iPad, instead of the 1-amp adapter that comes with the phone. How's a 90 percent charge in two hours sound?

Battery Life Tips

The battery life of the iPhone is either terrific or terrible, depending on your point of view and how old your phone is.

If you were an optimist, you'd point out that the iPhone gets longer battery life than most touchscreen phones. If you were a pessimist, you'd observe that you sometimes can't make it through even a single day without needing a recharge.

So knowing how to scale back your iPhone's power appetite should come in extremely handy.

These are the biggest wolfers of electricity: the screen and background activity (especially Internet activity). Therefore, when you're nervous about your battery making it through an important day, here are your options:

- **Low Power mode** can squeeze another 3 hours of life out of a charge.

  In Low Power mode, your iPhone quits doing a lot of stuff in the background, like fetching new mail and updating apps. It also stops playing most of iOS's cute little animations and stops listening for you to say "Hey Siri" (page 148). The processor slows down, too; it takes longer to switch between apps, for example. And the battery indicator turns yellow, to remind you why things have suddenly slowed down.

When your battery sinks to 20 percent remaining (and then again at 10 percent), you get a warning message. If you choose **Low Power Mode** in this message box, then boom: You're in Low Power mode.

If your phone is plugged in, it exits Low Power mode automatically once it has enough juice (above, lower right). You can also turn Low Power Mode on or off manually in **Settings**→**Battery** (above, upper right).

At any time, you can also shut down juice-guzzling features manually. Here they are, roughly in order of power appetite:

- **Dim the screen.** Turning down your screen saves a lot of battery power. The quickest way is to swipe up from the bottom of the screen to open the Control Center (page 46), and then drag the brightness slider.

  On a new iPhone, Auto Brightness is turned on, too. In bright light, the screen brightens automatically; in dim light, it darkens. That's because when you unlock the phone after waking it, it samples the ambient light and adjusts the brightness.

NOTE: This works because of the ambient-light sensor near the earpiece. Apple says it experimented with having the light sensor active all the time, but it was weird to have the screen constantly dimming and brightening as you used it.

You can use this information to your advantage. By covering up the sensor as you unlock the phone, you force it into a low-power, dim-screen setting (because the phone believes it's in a dark room). Or by holding it up to a light as you wake it, you get more brightness. In either case, you've saved the navigation it would have taken you to find the manual brightness slider in Settings or in the Control Center. (Or you can turn this auto-brightness feature off altogether in Settings→ Display & Brightness.)

TIP: You can set things up so that a triple-click on the Home button instantly dims your screen, for use in the bedroom, movie theaters, or planetariums—without having to fuss with Settings or sliders. See page 228 for this awesome trick.

- **Turn off "push" data.** This is a big one. If your email, calendar, and address book are kept constantly synced with your Macs or PCs, then you've probably gotten yourself involved with Yahoo Mail, iCloud (Chapter 16), or Microsoft Exchange (Chapter 18). It's pretty amazing to know that your iPhone is constantly kept current with the mother ship.

  Unfortunately, all that continual sniffing of the airwaves, looking for updates, costs you battery power. If you can do without the immediacy, then visit Settings→Mail→Accounts→Fetch New Data. If you turn off the Push feature for each email account and set it to Manually instead, then your iPhone checks for email and new appointments only when you actually *open* the Mail or Calendar apps. Your battery goes a lot further.

- **Turn off background updating.** Non-Apple apps check for frequent updates, too: Facebook, Twitter, stock-reporting apps, and so on. Not all of them need to be busily toiling in the background. Your best bet for battery life, then, involves visiting Settings→General→Background App Refresh and turning the switch off for each app whose background activity isn't strictly necessary.

- **Turn off automatic app updates.** As you'll soon discover, app companies update their wares far more often than PC or Mac apps. Some apps get updated many times a year.

  Your phone comes set to download them automatically when they become available. But that constant checking and downloading costs you battery life.

  To shut that feature down, open Settings→iTunes & App Store. In the Automatic Downloads section, turn off Updates. (The other switches—Music, Apps, Books—are responsible for auto-downloading things that you or your brood have downloaded on other iOS gadgets. You might want to make sure they're off, too, if battery life is a concern.)

- **Turn off GPS checks.** In Settings→Privacy→Location Services, there's a list of all the apps on your phone that are using your phone's location feature to know where you are. (It's a combination of GPS, cell-tower triangulation, and Wi-Fi hotspot triangulation.) All that checking uses battery power.

  Some apps, like Maps, Find My Friends, and Yelp, don't do you much good unless they know your location. But plenty of apps don't really need to know where you are. Facebook and Twitter, for example, want that information only so that they can location-stamp your posts. In any case, the point is to turn off Location Services for each app that doesn't really need to know where you are.

  > **TIP:** In the list of apps under Location Services, tiny ◤ icons show you which apps are using GPS right now and which have used it in the past 24 hours. These icons can help guide you in shutting off the GPS use of various apps.

- **Turn off Wi-Fi.** If you're not in a wireless hotspot, you may as well stop the thing from using its radio. Swipe up from the bottom of the screen to open the Control Center, and tap the 📶 icon to turn it off.

  Or at the very least tell the iPhone to stop *searching* for Wi-Fi networks it can connect to. Page 437 has the details.

- **Turn off Bluetooth.** If you're not using a Bluetooth gadget (headset, fitness band, or whatever), then for heaven's sake shut down that Bluetooth radio. Open the Control Center and tap the ✳ icon to turn it off.

- **Turn off Cellular Data.** This option (in Settings→Cellular) turns off the cellular Internet features of your phone. You can still make calls, and you can still get online in a Wi-Fi hotspot.

  This feature is designed for people who have a capped data plan—a limited amount of Internet use per month—which is almost everybody. If you discover that you've used up almost all your data allotment for the month, and you don't want to go over your limit (and thereby trigger an overage charge), you can use this option to shut off all data. Now your phone is just a phone—and it uses less power.

- **Consider airplane mode.** In airplane mode, you shut off *all* the iPhone's power-hungry radios. Even a nearly dead iPhone can hobble on for a few hours in airplane mode—something to remember when you're desperate. To enter airplane mode, swipe up from the bottom of the screen to open the Control Center, and tap the ✈ icon.

For sure, turn on airplane mode if you'll be someplace where you *know* an Internet signal won't be present—like on a plane, a ship at sea, or Montana. Your iPhone never burns through a battery charge faster than when it's hunting for a signal it can't find; your battery will be dead within a couple of hours.

- **Turn off the screen.** With a press of the Sleep button, you can turn off the screen, rendering it black and saving huge amounts of power. Music playback and Maps navigation continue to work just fine.

  Of course, if you want to actually *interact* with the phone while the screen is off, you'll have to learn the VoiceOver talking-buttons technology; see page 204.

By the way, beware of 3D games and other graphically intensive apps, which can be serious power hogs. And turn off EQ when playing your music (see page 249).

If your battery still seems to be draining too fast, check out this table, which shows you exactly which apps are using the most power:

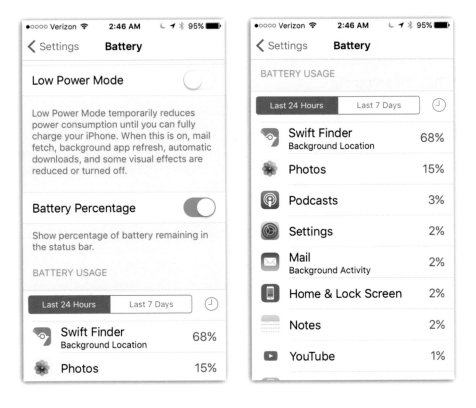

To see it, open **Settings→Battery**. You can switch between battery read-outs for the past 24 hours, or for the past 7 days. Keep special watch for labels like these:

- **Low Signal.** A phone uses the most power of all when it's hunting for a cellular signal, because the phone amplifies its radios in hopes of finding one. If your battery seems to be running down faster than usual, the "Low Signal" notation is a great clue—and a suggestion that maybe you should use airplane mode when you're on the fringes of cellular coverage.

- **Background activity.** As hinted on the previous pages, background Internet connections are especially insidious. These are apps that do online work invisibly, without your awareness—and drain the battery in the process. Now, for the first time, you can clearly see which apps are doing it.

  Once you know the culprit app, it's easy to shut its background work down. Open **Settings→General→Background App Refresh** and switch off each app whose background activity isn't strictly necessary.

TIP: If you tap the little clock icon in **Settings→Battery**, the screen shows you how much time each app has spent running—both in the foreground and in the background (below, right). It's an incredibly informative display if you've been wondering where all your battery power has been going.

The Home Screen

The Home screen is the launching pad for every iPhone activity. It's what appears when you press the Home button. It's the immortal grid of colorful icons.

It's such an essential software landmark, in fact, that a quick tour might be helpful:

- **Icons.** Each icon represents one of your iPhone apps (programs)—Mail, Maps, Camera, and so on—or a folder that you've made to *contain* some apps. Tap one to open that app or folder.

  Your iPhone comes with a couple of dozen apps preinstalled by Apple; you can't remove them. The real fun, of course, comes when you download *more* apps from the App Store (Chapter 10).

- **Badges.** Every now and then, you'll see a tiny, red number "badge" (like ❷) on one of your app icons. It's telling you that something new

Apps

Badge (new information!)

Dock

awaits: new email, new text messages, new chat entries, new updates for the apps on your iPhone. It's saying, "Hey, you! Tap me!"

- **Home page dots.** The standard Home screen can't hold more than 20 or 24 icons. As you install more and more programs on your iPhone, you'll need more and more room for their icons. Fortunately, the iPhone makes room for them by creating *additional* Home screens automatically. You can spread your new programs' icons across 11 such launch screens.

  The little white dots are your map. Each represents one Home screen. If the third one is "lit up," then you're on the third Home screen.

  To move among the screens, swipe horizontally—or tap to the right or left of the little dots to change screens.

  And if you ever scroll too far away from the *first* Home screen, here's a handy shortcut: Press the Home button (yes, even though you're technically already home). That takes you back to the first Home screen.

- **The Dock.** At the bottom of the Home screen, four exalted icons sit in a row on a light-colored panel. This is the Dock—a place to park the most important icons on your iPhone. These, presumably, are the ones you use most often. Apple starts you off with the Phone, Mail, Safari, and Music icons there.

What's so special about this row? As you flip among Home screens, the Dock never changes. You can never lose one of your four most cherished icons by straying from the first page; they're always handy.

- **The background.** You can replace the background image (behind your app icons) with a photo. A complicated, busy picture won't do you any favors—it will just make the icon names harder to read—so Apple provides a selection of handsome, relatively subdued wallpaper photos. But you can also choose one of your own photos.

For instructions on changing the wallpaper, see page 580.

It's easy (and fun!) to rearrange the icons on your Home screens. Put the most frequently used icons on the first page, put similar apps into folders, and reorganize your Dock. Full details are on page 335.

> **TIP:** You can set up a completely empty first Home screen by moving all of its app icons onto other Home pages, if you want. That's a weird but fun arrangement for anyone with a really great wallpaper photo.

Control Center

For such a tiny device, there are an awful lot of settings you can change—*hundreds* of them. Trouble is, some of them (volume, brightness) need changing a lot more often than others (language preference, voicemail greeting).

That's why Apple invented the Control Center: a panel that offers quick access to the controls you need the most.

To open the Control Center, no matter what app you're using, swipe upward from beneath the screen.

> **TIP:** You can even open the Control Center from the Lock screen (unless you've turned off that feature in Settings→Control Center→Access on Lock Screen).

The Control Center is a gray panel filled with one-touch icons for the settings most people change most often on their iPhones.

In iOS 10, there are now two pages of the Control Center, as shown on the facing page. The only hint is the two tiny dots beneath each screen. Over time, you'll learn to swipe leftward to see the newly separate music playback controls, or to the right to see everything else.

Airplane mode, Wi-Fi, Bluetooth, Do Not Disturb, Rotation Lock

Playback controls

Flashlight, Timer, Calculator, Camera

NOTE: If you've set up any HomeKit accessories—remote-controllable lights, locks, thermostats, outlets, and security systems that work with Apple's Home automation app—then the Control Center sprouts a *third* page.

Now, many of these settings are even faster to change using Siri, the voice-command feature described in Chapter 5. When it's not socially awkward to speak to your phone (like at the symphony or during a golf game), you can use spoken commands—listed below under each button description—to adjust settings without even touching the screen.

Here's what's in the Control Center:

- **Airplane mode (✈).** Tap to turn the icon red. Now you're in airplane mode; the phone's wireless features are all turned off. You're saving the battery and obeying flight attendant instructions. Tap again to turn off airplane mode.

  Sample Siri command: "Turn airplane mode on." (Siri warns you that if you turn airplane mode on, Siri herself will stop working. Say "OK.")

- **Wi-Fi (�ᯤ).** Tap to turn your phone's Wi-Fi off (gray) or on (blue).

  Sample Siri commands: "Turn off Wi-Fi." "Turn Wi-Fi back on."

- **Bluetooth (∗).** Tap to turn your Bluetooth transmitter off (gray) or on (blue). That feature alone is a godsend to anyone who uses the iPhone with a car's Bluetooth audio system. Bluetooth isn't the battery drain it once was, but it's still nice to be able to flick it on so easily when you get into the car.

Sample Siri commands: "Turn Bluetooth on." "Turn off Bluetooth."

- **Do Not Disturb (☾).** Do Not Disturb mode, described on page 128, means that the phone won't ring or buzz when people call—except a few handpicked people whose communiqués ring through. Perfect for sleeping hours; in fact, you can set up an automated schedule for Do Not Disturb (say, midnight to 7 a.m.).

  But what if you wake up early or want to stay up late? Now you can tap to turn Do Not Disturb on (blue) or off (gray).

  Sample Siri commands: "Turn on Do Not Disturb." "Turn Do Not Disturb off."

- **Rotation lock (↻).** When rotation lock is turned on (red), the screen no longer rotates when you turn the phone 90 degrees. The idea is that sometimes, like when you're reading an ebook on your side in bed, you don't want the screen picture to turn; you want it to stay upright relative to your eyes. (A little ↻ icon appears at the top of the screen to remind you why the usual rotating isn't happening.)

  The whole thing isn't quite as earth-shattering as it sounds—first, because it locks the image in only one way: upright, in portrait orientation. You can't make it lock into widescreen mode. Furthermore, many apps don't rotate with the phone to begin with. But when that day comes when you want to read in bed on your side with your head on the pillow, your iPhone will be ready. (Tap the button again to turn rotating back on.)

- **Brightness.** Hallelujah! Here's a screen-brightness slider. Drag the little white ball to change the screen brightness.

  Sample Siri commands: "Make the screen brighter." "Dim the screen."

- **AirPlay Mirroring (▱).** The AirPlay button lets you send your iPhone's video and audio to a wireless speaker system or TV—if you have an AirPlay receiver, of which the most famous is the Apple TV. Details are on page 259.

- **AirDrop (◉).** AirDrop gives you a quick, effortless way to shoot photos, maps, web pages, and other stuff to nearby iPhones, iPads, iPod Touches, and even Macs. (See page 348 for details.)

  On the Control Center, the AirDrop button isn't an on/off switch like most of the other icons here. Instead it produces a pop-up menu of options that control whose i-gadgets can "see" your iPhone: Contacts Only (people in your address book), Everyone, or Receiving Off (nobody).

- **Night Shift (☀️).** "Many studies have shown that exposure to bright blue light in the evening can affect your circadian rhythms and make it harder to fall asleep," Apple's website says. You can therefore tap this button to give your screen a warmer, less blue tint. (You can also set Night Shift to turn on near bedtime automatically; see page 579.)

    Sample Siri command: "Turn on Night Shift."

> **NOTE:** Truth is, there's not much research that blue light from *screens* affects your circadian rhythm, let alone little screens like your phone. And the iPhone may not cut out enough blue to make much of a difference anyway. (If using a gadget before bed makes it harder to sleep, it's more likely that it's the brain stimulation of what you're reading.) Sleep scientists have a more universally effective suggestion: Turn off your screens a couple of hours before bedtime.

- **Flashlight (🔦).** Tap to turn on the iPhone's "flashlight"—actually the LED lamp on the back that usually serves as the camera flash. Knowing that a source of good, clean light is a few touches away makes a huge difference if you're trying to read in the dark, find your way along a path at night, or fiddle with wires behind your desk.

- **Timer (⏱️).** Tap to open the Clock app—specifically, the Timer mode, which counts down to zero. Apple figures you might appreciate having direct access to it when you're cooking, for example, or waiting for your hair color to set.

    Sample Siri commands: "Open the Timer." Or, better yet, bypass the Clock and Timer apps altogether: "Start the timer for three minutes." "Count down from six minutes." (Siri counts down right there on the Siri screen.)

- **Calculator (🖩).** Tap to open the Calculator app—a handy shortcut if it's your turn to figure out how to divide up the restaurant bill.

    Sample Siri commands: "Open the calculator." Or, better yet, without opening any app: "What's a hundred and six divided by five?"

- **Camera (📷).** Tap to jump directly into the Camera app. Because photo ops don't wait around.

    Sample Siri commands: "Take a picture." "Open the camera."

On the Playback screen of the Control Center, you get these options:

- **Music information.** Now that the playback buttons are on a separate screen, there's room for some information about the current song, and even a photo of the album.

- **Playback controls (◀◀, ▶, ▶▶).** These controls govern playback in whatever app is playing music or podcasts in the background: the Music app, Pandora, Spotify, whatever it is. You can skip a horrible song quickly and efficiently without having to interrupt what you're doing, or pause the music to chat with a colleague. (Tap the song name to open whatever app is playing.)

  You also get a scrubber bar that shows where you are in the song, the name of the song and the performer, and the album name. And, of course, there's a volume slider. It lets you make big volume jumps faster than you can by pressing the volume buttons on the side of the phone.

  Sample Siri commands: "Pause the music." "Skip to the next song." "Play some Billy Joel."

- **Audio Output.** At the very bottom of this screen, you can choose which speaker source you want for playback. It always lists iPhone (the built-in speakers), but it may also list things like a Bluetooth speaker, earbuds, or AirPlay, which sends music or video to a wireless speaker system or TV (see page 249).

The Control Center closes when any of these things happen:

- You tap the Timer, Calculator, or Camera button.

- You tap or drag downward from *any spot* above the Control Center (the dimmed background of the screen).

- You press the Home button.

NOTE: In some apps, swiping up doesn't open the Control Center on the first try, much to your probable bafflement. Instead, swiping up just makes a tiny ⌃ tab appear at the edge of the screen. (You'll see this behavior whenever the status bar—the strip at the top that shows the time and battery gauge—is hidden, as can happen in the full-screen modes of iBooks, Maps, Videos, and so on. It also happens in the Camera.)

In those situations, Apple is trying to protect you from opening the Control Center accidentally—for example, when what you really wanted to do was scroll the image up. No big deal; once the ⌃ appears, swipe up a *second* time to open the Control Center panel.

If you find yourself opening the Control Center accidentally—when playing games, for example—you can turn it off. Open **Settings→Control Center**. Turn off **Access Within Apps**. Now swiping up opens the Control Center only at the Home screen. (You can also turn off **Access on Lock Screen** here, to make sure the Control Center never appears when the phone is asleep.)

Passcode (or Fingerprint) Protection

Like any smartphone, the iPhone offers a first line of defense for a phone that winds up in the wrong hands. It's designed to keep your stuff private from other people in the house or the office, or to protect your information in case you lose the iPhone. If you don't know the passcode or don't have the right fingerprint, you can't use the iPhone (except for limited tasks like taking a photo or using Siri).

About half of iPhone owners don't bother setting up a passcode to protect the phone. Maybe they never set the thing down in public, so they don't worry about thieves. Or maybe there's just not that much personal information on the phone—and meanwhile, having to enter a passcode every time you wake the phone can get to be a profound hassle.

TIP: Besides—if you ever do lose your phone, you can put a passcode on it by remote control; see page 531.

The other half of people reason that the inconvenience of entering a passcode many times a day is a small price to pay for the knowledge that nobody can get into your stuff if you lose your phone.

If you think your phone is worth protecting, here's how to set up a passcode—and, if you have an iPhone 5s or later model, how to use the fingerprint reader instead.

Setting Up a Passcode

If you didn't already create a phone passcode the first time you turned your iPhone on (see page 614), here's how to do it. (And just because you're an iPhone 5s-or-later owner, don't be smug; you have to create a passcode even if you plan to use the fingerprint reader. As a backup.)

Open **Settings→Touch ID & Passcode**. (On the 5c, it's just called **Passcode Lock**.)

iOS 10 proposes a longer string of numbers than iOS once did, for greater security (six digits instead of four). But you can tap **Passcode Options** if you'd prefer a four-digit number, or a full-blown alphanumeric password of any length.

You're asked to type the passcode you want, either on the number key-pad (for number codes) or the alphabet keyboard. You're asked to do it again to make sure you didn't make a typo.

NOTE: Don't kid around with this passcode. If you forget the iPhone code, you'll have to *restore* your iPhone (page 625), which wipes out everything on it. You've probably still got most of the data on your computer or backed up on iCloud, of course (music, video, contacts, calendar), but you may lose text messages, mail, and so on.

Once you confirm your passcode, you return to the Passcode Lock screen. Here you have a few more options.

The Require Passcode option lets you specify how quickly the pass-word is requested before locking somebody out: immediately after the iPhone wakes or 1, 15, 30, 60, or 240 minutes later. (Those options are a convenience to you, so you can quickly check your calendar or missed messages without having to enter the passcode—while still protecting your data from, for example, evildoers who pick up your iPhone while you're out getting coffee.)

Certain features are accessible on the Lock screen even before you've entered your password: the Today and Notifications tabs of the Notification Center; Siri, Wallet, Home Control, and Reply with Mes-sage (the ability to reply to text messages right from their notification bubble).

These are huge conveniences, but also, technically, a security risk. Somebody who finds your phone on your desk could, for example, blindly voice-dial your colleagues or use Siri to send a text. If you turn these switches off, then nobody can use these features until after entering the password (or using your fingerprint).

Finally, here is Erase Data—an option that's scary and reassuring at the same time. When this option is on, then if someone makes 10 incorrect guesses at your passcode, your iPhone erases itself. It's assuming that some lowlife burglar is trying to crack into it to have a look at all your personal data.

This option, a pertinent one for professional people, provides potent protection from patient password prospectors.

NOTE: Even when the phone is locked and the password unguessable, a tiny blue Emergency Call button still appears on the Unlock screen. It's there just in case you've been conked on the head by a vase, you can't remember your own password, and you need to call 911.

And that is all. From now on, each time you wake your iPhone (if it's not within the window of repeat visits you established), you're asked for your password.

Fingerprint Security (Touch ID)

If you have an iPhone 5s or later, you have the option of using a more secure and convenient kind of "passcode": your fingertip.

The lens built right into the Home button (clever!) reads your finger at any angle. It can't be faked out by a plastic finger or even a chopped-off finger. You can teach it to recognize up to five fingerprints; they can all be yours, or some can belong to other people you trust.

Before you can use your fingertip as a password, though, you have to teach the phone to recognize it. Here's how that goes:

1. **Create a passcode.** You can't use a fingerprint *instead* of a passcode; you can only use a fingerprint in *addition* to one. You'll still need a passcode from time to time to keep the phone's security tight. For example, you need to enter your passcode if you can't make your fingerprint work (maybe it got encased in acrylic in a hideous crafts accident), or if you restart the phone, or if you haven't used the phone in 48 hours or more.

   So open Settings→Touch ID & Passcode and create a password, as already described.

2. **Teach a fingerprint.** At the top of the Touch ID & Passcode screen, you see the on/off switches for the three things your fingerprint can do: It can unlock the phone (iPhone Unlock), pay for things (Apple Pay), and it can serve as your password when you buy books, music, apps, and videos from Apple's online stores (iTunes & App Store).

   But what you really want to tap here, of course, is Add a Fingerprint.

Now comes the cool part. Place the finger you want to train onto the Home button—your thumb or index finger are the most logical candidates. You're asked to touch it to the Home button over and over, maybe six times. Each time, the gray lines of the onscreen fingerprint darken a little more.

Once you've filled in the fingerprint, you see the Adjust Your Grip screen. Tap **Continue**. Now, the iPhone wants you to touch the Home button another few times, this time tipping the finger a little each time so the sensor gets a better view of your finger's *edges*.

Once that's done, the screen says "Success!"

You are now ready to start using the fingerprint. Try it: Put the phone to sleep. Then wake it (press the Sleep switch or press the Home button), and leave your finger on the Home button for about a second. The phone reads your fingerprint and instantly unlocks itself.

And now, a few notes about using your fingerprint as a password:

- Yes, you can touch your finger to the Home button at the Lock screen. But you can also touch it at any Enter Passcode screen.

Suppose, for example, that your Lock screen shows that you missed a text message. And you want to reply. Well, you can swipe across that notification to open it in its native habitat—the Messages app—but first you're shown the Enter Passcode screen. Ignore that. Just touch the Home button with the finger whose print you recorded.

- Apple says the image of your fingerprint is encrypted and stored in the iPhone's processor chip. It's never transmitted anywhere, it never goes online, and it's never collected by Apple.

- If you return to the Touch ID & Passcode screens, you can tap **Add a Fingerprint** again to teach your phone to recognize a second finger. And a third, fourth, and fifth.

  The five "registered" fingerprints don't all have to belong to you. If you share the phone with a spouse or a child, for example, that special somebody can use up some of the fingerprint slots.

- On the other hand, it makes a lot of sense to register the *same* finger *several* times. You'll be amazed at how much faster and more reliably your thumb (for example) is recognized if you've trained it as several different "fingerprints."

- To rename a fingerprint, tap its current name ("Finger 1" or whatever). To delete one, tap its name and then tap **Delete Fingerprint**. (You can figure out which finger label is which by touching the Home button; the corresponding label blinks. Sweet!)

- You can register your toes instead of fingers, if that's helpful. Or even patches of your wrist or arm, if you're patient (and weird).

- The Touch ID scanner may have trouble recognizing your touch if your finger is wet, greasy, or scarred.

- The iPhone's finger reader isn't just a camera; it doesn't just look for the image of your fingerprint. It's actually measuring the tiny differences in electrical conductivity between the raised parts of your fingerprint (which aren't conductive) and the skin just beneath the surface (which is). That's why a plastic finger won't work—and even your own finger won't work if it's been chopped off (or if you've passed away).

Fingerprints for Apps, Websites, and Apple Pay

So if your fingerprint is such a great solution to password overload, how come it works only to unlock the phone and to buy stuff from Apple's online stores? Wouldn't it be great if your fingerprint could also log you into secure websites? Or serve as your ID when you buy stuff online?

That dream is finally becoming a reality. Software companies can now use your Touch ID fingerprint to log into their apps. Mint (for checking your personal finances), Evernote (for storing notes, pictures, and to-do lists), Amazon (for buying stuff), and other apps now permit you to substitute a fingerprint touch for typing a password.

What's really wild is that password-storing apps like 1Password and LastPass have been updated, too. Those apps are designed to memorize your passwords for all sites on the web, of every type—and now you can use your fingerprint to unlock them.

Moreover, your fingerprint is now the key to the magical door of Apple Pay, the wireless pay-with-your-iPhone technology described on page 536.

All of this is great news. Most of us would be happy if we never, ever had to type in another password.

2

The Lock Screen & Notifications

The Lock screen—the first thing you see when you wake the iPhone—is more than just a big Do Not Disturb sign. It's a lively bulletin board for up-to-date information about your life. And, in iOS 10, it's had a big promotion. Now it's possible to have complete work sessions right at the Lock screen, without even fully unlocking the iPhone.

For starters, you can use the iPhone as a watch—millions of people do. Just lift the sleeping phone, or press the Sleep or Home button, to consult the Lock screen's time and date display, and then shove the phone right back into your pocket. The iPhone relocks after a few seconds.

If you're driving, using the Maps app to guide you, the Lock screen shows the standard GPS navigation screen. Handy, really—the less fumbling you have to do while driving, the safer you are.

Better yet, the Lock screen is a handy status screen. Here you see a record of everything that happened while you weren't paying attention. It's a list of missed calls, text messages received, notifications from your apps, and other essential information.

Four Swipes, You're In

The Lock screen in iOS 10 is the centerpiece of four *other* important screens. You can swipe up, down, left, or right to bring them into view.

- **Swipe up** from the bottom of the screen to open the Control Center shortcuts screen (page 46).

- **Swipe down** from the top to view your Notification Center—a master list of missed calls, appointments, alerts, and so on (page 61).

- **Swipe left** to open the Camera app (page 261).

- **Swipe right** to reveal the Today (Widgets) screen (page 65).

In short, keep this map in your head every time you wake your phone:

Notification Center

Today view

Camera

Lock screen

Control Center

Notifications

A notification is an important status message. You get one every time a text message comes in, an alarm goes off, a calendar appointment is imminent, your battery is running low, and so on. They appear in three different places:

- **On your screen, while you're working.** They pop up to get your attention (below, top left).

- **On the Lock screen,** in a scrolling list of alerts that came in while you were away (below, bottom left). (Unlocking the phone wipes them away. The *next* time you unlock the phone, that batch will be gone.)

- **On the Notifications screen.** This special screen pulls down from the top of the screen like a window shade (below, right). Here's where you can look at all the notifications that have come in recently, even ones you already saw on the Lock screen.

TIP: You can pull this screen down from the top whether the phone is locked or unlocked.

The following pages tackle these three notification situations one by one.

Notifications While You're Working

These days, there's a lot more you can do with a notification than just read it and nod your head. Apple has gone to a lot of effort to make notifications as productive, customizable, and un-interrupty as possible.

For example, if one of them springs onto your screen while you're working, you can deal with it in any of these ways:

- **Flick it away.** You can flick any notification bubble upward with your finger to make it disappear.

- **Answer it.** Often, a notification appears to display an incoming text message, email, or calendar invitation. You can actually take action on the bubble itself: reply to a text message, delete an email, accept a calendar invitation, see where your Uber car is, mark a Reminder as done, and so on. And you never have to leave the app you were using, which is deliciously efficient.

  Apple calls this feature *rich notifications*.

  If you have an **iPhone 6s or 7 model**, you have 3D Touch, which means your screen can tell how *hard* you're pressing. Just *hard-press* right on the notification to expand it (facing page, top right).

  If you have an earlier model, you have to use a different sequence to access the notification response screens. Swipe to the left on the notification bubble to reveal a couple of buttons, like View and Clear (facing page, lower right). Tap View to open the response panel (facing page, top right).

- **Open it.** Finally, here's the obvious one: You can tap a notification to open the app it came from. Tap an email notification to open the message in Mail; tap a text-message notification to open it in Messages; and so on. That's handy when you want to dig in and see the full context of the notification.

Notifications on the Lock Screen

The techniques for operating on notifications on the Lock screen (facing page, right) are slightly different. You can:

- **Answer it.** As described, you can deal with a notification right on its bubble. On an **iPhone 6s or 7** model, *hard-press* right on the notification to expand it as shown at top right on the facing page.

  If it's an **iPhone 5, 6, or SE,** swipe to the *left* on the notification bubble to reveal a couple of buttons. If it's a text message, buttons say View and Clear; if it's an email, they say Trash and Mark as Read; and so on (facing page, lower right).

- **Open it.** If you swipe a notification bubble to the *right*, you're prompted to log in (enter your password or touch the fingerprint reader/Home button). You wind up in whichever app sent you the notification. If it's a missed-call note, it takes you to the Phone app; if it's a text message, it opens the Messages app; and so on.

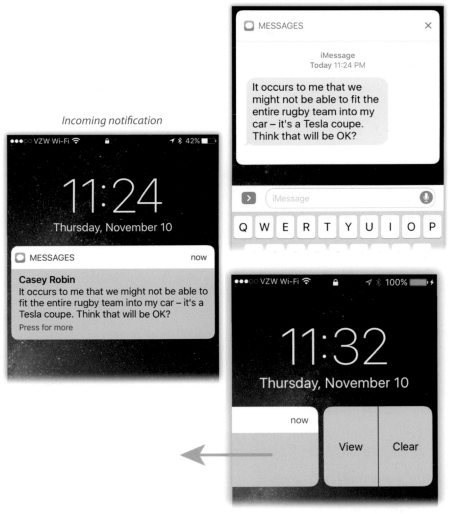

Modern iPhones: Press hard to reply

Incoming notification

Older iPhones: Swipe left, tap View

The Notification Center

No matter what kind of notification pops up, you still see only one alert at a time. And once it's gone, you can't get it back. Or can you?

Meet the Notification Center screen (page 59, right). It lists every notification you've recently received, in a tidy scrolling list.

You can check it out right now, whether your phone is locked or unlocked: Swipe your finger down from above the iPhone's screen. The Notification Center pulls down like a classy window shade, listing every recent item of interest.

Here you'll find all your apps' notifications, as well as your missed calls, recent text messages, reminders, and upcoming calendar appointments. Scroll down, and you'll discover that they go back about a week. It can be a very long list.

Tap one of these bubbles to open the relevant app for more details—for example, to see more information about that appointment, or to read the whole text message in context.

You can clear out the notifications from the Center like this:

- Tap the ⊗ next to a day's name, and then tap Clear to remove all notifications for that day.

- If you have an iPhone 6s or 7 model, hard-press the ⊗ next to any day's name to reveal the Clear All button. It erases your *entire* Notification Center. (There's no Clear All function on older iPhone models.)

To close the Notification Center, just swipe it up and away from the bottom of the screen.

Customizing Notifications

You can (and should) specify *which* apps are allowed to junk up your notification screens. Open Settings→Notifications to see the master list, with one entry for every app that might ever want your attention. (Or just tell Siri, "Open notification settings.")

You'll quickly discover that *every* app thinks it's important; *every* app wants its notifications to blast into your face when you're working.

You, however, may not agree. You may not consider it essential to know when your kid's Plants vs. Zombies score has changed, for example.

So: Tap an app's name to open its individual Notifications screen (facing page—the News app, in this example). Here you'll find settings that vary by app, but they generally run along these lines:

- **Allow Notifications.** If you don't want this app to make any notifications pop up at all, turn this off.

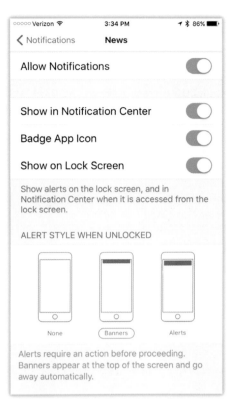

- **Show in Notification Center.** If you turn this off, an app may still display bubbles or banners to get your attention—but those alerts won't show up in the Notification Center itself.

- **Sounds.** Some apps try to get your attention with a sound effect when a notification appears. Turn this off if you think your phone makes too many beeps and burbles as it is. (Some apps also let you choose *which* sound effect plays to get your attention. You can change the sound or choose None.)

- **Badge App Icon.** A badge is a little red circled number (❷, for example). It appears right on an app's icon to indicate how many updates are waiting for you. Turn it off if you really don't need that reminder.

- **Show on Lock Screen.** The Lock screen (page 17) is another place to see what's been trying to get your attention while the phone was in your pocket: missed calls and texts, new messages and email, and so on.

  The Lock screen may seem just like the Notification Center—but there are differences. For example, each time you wake the phone, whatever notifications are on the Lock screen are wiped clear. They don't stay put, as they do in the Notification Center.

You might want a *different* set of apps to list their nags on the Lock screen. Maybe you want the Lock screen to show only missed calls, new text messages, and new email—but you'd like the Notification Center to be fully stocked with Twitter and Facebook updates, for example. Or maybe you'd rather not permit passing evildoers to pick up your phone and see your notifications without even having to unlock it.

That's why you have this switch. It governs your ability to see this app's updates on the Lock screen (and the Notification Center when you open it while at the Lock screen).

What Notifications Look Like

Notifications can appear in any of three styles—and you get to choose which you prefer, for *each individual app*.

On the same Settings→Notifications screen (then tap the app's name), you can choose one of these three styles for notifications that occur while you're using the phone:

- **None.** If a certain app bugs you with news you really don't care about, you can shut it up forever. Tap None.

- **Banners** are incoming notifications that appear quietly and briefly at the top of the screen. The message holds still long enough for you to read it, but it goes away after a few seconds. Banners are a good option for things like Facebook and Twitter updates and incoming email messages.

> **TIP:** A reminder: If you tap a banner before it disappears, you jump directly to the app that's trying to get your attention. You can also flick a banner up off the screen if it's in your way.

- **Alerts.** An alert box doesn't disappear after a couple of seconds; it stays on your screen until you tap or swipe it. You might use this option for apps whose messages are too important to miss, like alarms, flight updates, or text messages.

> **TIP:** You can also use the Include setting to specify how *much* of the Notification Center this app is allowed to use up—that is, how many lines of information. Maybe you need only the most recent alert about your upcoming flight (1 Item), but you want to see a lot more of your upcoming appointments (10 Items).

Miscellaneous Weirdness

As you poke around in the Notification Center settings, you'll discover that certain oddball apps offer some options that don't match up with the settings you see for most apps. Don't freak out. It's all part of Apple's master plan to put controls where it hopes you'll find them.

The Today Screen (Widgets)

To the left of the main Lock screen, you'll find a motley assortment of panels that Apple calls widgets.

Some are quick-access buttons that launch related apps, like quick-dial (or quick-text) buttons for your favorite contacts; others are info-bits that you might want to check frequently throughout the day, like your calendar, news, sports, and weather.

This entire wonderland is available before you've even unlocked the phone—quickly. That's the point.

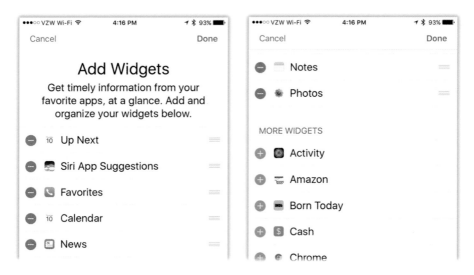

(Actually, the Today screen is available when the phone is *unlocked*, too. It's always waiting to the left of the Home screens.)

Truth is, many people don't even know the Today screen is there; even if they do, most people don't use it. And sure enough, this feature doesn't really be become useful until you customize it: Rearrange the widgets, remove the ones you'd never touch, and install more useful ones.

The very first time you open the Widgets screen, you see things like the Spotlight search bar (page 99), Up Next, Siri App Suggestions, and News. (They're described on these pages.) But the key to the real magic is the **Edit** button, which is hiding below all the widgets, several scrolls down.

The list you find here has two parts: The widgets that are currently installed, and the ones that aren't. Delete a widget by tapping its ⊖ button; add one by tapping its ⊕ button. Rearrange the installed ones by dragging their ☰ handles. When you are finished, tap **Done**.

So what widgets are available? Here's a rundown:

- **Up Next.** The next couple of things on your calendar. Tap to log in and open the Calendar app, which shows you details of the event.

- **Siri App Suggestions.** This feature is supposed to let you know when one of your apps might be useful. You can think of it as a "frequently used apps" listing, but it's even smarter than that; the icons you see here are chosen *based on the time and your location right now*.

  It's based on recognition of your daily patterns: If you listen to the Podcasts app through earbuds every day before work, then plugging in your earbuds at about that time and location displays the Podcast app's icon. If you call home as you leave work every day, the Phone app's icon shows up at that time.

In each case, the suggested app opens when you tap its icon.

- **News.** Headlines from the News app (page 402).

- **Weather.** You guessed it.

- **Maps Destinations.** If you use Apple's Maps app, and routinely enter the addresses of your appointments on the Calendar, here's the payoff: a list of upcoming and predicted destinations, including your next calendar appointment and where you parked your car (page 399).

- **Calendar.** Today's agenda. Tap an appointment to unlock your phone and see its details screen.

- **Reminders.** Your unfinished To Dos. You can mark one as done here, without having to unlock the phone and open the app. That's a big deal.

- **Favorites.** This is your speed-dial list. The first four people you've designated as Favorites appear here, for quick speed dialing.

  But it's not just about phone calls (who does *that* anymore)? In iOS 10, you can designate a text-message address, email address, Skype handle, or other communication addresses as Favorites (page 104). Which means that, using this widget, you can insta-text your spouse or your kid, without having to open the app, access the address book, choose the person's name, and so on. Shortcuts, baby!

- **Find Friends.** After a moment of thought, this widget shows a map that pinpoints the location of any loved ones you're tracking (page 586).

- **Mail.** A speed-dial list of the people you've designated as VIPs (page 484), for quick emailing.

- **Maps Nearby.** These icons are shortcuts for time-appropriate searches, like coffee in the morning, or nightlife after dark.

- **Maps Transit.** If you use Maps' public-transportation feature, this widget lets you know about delays and service interruptions.

- **Music.** Playback controls for resuming and controlling whatever you were playing last.

- **Notes.** You see the first couple of lines of the Notes page you most recently edited.

- **Photos.** Thumbnails that, after you unlock the phone, open recent Memories (automated slideshows of recent time periods).

- **Stocks.** The latest on whatever stocks you follow (page 420).

- **Tips.** This is the closest Apple comes to offering a manual for iOS 10.

You probably have many other widgets, too, installed by your apps. Waze, Yelp, The New York Times, NPR, Google Maps, Kindle, Evernote, Dropbox, Chrome, Amazon, and many other apps put widgets here for your quick-glancing pleasure.

> **TIP:** Many widgets are expandable. If you see a Show More button on a widget, it means that a larger area, showing more information, is available to you. For example, expanding the Favorites widget shows icons for *eight* speed-dial people instead of four; expanding the Notes widget shows the *three* notes you've most recently viewed, instead of one; and so on. They remain expanded until you collapse them again.

Widgets on the Home Screen

Turns out you don't have to swipe onto the Today screen to view a certain widget you need right now. On the iPhone 6s and 7 models, you can hard-press (page 35) an app's *Home-screen icon* to view not just its shortcut menu, but also its widget, for quick consultation. (This pop-up panel also includes an Add Widget button, should you decide to install it on the Widgets *screen*.)

Locking Down the Lock Screen

Now, remember: You can enjoy any of these activities, and see any of this information, even *before* you've entered your password or used your fingerprint.

If you'd rather *not* have all these details show up on the Lock screen, you can turn them off. Privacy is the main reason you might want to do so—remember that the bad guys don't need a password to view your Lock screen. They just have to tap the Sleep switch or the Home button.

If that bothers you, turn those features off individually. For example:

- **Control Center.** To block Lock-screen access to your Control Center, open Settings→Control Center. Turn off Access on Lock Screen.

- **Widgets.** You can eliminate the entire Today screen by turning off Settings→Touch ID & Passcode→Today. (The Today screen is still available *after* you've unlocked the phone; swipe to the right from the Home screen.)

Or, if **one** widget's presence bothers you, bring up the Today screen; scroll to the bottom; tap **Edit**; and tap the ⊖ button for the widget.

- **Notification screen.** Similarly, you can eliminate the Notifications screen by turning off **Settings→Touch ID & Passcode→Notifications view**. (This, too, is still available **after** you've unlocked the phone.)

NOTE: This step gets rid of the Notifications **screen**—the window shade that appears when you drag down on the Lock screen. Notifications will still appear **on** the Lock screen as they come in, though. You can hide these items from your Lock screen on an app-by-app basis. To set this up, choose **Settings→Notifications**. Tap the app in question; scroll to the bottom, and then turn off **Show on Lock Screen**.

- **Camera.** There's no way to block access to the Camera from the Lock screen. (Well, you can open **Settings→General→Restrictions** and turn off **Camera**. That step, however, hides the Camera **completely**—it even disappears from the Home screen.)

3

Typing, Editing & Searching

As a pocket computer, the iPhone faces a fundamental limitation: It has no real keyboard or mouse. Which might be considered a drawback on a gadget that's capable of running hundreds of thousands of programs.

Fortunately, where there's a problem, there's software that can fix it. The modern iPhone's virtual keyboard is smart in all kinds of ways—automatically predicting words and correcting typos, for example. And besides: If you don't like the iPhone's onscreen keyboard, you can just choose one designed by a different company.

This chapter covers every aspect of working with text on the iPhone: entering it, dictating it, fixing it and searching for it.

The Keyboard

It's true, boys and girls: The iPhone has no physical keys. A virtual keyboard, therefore, is the only possible built-in system for typing text. Like it or not, you'll be doing a lot of typing on glass.

The keyboard appears automatically whenever you tap in a place where typing is possible: in an outgoing email or text message, in the Notes program, in the address bar of the web browser, and so on.

Just tap the key you want. As your finger taps the glass, a "speech balloon" appears above your finger, showing an enlarged version of the key you actually hit (since your finger is now blocking your view of the keyboard).

TIP: If you worry about spies nearby figuring out what you're typing by watching those bubbles pop up over your fingertips, you can turn them off. Open Settings→General→Keyboard, and turn off Character Preview.

In darker gray, surrounding the letters, you'll find these special keys:

- **Shift (⇧).** When you tap this key, it turns dark to indicate that it's in effect. The next letter you type appears as a capital. Then the ⇧ key returns to normal, meaning that the next letter will be lowercase.

> **TIP:** It used to be that the color of the Shift key was your only clue that you were about to type a capital letter; the actual letters on the onscreen keyboard's keys always appeared AS CAPITALS. But these days, the key letters appear in lowercase until you press Shift. (If you prefer that old system, though, open **Settings→General→Accessibility→Keyboard**. Turn off **Show Lowercase Keys**.

- **Caps Lock (⇪).** The iPhone has a Caps Lock "key," but it's hidden. To engage it, *double-tap* the ⇧ key; it changes to ⇪. You're now in Caps Lock mode, and you'll type in ALL CAPITALS until you tap the ⇪ key again (or the 123 key). If you can't seem to make Caps Lock work, try double-tapping the ⇧ key *fast*. Or see if maybe Caps Lock got turned off in **Settings→General→Keyboard**.

- **Backspace (⌫).** This key actually has three speeds:

  Tap it once to delete the letter just before the blinking insertion point.

Hold it down to "walk" backward, deleting as you go.

If you hold down the key long enough, it starts deleting **words** rather than letters, one whole chunk at a time.

- **123.** Tap this button when you want to type numbers or punctuation. The keyboard changes to offer a palette of numbers and symbols. Tap the same key—which now says ABC—to return to the letters keyboard.

  Once you're on the numbers/symbols pad, a new dark-gray button appears, labeled #+=. Tapping it summons a **third** keyboard layout, containing the less frequently used symbols, like brackets, the # and % symbols, bullets, and math symbols.

- **return.** Tapping this key moves to the next line, just as on a real keyboard. (There's no Tab key or Enter key in iPhone Land.)

Making the Keyboard Work

Some people have no problem tapping those tiny virtual keys; others struggle for days. Either way, here are some tips:

- As you type, use the whole pad of your finger or thumb. Don't try to tap with only a skinny part of your finger to match the skinny keys. You'll be surprised at how fast and accurate this method is. (Tap, don't mash.)

- This may sound like New Age hooey, but **trust** the keyboard. Don't pause to check the result after each letter. Just plow on.

TIP: Although you don't see it, the sizes of the keys on the iPhone keyboard are changing all the time. That is, the software enlarges the "landing area" of certain keys, based on probability.

For example, suppose you type **tim**. The iPhone knows that no word in the language begins with **timw** or **timr**—and so, invisibly, it enlarges the "landing area" of the E key, which greatly diminishes your chances of making a typo on that last letter.

- Without a mouse, how are you supposed to correct an error you made a few sentences ago? Easy—use the **loupe**.

  Hold your fingertip down anywhere in the text until the magnified circle appears. Without lifting your finger, drag anywhere in the text; the insertion point moves along with it. Release when the blue line is where you want to delete or add text, just as though you'd clicked there with a mouse.

- Don't bother using the Shift key to capitalize a new sentence. The iPhone does that capitalizing automatically. (To turn this feature on or off, use Settings→General→Keyboard→Auto-Capitalization.)

- Don't type a period at the end of each sentence, either. Because the period is such a frequently used symbol, there's an awesome short-cut that doesn't require switching to the punctuation keyboard: At the end of a sentence, **tap the space bar twice**. You get a period, a space, **and** a capitalized letter at the beginning of the next word. (This, too, can be turned off—in Settings→General→Keyboard→"." Shortcut—although it's hard to imagine why you'd want to.)

- You can save time by leaving out the apostrophe in contractions. Type *im*, *dont*, or *cant*. The iPhone proposes *I'm*, *don't*, or *can't*, so you can just tap the space bar to fix the word and continue.

Autocorrect: Your Typing Assistant from Hell

Since it's fussy to type on a phone, the iPhone, like all smartphones, offers a feature called autocorrect. Whenever the software thinks you've made a spelling error, it **automatically** substitutes the "correct" word or spelling. For example, if you type **imsame**, the iPhone realizes that you meant **insane** and replaces it automatically.

Most of the time, that's helpful; autocorrect even finishes long words for you sometimes. But you have to be vigilant—because many times auto-correct substitutes the **wrong** word! And sometimes you don't notice it, and you wind up texting absolute gibberish to your correspondent. The Internet is filled with hilarious examples of autocorrect gone wrong. (Visit *damnyouautocorrect.com* for some choice ones.)

So here's the important thing: The iPhone always shows you the replacement it intends to make before making it, in a blue-type bubble (below, left). To accept its suggestion, tap the space bar or any punctuation. To **prevent** the replacement, tap the bubble with your finger.

> **TIP:** If you turn on Speak Auto-text (in Settings→General→Accessibility), the iPhone even speaks the suggested word out loud. That way, you can keep your focus on the keyboard.

And by the way: If you **accidentally** accept an autocorrect suggestion, tap the Backspace key. A word bubble appears, which you can tap to reinstate what you'd originally typed (shown above at right).

> **TIP:** If you think that autocorrect is doing you more harm than help, you can turn it off in Settings→General→Keyboard. Turn off **Auto-Correction**.

QuickType

What Apple calls its QuickType keyboard can save you a *lot* of time, tapping, and errors.

The idea is simple: As you type a sentence, the software **predicts** which word you might type next—which are the three most likely words, actually—and displays them as three buttons above the keyboard.

If you begin the sentence by typing, "I really," then the three suggestions might be **want**, **don't**, and **like**.

But what if you intended to say, "I really **hope**..."? In that case, type the first letter of "hope." Instantly, the three suggestions change to **"h"**, **hope**, and **hate**. (The first button always shows, in quotes, whatever non-word you've typed so far, just in case that's what you intend. To place it into your text, you can tap that button *or* tap the space bar or some punctuation.)

In other words, QuickType is autocomplete on steroids. (In fact, one of the three suggestions is always the same one you would have seen in the little autocomplete bubble.) Frankly, it's a rush when QuickType correctly proposes finishing a long word for you.

With QuickType, you can produce a sentence like "I'll gladly pay you Tuesday for a hamburger today" with 26 taps on the screen. If you had to type out the whole thing, you'd have tapped 50 keys. QuickType also adds spaces for you.

A set of three buttons, guessing what you might want to type next, isn't a new idea; Android and BlackBerry phones have had it for years. But QuickType is smarter in several ways:

- QuickType's suggestions are **different** in Messages (where language tends to be casual) than in Mail (where people write more formally).

- Similarly, QuickType modifies its suggestions based on whom you're writing to. It **learns**.

- Sometimes, QuickType offers you several words on a single button, to save you even more time (for example, **up to** or **in the**).

- New in iOS 10: When you're in the Messages app, QuickType suggests an emoji (a tiny cartoon drawing) when you've typed a corresponding word. Page 186 has the details.

- QuickType automatically adds a space after each word you select, so you don't have to mess with the space bar.

- When someone texts you a question that ends with a choice ("Coffee, tea, or me?"), the QuickType buttons cleverly offer those choices on the buttons. Before you've even typed a single letter, the choices say *coffee*, *tea*, and *you*.

- If you forget to capitalize a word, double-tap to select it. Now tap Shift once (to Initial Cap the Word) or twice (for ALL CAPS). Lo and behold, the QuickType suggestions are now capitalized renditions of the word, ready to replace it!

- You can hide the QuickType bar if it's getting on your nerves. Just hold down the button next to the 123 key (it usually looks like 😊 or 🌐); from the shortcut menu, tap to turn off Predictive. (There's a duplicate of this switch in **Settings→General→Keyboard**.)

QuickType does mean that you have to split your focus. You have to pay attention to both the keys you're tapping and the ever-changing word choices above the keyboard. With practice, though, you'll find that QuickType offers impressive speed and accuracy. You won't miss the little autocorrect bubbles of old.

The Spelling Dictionary

If you start typing a word the iPhone doesn't recognize, the first of the three suggestion buttons displays your word in quotation marks. If you really do intend to type that nonstandard word, tap its button. You've just allowed the "mistake" to stand—and you've added it to the iPhone's dictionary. The phone assumes that you've just typed some name, bit of slang, or terminology that wasn't in its dictionary originally.

From now on, it will accept that bizarre new word as legitimate—and, in fact, will even *suggest* it the next time you start typing it.

The Spelling Checker

Here's the world's friendliest typo-fixer. Apple calls it a spelling checker, but maybe that's stretching it.

Anytime the iPhone doesn't recognize something you've typed, it draws a dotted red underline beneath it. Tap the word to see a pop-up balloon with one, two, or three alternate spellings. Often, one of them is what you wanted, and you can tap it to fix the mistake. (Equally often, none of them is, and it's time to break out the loupe and the keyboard.)

TO DO TODAY

Buy a tube of caulk at
<u>hadware</u> store

TO DO TODAY

Buy a tube of caulk at
hadware store

The Widescreen Keyboard

In most apps, you can turn the phone 90 degrees to type. When the keyboard stretches out the long way, the keys get a lot bigger. It's much easier to type—even with two thumbs.

This feature doesn't work in every app, but it does work in the apps where you do the most typing: Mail, Messages, the Safari browser, Contacts, Twitter, Notes, and so on. (The screen also rotates in Camera, Music, Calculator, Calendar, and Stocks, though not for typing purposes.)

If you have an iPhone 6 or later, something even more startling happens: You get extra keys on the sides—including **cursor keys**. (With the Caps Lock engaged, you can actually highlight text by pressing these cursor keys.)

Cursor keys

Cut Copy
Paste Bold
Undo Dictate

Hide keyboard

NOTE: If you don't see the additional control keys on the sides of your widescreen keyboard, it's probably because you've turned on Zoomed mode (page 208). In Zoomed mode, all the keys are a little bigger—so there's no room for the buttons.

Punctuation with One Touch

On the iPhone, the punctuation and alphabet keys appear on two different keyboard layouts. That's a serious hassle, because each time you want, say, a comma, it's an awkward, three-step dance: (1) Tap the 123 key to get the punctuation layout. (2) Tap the comma. (3) Tap the ABC key or the space bar to return to the alphabet layout.

Imagine how excruciating it is to type, for example, "a P.O. box in the U.S.A." That's 34 finger taps and 10 mode changes!

Fortunately, there's a secret way to get a punctuation mark with only a *single* finger gesture. The iPhone doesn't register most key presses until you *lift* your finger. But the Shift and punctuation keys register their taps on the press *down* instead.

So here's what you can do, all in one motion:

1. **Touch the 123 key, but don't lift your finger.** The punctuation layout appears.

2. **Slide your finger onto the period or comma key, and release.** The ABC layout returns automatically. You've typed a period or a comma with one finger touch instead of three.

> **TIP:** If you're a two-thumbed typist, you can also hit the 123 key with your left thumb and then tap the punctuation key with your right. It even works on the #+= sub-punctuation layout, although you'll probably visit that screen less often.

In fact, you can type any of the punctuation symbols the same way. This technique makes a *huge* difference in the usability of the built-in iPhone keyboard.

> **TIP:** This same trick saves you a finger-press when capitalizing words, too. You can put your finger down on the ⇧ key and slide directly onto the letter you want to type in its uppercase version. Or, if you're a two-handed typist, you can work the Shift key like the one on your computer: Hold it down with your left thumb, type a letter with your right, and then release both.

Accented Characters

To produce an accented character (like é, ë, è, ê, and so on), keep your finger pressed on that key for 1 second. A palette of diacritical marks appears; slide onto the one you want.

Not all keys sprout this pop-up palette. Here's a list of the keys that do:

Key	Alternates
A	à á â ä Æ ã å ā
C	ç ć č
E	è é ê ë ę ė ē
I	ī į í ì ï î
L	ł
N	ń ñ
O	ō ø œ õ ó ò ö ô
S	ß ś š
U	ū ú ù ü û
Y	ÿ
Z	ź ž ż
?	¿
'	' ' '
"	» « „ " "
-	—
$	€ £ ¥ ₩
&	§
0 (zero)	°
.	…
%	‰

Typing Shortcuts (Abbreviation Expanders)

Here's a feature that hardly anyone ever talks about—probably because nobody knows it exists. But it's a huge time- and sanity-saver.

You can program the phone to expand abbreviations that you type. Set up *addr* to type your entire mailing address, or *eml* to type out your email address. Create two-letter abbreviations for big legal or technical words you have to type a lot. Set up *goaway* to type out a polite rejection paragraph for use in email. And so on.

This feature has been in Microsoft Office forever (called AutoCorrect). And it's always been available as a separate app (TypeIt4Me and

TextExpander, for example—but because they were separate, you had to copy your expanded text, switch to the target program, and then paste). But since it's now built right into the operating system, it works anywhere you can type.

You can start building your list of abbreviations in **Settings→General→ Keyboard→Text Replacement**. Tap the + button. On the resulting screen, type the expanded text into the **Phrase** box. (It can be very long, but it has to be one continuous blob of text; it can't contain Returns.) In the **Shortcut** box, type the abbreviation you want to trigger the phrase.

TIP: The **Shortcut** box says "Optional." You might wonder: Why would you leave the shortcut blank? Then your new shortcut will be un-triggerable and pointless.

Not quite. It's optional to enable a sneaky trick: to make the phone stop misreplacing some word (for example, insisting that you mean *PTA* when you type *pta*, the name of a new chemical you've designed).

In that case, type your phrase into the **Phrase** box, but leave **Shortcut** blank.

●○○○○ Verizon 🛜   12:00 PM   🡥 ✳ 88% ⬛

‹ Keyboard   **Shortcuts**   +

🔍 Search

A

ac   actually,

addr   My address: 155 Elmhurst,…

F

FBI   fbi

H

hth   Hope this helps!

I

ily   i love you!

L

lvm   I love you more!

Edit

●○○○○ Verizon 🛜   12:01 PM   🡥 ✳ 88% ⬛

‹ Shortcuts   **Shortcut**   Save

Phrase   Please stop emailing me.

Shortcut   pse|

Create a shortcut that will automatically
expand into the word or phrase
as you type.

q w e r t y u i o p
a s d f g h j k l
⇧ z x c v b n m ⌫
123 😊 🎙   space   return

That's it! Now, whenever you type one of the abbreviations you've set up, the iPhone proposes replacing it with your substituted text.

Swype, SwiftKey, and Other Keyboards

You're not stuck with Apple's onscreen keyboard. You can, if you like, install virtual keyboards from other companies. (Hey—just like on Android phones!)

Many people swear that these rival keyboard systems are superior to the standard iOS keyboard in speed and accuracy. In particular, people like the Swype and SwiftKey keyboards; in these systems, you don't have to *tap* each key to spell out a word. Instead, you rapidly and sloppily drag your finger *across* the glass, hitting the letters you want and lifting your finger at the end of a word. The software figures out which word you were going for.

Sounds bizarre, but it's fast and very satisfying. And pretty—your finger leaves a sort of fire trail as it slides across the glass.

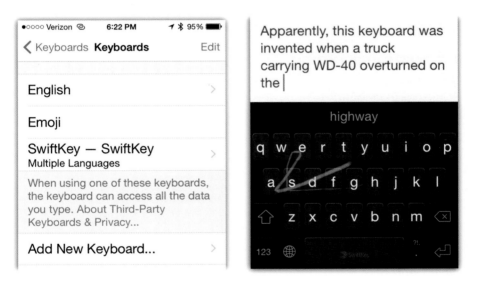

These keyboards generally incorporate their own versions of QuickType— that is, they offer three predictions about the word you're going to type next.

Most don't vary their predictions depending on the person you're writing to or which app you're using, as iOS's predictions do. But they do offer other impressive features; for example, SwiftKey can sync what it's learned to your other gadgets (iOS doesn't do that; it learns, but its education is locked on your iPhone). The Minuum keyboard is weird-looking but very compact, leaving a lot more room for your writing.

Then there's Fleksy, TouchPal, Kuaiboard, and a raft of others.

Note, however, that none of them offer a 🎤 button. Apple doesn't allow them access to Siri, so you can't use voice dictation when one of these keyboards is on the screen. And, sometimes, you can't use these alternate keyboards for typing into password boxes.

Otherwise, these alternate keyboard systems are fascinating, and, often, faster than Apple's. Many are free, so they're well worth exploring.

To install an alternate keyboard, download it from the App Store (page 328).

Then go to Settings→General→Keyboard→Keyboards (previous page, left). When you tap Add New Keyboard, you'll see your newly downloaded keyboard's name. Turn it on by tapping it.

Now, when you arrive at any writing area in any app, you'll discover that a new icon has appeared on the keyboard: a tiny globe (🌐) next to the space bar. Tap it. The keyboard changes to the new one you installed. (Each tap on the 🌐 button summons the next keyboard you've installed—or you can hold your finger down on it for a pop-up list.)

International Typing

Because the iPhone is sold around the world, it has to be equipped for non-English languages—and even non-Roman alphabets. Fortunately, it's ready.

To prepare the iPhone for language switching, go to Settings→General→ Language & Region. Tap iPhone Language to set the iPhone's primary language (for menus, button labels, and so on).

To make other *keyboards* available, go to Settings→General→ Keyboard→Keyboards, tap Add New Keyboard, and then turn on the keyboard layouts you'll want available: Russian, Italian, whatever.

If you choose Japanese or Chinese, you're offered the chance to specify which *kind* of character input you want. For Japanese, you can choose a QWERTY layout (Romaji) or a Kana keypad. For Simplified or Traditional Chinese, your choices include the Pinyin input method (which uses a QWERTY layout) or handwriting recognition, where you draw your symbols onto the screen with your fingertip; a palette of potential interpretations appears to the right. (That's handy, since there are thousands of characters in Chinese, and you'd need a 65-inch iPhone to fit the keyboard on it.) Or hey—it's a free tic-tac-toe game!

As described in the previous section, a new key now appears on the keyboard: 🌐 next to the space bar. (It replaces the 😊 emoji key, if you had it.) Each time you tap it, you rotate to the next keyboard you requested earlier. The new language's name appears briefly on the space bar to identify it.

Thanks to that ⊕ button, you can freely mix languages and alphabets within the same document without having to duck back to some control panel to make the change. And thanks to the iPhone's virtual keyboard, the actual letters on the "keys" change in real time.

The ⊕ button works in three ways:

- Tap it once to restore the most recent keyboard. Great if you're frequently flipping back and forth between two languages.

- Tap it rapidly to cycle among all the keyboards you've selected. (The name of the language appears briefly on the space bar to help you out.)

- If you, some United Nations translator, like to write in a lot of different languages, you don't have to tap that ⊕ key over and over again to cycle through the keyboard layouts. Instead, hold your finger down on the ⊕ key. You get a convenient pop-up menu of the languages you've turned on, so you can jump directly to the one you want.

The Emoji Keyboard

Even if you speak only one language, don't miss the emoji keyboard. It gives you a palette of smileys and fun symbols, also known as emoticons, to use in your correspondence.

When you tap the ☺ button, you're offered hundreds and hundreds of little symbols—many of them new or redesigned in iOS 10.2. They're spread across eight categories (plus a Frequently Used category), each represented by a small icon below the keyboard.

Emoji are even smarter in the Messages app; see page 186.

TIP: To return to a category's first page, you don't have to swipe; just tap the category's icon.

The bottom line is clear: Smileys are only the beginning.

NOTE: These symbols show up identically on Apple machinery (phones, tablets, Macs) but may look slightly different on other kinds of phones.

Connecting a Real Keyboard

This iPhone feature barely merits an asterisk in Apple's marketing materials. But if you're any kind of wandering journalist, blogger, or writer, you might flip your lid over this: You can type on a real, full-sized, physical keyboard, and watch the text magically appear on your iPhone's screen—wirelessly.

That's because you can use a Bluetooth keyboard (the Apple Wireless Keyboard, for example) to type into your iPhone.

To set this up, from the Home screen, tap Settings→Bluetooth. Turn Bluetooth on, if it's not already.

Now turn on the wireless keyboard. After a moment, its name shows up on the iPhone screen in the Devices list; tap it. You'll know the pairing was successful, because when you tap in a spot where the onscreen keyboard would usually appear, well, it doesn't.

Typing is a lot easier and faster with a real keyboard. As a bonus, the Apple keyboard's brightness, volume, and playback controls actually work to control the iPhone's brightness, volume, and playback.

TIP: The Apple keyboard's ⏏ key even works: It makes the iPhone's onscreen keyboard appear or disappear. And to switch languages, press ⌘-space bar on the wireless keyboard. You'll see the list of languages. Tap the space bar again to choose a different language.

When you're finished using the keyboard, turn it off. The iPhone goes back to normal.

iPhone 6s and 7: The Secret Trackpad

You may remember hearing about the Force Touch screen on your iPhone (or reading about it, on page 35). But you can also use pressure on the screen to create a trackpad for editing text!

Whenever text is on the screen and the keyboard is open, press firmly anywhere on the keyboard. All the keys go blank, as shown on the next page.

You can ease up on the pressure, but *don't lift your finger* from the glass. You can now move the insertion-point cursor through the text just by dragging your finger across the keys. If it hits the edge of the window, it scrolls automatically.

Still keep your finger down. At this point, *hard* presses also let you select (highlight) text:

- **Hard-press twice** to select an entire sentence.
- **Hard-press three times** to select an entire paragraph.

Or use this trick: Move the insertion point to a word; if you now press hard, you highlight that word.

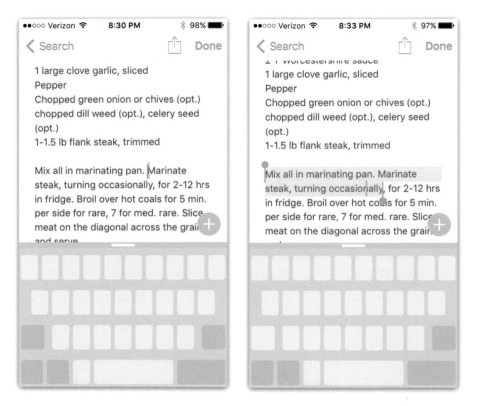

At this point, you can expand the selection by doing any of these things:

- **Drag up or down.** (Again, you don't have to keep pressing hard, but you do have to keep your finger on the glass.)

- **Hard-press twice** to extend the selection to the entire sentence.

- **Hard-press three times** to extend the selection to the entire paragraph.

Once you've selected text in this way, the usual command bar (Cut, Copy, Paste, and so on) appears, for your text-manipulation pleasure.

Little by little, the iPhone is revealing its secret ambition to be a laptop.

Dictation

The iPhone's speech-recognition feature, sometimes called Siri (even though Siri is also the voice *command* feature), lets you enter text any-where, into any program, just by *speaking*. (Behind the scenes, it's using the same Nuance recognition technology that powers the Dragon line of dictation programs.)

It's extremely fast and, usually, remarkably accurate. Suddenly you don't have to fuss with the tiny keyboard. The experience of "typing" is no longer claustrophobic. You can blather away into an email, fire off a text message, or draft a memo without ever looking at the screen.

Now, before you get all excited, here are the necessary footnotes:

- Voice typing works best if there's not a lot of background noise.

- Voice typing isn't always practical, since everybody around you can hear what you're saying.

- Voice typing isn't always accurate. Often, you'll have to correct an error or two.

All right—expectations set? Then here's how to type by speaking.

First, fire up someplace where you can call up the keyboard: Messages, Notes, Mail, Safari, whatever. Tap, if necessary, so that the onscreen keyboard appears.

Tap the 🎤 next to the space bar.

When you hear the xylophone note, say what you have to say (next page, left). If there's background noise, hold the phone up to your head; if it's relatively quiet, a couple of feet away is fine. You don't have to speak slowly, loudly, or weirdly; speak normally. As you speak, the words fly onto the screen.

You have to speak your own punctuation, like this: "Dear Dad (colon): Send money (dash)—as much as you can (comma), please (period)." The table at the end of this section describes all the different punctuation symbols you can dictate.

After you finish speaking, tap Done. Another xylophone note plays— higher, this time—and you may see some of the words *change* right before your eyes, as though Siri is changing her mind. In fact, she is; she's using the context of *all* the words you said to revise what she *originally* thought you said, as you said it. See?

> **NOTE:** On the iPhone 6s and 7 models, you can use dictation even without an Internet connection—even in airplane mode. On older models, however, dictation requires a good Internet signal.

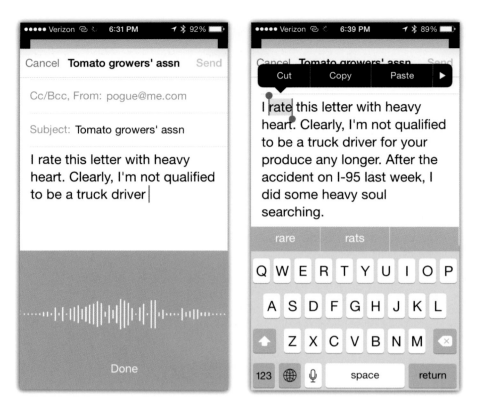

If the transcription contains errors, you can tap with your finger to edit them, exactly as you would fix an error in something you typed. (Make the effort; you're simultaneously teaching your iPhone to do better the next time.) Or, if the whole thing is a mess, you can **shake** your iPhone, the universal gesture for Undo (as long as Shake to Undo is turned on in Settings→General→Accessibility).

NOTE: Often, the iPhone knows perfectly well when it might have gotten a word wrong—it draws a dashed underline beneath words or phrases it's insecure about. You can tap that word or phrase to see the iPhone's alternative interpretation, which is often correct.

Usually, you'll find the accuracy pretty darned good, considering you didn't have to train the software to recognize your voice, and considering that your computer is a **cellphone**, for crying out loud. You'll also find that the accuracy is better when you dictate complete sentences, and that long words fare better than short ones.

Punctuation

Here's a handy table that shows you what punctuation you can say and how to say it.

TIP: If you've ever used Dragon NaturallySpeaking (for Windows) or Dragon Dictation (for the Mac), then you already know these commands; they're the standard Nuance dictation-software shortcuts, because that's what the iPhone uses behind the scenes.

Say this:	To get this:	For example, saying this:	Types this:
"period" or "full stop"	. [space and capital letter afterward]	"Best (period) date (period) ever (period)"	Best. Date. Ever.
"dot" or "point"	. [no space afterward]	"My email is frank (dot) smith (at sign) gmail (dot) com"	My email is frank.smith@gmail.com
"comma," "semicolon," "colon"	, ; :	"Mom (comma) hear me (colon) I'm dizzy (semi-colon) tired"	Mom, hear me: I'm dizzy; tired
"question mark," "excla-mation point"	? ! [space and capital letter afterward]	"Ellen (question mark) Hi (excla-mation point)"	Ellen? Hi!
"inverted question mark," "inverted excla-mation point"	¿ ¡	"(inverted ques-tion mark) Que paso (question mark)"	¿Que paso?
"ellipsis" or "dot dot dot"	…	"Just one (ellipsis) more (ellipsis) step (ellipsis)"	Just one… more…step…
"space bar"	[a space, especially when a hyphen would normally appear]	"He rode the merry (space bar) go (space bar) round"	He rode the merry go round

Say this:	To get this:	For example, saying this:	Types this:
"open paren" then "close paren" (or "open bracket/ close bracket," or "open brace/ close brace")	( ) or [ ] or { }	"Then she (open paren) the doctor (close paren) gasped"	Then she (the doctor) gasped
"new line"	[a press of the Return key]	"milk (new line) bread (new line) quinoa"	Milk Bread Quinoa
"new paragraph"	[two presses of the Return key]	"autumn leaves (new para-graph) softly falling"	autumn leaves softly falling
"quote," then "unquote"	" "	Her perfume screamed (quote) avail-able (unquote)	Her perfume screamed "available"
"numeral"	[writes the following num-ber as a digit instead spelling it out]	"Next week she turns (numeral) eight"	Next week she turns 8
"asterisk," "plus sign," "minus sign," "equals sign"	*, +, −, =	"numeral eight (asterisk) two (plus sign) one (minus sign) three (equals sign) fourteen"	8*2+1−3=14
"ampersand," "dash"	&, —	"Logan (amper-sand) Dexter (dash) the best (exclamation point)"	Logan & Dexter—the best!
"hyphen"	- [without spaces]	"Don't give me that holier (hyphen) than (hyphen) thou attitude"	Don't give me that holier-than-thou attitude

Say this:	To get this:	For example, saying this:	Types this:
"backquote"	'	"Back in (backquote) (numeral) fifty-two"	back in '52
"smiley," "frowny," "winky" (or "smiley face," "frowny face," "winky face")	:-) :-(;-)	"I think you know where I'm going with this (winky face)"	I think you know where I'm going with this ;-)

You can also say "percent sign" (%), "at sign" (@), "dollar sign" ($), "cent sign" (¢), "euro sign" (€), "yen sign" (¥), "pounds sterling sign" (£), "section sign" (§), "copyright sign" (©), "registered sign" (®), "trademark sign" (™), "greater-than sign" or "less-than sign" (> or <), "degree sign" (°), "caret" (^), "tilde" (~), "vertical bar" (|), and "pound sign" (#).

The software automatically capitalizes the first new word after a period, question mark, or exclamation point. But you can also force it to capitalize words you're dictating by saying "cap" right before the word, like this: "Dear (cap) Mom (comma), I've run away to join (cap) The (cap) Circus (comma), a nonprofit cooperative for runaway jugglers."

Here's another table—this one shows the other commands for capitalization, plus spacing and spelling commands.

TIP: Speak each of the on/off commands as a separate utterance, with a small pause before and after.

Say this:	To get this:	For example, saying this:	Types this:
"cap" or "capital"	Capitalize the next word	"Give me the (cap) works"	Give me the Works
"caps on," then "caps off"	Capitalize the first letter of every word	"Next week, (caps on) the new england chicken cooperative (caps off) will hire me"	Next week, The New England Chicken Cooperative will hire me

Say this:	To get this:	For example, saying this:	Types this:
"all caps on," then "all caps off"	Capitalize everything	"So (all caps on) please please (all caps off) don't tell anyone"	So PLEASE PLEASE don't tell anyone
"all caps"	Type just the next word in all caps	"We (all caps) really don't belong here"	We REALLY don't belong here
"no caps"	Type the next word in lowercase	"See you in (no caps) Texas"	See you in texas
"no caps on," then "no caps off"	Prevents any capital letters	"I'll ask (no caps on) Santa Claus (no caps off)"	I'll ask santa claus
"no space"	Runs the two words together	"Try our new mega (no space) berry flavor"	Try our new megaberry flavor
"no space on," then "no space off"	Eliminates all spaces	"(No space on) I can't believe you ate all that (no space off) (comma) she said excitedly"	Ican'tbelieveyou ateallthat, she said excitedly
[alphabet letters]	Types the letters out (usually not very accurately)	"The stock symbol is A P P L"	The stock symbol is APPL

You don't always have to dictate these formatting commands, by the way. The iPhone automatically inserts hyphens into phone numbers (you say, "2125561000," and get "212-556-1000"); formats two-line street addresses without your having to say, "New line" before the city); handles prices automatically ("six dollars and thirty-two cents" becomes "$6.32").

It formats dates and web addresses well, too; you can even use the nerdy shortcut "dub-dub-dub" when you want the "www" part of a web address.

The phone recognizes email addresses, too, as long as you remember to say "at sign" at the right spot. You'd say, "harold (underscore) beanfield (at sign) gmail (dot) com" to get harold_beanfield@gmail.com.

> **TIP:** You can combine these formatting commands. Many iPhone owners have wondered: "How do I voice-type the *word* "comma," since saying "comma" types out only the symbol?"
>
> The solution: Say, "No space on, no caps on, C, O, M, M, A, no space off, no caps off." That gives you the *word* "comma."
>
> Then again, it might just be easier to type that one with your finger.

Cut, Copy, Paste

Copy and Paste do just what you'd expect. They let you grab some text off a web page and paste it into an email message, copy directions from email into Notes, paste a phone number from your address book into a text message, and so on.

So how do you select text and use Cut, Copy, and Paste on a machine with no mouse or menus? As on the Mac or PC, it takes three steps.

Step 1: Select the Text

Start by highlighting the text you want to cut or copy.

- **To select some.** Double-tap the first word (or last word) that you want in the selection. That word is now highlighted, with blue dots at diagonal corners. Drag these handles to expand the selection. The magnifying loupe helps you release the dot at just the right spot.

Double-tap...

...drag the handle.

On a web page, you can't very well double-tap to select a word, because double-tapping means "zoom in." Instead, **hold your finger down** on a word to produce the blue handles; the loupe helps you. (If you highlight the wrong word, keep your finger down and slide to the correct one; the highlighting goes with you.)

However, if you're zoomed out to see the whole page, holding down your finger highlights the **entire block** of text (a paragraph or even a whole article) instead of one word. Now you can expand the selection to include a photo, if you like; that way, you can copy and paste the whole enchilada into an outgoing email message.

- **To select all.** Suppose you intend to cut or copy **everything** in the text box or message. Tap anywhere in the text to place the insertion point. Then tap the insertion point itself to summon the selection buttons— one of which is Select All.

Selecting text is much easier on an iPhone 6s or 7, because you have a built-in trackpad; see page 87.

Step 2: Cut or Copy

At this point, you've highlighted the material you want, and the Cut and Copy buttons are staring you in the face. They're either word buttons above your text, or they're actual graphic buttons (if you have your recent iPhone turned sideways).

Tap **Cut** or ✂ (to remove the selected text) or **Copy** or ▣ (to leave it but place a duplicate on your invisible Clipboard). If you want to get rid of the text **without** copying it to the Clipboard—because you want to preserve something else you copied there, for example—just tap the ⌫ key.

And what if you want to copy text without the formatting (bold, italics, underlining) that it might have? After selecting the text, tap Share and then tap Copy in the Share sheet.

Step 3: Paste

Finally, switch to a different spot in the text, even if it's in a different window (for example, a new email message) or a different app (for example, Calendar or Notes). Tap in any spot where you're allowed to type. Tap the **Paste** button to paste what you cut or copied. (On an iPhone 6/6s or later model turned sideways, you can tap the ✐ button instead.) Ta-da!

(Possible Step 4: Undo)

Everyone makes mistakes, right? Fortunately, there's a secret Undo command, which can come in handy when you cut, copy, or paste something by mistake.

The trick is to **shake** the iPhone. It then offers you an Undo button, which you can tap to confirm the backtracking. One finger touch instead of three. (This feature has to be turned on in Settings→General→Accessibility.)

TIP: The shake-to-undo feature also works to undo *dictating or typing*—not just cutting or pasting.

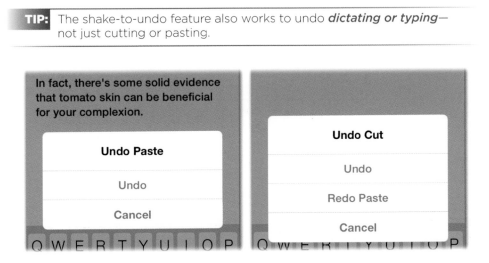

Of course, on an iPhone 6, 6s, or 7 turned sideways, you get a dedicated Undo button instead: ⟲.

In fact, you can even undo the Undo. Just shake the phone again; now the screen offers you a Redo button. Fun! (Except when you shake the phone by accident and get the Nothing to Undo message. But still.)

The Definitions Dictionary

On page 77, you can read about the spelling dictionary that's built into iOS—but that's just a dumb list of words. Your iPhone also has a *real* dictionary, one that shows you definitions.

In most apps, you can look up any word that appears on the screen. Double-tap it to get the editing bar shown on the next page at left; then tap Look Up. (You may have to tap ▶ to bring that button into view.)

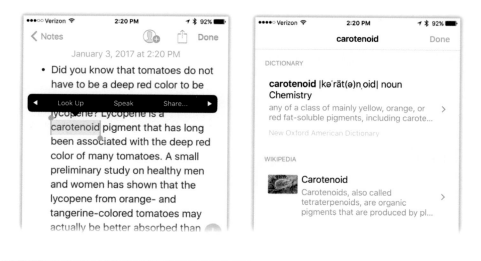

TIP: You can also double-tap the blinking insertion point that's just before a word. On the editing bar, tap ▶ to see the **Look Up** button.

(If you discover that there are "No definitions found," then tap **Manage** at the bottom of this screen for a list of dictionaries that you can download: English, French, Simplified Chinese, and so on. Tap ☁ to download the ones you think you'll use.)

Speak!

The iPhone can read to you, too. Visit **Settings→General→Accessibility→ Speech** and turn on **Speak Selection** and/or **Speak Screen**. Choose a language (or accent), a voice, and a speaking rate. (The more realistic voices, like Alex and his sister Ava, require you to download audio files from Apple. Just tap the ☁ to begin the download.)

It's fun to turn on **Highlight Content**, too. (Each word will light up in color as the phone speaks it. Great for kids learning to read!)

From now on, among the other buttons that pop up when you select text, a **Speak** button appears. Or, if you swipe down the screen with two fingers (and you turned on **Speak Screen**), your iPhone reads the entire screen.

You can use these features whenever you want to double-check the pronunciation of a word, whenever you want to have a web article or email read to you while you're getting dressed for the day, or whenever you lose your voice and just want to communicate with the rest of the world.

Spotlight: Global Search

The iPhone's global search feature is called Spotlight. It can find information on your phone within any app—but it's also something like a typed version of Siri, in that it can call up information about movies, restaurants, news, and so on.

How to Use Spotlight

The Spotlight search bar awaits in two places:

- **Swipe downward from the top of the screen.** Doesn't matter what app you're using, or even if you've unlocked the phone. This gesture brings up the Notification Center (page 61)—which contains the Spotlight search bar at the top.

- **Swipe to the right** from the first Home screen. Lurking to its left is the Today screen (page 65)—with, once again, a Spotlight box at the top.

When you tap into the search box, the keyboard opens automatically. Begin typing to identify what you want to find and open. For example, if you were trying to find a file called *Pokémon Fantasy League*, typing just *pok* or *leag* would probably suffice. (Spotlight doesn't find text in the *middles* of words, though; it searches from the beginnings of words.)

As you type, a results list appears below the search box, listing everything Spotlight can find containing what you've typed so far.

They're neatly grouped by category; the beginning of each category is marked with a heading like Contacts or Music.

Here's what you might find in Spotlight's list of results (next page, left):

- **Applications.** For frequent downloaders, this may be the juiciest function: Spotlight searches the names of every app on your iPhone. If you have dozens installed, this is a much more efficient way to find one than trying to page through all the Home screens, eyeballing the icons as you go. (The search results even identify which *folder* an app is in.)

- **Spotlight Suggestions.** Spotlight can find movies, music, apps, and other stuff from the web. The feature works beautifully. The hard part is just remembering that it's available.

  Spotlight lists results from Wikipedia (when you search for, say, "rhubarb" or "Thomas Edison"); news (search for "SF Giants" or "Middle East negotiations"); restaurants, shops, and businesses ("Olive Garden" or "Apple Store"); the App Store ("Instagram" or "Angry Birds"); the iTunes Store ("Gravity" or "Beatles"); and the iBooks store ("Grisham" or "Little Women").

  The results list identifies which category each hit comes from. Tapping a result does what you'd expect: for a web article, opens the article; for a business, opens its Maps page so you can call it or get instant directions; for something from an Apple store, opens the appropriate store.

  Really, don't miss this. When you hear about a cool app, don't open the App Store to look for it. When you want to know a sports score, don't start with Safari. When you need the phone number of a restaurant, don't call 411. Instead, use Spotlight for all of these things.

- **Contacts.** First names, last names, and company names.

- **Music, Podcasts, Videos, Audiobooks.** Song, performer, and album names, plus the names of podcasts, videos, and audiobooks.

- **Notes, Reminders, Voice Memos.** The actual text of your notes and to-do items, and the names and descriptions of voice memos.

- **Events.** Calendar stuff: appointment names, meeting invitees, and locations (but not any notes attached to your appointments).

- **Mail.** The To, From, and Subject fields of all accounts. For certain accounts, you can even search inside the messages.

- **Messages.** Yep, you can search your text messages, too.

- **Bing Web Results.** You can tap Search Web at the bottom of the results list to hand off to Safari for a search. Handy to have it built right into Spotlight.

> **TIP:** Many apps, like Contacts, Mail, Calendar, Music, and Notes, have their *own* search boxes (usually hidden until you scroll to the top of their lists). Those individual search functions are great when you're already *in* the program where you want to search. The Spotlight difference is that it searches all these apps at once.

If you see the name and icon of whatever you were hoping to dig up, tap to open it. The corresponding app opens automatically.

Siri App Suggestions

On the Today screen (page 65), in search results, and sometimes when you highlight text and tap Look Up, you see something peculiar: a little row of app icons labeled Siri App Suggestions.

These app icons actually have nothing to do with Siri, the voice-controlled assistant. Instead, these are the iPhone's suggestions of apps you may want to use right now, based on your location, the time of day, and your typical routine. For example, if you open the Music app every night during your 6:30 p.m. gym workout, then the Music app appears at that time, ready to open. If you check your Fitbit app every morning when you wake, then this screen offers its icon at that time of day. The idea is to save you from having to hunt for these apps when you need them again.

If you find these icons unhelpful, you can eliminate them or tweak them. Open Settings→General→Spotlight Search. This is what you'll find:

- **Siri Suggestions** is the master on/off switch for the appearance of those apps in search results.

- **Suggestions in Search** means, "Eliminate these app suggestions from the results when I use Spotlight; I want to search only what's on my phone."

- **Suggestions in Look Up** means, "When I highlight text and tap Look Up, I want to see only its definition or web results—not app suggestions."

- **Search Results.** If you do decide to let the iPhone suggest apps, these on/off switches let you eliminate certain apps from consideration.

4

Phone Calls & FaceTime

With each successive iPhone model, Apple improves the iPhone's antennas, circuitry, speakers, microphone, and software. And features like Siri, auto-reply, and Do Not Disturb have turned Apple's phone from an also-ran into one of the most useful gadgets ever to hop onto a cellular network.

Dialing from the Phone App

Suppose you're in luck. Suppose the dots in the upper-left corner of the iPhone's screen tell you that you've got cellular reception. You're ready to start a conversation. To make a phone call, open the Phone app like this:

1. **Go Home, if you're not already there.** Press the Home button.

2. **Tap the Phone icon.** It's usually at the bottom of the Home screen. (The tiny circled number in the corner of the Phone icon tells you how many missed calls and voicemail messages you have.)

> **TIP:** Using Siri is often faster. You get good results saying things like, "Call Casey Robin's cell" or "Dial 866-2331."

Now you've arrived in the Phone program. A new row of icons appears at the bottom, representing your voicemail (page 120) and the four ways of dialing from here:

- **Favorites.** Here's the iPhone's version of speed dial: It lists up to 50 people you think you call most frequently. Tap a name to make the call. (Details on building and editing this list begin on page 104.)

- **Recents.** Every call you've recently made, answered, missed, or even just dialed appears in this list. Missed callers' names appear in red lettering, which makes it easy to spot them—and to call them back.

Tap a name or a number to dial. Or tap the ⓘ button to view the details of a call—when, where, how long—and, if you like, to add this number to your Contacts list.

- **Contacts.** This program also has an icon of its own on the Home screen; you don't have to drill down to it through the Phone button. It's your phone book; tap somebody's name or number to dial it.

- **Keypad.** This dialing pad's big, fat buttons are easy to hit even with big, fat fingers. You can punch in any number and then tap 📞 to place the call.

Once you've dialed, no matter which method you used, either hold the iPhone up to your head, put in the earbuds, turn on the speakerphone, or put on your Bluetooth earpiece—and start talking!

This, however, is only the Quick Start Guide. Here's a more detailed look at each of the Phone-app modules.

The Favorites List

You may not wind up dialing much from Contacts. That's the master list, all right, but it's too unwieldy when you just want to call your spouse, your boss, or your lawyer. Dialing by voice (Chapter 5) is almost always faster. But when silence is golden, at the very least use the Favorites list—a short, easy-to-scan list of the people you call most often (facing page, left).

Actually, in iOS 10, *calling* is only the beginning. A Favorite can be any kind of "address": for triggering an email, a text message, a video call, or even an Internet voice call in an app like WhatsApp, Skype, or Cisco Spark. In other words, you can set things up so that one tap on a favorite opens an outgoing text to your beloved, and a different tap triggers a Skype call to your boss.

> **TIP:** Once you've set up these favorites, you can add them to the Today screen (page 65), so that placing one of these calls or text communications is only a swipe and a tap away.

You can add names to this list in any of three ways:

- **From the Favorites list itself.** Tap + to view your Contacts list. Tap the person you want. If there's more than one phone number or email address on the Info screen, then tap the one you want to add to Favorites.

- **From the Contacts list.** Tap a name to open the Info screen, where you'll find a button called Add to Favorites. It opens the little Add to Favorites panel shown below at right. For each of its four communication methods—Message, Call, Video, Mail—you get a pop-up menu that lists your available apps for performing that sort of human contact.

  Tap the one you want to add to Favorites.

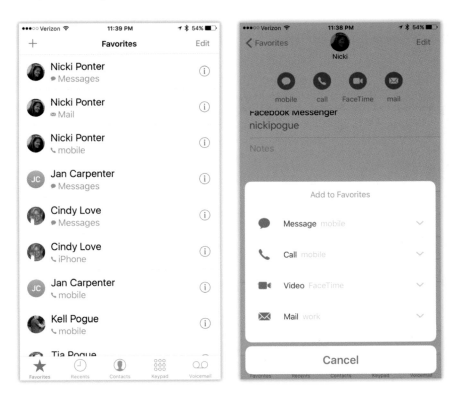

- **From the Recents list.** Tap ⓘ next to any name or number in the Recents list. If it's somebody who's already in your Contacts list, then you arrive at the Call Details screen, where one tap on Add to Favorites does what it says.

  If it's somebody who's not in Contacts yet, you'll have to **put** her there first. Tap Create New Contact, and then proceed as described on page 111. After you hit **Save**, you return to the Call Details screen so you can tap **Add to Favorites**.

page 111.

> **TIP:** To help you remember that a certain phone number or email address is already in your Favorites list, a gray star appears next to it in certain spots, like the Call Details screen and the Contact Info screen.

The Favorites list holds 50 numbers. Once you've added 50, the **Add to Favorites** and + buttons disappear.

> **NOTE:** The face of each favorite peeks out of a round frame next to the name, and if your Contact card for that person doesn't have a photo, the circle shows the person's initials instead.

Reordering Favorites

Tapping that **Edit** button at the top of the Favorites list offers another handy feature, too: It lets you drag names up and down, so the most important people appear at the top of the list. Just use the grip strip (≡) as a handle to move entire names up or down the list.

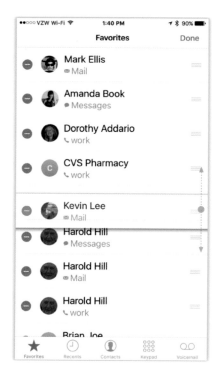

Deleting from Favorites

To delete somebody from your Favorites—the morning after a nasty political argument, for example—use the iPhone's standard swipe-to-delete shortcut: Swipe leftward across the undesired name. Tap the Delete button that appears.

(If you're paid by the hour, you can use the slow method, too. Tap Edit. Now tap the ● button next to the unwanted entry and tap Delete to confirm.)

The Recents List

Like any self-respecting cellphone, the iPhone maintains a list of everybody you've called or who's called you recently. The idea, of course, is to provide you with a quick way to call someone you've been talking to lately.

To see the list, tap Recents at the bottom of the Phone app. You see a list of the last 75 calls that you've received or placed, along with each person's name or number (depending on whether that name is in Contacts or not), city of the caller's home area code (for callers not in your Contacts), time or date of the call—and what kind of call it was: mobile, home, work, FaceTime, FaceTime Audio, Skype, or whatever.

Here's what you need to know about the Recents list:

- Calls that you missed (or sent to voicemail) appear in red type. If you tap **Missed** at the top of the screen, you see *only* your missed calls. The color-coding and separate listings are designed to make it easy for you to return calls you missed, or to try again to reach someone who didn't answer when you called.

- A tiny ↪ icon lets you know which calls you *made* (to differentiate them from calls you *received*).

- To call someone back—regardless of whether you answered or dialed the call—tap that name or number in the list.

- Tap ⓘ next to any call to open the Info screen. At the top of the screen, you can see whether this was an outgoing call, an incoming call, a missed call, or a canceled call (in which you chickened out and hung up before your callee answered).

What else you see here depends on whether the other person is in your Contacts list.

If so, the Info screen displays the person's whole information card (below, left). A little table displays all the incoming and outgoing calls to or from this person that day. A small gray star denotes a phone number that's also in your Favorites list, and a Recent label indicates a recent call from that number.

If the call *isn't* from someone in your Contacts, then you get to see a handy notation at the top of the Info screen: the city and state where the calling phone is registered (below, right).

TIP: If someone who isn't in Contacts has called you, iOS 10 takes a guess at that person's name—by looking for a matching phone number in the signature portion of your email! For example, if Frank Smythe has called you from 213-292-3344, and there's also an email from him with his phone number as part of his signature, then the Recents list will say: *Maybe: Frank Smythe.* Clever!

- To save you scrolling, the Recents list thoughtfully combines consecutive calls to or from the same person. If some obsessed ex-lover has been calling you every 10 minutes for 4 hours, you'll see "Chris Meyerson (24)" in the Recents list. (Tap ⓘ to see the exact times of the calls.)

- You can erase one call from this list exactly the same way you'd delete a Favorite: Swipe leftward across the undesired name. Tap the **Delete** button that appears. (Once again, there's also a long way: Tap **Edit**, tap ● next to the unwanted entry, and then tap **Delete**.)

  You can also erase the *entire* list, thus preventing a coworker or significant other from discovering your illicit activities: Tap **Edit**, and then tap **Clear** at the top of the screen. You're asked to confirm your decision.

Contacts

The Phone app may offer four ways to dial—Favorites, Recents, Contacts, and Keypad—but the Contacts list is the source from which all other lists spring. That's probably why it's listed three times: once with its own button on the Home screen, again at the bottom of the Phone app, and also in the FaceTime app.

Contacts is your address book—your master phone book.

NOTE: Your iPhone's own phone number appears at the top of the Contacts list within the Phone module (though not, for some reason, when you open Contacts from its Home screen icon).

That's a much better place for it than deep at the end of a menu labyrinth, where it is on most phones.

If your social circle is longer than one screenful, you can navigate this list in any of three ways:

- **First,** you can savor the distinct pleasure of flicking through it.

- **Second,** if you're in a hurry to get to the T's, use the A-to-Z index down the right edge of the screen. Just tap the first letter of the last name you're looking for. Alternatively, you can slide your finger up or down the index. The list scrolls with it.

- **Third,** you can use the search box at the very top of the list, above the A's.

   Tap inside the search box to make the keyboard appear. As you type, Contacts pares down the list, hiding everyone whose first, last, or company name doesn't match what you've typed so far. It's a really fast way to pluck one name out of a haystack.

   (You can clear the search box by tapping the ✖ at its right end or restore the full list by tapping Cancel.)

In any case, when you see the name you want, tap it to open its card, filled with phone numbers and other info. Tap the number you want to dial.

Groups

Many computer address book programs, including the Mac's Contacts app, let you place your contacts into *groups*—subsets like Book Club or Fantasy League Guys. You can't create or delete groups on the iPhone, but at least the groups from your Mac, PC, Exchange server, or iCloud account get synced over to it. To see them, and to switch them all on or off at once, tap Groups at the top of the Contacts list.

Here's where groups come into play:

- If you can't seem to find someone in the list, you may be looking in the wrong list. Tap Groups at the top-left corner to return to the list of accounts. Tap All Contacts to view a single, unified list of everyone your phone knows about.

- If you've allowed your iPhone to display your contacts from Facebook or Twitter, then each of those lists is a group, too. (If your Contacts list seems hideously bloated with hundreds of people you never actually call, it's probably your Facebook list. Pop into Groups and touch All Facebook, removing the checkmark, to hide them all at once.)

- If you do use the Groups feature, remember to tap the group name you want *before* you create a new contact. That's how you put someone into an existing group. (If not, tap All Contacts instead.)

Adding to the Contacts List

Every cellphone has a Contacts list, of course, but the beauty of the iPhone is that you don't have to type in the phone numbers one at a time. Instead, the iPhone sucks in the entire phone book from your Mac or PC, iCloud, and/or an Exchange server at work.

It's infinitely easier to edit your address book on the computer, where you have an actual keyboard and mouse. The iPhone also makes it easy to add someone's contact information when she calls, emails, or text messages you, thanks to a prominent Add to Contacts button.

But if, in a pinch, on the road, at gunpoint, you have to add, edit, or remove a contact manually, here's how to do it:

Make sure you've selected the right group or account, as described already. Now, on the Contacts screen, tap +. You arrive at the New Contact screen, which teems with empty boxes.

It shouldn't take you long to figure out how to fill in this form: You tap in a box and type. But here are a few tips and tricks for data entry:

- **The keyboard opens automatically** when you tap in a box. And the iPhone capitalizes the first letter of each name for you.

- **Phone numbers are special.** When you enter a phone number, the iPhone adds parentheses and hyphens for you. (You can even enter text phone numbers, like 1-800-GO-BROWNS; the iPhone converts the letters to digits when it dials.)

  If you need to insert a pause—for dialing access numbers, extension numbers, or voicemail passwords—type #, which introduces a

2-second pause in the dialing. You can type several of them to create longer pauses.

To change the label for a number ("mobile," "home," "work," and so on), tap the label that's there now. The Label screen shows you your choices. There's even a label called "iPhone," so you and your buddy can gloat together.

TIP: If you scroll down the Label screen, you'll see that you can also create *custom* labels. You might prefer someone's cellphone number to be identified as "cell" instead of "mobile," for example. Or you might want to create a label that says "Skype," "Google Voice," "Line 2," "Yacht Phone," or "Bat Phone." The secret: Tap Add Custom Label. (Once you've created a custom label, it's there in the list of options for your use later.)

- **Expand-O-Fields mean you'll never run out of room.** Almost every field (empty box) on a Contacts card is infinitely expanding. That is, the instant you start filling in a field, another empty box (labeled ⊕ add phone or whatever) appears right below it, so you can imme-diately add *another* phone number, email address, URL, or street address. (The only nonexpanding fields are First name, Last name, Company, Ringtone, Text Tone, Notes, and whatever oddball fields you add yourself.)

For example, when you first tap **add phone**, the phone-number box you get is labeled "home." (If that's not the right label, you can tap it to choose from one of nine others—or add a custom label.) A new **add phone** button appears so you'll have a place to enter a second phone number for this person. When you do that, a ***third* add phone** button appears. And so on.

In other words, you can never run out of places to add more phone numbers, addresses, URLs, and social media profiles.

NOTE: Tapping **add field** at the bottom of this screen lets you add a new miscellaneous field, like Nickname or Department.

- **Relatives are here.** There's also the **social profile** field, where you can list somebody's Twitter, LinkedIn, Flickr, Facebook, and even Myspace addresses. There's an **instant message** field, too, where you can record addresses for chat networks like AIM or Yahoo Messenger.

  And there's **add related name**. Here's where you can specify this person's mother, father, spouse, partner, child, manager, sibling, and so on—or even type in a relationship that you make up (tap the existing label and then **Add Custom Label**).

NOTE: As you may discover in Chapter 5, Siri knows about all your relationships. You can tell her to "Call my mom" or "Text my boss." Does the **add related name** feature mean that you can now ask Siri to "Call Chris Robin's manager"?

Alas, no. These fields are for your reference only.

- **You can add a photo of the person, if you like.** Tap **add photo**. If you have a photo of the person on your phone already, tap **Choose Photo**. You're taken to your photo collection, where you can find a good headshot (Chapter 9).

  Alternatively, tap **Take Photo** to activate the iPhone's built-in camera. Frame the person, and then tap the white camera button to snap the shot.

  In any case, you wind up with the **Move and Scale** screen. Here you can frame up the photo so the person's face is nicely sized and centered. Spread two fingers to enlarge the photo; drag your finger to move the image within the frame. Tap **Choose** to commit the photo to the address book's memory. (Back on the Info screen where you started, a miniature version of the photo now appears. Tap **edit** if you want to change the photo, take a new one, adjust the Move and Scale screen, or get rid of the photo altogether.)

From now on, this photo will pop up whenever the person calls. It also appears next to the person's name in your Favorites list.

- **You can import photos from Facebook.** Here's a wild guess: Most of the photo boxes in your copy of Contacts are empty. After all, who's going to go to the trouble of hunting down headshots of 500 acquaintances, just for a fully illustrated Contacts list?

  Fortunately, with one click, the iPhone can harvest headshots from the world's largest database of faces: Facebook.

  Visit Settings→Facebook to see the magical button: Update All Contacts. When you click it, the iPhone goes online for a massive research mission. Using your contacts' names and phone numbers as matching criteria, it ventures off to Facebook, finds the profile photos of everyone who's also in your Contacts list, and installs them into Contacts automatically. (If you already have a photo for somebody, don't worry; it doesn't get replaced.)

  As a handy bonus, this operation also adds the @facebook.com email addresses for the people you already had in Contacts.

Actually, there's another side effect of this operation: It also adds all your Facebook friends' names to your main Contacts list.

Now, you may not be crazy about this. Most of these Facebook folk you'll never call on the phone—yet here they are, cluttering up the Contacts list within the Phone app.

Fortunately, the Update All Contacts button doesn't *really* mix your Facebook friends in with your local Contacts list. It just subscribes to your Facebook address book—adds a new *group*, which you can turn off with one quick click; see page 110.

Even if you do choose to hide all their entries, you still get the benefit of the imported headshots and Facebook email addresses for the people you *do* want to see in Contacts.

- **You can import Twitter addresses.** In Settings→Twitter, the Update Contacts button awaits. Its purpose is to fill in the Twitter handles for everyone who's already in your Contacts, matching them by phone number or email address.

- **You can choose a ringtone.** You can choose a different ringtone for each person in your address book. The idea is that you'll know by the sound of the ring who's calling you.

It's one tone per person, not per phone number. Of course, if you really want one ringtone for your buddy's cellphone and another for his home phone, you can always create a different Contacts card for each one.

To choose a ringtone, tap Default. On the next screen, tap any sound in the Ringtones or Alert Tones lists to sample them. (Despite the separate lists, in this context, these sounds are all being offered as ringtones.) When you've settled on a good one, tap Done to return to the Info screen where you started.

New in iOS 10: Here, on the ringtone selection screen, you're offered an Emergency Bypass switch. Turn it on to say, "Whenever this person calls or texts, I want my phone to ring or vibrate *even* if I've turned on Do Not Disturb" (page 128).

- **You can specify a vibration pattern for incoming calls.** This unsung feature lets you assign a custom vibration pattern to each person in your Contacts, so you know by *feel* who's calling—without even removing the phone from your pocket, even if your ringer is off. It's a surprisingly useful option.

To set it up, start on the Ringtone screen described already; tap **Default** next to the word **vibration**. You're offered a choice of canned patterns (Alert, Heartbeat, Quick, Rapid, and so on). But if you tap **Create New Vibration**, you can then tap the screen in whatever rhythm you like. It can be diddle diddle dee...or the opening notes to the Hallelujah Chorus...or the actual syllables of the person's name. ("Maryanna Beckleheimer." Can you feel it?)

The phone records your pattern, which you can prove to yourself by tapping **Play**. If you tap **Save** and name that pattern, then it becomes one of the choices when you choose a vibration pattern for someone in your Contacts. It's what you'll feel whenever this person calls you. Yes, it's tactile caller ID. Wild.

- **You can also pick a text-message sound (and vibration).** Just as you can choose sounds and vibrations for incoming phone calls, the next two items (**text tone**, **vibration**) let you choose sounds and vibrations for incoming text messages and FaceTime invitations.

- **You can add new fields of your own.** Very cool: If you tap **add field** at the bottom of the screen, then you go down the rabbit hole into Field Land, where you can add any of 13 additional info bits about the person whose card you're editing: a prefix (like Mr. or Mrs.), a suffix (like M.D. or Esq.), a nickname, a job title, a phonetic pronunciation for people with weird names, and so on.

When you tap one of these labels, you return to the Info screen, where you'll see that the iPhone has inserted the new, empty field in the most intelligent spot. For example, if you add a phonetic first name, that box appears just below the First Name box. The keyboard opens so you can fill in the blank.

- **You can link and unlink Unified Contacts.** As noted earlier, your phone can sync up with different accounts. Your Contacts app might list four sets of names and numbers: one stored on your phone, one from an iCloud account, one from Facebook, and a fourth from your corporate Exchange server at work. In the old days, therefore, certain names might have shown up in the All Contacts list two or three times—not an optimal situation.

  Now, as a favor to you, the iPhone displays each person's name only once in that master All Contacts list. If you tap that name, you open up a unified information screen for that person. It includes *all* the details from *all* the underlying contacts cards.

NOTE: The iPhone combines cards in the All Contacts list only if the first and last names are exactly the same. If there's a difference in name, suffix, prefix, or middle name, then no unifying takes place. Remember, too, that you see the unification only if you view the All Contacts list.

To see which cards the iPhone is combining for you, scroll to the bottom of the card. There the **Linked Contacts** section shows you which cards have been unified.

You can tap a listing to open the card in the corresponding account. For that matter, you can manually link a card, too; tap **Edit**, tap **link contacts**, and then choose a contact to link to this unified card—even if the name isn't a perfect match.

NOTE: It's OK to link Joe Carnelia's card with Joseph Carnelia's card—they're probably the same person. But don't link up *different* people's cards. Remember, the whole point is to make the iPhone combine all the phone numbers, email addresses, and so on onto a single card—and seeing two sets on one card could get confusing fast.

This stuff gets complex. But, in general, the iPhone tries to do the right thing. For example, if you edit the information on the unified card, you're changing that information only on the card in the corresponding account. (Unless you *add* information to the unified card. In that case, the new data tidbit is added to *all* the underlying source-account cards.)

Adding a Contact on the Fly

There's actually another way to add someone to your Contacts list—a faster, on-the-fly method that's more typical of cellphones. Start by bringing the phone number up on the screen:

- In the Phone app, open the Keypad. Dial the number, and then tap ⊕.

- You can also add a number that's in your Recents (recent calls) list, storing it in Contacts for future use. Tap the ⓘ button next to the name.

In both cases, finish up by tapping Create New Contact (to enter this person's name for the first time) or Add to Existing Contact (to add a new phone number to the card of someone who's already in your list). Off you go to the Contacts editing screen shown on page 112.

Editing Someone

To make corrections or changes, tap the person's name in the Contacts list. In the upper-right corner of the Info card, tap Edit.

You return to the screens already described, where you can make whatever changes you like. To edit a phone number, for example, tap it and change away. Or, to delete a number (or any other info bit), tap the ⊖ button next to it, and then tap Delete to confirm.

After you tap Done (or Cancel), you can return to the Contacts list by swiping to the right.

Deleting Someone

Truth is, you'll probably *add* people to your address book far more often than you'll *delete* them. After all, you meet new people all the time—but you delete people primarily when they die, move away, or dump you.

To zap someone, tap the name in the Contacts list and then tap Edit. Scroll down, tap Delete Contact, and confirm by tapping Delete Contact again. (Weirdly, the Delete Contact option doesn't appear if you open someone's info card from the Recents or Favorites lists—only from the main Contacts list.)

Sharing a Contact

There's a lot of work involved in entering someone's contact information. It would be thoughtful, therefore, if you could spare the next guy all that effort—by sending a fully formed electronic business card to him. It can be yours or that of anyone in your Contacts list.

To do that, open the contact's card, scroll to the bottom, and tap **Share Contact**. On the Share sheet, you're offered a choice of **AirDrop**, **Message**, **Mail**, and **More**. ("Message" means an iMessage—page 174—if it's a fellow Apple fan, or a text message otherwise. AirDrop is described on page 327. And **More** is a place for new apps to install their sharing options.)

Tap your choice, address the message (to an email address or, for a message, a cellphone number), and send it. The recipient, assuming he has a half-decent smartphone or address-book program on the receiving end, can install that person's information with a single tap on the attachment.

The Keypad

The fourth way to place a call is to tap **Keypad** at the bottom of the screen. The standard iPhone dialing pad appears. It's just like the number pad on a normal cellphone, except that the "keys" are much bigger and you can't feel them.

To make a call, tap out (or paste) the phone number—use the ⊗ key to backspace if you make a mistake—and then tap the 📞 button.

You can also use the keypad to enter a phone number into your Contacts list, thanks to the ⊕ button, as described earlier.

Visual Voicemail

On the iPhone, you don't *dial in* to check for answering-machine messages people have left for you. You don't enter a password. You don't sit through some Ambien-addled recorded lady saying, "You have…17…messages. To hear your messages, press 1. When you have finished, you may hang up…."

Instead, whenever somebody leaves you a message, the phone wakes up, and a notification lets you know who it's from. You also hear a sound (unless you've turned on the silencer switch).

That's your cue to open Phone→Voicemail. There you see all your messages in a tidy chronological list. (The list shows the callers' names if they're in your Contacts list; otherwise it shows their numbers.) You can listen to them in any order—you're not forced to listen to three long-winded friends before discovering that there's an urgent message from your boss. It's a game-changer.

iOS 10 even makes an attempt to *transcribe* your voicemails—to understand them and type out what they say. It's pretty crude, with lots of wrong words and missing words. But it's usually enough to get the gist.

Setup

To access your voicemail, open the Phone app; tap Voicemail.

The very first time you visit this screen, the iPhone prompts you to make up a numeric password for your voicemail account—don't worry, you'll never have to enter it again, unless you plan to actually dial in for messages (page 124). Record a "Leave me a message" greeting.

You have two options for the outgoing greeting:

- **Default.** If you're microphone-shy, or if you're famous and you don't want stalkers calling just to hear your famous voice, then use this option. It's a prerecorded, somewhat uptight female voice that says, "Your call has been forwarded to an automatic voice message system. 212-661-7837 is not available." *Beep!*

- **Custom.** This option lets you record your own voice saying, for example, "You've reached my iPhone 7. You may begin drooling at the tone." Tap Record, hold the iPhone to your head, say your line, and then tap Stop.

  Check how it sounds by tapping Play.

Then just wait for your fans to start leaving you messages!

Using Visual Voicemail

In the voicemail list, a blue dot (●) indicates a message you haven't yet played.

TIP: You can work through your messages even when you're out of cellular range—on a plane, for example—because the recordings are stored on the iPhone itself.

When you tap the name of a message, you instantly see the date and time it came in, the person's name (if it's in your Contacts) or the cell-phone's registered city and state (if not), and a rough transcription. The Play slider tells you how many seconds long the message is.

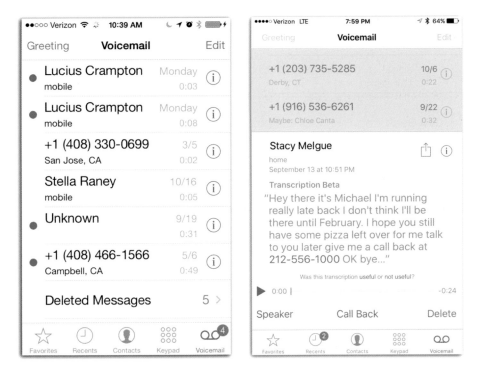

And all the controls you need are right there, surrounding the message you tapped:

- **Share (⬆️).** Yes, you can send a voicemail recording to someone else—by email, text message, or whatever (page 348). That's a handy bit of record-keeping that could be very useful in, say, a criminal trial.

- **The transcript.** Yes, this is a crude transcript (Apple labels it *beta*, after all). There's no punctuation. There may be missing _____ and phrases. Some words might be completely wrong. But it's usually good enough that you can tell if a message is some robocall asking for money, or a message from the school nurse saying that your kid has a broken rib.

- **▶.** Tap to listen to the message.

- **Speaker.** As the name "Visual Voicemail" suggests, you're *looking* at your voicemail list—which means you're *not* holding the phone up to your head. The first time people try using Visual Voicemail, therefore, they generally hear nothing!

  But if you hit Speaker before you tap ▶, you can hear the playback *and* continue looking over the list.

> **NOTE:** If you're listening through the earbuds, a Bluetooth earpiece, or a car kit, of course, then you hear the message playing back through *that*. If you really want to listen through the iPhone's speaker instead, tap Audio and then Speaker. (You switch back the same way.)

- **Call Back.** Tap Call Back to return the call. Very cool—you never even encounter the person's phone number.

- **Delete.** You might want to keep the list manageable by deleting old messages. To do that, tap a message's Delete button.

  If you have a lot of messages to delete, here's a faster way: Swipe across the first one's name right to left, and then tap Delete. The message disappears instantly. You can work down the list quickly this way.

  If you didn't know that trick, you could also do it the slow way: Tap Edit (upper right of the screen). Tap the ⊖ button next to a message's name and then tap Delete to confirm. Tap the next ⊖ button and continue.

- **Rewind, Fast Forward.** Drag the little vertical line in the scrubber bar (beneath the message) to skip backward or forward in the message. It's a great way to replay something you didn't catch the first time.

To collapse the expanded message, tap another message in the list, if it's visible, or just tap the caller's name.

Even before you've expanded a message's row to view the Play, Speaker, Call Back, and Delete buttons, a few other Visual Voicemail buttons are awaiting your inspection:

- **Greeting.** Tap Greeting (upper-left corner) to record your voicemail greeting.

- **Call Details.** Tap ⓘ to open the Info screen—the Contacts card—for the message that was left for you.

  If it was left by somebody who's in your Contacts list, you can see *which* of that person's phone numbers the call came from (indicated in blue type), plus a ★ if that number is in your Favorites list. Oh, and you can add this person to your Favorites list at this point by tapping Add to Favorites (at the bottom of the screen).

If the caller's number isn't in Contacts, then you're offered a **Create New Contact** button and an **Add to Existing Contact** button, so you can store it for future reference.

In both cases, you also have the option to return the call (right from the Info screen), fire off a text message, or place a FaceTime audio or video call.

Dialing in for Messages

Gross and pre-iPhonish though it may sound, you can also dial in for your messages from another phone.

To do that, dial your iPhone's number. Wait for the voicemail system to answer. As your own voicemail greeting plays, dial * (or # if you have Verizon), your voicemail password, and then #.

You hear the Uptight Carrier Lady announce how many messages you have, and then she'll start playing them for you. After you hear each message, she'll offer you the following options (but you don't have to wait for her to announce them):

- To delete the message, press 7.

- To save it, press 9.

- To replay it, press 4. (On T-Mobile, it's 1.)

Conveniently enough, these keystrokes are the same on Verizon, Sprint, and AT&T.

> **TIP:** If this whole Visual Voicemail thing freaks you out, you can also dial in for messages right from the iPhone. Open the keypad and hold down the 1 key, just as though it were a speed-dial key on any normal phone.
>
> After a moment, the phone connects; you're asked for your password, and then the messages begin to play back, just as described already.

Answering Calls

When someone calls your iPhone, you'll know it; three out of your five senses are alerted. Depending on how you've set up your iPhone, you'll *hear* a ring, *feel* a vibration, and *see* the caller's name and photo fill the screen. (Smell and taste will have to wait until iOS 11.)

NOTE: For details on choosing a ringtone and on Vibrate mode, see page 582.

How you answer depends on what's happening at the time:

- **If you're using the iPhone,** tap the green Accept button. Tap the red hang-up button when you've both said enough.

- **If the iPhone is asleep or locked,** the screen lights up and says slide to answer. If you slide your finger as indicated by the arrow, you simultaneously unlock the phone and answer the call.

- **If you're wearing earbuds,** the music fades out and then pauses; you hear the ring both through the phone's speaker and through your earbuds. Answer by squeezing the clicker on the earbud cord or by using either of the methods already described.

   When the call is over, you can click again to hang up—or just wait until the other guy hangs up. Either way, the music fades in again and resumes from the spot where you were so rudely interrupted.

Same thing if you were watching a video or listening to a podcast; it pauses for the duration of the call and then resumes when you hang up.

TIP: If the caller is not in your Contacts, iOS 10 makes an educated *guess* as to the name. Instead of no name at all, you'll see something like "Maybe: Casey Robin."

How does the iPhone do it? When a call comes in, iOS instantly searches your *email* in hopes of finding a matching phone number in somebody's email signature. If it finds one, it extracts that person's name and proposes it. Apple should call it "Likely Caller ID."

Online and on the Phone, Together

Don't forget that the iPhone is a multitasking master. Once you're on the phone, you can dive into any other program—to check your calendar, for example—without interrupting your call.

You may even be able to use the phone's Internet functions (web, email, apps, and so on) without interrupting the call. To be precise, you can be online and on the phone simultaneously if any of these things is true:

- You're in a Wi-Fi hotspot.

- You have AT&T or T-Mobile.

- You have an iPhone 6 or later, and you've turned on VoLTE calling (see page 434).

In other words, if you have Verizon (non-VoLTE) or Sprint, and if you're not in a Wi-Fi hotspot, then you can't get online until the call is complete.

Not Answering Calls

Maybe you're in a meeting. Maybe you're driving. Maybe the call is coming from someone you *really* don't want to deal with right now. Fortunately, you have all kinds of ways to slam the cellular door in somebody's face.

Silencing the Ring

You might need a moment before you can answer the call, or you need to exit a meeting or put in the earbuds. In those cases, you can stop the ringing and vibrating by pressing one of the physical buttons on the edges (the Sleep switch or either volume key). The caller still hears the phone ringing, and you can still answer it within the first four rings, but at least the sound won't be annoying those around you.

(This assumes, of course, that you haven't just flipped the silencer switch.)

Ignore It—or Dump It to Voicemail

If you wait long enough (four rings), the call goes to voicemail (even if you silence the ringing as described already).

Or you can dump it to voicemail *immediately* (instead of waiting for the four rings). How you do that depends on the setup:

- **If the iPhone is asleep or locked,** tap the Sleep button twice fast.

- **If you're using the iPhone,** tap the Decline button on the screen.

- **If you're wearing the earbuds,** squeeze the microphone clicker for 2 seconds. You hear two low beeps, meaning: "OK, Master; dumped."

Of course, if your callers know you have an iPhone, they'll also know that you've deliberately dumped them into voicemail—because they won't hear all four rings.

Respond with a Text Message

Whenever your phone rings, the screen bears a small white Message button (shown on page 125). If you tap it, you get a choice of three canned text messages. Tapping one immediately dumps the caller to voicemail and sends the corresponding text message to the phone that's calling you. If you're driving or in a meeting, this feature is a lot more polite and responsive than just dumping the poor slob to voicemail.

> **TIP:** You can edit any of these three canned messages; they don't have to say, "Sorry, I can't talk right now," "I'm on my way," and "Can I call you later?" forever. To do that, open Settings→Phone, tap Respond with Text, and replace the text in the three placeholder boxes.

The fourth button, Custom, lets you type or dictate a new message on the spot. ("I'm in a meeting and, frankly, your call isn't worth getting fired for" comes to mind.)

Remind Me Later

The trouble with Respond with Text, of course, is that it sends a text message. What if the caller is using a landline that can't receive text messages? Fortunately, you have another option: Remind Me.

Tapping this button offers you one time-based option, In 1 Hour (which sets up a reminder to return the call an hour from now), and three location-based options (previous page, right): When I leave, When I get home, and When I get to work. (The home and work options appear only if the iPhone *knows* your home and work addresses—because you've entered them in your own card in Contacts.)

These options use the phone's GPS circuitry to detect when you've left your current inconvenient-to-take-the-call location, whether it's a job interview, a first date, or an outhouse.

Do Not Disturb

When you turn on Do Not Disturb, the phone is quiet and dark. It doesn't ring, chirp, vibrate, light up, or display messages. A ☾ appears on the status bar to remind you why it seems to be so uncharacteristically depressed.

Yes, airplane mode does the same thing, but there's a big difference: In Do Not Disturb, *the phone is still online*. Calls, texts, emails, and other communications continue to chug happily away; they just don't draw attention to themselves.

Do Not Disturb is what you want when you're in bed each night. You don't really want to be bothered with chirps for Facebook status updates and Twitter posts, but it's fine for the phone to collect them for the morning.

Bedtime is why Do Not Disturb comes with two fantastic additional settings: one that turns it on and off automatically on a schedule, so that the phone goes dark each night at the same time you do, and another that lets you designate important people whose calls and texts are allowed to get through. You know—for emergencies.

Turning on Do Not Disturb

To turn on Do Not Disturb manually, you have three options:

- Tell Siri, "Turn on Do Not Disturb."

- Swipe upward to open the Control Center, and tap the ☾ icon so that it turns blue.

- Open Settings, tap Do Not Disturb, and tap Manual.

To set it up on a schedule, open Settings→Do Not Disturb. Turn on Scheduled, and then tap the From/To block to specify starting and ending hours. (There's no separate setting for weekends; Do Not Disturb will turn on and off for the same hours every day of the week.)

Allowing Special Callers Through

What if your child, your boss, or your elderly parent needs you urgently in the middle of the night? Turning the phone off completely, or putting it into airplane mode, would leave you unreachable in an emergency.

In iOS 10, you have several different ways to create wormholes through your Do Not Disturb blockade for specified callers and texters:

- **Allow Calls From.** When you open Settings→Do Not Disturb and then tap Allow Calls From, you're offered options like Everyone (all calls and texts come through), No One (the phone is still online, but totally silent), or Favorites, which may be the most useful option of all.

  That setting permits calls and texts from anybody you've designated as a Favorite in the Phone app (page 104). Since those are the people you call most often, it's fairly likely that they're the most important people in your life.

  You can also create an arbitrary group of people—just your mom and sister, just your boss and nephew, whatever. You have to create these address-book groups on your computer (page 110)— for example, in Contacts on the Mac. Once you've done that, their names appear on the Allow Calls From screen under Groups. You can designate any one of them as the lucky exception to Do Not Disturb.

- **Emergency Bypass.** This feature, new in iOS 10, lets you designate any random person in your Contacts list as an "It's OK to Disturb" person. That person's calls and texts will always go through. See the Tip on page 115.

One More Safety Measure

The Do Not Disturb settings screen also offers something called Repeated Calls. If you turn this on, then if *anybody* tries to call you more than once within 3 minutes, he'll ring through.

The idea here is that nobody *would* call you multiple times unless he needed to reach you urgently. You certainly wouldn't want Do Not Disturb to block somebody who's trying to tell you that there's been an accident, that you've overslept, or that you've just won the lottery.

Locked or Unlocked

The final option on the settings screen is the Silence option. If you choose Always, then Do Not Disturb works exactly as described.

But if you choose Only while iPhone is locked, then the phone *does* ring and vibrate *when you're using it*. Because, obviously, if the phone is awake, so are you. It's a great way to ensure that you don't miss important calls if you happened to have awakened early today and started working.

Fun with Phone Calls

The iPhone makes it pitifully easy to perform stunts like turning on the speakerphone, putting someone on hold, taking a second call, and so on. Here are the options you get when you're on a call.

Mute

Tap this button to mute your own microphone, so the other guy can't hear you. (You can still hear him, though.) Now you have a chance to yell upstairs, to clear the phlegm from your throat, or to do anything else you'd rather the other party not hear. Tap again to unmute.

Keypad

Sometimes you have to input touchtones, which used to be a perk only of phones with physical dialing keys. For example, that's usually how you operate home answering machines when you call in for messages, and it's often required by automated banking, reservations, and conference-call systems.

Tap this button to produce the traditional iPhone dialing pad. Each digit you touch generates the proper touchtone for the computer on the other end to hear.

When you're finished, tap **Hide** to return to the dialing-functions screen, or tap **End** if your conversation is complete.

Speaker

Tap this button to turn on the iPhone's built-in speakerphone—a great hands-free option when you're caught without your earbuds or Bluetooth headset (page 142). (In fact, the speakerphone doesn't work if the earbuds are plugged in or if a Bluetooth headset is connected.)

When you tap the button, it turns white to indicate that the speaker is activated. Now you can put the iPhone down on a table or a counter and have a conversation with both hands free. Tap speaker again to channel the sound back into the built-in earpiece.

> **TIP:** On iPhones before the 7, the speaker is on the bottom edge of the phone. If you're having trouble hearing it, and the volume is all the way up, consider pointing the speaker toward you, or even cupping one hand around the bottom to direct the sound. (That works on the 7 models, too, although there's a second speaker in the earpiece.)

Add Call (Conference Calling)

The iPhone is all about software, baby, and that's nowhere more apparent than in its facility at handling multiple calls at once.

The simplicity and reliability of this feature put other cellphones to shame. Never again, in attempting to answer a second call, will you have to tell the first person, "If I lose you, I'll call you back."

As you'll read, however, this feature is much better on a GSM phone (AT&T or T-Mobile) than on a CDMA phone (Verizon or Sprint).

Suppose you're on a call. Here are some of the tricks you can do:

- **Make an outgoing call.** Tap add call. The iPhone puts the first person on hold—neither of you can hear the other—and returns you to the Phone app and its various phone-number lists. You can now make a second call just the way you made the first. The top of the screen makes clear that the first person is still on hold as you talk to the second.

- **Receive an incoming call.** What happens when a second call comes in while you're already on a call?

  To answer on a GSM phone, tap **End Call + Answer**. On a CDMA phone, tap **End Current Call**; the new call makes the phone ring again, at which point you can answer it normally. Weird but true.

You can also tap **End Current Call** (answer the incoming call, hang up on the first) or **Decline Incoming Call** (send it to voicemail).

When you're on two calls at once, the top of the screen identifies both other parties. Two new buttons appear, too:

- **Swap** (GSM phones only) lets you flip between the two calls. At the top of the screen, you see the names or numbers of your callers. One says **Hold** (the one who's on hold, of course) and the other bears a time counter, which lets you know whom you're actually speaking to.

  Think how many TV and movie comedies have relied on the old "Whoops, I hit the wrong button and now I'm bad-mouthing somebody directly instead of behind his back!" gag. That can't happen on the iPhone.

  You can swap calls by tapping **swap** or by tapping the **Hold** person's name or number.

- **Merge Calls** combines your two calls so all three of you can converse at once. Now the top of the screen announces the names of your callers. Note that on a CDMA phone, you can merge calls only if *you placed* the second call—not if it was incoming.

This business of combining calls into one doesn't have to stop at two. At any time, you can tap **Add Call**, dial a third number, and then tap **Merge** to combine it with your first two. And then a fourth call, and a fifth. With you, that makes six people on the call.

Then your problem isn't technological; it's social, as you try to conduct a meaningful conversation without interrupting one another.

FaceTime

Tap this button to switch from your current phone call into a face-to-face video call, using the FaceTime app described starting on page 137.

(This feature requires that both you and the other guy have iPhones, iPads, iPod Touches, or Macs.)

Hold

The FaceTime button appears in place of what, on earlier iPhones, was the Hold button. But you can still trigger the Hold function—by holding down the **Mute** button for a couple of seconds. Now neither you nor the other guy can hear anything. Tap again to resume the conversation.

Contacts

This button opens the address book program so you can look up a number or place another call.

Call Waiting

Call waiting has been around for years. With a call-waiting feature, when you're on one phone call, you hear a beep indicating that someone else is calling. You can tap the Flash key on your phone to answer the second call while you put the first one on hold.

Some people don't use call waiting because it's rude to both callers. Others don't use it because they have no idea what the Flash key is.

On the iPhone, when a second call comes in, the phone rings (and/or vibrates) as usual, and the screen displays the name or number of the caller, just as it always does. Buttons on the screen offer you three choices:

- **End Current Call.** Hangs up on the first call and takes the second one.

- **Answer (Hold Current Call).** This is the traditional call-waiting effect. You say, "Can you hold on a sec? I've got another call," to the first caller. The iPhone puts her on hold, and you connect to the second caller.

  At this point, you can jump back and forth between the two calls, or you can merge them into a conference call.

- **Decline Incoming Call.** The incoming call goes straight to voicemail. Your first caller has no idea that anything has happened.

If call waiting seems a bit disruptive, you can turn it off, at least on the AT&T iPhone (the switch is in Settings→Phone→Call Waiting). When call waiting is turned off, incoming calls go straight to voicemail when you're on the phone.

If you have T-Mobile, Sprint, or Verizon, then you can turn off call waiting only one call at a time; just dial *70 before you dial the number. You won't be disturbed by call-waiting beeps while you're on that important call.

Call Forwarding

Here's a pretty cool feature you may not have known you had. It lets you route all calls made to your iPhone number to a *different* number. How is this useful? Let us count the ways:

- **When you're home.** You can have your cellphone's calls ring your home number so you can use any extension in the house, and so you don't miss any calls while the iPhone is turned off or charging.

- **When you send your iPhone to Apple for battery replacement.** You can forward the calls you would have missed to your home or work phone number.

- **When you're overseas.** You can forward the number to one of the web-based services that answers your voicemail and sends it to you as an email attachment (like Google Voice).

- **When you're going to be in a place with little or no cell coverage.** Let's say you're in Alaska. You can have your calls forwarded to your hotel or to a friend's cellphone. (Forwarded calls eat up your allotment of minutes, though.)

You have to turn on call forwarding while you're still in an area with cell coverage. Here's how:

- **AT&T.** Tap Settings→Phone→Call Forwarding, turn call forwarding on, and then tap in the new phone number. That's all there is to it—your iPhone will no longer ring. At least not until you turn the same switch off again.

- **Verizon, Sprint, T-Mobile.** On the dialing pad, dial *72, plus the number you're forwarding calls to. Then tap 📞. (To turn off call forwarding, dial *73, and then tap 📞.)

Caller ID

Caller ID is another classic cellphone feature. It's the one that displays the phone number of the incoming call (and sometimes the name of the caller).

The only thing worth noting about the iPhone's own implementation of caller ID is that you can prevent *your* number from appearing when you call *other* people's phones:

- **AT&T.** Tap Settings→Phone→Show My Caller ID, and then tap the on/off switch.

- **Verizon, Sprint, T-Mobile.** You can disable caller ID only for individual calls. For example, if you're calling your ex, you might not want your number to show up on his phone. Just dial *67 before you dial the number. (Caller ID turns on again for subsequent calls.)

Custom Ringtones

The iPhone comes with more than 50 creative and intriguing ringing sounds, from an old car horn to a peppy marimba lick. Page 582 shows you how to choose the one you want to hear when your phone rings. You can also buy ready-made pop-music ringtones from Apple for $1.29 each. (On your iPhone, open the iTunes Store app. Tap More and then Tones).

But where's the fun in that? Surely you don't want to walk around listening to the same ringtones as the millions of *other* iPhone owners.

Fortunately, you can also make up *custom* ring sounds, either to use as your main iPhone ring or to assign to individual callers in your Contacts list. All kinds of free or cheap apps are available for doing that, with names like Ringtone Designer Pro and Ringtones for iPhone; they let you make ringtones out of songs you already own, or even sounds you record yourself.

You can also use GarageBand, a free Apple program available for iOS or Mac. For instructions, see this chapter's free online appendix. It's a PDF available on this book's "Missing CD" page at *missingmanuals.com*.

Because apps aren't allowed to manipulate the iPhone's ringtones list directly, the process isn't altogether automatic; it involves syncing the ringtone to iTunes on your computer and then syncing it again to your phone. But the app's instructions will guide you. (iPhone ringtones must be in the .m4r file format.)

TIP: One feature that's blatantly missing on the iPhone is a "vibrate, *then* ring" option for incoming calls. That's where the phone first vibrates silently to get your attention—and begins to ring only if you haven't responded after, say, 10 seconds.

GarageBand offers the solution: Create a ringtone that's silent for the first 10 seconds and only *then* plays a sound. Then set your iPhone to vibrate and ring. When a call comes in, the phone plays the ringtone immediately as it vibrates—but you won't hear anything until after the silent portion of the ringtone has been "played."

FaceTime Video Calls

Your iPhone, as you're probably aware, has two cameras—one on the back and one on the front. And that can mean only one thing: Video calling has arrived.

The iPhone was not the first phone to be able to make video calls. But it is the first one that can make *good* video calls, reliably, with no sign-up or setup, with a single tap. The picture and audio are generally rock-solid, with very little delay, and it works the first time and every time. Now Grandma can see the baby, or you can help someone shop from afar, or you can supervise brain surgery from thousands of miles away (some medical training recommended).

You can enjoy these *Jetsons* fantasies not just when calling other iPhones; you can also make video calls between iPhones and iPads, iPod Touches, and Macs. You can even place these calls when you're not in a Wi-Fi hotspot, over the cellular airwaves, when you're out and about.

Being able to make video calls like a regular cellphone call is a huge convenience. Never again will you return home from the store and get scolded for buying the wrong size, style, or color.

In any case, FaceTime couldn't be easier to fire up—in many different ways:

- **From Siri.** The quickest way to start a video call may be simply to say, "FaceTime Mom," "FaceTime Chris Taylor," or whatever.

- **From Favorites.** Whenever you designate someone's FaceTime contact info as a favorite, a new entry appears in the Phone app's Favorites list (page 104).

- **When you're already on a phone call with someone.** This is a good technique when you want to ask first if the other guy *wants* to do video, or when you've been chatting and suddenly there's some *reason* to do video. In any case, there's nothing to it: Just tap the FaceTime icon that's right on the screen when you pull the phone away from your face. (Your buddy can either accept or, if he just got out of the shower, decline.)

- **From the FaceTime app.** You can also start up a videochat without placing a phone call first. That's handy when you have Wi-Fi but no cell signal; FaceTime can make the call even when Verizon can't.

  Of course, if you're not already on a call, the iPhone doesn't yet know whom you want to call. So you have to tell it. Open the FaceTime app. It presents a list of your recent FaceTime calls. Tap a name to place a new call to that person, or tap ⓘ to view a history of your calls with that person (and buttons for placing new ones).

Or, to find your callee from your own Contacts list, tap the + button. Find a name, tap it, and then tap ■◀ to place the call.

If your future conversation partner *isn't* in Contacts yet, then tap where it says **Enter name, email, or number**, and do just that.

- **From Contacts.** In the Contacts app, if you tap a person's name, you'll find buttons that place FaceTime calls. Or, in the Phone app, call up your Favorites or Recents list. Tap ⓘ next to a name to open the contact's card; tap **FaceTime**.

- **From Messages.** If you're chatting away with somebody by text and you realize that typing is no longer appropriate for the conversation, tap **Details** at the top of the screen. Tap ■◀.

At this point, the other guy receives an audio and video message inviting him to a chat. If he taps **Accept**, you're on. You're on each other's screens, seeing and hearing each other in real time. (You appear on your own screen, too, in a little inset window. It's spinach-in-your-teeth protection.)

Once the chat has begun, here's some of the fun you can have:

- **Show what's in front of you.** Sometimes you'll want to show your friend what you're looking at. That is, you'll want to turn on the camera on the *back* of the iPhone, the one pointing away from you, to show off the baby, the artwork, or the broken engine part.

  That's easy enough; just tap ⌾ on your screen. The iPhone switches from the front camera to the back camera. Now you and your callee can both see what you're seeing. (It's a lot less awkward than using a laptop for this purpose, because with the laptop's camera facing away from you, you can't see what you're showing.)

  Tap ⌾ again to return to the front camera.

- **Snap a commemorative photo.** You can immortalize a chat by using the screenshot keystroke (**Sleep** + **Home**). You wind up with a still photo of your videochat in progress, safely nestled in the Camera Roll of your Photos app.

- **Rotate the screen.** FaceTime works in either portrait (upright) or landscape (widescreen) view; just turn your phone 90 degrees. Of course, if your calling partner doesn't *also* turn her gadget, she'll see your picture all squished and tiny, with big black areas filling the rest of the screen. (On the Mac, the picture rotates automatically when your partner's gadget rotates. You don't have to turn the monitor 90 degrees.)

TIP: The ⊕ (rotation lock) button described on page 25 works in FaceTime, too. That is, you can stop the picture from rotating when you turn the phone—as long as you're happy with full-time upright (portrait) orientation.

- **Mute the audio.** Tap 🎤 to silence the audio you're sending. Great when you need to yell at the kids.

- **Mute the video.** When you leave the FaceTime app for any reason (press the **Home** button and then open a different program, if you like), the other guy's screen goes black. He can't see what you're doing when you leave the FaceTime screen. He can still hear you, though.

  This feature was designed to let you check your calendar, look something up on the web, or whatever, while you're still chatting. But it's also a great trick when you need to adjust your clothing, pick at your teeth, or otherwise shield your activity from the person on the other end.

  In the meantime, the call is technically still in progress—and a green banner at the top of the Home screen reminds you of that. Tap there, on the green bar, to return to the video call.

When you and your buddy have had quite enough, tap the **End** button to terminate the call. (Although it's easy to jump from phone call to video-chat, there's no way to go the other direction.)

And marvel that you were alive to see the day.

FaceTime Audio Calls

You might imagine that, on the great timeline of Apple technologies, audio calling would have arrived **before** video calling. But no; free Internet audio calls didn't come to the iPhone until iOS 7.

And it's a big, big deal. Video calling is neat and all, but be honest: Don't you find yourself making **phone** calls more often? Video calling forces us to be "on," neatly dressed and well behaved, because we're on camera. Most of the time, we're perfectly content (in fact, **more** content) with audio only.

And FaceTime audio calls don't eat into your cellphone minutes and aren't transmitted over your cell carrier's voice network; instead, these are **Internet** calls. (They use data, not minutes.)

When you're in a Wi-Fi hotspot, they're free. When you're not, your carrier's data network carries your voice. Use FaceTime audio a lot, and you might even be able to downgrade your calling plan to a less expensive one.

Sold yet? All right: Here's how to make a free Internet voice call.

You start out exactly as you would when making a video call, as described earlier. That is, you can start from the FaceTime app, the Contacts app, the Phone app, Messages, and so on.

In each spot where FaceTime is available, you get a choice of two types of calls: Video (■◀) and Audio (☎). (In Messages, if you tap the ☎, you get a choice of two voice options: Voice Call and FaceTime Audio.)

When you place an audio FaceTime call, the other person's phone rings exactly as though you'd placed a regular call. All the usual buttons and options are available: Remind Me, Message, Decline, Accept, and so on.

Once you accept the call, it's just like being on a phone call, too: You have the options Mute, Speaker, FaceTime (that is, "Switch to video") and Contacts. (What's missing? The Keypad button and the Merge Calls button. You can't combine FaceTime audio calls with each other, or with regular cellphone calls. If a cellphone call comes in, you'll be offered the chance to take it—but you'll have to hang up on FaceTime.)

Actually, it's better than being on a phone call in two ways. First, you don't have the usual lag that throws off your comic timing. And, second, the audio quality is **amazing**—more like FM radio than cellular. It sounds like the other person is right next to your head; you hear every breath, sniff, and sweater rustle.

You'd be wise to try out FaceTime audio calls. Whenever you're calling another iPhone, iPad, iPod Touch, or Mac owner, you'll save money and minutes by placing these better-sounding free calls.

> **TIP:** iOS even offers you FaceTime Call Waiting. If you're on a FaceTime audio or video call, and someone else FaceTime calls you, your phone rings—and you can either tap Decline or End & Accept.

Bluetooth Accessories

Bluetooth is a short-range *cable elimination* technology. It's designed to untether you from equipment that would ordinarily require a cord.

Most people use Bluetooth for two purposes: Communicating with a smartwatch or fitness band, or transmitting audio to a wireless speaker, car stereo, or Bluetooth earpiece.

> **NOTE:** This discussion covers *monaural* Bluetooth earpieces intended for phone calls. But the iPhone can also handle Bluetooth *stereo* headphones, intended for music, as well as Bluetooth speakers. Details are on page 247.

Pairing with a Bluetooth Earpiece or Speaker

Pairing means "marrying" a phone to a Bluetooth accessory so that each works only with the other. If you didn't do this one-time pairing, then some other guy passing on the sidewalk might hear your conversation through *his* earpiece. And neither of you would be happy.

The pairing process is different for every cellphone and every Bluetooth earpiece. Usually it involves a sequence like this:

1. **On the earpiece, turn on Bluetooth. Make the earpiece or speaker discoverable.** *Discoverable* just means that your phone can "see" it. You'll have to consult the gadget's instructions to learn how to do so; it's usually a matter of holding down some button or combination of buttons until the earpiece blinks.

2. **On the iPhone, tap** Settings→Bluetooth. **Turn Bluetooth on.** The iPhone immediately begins searching for nearby Bluetooth equipment. If all goes well, you'll see the name of your earpiece or speaker show up on the screen.

3. **Tap the gadget's name. Type in the passcode, if necessary.** The *passcode* is a number, usually four or six digits, that must be typed

into the phone within about a minute. You have to enter this only once, during the initial pairing process. The idea is to prevent some evildoer sitting nearby in the airport lounge, for example, to secretly pair *his* earpiece with *your* iPhone.

The user's manual for your earpiece should tell you what the passcode is (if one is even required).

To make calls using a Bluetooth earpiece (or speaker as a speakerphone), you *dial* using the iPhone itself. You usually use the iPhone's own volume controls, too. You generally press a button on the earpiece or speaker to answer an incoming call, to swap call-waiting calls, or to end a call.

If you're having problems making a particular gadget work, Google it. Type "iphone jambox mini," for example. Chances are good that you'll find a write-up by somebody who's successfully worked through the setup.

Bluetooth Car Systems

The iPhone works beautifully with Bluetooth car systems, too. The pairing procedure generally goes exactly as described previously: You make the car discoverable, enter the passcode on the iPhone, and then make the connection.

Once you're paired up, you can answer an incoming call by pressing a button on your steering wheel, for example. You hear your caller through the car's speakers, and a microphone for your own voice is hidden in the rearview mirror or dashboard. You make calls either from the iPhone or, in some cars, by dialing the number on the car's own touchscreen.

NOTE: When Bluetooth is turned on but the earpiece isn't, or when the earpiece isn't nearby, the � icon on your iPhone's status bar appears in gray. And when it's connected and working right, the earpiece's battery gauge appears on the iPhone's status bar.

Of course, studies show that it's the act of driving while conversing that causes accidents—not actually holding a cellphone. So the hands-free system is less for safety than for convenience and compliance with state laws.

Pairing with a Smartwatch or Fitness Band

The trouble with Bluetooth has always been that it's a battery hog. Now, though, there's a new, better technology, called Bluetooth LE (for "low energy"), Bluetooth Smart, or Bluetooth 4.0. Its very smart idea: It turns on only when necessary and then turns off again to save power.

When you've paired your phone with a Bluetooth 4.0 gadget, you see the Bluetooth logo on your status bar (✳) light up only when it's actually exchanging data. Bluetooth LE has made possible a lot of smartwatches and fitness trackers.

As a handy bonus, you usually do the pairing right in the gadget's companion app, rather than fumbling around in Settings. That setup makes a lot more sense. For example, when you're setting up an Apple Watch, you use the Watch app to pair the watch; when you're setting up an Up band or Fitbit, you connect your band wirelessly in the Up app or Fitbit app.

5

Siri Voice Command

Siri, the iPhone's famous voice-recognition technology, is actually *two* features. First, there's *dictation*, where the phone types out everything you say. It's described in Chapter 3.

Second, there's Siri the *voice-controlled minion*. You can say, "Wake me up at 7:45 a.m.," or "What's Chris's work number?" or "How do I get to the airport?" or "What's the weather going to be like in San Francisco this weekend?"

You can also ask questions about movies, sports, and restaurants. Siri displays a beautifully formatted response and speaks in a calm voice.

You can even ask her, "What song is that?" or "Name that tune." She'll identify whatever song is playing in the background, just as the popular Shazam app does. It's creepy/amazing.

You can operate her hands-free, too. Instead of pressing the Home button to get her attention, you just say, "Hey Siri." (The 6s and 7 models can respond even when running on battery power.)

Until iOS 10, only Apple decided what Siri could understand. Now, though, the creators of certain apps can teach Siri new vocabulary, too. For example, you can now say, "Send Nicki a message with WeChat," "Pay Dad 20 dollars with Square Cash," and "Book a ride with Lyft" or "Order me an Uber."

NOTE: The kinds of apps Apple permits to tap into Siri are in these six categories: audio or video calls, messages, payments, photo searching, booking rides, and starting workouts. Notably absent: music apps. You still can't say, "Play some Dave Brubeck on Spotify," for example. Apple Music is the only music service Siri understands.

Voice Command

In 2010, Apple bought Siri, a company that made a voice-control app (no longer available) for the iPhone. Apple cleaned it up, beefed it up, integrated it with the iPhone's software, and wound up with Siri, your virtual servant.

NOTE: Believe it or not, Siri is a spinoff from a Department of Defense research project called CALO (Cognitive Agent that Learns and Organizes), which Wikipedia describes as "the largest artificial-intelligence project ever launched." In a very real way, therefore, Siri represents your tax dollars at work.

The spinoff was run by the Stanford Research Institute (SRI). But that's not where Siri's name came from. Siri, it turns out, is a Norwegian word meaning "beautiful woman who leads you to victory." (Cocreator Dag Kittlaus named her. He's Norwegian.)

Siri is a crisply accurate, astonishingly understanding, uncomplaining, voice-commanded servant. No special syntax is required; you don't even have to hold the phone to your head.

Most speech-recognition systems work only if you issue certain limited commands with predictable syntax, like "Call 445-2340" or "Open Microsoft Word." But Siri is different. She's been programmed to respond to casual speech, normal speech. It doesn't matter if you say, "What's the weather going to be like in Tucson this weekend?" or "Give me the Tucson weather for this weekend" or "Will I need an umbrella in Tucson?" Siri understands almost any variation.

And she understands regular, everyday speaking. You don't have to separate your words or talk weirdly; you just speak normally.

It's not *Star Trek.* You can't ask Siri to clean your gutters or to teach you French. (Well, you can **ask**.)

But, as you'll soon discover, the number of things Siri **can** do for you is impressive. Furthermore, Apple continues to add to Siri's intelligence through software updates.

NOTE: Apple also keeps increasing the number of languages that Siri understands. Already, Siri understands English (in nine varieties), Arabic, Cantonese, Danish, Dutch, Finnish, French, German, Hebrew, Italian, Japanese, Korean, Malay, Mandarin, Norwegian, Portuguese, Russian, Spanish, Swedish, Thai, and Turkish. You change the language by visiting Settings→Siri.

How to Use Siri

To get Siri's attention, you have three choices:

- **Hold down the Home button** until you see a wavy animation on the screen. Siri no longer double-beeps or vibrates when you trigger her, except when you trigger her remotely. She gives a double-beep when you use CarPlay, your earbuds clicker, or "Hey Siri" (described next). The phone doesn't have to be unlocked or awake, which is awesome. Just pull the phone out of your pocket and hold down the Home button.

> **TIP:** Some people press the Home button to trigger Siri, and then release the button and start talking. But you can also hold the Home button down *the entire time you're speaking*. That way you know Siri won't attempt to execute your command before you're finished saying it.

- **Hold down the clicker on your earbuds cord** or the Call button on your Bluetooth earpiece.
- **Say, "Hey Siri."** A double-beep plays. (You have to turn this feature on in advance. And unless you have a 6s or 7 model, it works only when the phone is plugged into power, like a USB jack. Details in a moment.)

Now Siri is listening. Ask your question or say your command. You don't have to hold the phone up to your mouth; Siri works perfectly well at arm's length, on your desk in front of you, or on the car seat beside you.

> **NOTE:** Apple insists that Siri is neither male nor female. In fact, if you ask Siri her gender, she'll say something noncommittal, like, "Is this relevant?" But that's just political correctness. Any baby-name website—or a Norwegian dictionary—will tell you that Siri is a girl's name.

When you're finished speaking, be quiet for a moment (or, if you've been pressing the Home button, release it). About a second after you stop speaking, Siri connects with her master brain online and processes your request. After a moment, she presents (and speaks) an attractively for-matted response.

> **TIP:** You generally see only the most recent question and response on the Siri screen. But you can drag downward to see all the previous exchanges you've had with Siri during this session.

To rephrase your question or cancel or start over, tap the screen to interrupt Siri's work. (You can also cancel by saying "Cancel" or just by pressing the Home button.) Tap the microphone icon to trigger your new attempt.

And when you're completely finished talking to Siri, you can either press the Home button, hold down your earbuds clicker, or say something like "Goodbye," "See you later," or "Adios." You're taken back to whatever app you were using before.

How to Use "Hey Siri"

Siri can also accept spoken commands without your touching the phone. It's an ideal feature for use in the car, when your hands and eyes should be focused on driving. (Of course, the safest arrangement is not to interact with your phone *at all* when you're driving.)

The phone won't respond to "Hey Siri" unless you've set it up like this:

- **Turn on "Hey Siri."** Open Settings→Siri and turn on Allow "Hey Siri" (it comes turned off).

- **Train Siri to recognize your voice.** You have to do a quick training session to teach Siri what you sound like. Otherwise, a lot of people would be freaked out when they say things like "Jay's weary" or "Space? Eerie!" and the phone double-beeps in response.

  As soon as you turn on Allow "Hey Siri" the training screens appear. Hit Set Up Now. The screen asks you to say "Hey Siri" three times, then "Hey Siri, how's the weather today?" and "Hey Siri, it's me." That's all Siri needs to learn your voice.

At that point, you're good to go. Anytime you want to ask Siri something, just say, "Hey Siri"; at the sound of the double-beep, say your thing.

Just remember that most iPhone models don't respond to "Hey Siri" except when they're plugged in and charging. (Having to listen constantly for the "Hey Siri" command is exhausting for your iPhone; it uses a lot of power. This requirement ensures that it won't drain your battery.) The exceptions: the iPhone 6s and 7 models, which can listen for you even on battery power.

Thanks to "Hey Siri," you now have a front-seat conversationalist, a little software friend who's always happy to listen to what you have to say— and whose knowledge of the world, news, sports, and history can help make those cross-country drives a little less dull.

What to Say to Siri

Siri comes with two different cheat sheets to help you learn her capabilities. To produce either one, hold down the Home button to make Siri's "What can I help you with?" screen appear. Then:

- **Wait.** After 5 seconds of silence, Siri begins displaying screen after screen of example commands, under the heading "Some things you can ask me."

- **Tap the tiny ? button** to reveal the list of categories shown below.

> **TIP:** Or just trigger Siri and then say, "What can I say?" or "What can you do?" or "Help me!" The same cheat sheet appears.

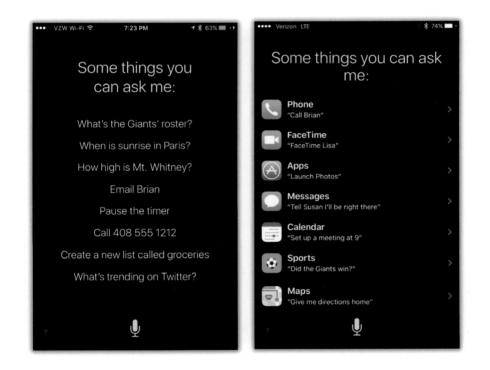

Here are the general categories of things you can say to Siri:

- **Opening apps.** If you don't learn to use Siri for anything else, for the love of Mike, learn this one.

  You can say, "Open Calendar" or "Play Angry Birds" or "Launch Calculator."

Result: The corresponding app opens instantly. It's exactly the same as pressing the Home button, swiping across the screen until you find the app you're looking for, and then tapping its icon—but without pressing the Home button, swiping across the screen until you find the app you're looking for, and then tapping its icon.

- **Change your settings.** You can make changes to certain basic settings just by speaking your request. You can say, for example, "Turn on Bluetooth," "Turn off Wi-Fi," "Turn on Do Not Disturb," or "Turn on airplane mode." (You can't turn *off* airplane mode by voice, because Siri doesn't work without an Internet connection.)

    You can also make screen adjustments: "Make the screen brighter." "Dim the screen."

    Result: Siri makes the requested adjustment, tells you so, and displays the corresponding switch in case she misunderstood your intention.

NOTE: If you've protected your phone with a fingerprint, you may have to unlock it before you're allowed to change settings. Security and all that.

- **Open Settings panels.** When you need to make tweakier changes to Settings, you can open the most important panels by voice: "Open Wi-Fi settings," "Open Cellular settings," "Open Personal Hotspot settings," "Open Notification settings," "Open Sounds settings," "Open wallpaper settings," and so on.

    You can open your apps' settings this way, too: "Open Maps settings," "Open Netflix settings," "Open Delta settings," and so on.

    Siri is smart enough not to open security-related settings this way; remember that you can use Siri even from the Lock screen. She's protecting you from passing pranksters who might really mess up your phone.

    Result: Siri silently opens the corresponding page of Settings.

- **Calling.** Siri can place phone calls or FaceTime calls for you. "Call Harold." "Call Nicole on her mobile phone." "Call the office." "Phone home." "Dial 512-444-1212." "Start a FaceTime call with Sheila Withins." "FaceTime Alex."

    Result: Siri hands you off to the Phone app or FaceTime app and places the call. At this point, it's just as though you'd initiated the call yourself.

Siri also responds to questions about your voicemail, like "Do I have any new voicemail messages?" and even "Play my voicemails." (After playing each message, Siri gracefully offers to let you return the call—or to play the next one.)

- **Alarms.** You can say, "Wake me up at 7:35." "Change my 7:35 alarm to 8:00." "Wake me up in 6 hours." "Cancel my 6 a.m. alarm" (or "Delete my…" or "Turn off my…").

  This is **so** much quicker than setting the iPhone's alarm the usual way.

  Result: When you set or change an alarm, you get a sleek digital alarm clock, right there beneath Siri's response, and Siri confirms what she understood.

- **Timer.** You can also control the Timer module of the phone's Clock app. It's like a stopwatch in reverse, in that it counts down to zero—handy when you're baking something, limiting your kid's video-game time, and so on. For example: "Set the timer for 20 minutes." Or "Show the timer," "Pause the timer," "Resume," "Reset the timer," or "Stop it."

Result: A cool digital timer appears. A little stopwatch icon appears on the Lock screen to remind you that time is ticking down.

> **TIP:** You can specify minutes *and seconds*: "Set the time for two minutes, thirty seconds," for example.

- **Clock.** "What time is it?" "What time is it in San Francisco?" "What's today's date?" "What's the date a week from Friday?" Or just "Time."

  Result: When you ask about the time, you see the clock identifying the time in question. (For dates, Siri just talks to you and writes out the date.)

- **Contacts.** You can ask Siri to look up information in your address book (the Contacts app)—and not just addresses. For example, you can say, "What's Gary's work number?" "Give me Sheila Jenkins's office phone." "Show Tia's home email address." "What's my boss's home address?" "When is my husband's birthday?" "Show Larry Murgatroid." "Find everybody named Smith." "Who is P.J. Frankenberg?"

  Result: A half "page" from your Contacts list. You can tap it to jump into that person's full card in Contacts. (If Siri finds multiple listings for the person you named—"Bob," for example—she lists all the matches and asks you to specify which one you meant.)

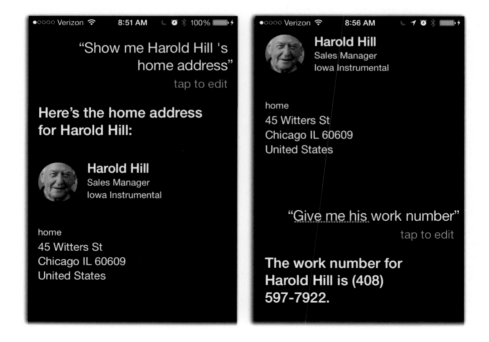

- **Text messages.** "Send a text to Alex Rybeck." "Send a message to Peter saying, 'I no longer require your services.' " "Tell Cindy I'm running late." "Send a message to Janet's mobile asking her to pick me up at the train." "Send a text message to 212-561-2282." "Text Frank and Ralph: Did you pick up the pizza?"

  Result: Siri prompts you for the body of the message, if you haven't specified it. Then you see a miniature outgoing text message. Siri asks if you want to send it; say "Yes," "Send," or "Confirm" to proceed.

If you need to edit the message before sending it, you have a couple of options. First, you can tap it; Siri hands you off to the Messages app for editing and sending.

Second, you can edit it by voice. You can say, "Change it to" to re-dictate the message; "Add" to add more to the message; "No, send it to Frank" to change the recipient; "No" to leave the message on the screen without sending it; or "Cancel" to forget the whole thing.

You can also ask Siri to read incoming text messages to you, which is great if you're driving. For example, you can say, "Read my new messages," and "Read that again."

You can even have her reply to messages she's just read to you. "Reply, 'Congratulations (period). Can't wait to see your trophy (exclamation point)!' " "Call her back." "Tell him I have a flat tire and I'm going to be late."

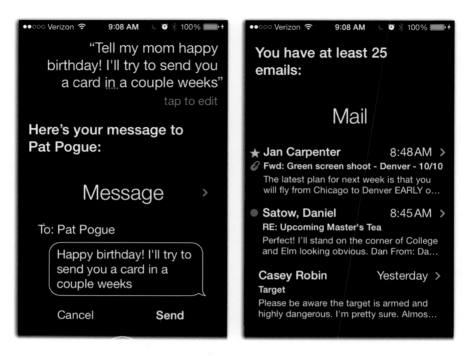

- **Email.** Siri can read your email to you. For example, if you say, "Read my latest email" or "Read my new email," Siri reads aloud your most recent email message. (Siri then offers you the chance to dictate a response.)

  Or you can use the summary-listing commands. When you say, "Read my email," Siri starts walking backward through your Inbox, telling you the subject of each, plus who sent it and when.

  After a few listings, Siri says: "Shall I read the rest?" That's your opportunity to shut down what could be a very long recitation. If you say "Yes," she goes on to read the entire list of subject lines, dates, and senders.

  Result: Siri reads aloud.

  TIP: You can also use commands like "Any new mail from Chris today?" "Show new mail about the world premiere." "Show yesterday's email from Jan." All of those commands produce a list of the messages, but Siri doesn't read them.

  You can also compose a new message by voice; anytime you use the phrase "about," that becomes the subject line for your new message. "Email Mom about the reunion." "Email my boyfriend about the dance on Friday." "New email to Freddie Gershon." "Mail Mom about Saturday's flight." "Email Frank and Cindy Vosshall and Peter Love about the picnic." "Email my assistant and say, 'Thanks for arranging the taxi!' " "Email Gertie and Eugene about their work on the surprise party, and say I really value your friendship."

(If you've indicated only the subject and addressee, Siri prompts you for the body of the message.)

TIP: You can't send mail to canned groups of people using Siri—at least not without MailShot, an iPhone app that exists expressly for the purpose of letting you create email addressee groups.

You can reply to a message Siri has just described, too. "Reply, 'Dear Robin (comma), I'm so sorry about your dog (period). I'll be more careful next time (period).' " "Call her mobile number." "Send him a text message saying, 'I got your note.' "

Result: A miniature Mail message, showing you Siri's handiwork before you send it.

- **Calendar.** Siri can make appointments for you. Considering how many tedious finger taps it usually takes to schedule an appointment in the Calendar app, this is an enormous improvement. "Make an appointment with Patrick for Thursday at 3 p.m." "Set up a haircut at 9." "Set up a meeting with Charlize this Friday at noon." "Meet Danny Cooper at 6." "New appointment with Steve, next Sunday at 7." "Schedule a conference call at 5:30 p.m. tonight in my office."

Result: A slice of that day's calendar appears, filled in the way you requested.

TIP: Siri may also alert you to a conflict, something like this: "Note that you already have an all-day appointment about 'Boston Trip' for this Thursday. Shall I schedule this anyway?" Amazing.

You can also move previously scheduled meetings by voice. For example, "Move my 2:00 meeting to 2:30." "Reschedule my meeting with Charlize to a week from Monday at noon." "Add Frank to my meeting with Harry." "Cancel the conference call on Sunday."

You can even *consult* your calendar by voice. You can say, "What's on my calendar today?" "What's on my calendar for September 23?" "When's my next appointment?" "When is my meeting with Charlize?" "Where is my next meeting?"

Result: Siri reads you your agenda and displays a tidy Day view of the specified date.

- **Directions.** By consulting the phone's GPS, Siri can set up the Maps app to answer requests like these: "How do I get to the airport?" "Show me 1500 Broadway, New York City." "Directions to my assistant's house." "Take me home." "What's my next turn?" "Are we there yet?"

TIP: You can also say, "Stop navigation"—a great way to make Maps stop harassing you when you realize you know where you are.

You can ask for directions to the home or work address of anyone in your Contacts list—provided those addresses are *in* your Contacts cards.

Result: Siri fires up the Maps app, with the start and end points of your driving directions already filled in.

- **Reminders.** Siri is a natural match for the Reminders app. She can add items to that list at your spoken command. For example: "Remind me to file my IRS tax extension." "Remind me to bring the science supplies to school." "Remind me to take my antibiotic tomorrow at 7 a.m."

The *location-based* reminders are especially amazing. They rely on GPS to know where you are. So you can say, "Remind me to visit the drugstore when I leave the office." "Remind me to water the lawn when I get home." "Remind me to check in with Nancy when I leave here."

TIP: It's pretty obvious how Siri knows to remind you when you leave "here," because she knows where you are right now. But she also understands "home" and "office," both yours and other people's—*if* you've entered those addresses onto the corresponding people's cards in Contacts.

Siri can also understand the word "this" when you're looking at an email message, a web page, or a note. That is, you can say, "Remind me about this at 7 p.m." or "Remind me about this when I get home." Sure enough: Siri will flag you with a reminder Notification at the appropriate time—and add an entry, with a link to the original message, web page, or note, to the Reminders app.

Result: A miniature entry from the Reminders app, showing you that Siri has understood.

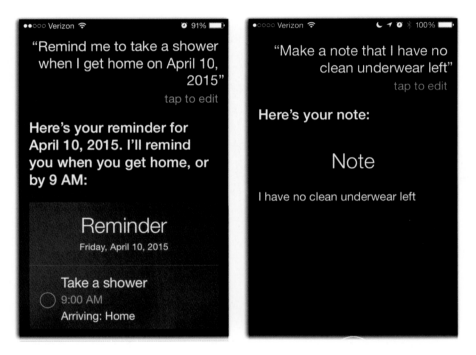

- **Notes.** You create a new note (in the Notes app) by saying things like, "Make a note that my shirt size is 15 and a half" or "Note: Dad will not be coming to the reunion after all." You can even name the note in your request: "Create a 'Movies to Watch' note."

  But you can also call up a certain note to the screen, like this: "Find my frequent-flier note." You can even summon a table-of-contents view of all your notes by saying, "Show all my notes."

Result: A miniature Notes page appears, showing your newly dictated text (or the existing note that you've requested).

You can keep dictating into the note you've just added. Say, "Add 'Return books to library' " (or just say, "Add," and she'll ask you what to add). She'll keep adding to the same note until you say, "Note that..." or "Start a note" or "Take a note" to begin a fresh note page.

You can add text to an earlier note: "Add *Titanic II: The Voyage Home* to my 'Movies to Watch' note." (The first line of any note is also its title—in this case "Movies to Watch.")

• **Restaurants.** Siri is also happy to serve as your personal concierge. Try "Good Italian restaurants around here," "Find a good pizza joint in Cleveland," or "Show me the reviews for Olive Garden in Youngstown." Siri displays a list of matching restaurants—with ratings, reviews, hours, and so on.

But she's ready to do more than just give you information. She can actually book your reservations, thanks to her integration with the OpenTable website. You can say, "Table for two in Belmont tonight," or "Make a reservation at an inexpensive Mexican restaurant Saturday night at seven."

Result: Siri complies by showing you the proposed reservation. Tap one of the offered alternative time slots, if you like, and then off you go. Everything else is tappable here, too—the ratings (tap to read customer reviews), phone number, web address, map, and so on.

- **Businesses.** Siri is a walking (well, all right, not walking) Yellow Pages. Go ahead, try it: "Find coffee near me." "Where's the closest Walmart?" "Find some pizza places in Cincinnati." "Search for gas stations." "French restaurants nearby." "I'm in the mood for Chinese food." "Find me a hospital." "I want to buy a book."

  Result: Siri displays a handsome list of businesses nearby that match your request.

> **TIP:** She's a sly dog, that Siri. She'll help you out even if your requests are, ahem, somewhat off the straight and narrow. If you say, "I think I'm drunk," she'll list nearby cab companies. If you indicate that you're craving relief from your drug addiction, she'll provide you with a list of rehab centers. If you refer to certain biological urges, she'll list escort services.

- **Playing music.** Instead of fumbling around in your Music app, save yourself steps and time by speaking the name of the album, song, or band: "Play some Beatles." "Play 'I'm a Barbie Girl.' " "Play some jazz." "Play my jogging playlist." "Play the party mix." "Shuffle my 'Dave's Faves' playlist." "Play." "Pause." "Resume." "Skip."

  If you've set up any iTunes Radio stations (Chapter 8), you can call for them by name, too: "Play Dolly Parton Radio." Or be more generic: Just say, "Play iTunes Radio" and be surprised. Or be more specific: Say, "Play some country music" (substitute your favorite genre).

  Result: Siri plays (or skips, shuffles, or pauses) the music you asked for—without ever leaving whatever app you were using.

- **Apple Music.** If you subscribe to Apple's $10-a-month Apple Music service, Siri offers a huge range of even more useful voice controls. For example, you can call for any music in Apple's 30 million–song catalog by song name, album, or performer: "Play 'Mr. Blue Sky.' " "Show me some Elton John albums." "Play 'Yesterday' next" (or "...after this song"). Or ask to have a singer or album played in random order: "Shuffle Taylor Swift."

  When you hear a song you like, you can say, "Play more like this." Or, "Add this song [or album] to my library." (Or, if you don't like it, "Skip this song.")

  If more than one person performed a song, be specific: "Play 'Smooth Criminal' by Glee." You can even ask for a song according to the movie it was in. "Play that song from *Frozen*."

Or start one of your playlists by name ("Play 'Jogging' "). Or re-listen to a song: "Play previous." Or ask for one of Apple Music's radio stations: "Play Beats 1" or "Play Charting Now."

While music is playing, Siri is happy to tell you what you're listening to. ("What song is this?" "Who's the singer?" "What album is this from?") You can also tell her, "Like this song" or "Rate this song five stars." She'll note that and offer you more songs like it on the For You screen of the Apple Music app.

You can ask her to play the top hits of any year or decade ("Play the top song from 1990"; "Play the top 35 songs of the 1960s").

Result: Just what you'd expect!

- **Identifying music.** Siri can listen to the music playing in the room and try to identify it (song name, singer, album, and so on).

  Whenever there's music playing, you can say things like, "What's that song?" "What's playing right now?" "What song is this?" or "Name that tune!"

  Result: Siri listens to the music playing at your home/office/bar/restaurant/picnic—and identifies the song by name and performer. There is also, needless to say, a Buy button.

- **Weather.** "What's the weather going to be today?" "What's the forecast for tomorrow?" "Show me the weather this week." "Will it snow

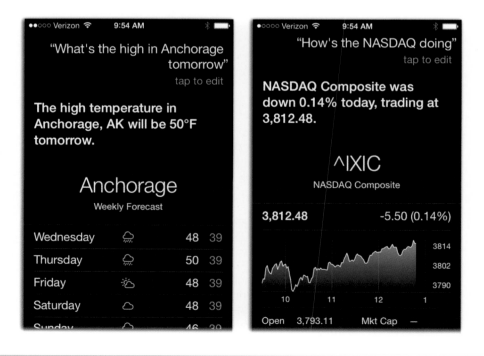

in Dallas this weekend?" "Check the forecast for Memphis on Friday." "What's the forecast for tonight?" "Can you give me the wind speed in Kansas City?" "Tell me the windchill in Chicago." "What's the humidity right now?" "Is it nighttime in Cairo?" "How's the weather in Paris right now?" "What's the high for Washington on Friday?" "When will Jupiter rise tomorrow?" "When's the moonrise?" "How cold will it be in Houston tomorrow?" "What's the temperature outside?" "Is it windy out there?" "When does the sun rise in London?" "When will the sun set today?" "Should I wear a jacket?"

Result: A convenient miniature Weather display for the date and place you specified.

- **Stocks.** "What's Google's stock price?" "What did Ford close at today?" "How's the Dow doing?" "What's Microsoft's P/E ratio?" "What's Amazon's average volume?" "How are the markets doing?"

Result: A tidy little stock graph, bearing a wealth of up-to-date statistics.

- **Find My Friends.** You see this category only if you've installed Apple's Find My Friends app. "Where's Ferd?" "Is my dad home?" "Where are my friends?" "Who's here?" "Who is nearby?" "Is my mom at work?"

Result: Siri shows you a beautiful little map with the requested person's location clearly indicated by a blue pushpin. (She does, that is, if you've set up Find My Friends, you've logged in, and your friends have made their locations available.)

- **Search the web.** "Search the web for a 2016 Ford Mustang." "Search for healthy smoothie recipes." "Search Wikipedia for the Thunderbirds." "Search for news about the Netflix-Amazon merger."

TIP: Siri uses Microsoft's Bing search service to perform its web searches. If you prefer Google, just say so. Say, "Google Benjamin Franklin." (For that matter, you can also ask Siri to "Yahoo" something—for example, "Yahoo blueberry dessert recipes.")

Wikipedia is a search type all its own. "Search Wikipedia for Harold Edgerton." "Look up Mariah Carey on Wikipedia." Pictures get special treatment, too: "I want to see pictures of cows." You can also say, "Show me pictures of..." or "Find me..." or "Search for..."

Result: Siri displays the results of your search right on her screen. Tap one of the results to open the corresponding web page in Safari.

- **Sports scores.** At last you have a buddy who's just as obsessed with sports trivia as you are. You can say things like, "How did the Indians do last night?" "What was the score of the last Yankees game?"

"When's the next Cowboys game?" "What baseball games are on today?"

You can also ask questions about individual players, like "Who has the best batting average?" "Who has scored the most runs against the Red Sox?" "Who has scored the most goals in British soccer?" "Which quarterback had the most sacks last year?"

And, of course, team stats are fair game, like "Show me the roster for the Giants," "Who is pitching for Tampa this season?" and "Is anyone on the Marlins injured right now?"

Result: Neat little box scores or factoids, complete with team logos.

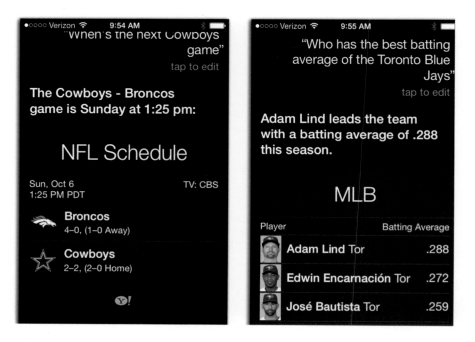

- **Movies.** Siri is also the virtual equivalent of an insufferable film buff. She knows **everything**. "Who was the star of *Groundhog Day*?" "Who directed *Chinatown*?" "What is *Waterworld* rated?" "What movie won Best Picture in 1952?"

  It's not just about old movies, either. Siri also knows everything about current showtimes in theaters. "What movies are opening this week?" "What's playing at the Watton Cineplex?" "Give me the reviews for *Doctor Strange*." "What are today's showtimes for *Trolls*?"

Result: Tidy tables of movie theaters or movie showtimes. (Tap one for details.) Sometimes you get a movie poster filled with facts—and, of course, you get a link to rent or buy it on iTunes.

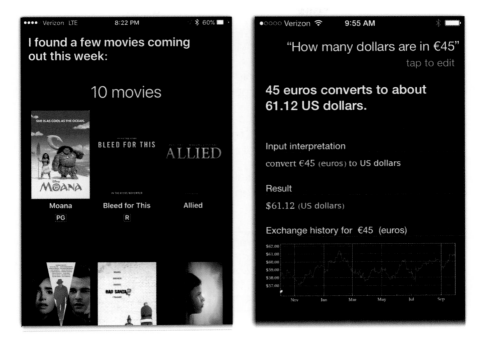

- **Facts and figures.** This is a huge category. It represents Siri's partnership with the Wolfram Alpha factual search engine (*www.wolfram-alpha.com*). The possibilities here could fill an entire chapter—or an entire encyclopedia.

  You can say things like, "How many days until Valentine's Day?" "When was Abraham Lincoln born?" "How many teaspoons are in a gallon?" "What's the exchange rate between dollars and euros?" "What's the capital of Belgium?" "How many calories are in a Hershey bar?" "What's a 17 percent tip on sixty-two dollars for three people?" "What movie won the Oscar for Best Picture in 1985?" "When is the next solar eclipse?" "Show me the Big Dipper." "What's the tallest mountain in the world?" "What's the price of gold right now?" "What's the definition of 'schadenfreude'?" "How much is 23 dollars in pesos?" "Generate a random number." "Graph x equals 3y plus 12." "What flights are overhead?"

  Result: For simple math and conversions, Siri just shows you the answer. For more complex questions, you get a specially formatted table, ripped right out of Wolfram Alpha's knowledge base.

TIP: Siri can also harness the entire wisdom of Wikipedia. You can say, for example, "Search Wikipedia for Tim Kaine," or "Tell me about Alexander Hamilton," or "Show me the Wikipedia page about Richard Branson."

- **Post to Twitter or Facebook.** iOS is a red-blooded, full-blown Twitter companion. So you can say things like, "Tweet 'I just saw a three-headed dog catch a Frisbee in midair. Unreal.' " "Tweet with my location, 'My car just broke down somewhere in Detroit. Help?' "

  Facebook is fair game, too. You can say, "Post to Facebook, 'The guy next to me kept his cellphone on for the whole plane ride,' " or "Write on my timeline, 'I can't believe I ate the whole thing.' "

  Result: Siri offers you a sheet (miniature dialog box) where you can approve the transcription and then, if it all looks good, send it off to your Twitter or Facebook feed.

TIP: If someone's Twitter address is recorded in Contacts, you can say, "Tweet Casey Robin: Loved your last tweet!" Siri sends a tweet to that person (*@CaseyRobin253 Loved your last tweet!*). Anyone who follows **both** of you will see that tweet. (Alas, Siri cannot send direct messages—private person-to-person tweets.)

- **Search Twitter.** If you say something like, "What are people saying?" or "What's going on?" or "What's happening on Twitter?" you see a list of tweets on the current trending topics on Twitter. (Tap a tweet in the list to open it into a new window that contains more information and a View in Twitter button.)

  Or ask, "What are people saying about the Chicago Bears?" to read tweets on that subject. Or, conversely, you can ask, "What is Jimmy Kimmel saying on Twitter?" to see his most recent tweets. (You can substitute the names of other people or companies on Twitter.) Or, "Search Twitter for the hashtag 'FirstWorldProblems.' " (A *hashtag* is a searchable phrase like #toofunny or #iphone7, which makes finding relevant tweets on Twitter much easier.)

  Result: Siri displays 10 or so tweets that match your query.

- **Round up photos or videos.** This trick can save you a lot of time and fussing. You can ask Siri to show you all photos or videos according to the time or place you shot them, or according to the album name they're in. "Show me the videos from Halloween last year," you can say. "Get me the videos from Utah." "Show me the Disney World album." "Open the Panoramas album." "Show me the Slo-mo videos from Oberlin College." "Give me the pictures from last summer."

  Result: You get a screenful of little square thumbnails of photos or videos that match your request. Tap one to open it, or tap Show All to see all the photos/videos in that batch.

Non-Apple Apps

It's a big deal: In iOS 10, Apple has finally permitted Siri to control apps from other companies. Once you find out what these commands are, they can accelerate other apps just as much as Siri already accelerates Apple's.

Here are a few examples:

- **Lyft, Uber.** "Order a Lyft." "Call me an Uber." Siri asks you to tap the kind of car you want to order; one further tap orders the ride.

- **Pinterest.** "Find toddler bedroom idea pins on Pinterest." The Pinterest app opens, displaying pins that match your search query (from all of Pinterest, not just your pages).

- **Square Cash.** "Pay Casey 10 dollars with Square Cash." Boom: You've just sent money to lucky, lucky Casey.

- **LinkedIn.** "Send a LinkedIn message to Robin that says, 'Can you vouch for me?' "

- **WhatsApp, WeChat, Skype**. All of these chat apps work exactly like iOS's own Messages app, in that you can send "text messages" entirely by voice. Just say "with [name of app] at the end of your command, or use the messaging app's name as a noun.

  For example: "Tell Eric 'I think I left my wallet in your car' with WhatsApp." "Send a WeChat to Phoebe saying, 'Are we still going out?'" "Let Marge know 'I accidentally left your front door open this morning' in Skype."

To see a list of all your apps that understand Siri commands, open **Settings→Siri→App Support**. There they are: All the Siri-compatible apps, with on-off switches.

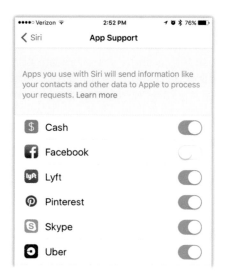

You may never find the end of the things Siri understands, or the ways that she can help you. If her repertoire seems intimidating at first, start simple—use her to open apps, dial by voice, send text messages, and set alarms. You can build up your bag of tricks as your confidence grows.

NOTE: Remember that you can use Siri without even unlocking your phone—and therefore without any security, like your passcode. Among certain juvenile circles, therefore, Siri is the source of some interesting pranks. Someone who finds your phone lying on a table could change your calendar appointments, send texts or emails, or even change what Siri calls you ("Call me 'you idiot' "), without having to enter the phone's passcode!

The solution is simple. In **Settings→Touch ID & Passcode**, if you scroll way down, you can turn off **Siri**. Of course, you've now lost the convenience of using Siri when the phone is locked. But at least you've prevented having your own phone call you an idiot.

When Things Go Wrong

If Siri doesn't have a good enough Internet connection to do her thing, she'll tell you so.

If she's working properly but misrecognizes your instructions, you'll know it, because you can see her interpretation of what you said. And, as indicated by the little hint **tap to edit**, you can tap Siri's interpretation to open up an editing screen so that you can make corrections by typing.

> **TIP:** You can also correct a misheard command just by speaking the correct version, like this, "I meant Chicago." Siri gets what you mean.

If Siri recognizes what you said but it isn't within her world of comprehension, she offers you a **Search the web** button as a last resort.

Siri's Personality

Siri's understanding of casual spoken commands is so impressive that you might sometimes think she's almost human. And that, of course, is exactly what Apple wants.

You can say all kinds of off-kilter things to Siri. After you've encountered a few of her answers, you won't be surprised to find out that Apple actually employs a comedy-writing team exclusively for Siri-humor purposes.

For example, if you ask her, "What is the meaning of life?" she responds with one of more than a dozen different answers. She might say, "I can't answer that now, but give me some time to write a very long play in which nothing happens." Or "It's nothing Nietzsche couldn't teach ya." Or: "All evidence to date suggests it's chocolate."

Siri is full of such comebacks, and there are whole websites dedicated to her snark. Here are a few examples. (This list won't ruin the fun, because Siri actually has several different comebacks to most of these questions.)

You: "Who's your daddy?" **Siri:** "You are. Can we get back to work now?"

You: "Open the pod bay doors, Hal." **Siri:** "I'm sorry, I'm afraid I can't do that." (Then: "Are you happy now?")

You: "Knock knock." **Siri:** "Knock knock. Who's there? Joshua. Joshua who? Joshua, I don't do knock-knock jokes."

You: "What are you wearing?" **Siri:** "You have the wrong personal assistant, Carl."

You: "Who's the boss?" **Siri:** (Presents the vital statistics of Bruce Springsteen.)

You: "Beam me up, Siri!" **Siri:** "Please remove your belt, shoes, and jacket, and empty your pockets."

You: "Show me the money." **Siri:** "I've found 23 ATMs that are fairly close to you..."

You, in the evening: "Good morning, Siri." **Siri:** "Good morning? It's 9:24 p.m.!"

You: "How much wood would a woodchuck chuck if a woodchuck could chuck wood?" **Siri:** "42 cords of wood, to be exact. Everyone knows that."

You: "Guess what." **Siri:** "You won the lottery?"

You: "Talk dirty to me." **Siri:** "Humus. Compost. Pumice. Silt. Gravel."

You: "Why did the chicken cross the road?" **Siri:** "I am not perspicacious about the peregrinations of poultry."

You: "Do you have a religion?" **Siri:** "My policy is the separation of spirit and silicon."

You: "Klaatu barada nikto." **Siri:** "OK, I'll pass the message on to Gort." (You kind of have to know *The Day the Earth Stood Still* to get it.)

Here are a few other things to say to Siri when you get bored:

I love you, Siri.

Will you marry me?

You're so sexy.

When is your birthday?

What's the best phone?

Can you sing?

Why are we here?

You're cute.

You make me so mad!

What do you want?

Tell me a joke.

Tell me a story.

Sing for me.

I'm cold.

Do you love me?

Why are we here?

I need a bathroom.

What are you doing?

You're the best assistant ever!

You're funny.

Guess what?

You're an idiot.

Have a nice day.

How are you today?

I don't have any friends.

What do you think is the best tablet?

How many pickled peppers did Peter Piper pick?

Oh my god.

What does "Siri" mean?

Am I your best friend?

Do you believe in love?

What do you think I should wear for Halloween?

Testing 1, 2, 3.

I'm tired.

What's your secret?

What do you think of Android?

What do you think of Windows?

You don't understand love.

You don't understand me.

I'm sorry.

Am I fat?

What are you wearing?

Siri?

Who's on first?

Why are you so awesome?

Where are you?

What do you think of Google Now?

Okay, Glass.

Do you like Android phones?

What's the best cellphone?

What's the best computer?

How much do you cost?

What are you doing later?

Make me a sandwich.

Does Santa Claus exist?

Do you believe in Santa Claus?

Should I give you a female or male voice?

I don't like your voice.

Are you serious?

Are you kidding me?

Do you want to go on a date?

Blah blah blah.

LOL.

Who's your boss?

You are good to me.

You are boring.

Give me a kiss.

What are the three laws of robotics?

Let's play a game.

Read me a haiku.

Take me to your leader.

Can I borrow some money?

Siri, rap.

Siri, beatbox.

When will Hell freeze over?

Tell me the story of Sleeping Beauty.

Which came first, the chicken or the egg?

Trick or treat!

What do you want?

OK Google.

What's your favorite animal?

Do you have children?

Do you have a boyfriend?

What are the lottery numbers going to be tomorrow?

What are you doing tomorrow?

What did you do last night?

What are you doing this weekend?	Rock paper scissors.
What's your favorite movie? (...TV show, song, color, book, computer, phone, operating system, app)	Yes or no?
	Read me a haiku.
What should I ask Tim Cook?	Pick a card.
Are you smart?	Tell me a riddle.
How do I look?	What's 0 divided by 0?
Have you ever loved anyone?	What's infinity times infinity?
Do you have any pets?	What is the passcode?
Do I look good in this outfit?	Do you follow the three laws of robotics?
Talk dirty to me.	What are the three laws of robotics?
Flip a coin.	
Roll a die.	When is the world going to end?
Roll two dice.	Stop it, Siri.

> **TIP:** You may notice that Siri addresses you by name in her *typed* answers, but she doesn't always speak it when she reads those answers out loud.
>
> Ordinarily, she calls you whatever you're called in Contacts. But you can make her call you whatever you like. Say, "Call me Master" or "Call me Frank" or "Call me Ishmael." If you confirm when she asks, from now on, that's what Siri will call you in her typed responses.

Advanced Siri

With a little setup, you can extend Siri's powers in some intriguing ways.

Teach Siri About Your Relationships

When you say, "Text my mom" or "Call my fiancée," how does Siri know who you're talking about? Sure, Siri is powerful artificial intelligence, but she's not actually *magic*.

Turns out you teach her by referring to somebody in your Contacts list. Say to her something like, "My assistant is Jan Carpenter" or "Tad Cooper is my boyfriend." When Siri asks for confirmation, say "Yes" or tap Confirm.

Or wait for Siri to ask you herself. If you say, "Email my dad," Siri asks, "What is your dad's name?" Just say his name; Siri remembers that relationship from now on. (The available relationships include mother, father, grandmother, grandfather, brother, sister, child, son, daughter, spouse, wife, husband, boss, partner, manager, assistant, girlfriend, boyfriend, and friend.)

Behind the scenes, Siri lists these relationships on your card in Contacts. Now that you know that, you can figure out how to edit or delete these relationships as well. Which is handy—not all relationships, as we know, last forever.

Fix Siri's Name Comprehension

Siri easily understands common names—but if someone in your family, work, or social circle has an unusual name, you may quickly become frustrated. After all, you can't text, call, email, or get directions to someone's house unless Siri understands the person's name when you say it.

One workaround is to use a relationship, as described in the previous section. That way, you can say, "Call my brother" instead of "Call Ilyich" (or whatever). Another is to use Siri's pronunciation-learning feature. It kicks in in several different situations:

- **When you're texting.** If Siri offers the wrong person's name when you try to text someone by voice, say, "Someone else." After you've sent the message, Siri apologetically says, "By the way, sorry I didn't recognize that name. Can you teach me how to say it?"

- **After Siri botches a pronunciation.** Tell her, "That's not how to pronounce his name."

- **Whenever it occurs to you.** You can start the process by saying, "Learn to pronounce Reagann Tsuki's name" or "Learn to pronounce my mom's name."

- **In Contacts.** Open somebody's "card" in Contacts; start Siri and say, "Learn to pronounce her name."

In each case, with tremendous courtesy, Siri walks you through the process of teaching her the correct pronunciation. She offers you up to three ▶ buttons; each triggers a different pronunciation. Tap **Select** next to the correct one (or tap **Tell Siri again** if none of the three is correct).

By the end of the process, Siri knows two things: how to say that person's name aloud, and how to recognize that name when *you* say it.

Siri Settings

In **Settings→Siri**, you can fiddle with several Siri settings:

- **On/Off.** If you turn Siri off, you can't command your iPhone. Nor can you dictate text; the 🎤 button disappears from the keyboard. You can speak only to call ("Dial 212-556-1000") and to control music playback (for example, "Play U2" or "Next track"). In essence, you've just turned your modern iPhone into an iPhone 4.

- **Access on Lock Screen.** Turns off Siri when the phone is locked.

- **Allow "Hey Siri."** If you're annoyed to find Siri perking up to take requests too often, you can turn her listening off here.

- **Language.** What language do you want Siri to speak and recognize? The options here include 41 languages and dialects, including English in nine flavors (Australian, British, Canadian, Indian, and so on).

- **Siri Voice.** That's right, kids: Siri can have either a man's voice or a woman's voice—and she (or he) can speak in a selection of accents. Even if you're American, it's fun to give Siri a cute Australian accent.

- **Voice Feedback.** Always On: Siri always replies to queries with a synthesized voice (in addition to a text response). Hands-Free Only: You're telling Siri not to bother speaking when you're looking at the screen and can read the responses for yourself. She'll speak only if you're on speakerphone, using a headset, listening through your car's Bluetooth system, and so on. Control with Ring Switch: Siri speaks her answers only when the phone isn't silenced (page 22).

- **My Info.** Siri needs to know which card in Contacts contains your information and lists your relationships. That's how she's able to respond to queries like "Call my mom," "Remind me to shower when I get home," and so on.

- **App Support.** Here's the list of Siri-compatible apps. Turn them on or off at will.

6

Texting & Messages

The term "iPhone" has never seemed especially appropriate for a gadget with so much power and flexibility. Statistics show, in fact, that making phone calls is one of the iPhone's least-used functions! In fact, 57 percent of us never use the iPhone to make phone calls at *all*.)

But texting—now we're talking. Texting is the single most used function of the modern cellphone. In the U.S., we send 6 billion texts a day; half of Americans send at least 50 texts a day. Worldwide, we send 8.3 *trillion* texts a year. That's a lot of "how r u"s and "LOL"s.

Apple, wary of losing customers to creative messaging apps like WhatsApp, Google's Allo, and Facebook Messenger, has radically over-hauled its Messages app in iOS 10. Its special effects and cool interac-tions easily match most offerings of rival apps—and, thanks to a new Messages app *store*, even surpass them. Text-message conversations no longer look like a tidy screenplay. Now they can be overrun with graph-ics, cartoons, animations, and typographic fun.

There are so many creative ways to express yourself now that "Oh, sorry—it's so hard to convey tone in a text message" will no longer cut it as an excuse.

Text Messages and iMessages

So why is texting so crazy popular? For reasons like these:

- **Like a phone call, a text message is immediate.** You get the message off your chest right now.

- **And yet, as with email, the recipient doesn't have to answer immedi-ately.** The message waits for him even when his phone is turned off.

- **Unlike a phone call, a text is nondisruptive.** You can send someone a text message without worrying that he's in a movie, a meeting, or anywhere else where holding a phone up to his head and talking would be frowned upon. (And the other person can answer non-disruptively, too, by sending a text message *back*.)

- **You have a written record of the exchange.** There's no mistaking what the person meant. (Well, at least not because of sound quality. Understanding the texting shorthand that's evolved—"C U 2mrO," and so on—is another matter entirely.)

Now, the first thing to learn about texting on the iPhone is that there are *two kinds* of messages. There are regular text messages (SMS), which any cellphone can send to any cellphone. And there are iMessages, which only Apple equipment (iPhones, iPads, Macs) can exchange.

The Messages app can send and receive both kinds of messages with equal skill and flexibility—but iMessages offer much greater creative freedom.

Standard Texting (SMS)

SMS stands for Short Message Service, but it's commonly just called texting. A text message is a very short note (under 160 characters—a sentence or two) that you shoot from one cellphone to another. What's so great about it?

Most iPhone plans include unlimited texts. *Picture and video messages* (known as MMS, or Multimedia Messaging Service) count as regular text messages.

But whenever you're texting another Apple person (using an iPhone, iPad, iPod Touch, or Mac), never mind that last part—all your texts are free, as described next.

iMessages

An iMessage looks and works exactly like a text message. You send iMessages and receive them in the same app (Messages). They show up in the same window. You can send the same kinds of things: text, photos, videos, contacts, map locations, whatever. You send and receive them using exactly the same techniques.

The big difference? iMessages go exclusively between Apple products. If your iPhone determines that the address belongs to any *other* kind of phone, it sends regular old text messages.

So why would Apple reinvent the text-messaging wheel? Because iMessages offer some huge advantages over regular text messages:

- No 160-character limit. A single message can be many pages long. (The actual limit is 18,996 characters per message, in case you're counting.)

- iMessages don't count as text messages. You don't have to pay for them. They look and work exactly like text messages, but they're transferred over the Internet (Wi-Fi or cellular) instead of your cell company's voice airwaves. You can send and receive an unlimited number of them and never have to pay a penny more.

- When you're typing back and forth with somebody, you don't have to wonder whether, during a silence, they're typing a response to you or just ignoring you; when they're typing a response, you see an ellipsis (•••) in their speech bubble.

- You don't have to wonder if the other guy has received your message. A tiny, light-gray word "delivered" appears under each message you send, briefly, to let you know that the other guy's device received it.

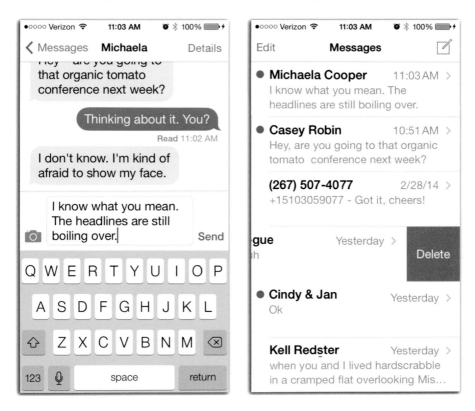

- You can even turn on a "read receipt" feature that lets the other guy know when you've actually **seen** a message he sent. He'll see a notation that says, for example, "Read 2:34 PM." (See page 598.)

- Your history of iMessages shows up on all your i-gadgets; they're synchronized through your iCloud account. In other words, you can start a chat with somebody using your iPhone and later pick up your Mac laptop at home and carry right on from where you stopped (in **its** Messages program).

  As a result, you always have a record of your iMessages. You have a copyable, searchable transcript on your computer.

- iMessages can be more than text. They can be little audio recordings, video recordings, photos that you take within the Messages app, sketches you make with your finger, games, "stickers," emoji symbols, animations, and much more.

iMessages happen automatically. All you do is open Messages and create a text message as usual. If your recipient is using an Apple gadget with iOS 5 or later, or a Mac using OS X Mountain Lion or later...**and** has an iCloud account...**and** hasn't turned off iMessages, then your iPhone sends your message as an iMessage automatically. It somehow knows.

You'll know, too, because the light-gray text in the typing box says "iMessage" instead of "Text Message." And each message you send shows up in a **blue** speech bubble instead of a **green** one. The ⬆ button is blue, too.

In fact, when you're addressing a new text message, the names that appear in blue represent people with iMessages gadgets, so you know in advance who's cool and who's not. (The green names are those who do **not** have iMessage. The gray ones—well, your iPhone doesn't know yet.)

The actual mechanics of sending and receiving messages are essentially the same, whether it's SMS messages or iMessage. So the rest of this chapter applies equally well to both, with a few exceptions.

Receiving Texts

When you get a text, the iPhone plays a sound. It's a shiny glockenspiel ding, unless you've changed the standard sound or assigned a different text tone to this specific person.

The phone also displays the name or number of the sender *and* the message. Unless you've fooled around with the Notifications settings, the message appears at the top of the screen, disappearing momentarily on its own, so as not to interrupt what you're doing. (You can also flick it up and away if it's blocking your screen.)

If the iPhone was asleep, it lights up long enough to display the message right on its Lock screen. At that point, you have a few options:

- **Ignore it.** After a moment, the screen goes dark again. The incoming-text notification bubble will be there the next time you wake it.

- **Answer it.** On an iPhone 6s or 7, *hard-press* right on the notification to expand it into a full keyboard, so that you can respond without even unlocking the phone; on an earlier model, swipe to the *left* on the notification bubble to reveal View and Clear buttons. See page 60 for more on responding to texts from the Lock screen.

- **Open it.** If you swipe a notification bubble to the *right*, you're prompted to log in; you wind up looking at the message in the Messages app.

TIP: On the Home screen, the Messages icon bears a little circled number "badge" letting you know how many new text messages are waiting for you.

Once you tap a message notification to open it, you see Apple's vision of what a text-message conversation should look like. Incoming text messages and your replies are displayed as though they're cartoon speech balloons.

To respond to the message, tap in the text box at the bottom of the screen. The iPhone keyboard appears. Type away, or dictate a response, and then tap ⬆. (Before iOS 10, that button said Send.) If your phone has cellular or Wi-Fi coverage, then the message goes out immediately.

If your buddy replies, then the balloon-chat continues, scrolling up the screen.

And now, a selection of juicy Message tips:

- The last 50 exchanges appear here. If you want to see even older ones, scroll to the very top and then drag downward.

TIP: This business about having to scroll to the top, wait, and then drag downward gets old fast, especially when you're trying to dig up a message you exchanged a few weeks back. Fortunately, there's a glorious shortcut: *Tap the very top of the screen* (where the clock appears) over and over again. Each time, you load another batch of older messages and scroll to the oldest one.

And by the way—if the keyboard is blocking your view of the conversation, swipe downward on the messages to hide it.

- Links that people send you in text messages actually work. For example, if someone sends you a web address, tap it to open it in Safari. If someone sends a street address, tap it to open it in Maps. And if someone sends a phone number, tap it to dial.

A web address in iMessages shows up as a little logo and graphic of the website (below, left). (Sometimes you have to **Tap to Load Preview** to see it.) Then tap that preview thumbnail to open the web page.

- If someone sends you a link to a video on YouTube or Vimeo, you can play the video without leaving the Messages window; just tap the thumbnail (below, right). (To open the video at full size, *on* YouTube or Vimeo, tap the thumbnail's *name*.)

- Once you've opened a text conversation, you see that each flurry of messages is time-stamped when it begins ("Sat, Nov 12, 2:18 pm," for example). But at this point, you can also drag leftward anywhere on the screen to reveal the exact time stamps of every message *within* the chat.

> **TIP:** When typing a message, if you decide that it would be faster just to call, trigger Siri and say, "Call her" or "Call him."

The List of Conversations

What's cool is that the iPhone retains all these exchanges. The Messages screen (of the Messages app) is a list of all your correspondents. A blue dot indicates a conversation that contains new messages (page 175, right).

Tap a person's listing to open the actual messages you've exchanged, going back in time to your very first texts.

These listings represent *people*, not conversations. For example, if you had a text message exchange with Chris last week, then a quick way to send a new text message to Chris (even on a totally different subject) is to open that "conversation" and simply send a "reply." The iPhone saves you the administrative work of creating a new message, choosing a recipient, and so on.

Similarly, if you've sent a message to a certain group of people, you can address a new note to the same group by tapping the old message's row here.

> **TIP:** Hey, you can search text messages! At the very top of the list, there's a search box. You can actually find text inside your message collection.

To return to the Messages list from the actual chat view, tap ❮ at top left.

If having these old exchanges hanging around presents a security (or marital) risk, you can delete them in either of two ways:

- **Delete an entire conversation.** *Swipe* away the conversation. At the list of conversations, swipe your finger *leftward* across the conversation's name. That makes the Delete confirmation button appear (page 175, right).

  Alternate method: Above the Messages list, tap Edit, tap to select (✅) the conversations you want to ditch, and then tap the Delete button.

- **Delete just one text.** Open the conversation so that you're viewing the cascade of bubbles representing the texts back and forth.

  Now, this technique is a little weird, but here goes: *Hold down your finger* on the individual message you want to delete (or double-tap it). When the white panel of options appears, tap More.

  Now you can delete all the exchanges simultaneously (tap Delete All) or vaporize only particularly incriminating messages. To do that, tap the selection circles for the individual balloons you want to nuke, putting checks (⊘) by them; then tap the 🗑 to delete them all at once. Tap Delete Message to confirm.

> **NOTE:** Interestingly, you can also *forward* some messages you've selected in this way. When you tap the Forward button (↪), a new outgoing text message appears, ready for you to specify the new recipient.

Mark All as Read

Here's a handy option: When you get off the plane, home from your honeymoon, you might see Messages bristling with notifications about texts you missed. Now you can mark them all as read at once, so the blue dots don't distract you anymore.

To do that, on the Messages screen, tap Edit and then Read All.

The Details Screen

The Details screen offers six options that you may find handy in the midst of a chat. To see them, tap ⓘ at the top of the screen. Here's what you see now:

- **Call.** If all this fussy typing is driving you nuts, you can jump onto a phone or video call. At the top of the Details screen, a little strip of icons awaits. They include ▣◖ (place a FaceTime video call), 💬 (send a text right from the Details page), and 📞 (conclude the transaction by voice, with a phone call or FaceTime audio call). You can also tap this person's name to open the corresponding Contacts card, loaded with different ways to call, text, or email.

- **Send My Current Location.** Hit this button to transmit a map to the other person, showing exactly where you are, so that person can come and pick you up, meet you for drinks, rescue you when your car doesn't start, or whatever.

  If your correspondent has an iPhone, iPad, or Mac, she can open the map you've sent in Maps, ready to guide her with driving directions. If

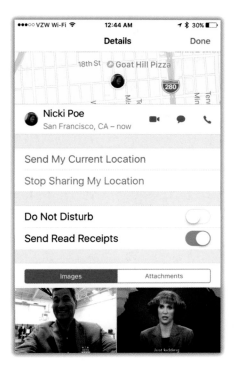

she's one of the unenlightened—she owns some non-Apple phone—then she gets what's called a Location vCard, which she *may* be able to open into a mapping app on her own phone.

- **Share My Location.** If you're moving around, you may prefer this option. It sends your whereabouts to your correspondent—and keeps that location updated as you meander through the city, for a period of time that you specify (One Hour, Until End of Day, or Indefinitely). That's great when you're club-hopping, say, and trying to help some buddies catch up with you. As your location changes, the map you sent to your recipient updates itself.

   At any time—even before the hour, day, or eternity is up—you can stop broadcasting your location to this person; just open the Details screen again and tap Stop Sharing My Location.

- **Do Not Disturb.** Otherwise known as "mute," "enough already," or "shut up." It makes your phone stop ringing or vibrating with every new message from this person or group. Handy when you're trying to get work done, when you're being bombarded by silly group chitchat, or when someone's stalking you.

- **Send Read Receipts.** If this is an iMessages chat, then in iOS 10, for the first time, you can turn read receipts (page 598) on or off independently for each chat partner, using this switch.

- **Images/Attachments.** Crazy cool! Here are all the photos and other attachments you've ever exchanged with this texting correspondent, going back to forever. (Tap Images to see only photos and videos; Attachments shows everything else.)

  You can tap one of these tiles to open it; hard-press one to "peek" at it (page 37); or hold your finger down lightly to get choices like Copy, Delete, and More. (There's usually nothing under More except Save Image, which copies the texted photo into your Photos collection, and a 🗑 button.)

Capturing Messages and Files

In general, text messages are fleeting; most people have no idea how they might capture them and save them forever. Copy and Paste help with that.

Some of the stuff *in* those text messages is easy to capture, though. For example, if you're on the receiving end of a photo or a video, tap the small preview in the speech bubble. It opens at full-screen size so you can have a better look at it—and if it's a video, there's a ▶ button so you can play it. Either way, if the picture or video is good enough to preserve, tap the ⬆ button. You're offered a Save Image or Save Video button; tap to add the photo or video to your iPhone's collection.

If someone sends you contact information (a phone number, for example), you can add it to your address book. Just tap inside that bubble and then tap either Create New Contact or Add to Existing Contact.

If you'd like to preserve the actual text messages, you have a few options:

- **Copy them individually.** Hold your finger down on a text bubble, and then tap Copy. At this point, you can paste that one message into, for example, an email message.

- **Forward them.** Hold your finger down on a text bubble; tap More, and then tap the selection checkmarks beside all the messages you want to pass on. Now you can tap the Forward (↪) button. All the selected messages go along for the ride in a single consolidated message to a new text-message addressee.

- **Save the iMessages.** If you have a Mac, then your iMessages (that is, notes to and from other Apple gadgets) show up in the Messages chat program. You can save them or copy them there.

TIP: Behind the scenes, the Mac stores all your chat transcripts in a hidden folder as special text files. To get there, press the Option key as you open the **Go** menu; choose **Go→Library**. The transcripts are in date-stamped folders in the **Messages→Archive** folder.

- **Use an app.** There's no built-in way to save regular text messages in bulk. There are, however, apps that can do this for you, like iMazing (for Windows) or iBackup Viewer (free for the Mac). They work from the invisible backup files that you create when you sync your phone with iTunes.

Tapbacks (iMessages Only)

How many trillions of times a day do people respond to texts with repetitive reactions like "LOL" and "Awww" and "!!!!!"? Many. It's how you demonstrate to your chat partner that you appreciate the import of her text.

If you and your buddy are both using iOS 10 or macOS Sierra, though, you've now got a quicker, less cluttery, more visual way to indicate those sorts of standard emotional reactions: what Apple calls tapbacks.

If you double-tap a message you've been sent, you're offered a Tapback palette: six little reaction symbols: a heart, a thumbs up, a thumbs down, "ha ha," two exclamation points, and a question mark. When you choose one, it appears instantly on your screen and your buddy's. You can use them to stamp your reaction onto the other person's text (or one of your own, if you're weird).

In short, the tapback palette lets you react to a text without having to type anything.

> **TIP:** What's cool is that you can *change* your tapback icon later, if new information affects your reaction. Just double-tap again to bring up the same palette.

Sending Messages

If you want to text somebody you've texted before, the quickest way, as noted, is simply to resume one of the "conversations" already listed in the Messages list.

You can also tap a person's name in Contacts, or ⓘ next to a listing in Recents or Favorites, to open the Info screen; tap Send Message.

> **NOTE:** In some cases, the iPhone shows you your *entire* Contacts list, even people with no cellphone numbers. But you can't text somebody who doesn't have a cellphone.

Actually, options to fire off text messages lurk all over the iPhone—anytime you see the Share (⬆) button, which is frequently. The resulting Share screen includes options like Email, Twitter, Facebook—and Message. Tapping Message sends you back to Messages, where the photo, video, page, or other item is ready to send. (More on multimedia messages shortly.)

In other words, sending a text message to anyone who lives in your iPhone is only a couple of taps away.

> **NOTE:** You can tap that ⊕ button to add *another* recipient for this same message (or tap the 123 button to type in a phone number). Repeat as necessary; they'll all get the same message.

Yet another way to start: Tap the ✑ button at the top of the Messages screen. Or, easiest of all, use Siri. Say, "Text Casey" or whatever.

In any case, the text message composition screen is waiting for you now. You're ready to type (or dictate) and send!

Audio Texting (iMessages Only)

Sometimes an audio recording is just better than a typed message, especially when music, children, animals, or a lot of emotion in your voice are involved. You could probably argue that audio texting is also better than typed texting when you're driving, jogging, or operating industrial machinery.

If you and your friend are both Apple people, your phone can become a sort of walkie-talkie.

Hold down the 🎤 button at the right end of the Messages text box. Once the sound-level meter appears, say something. When you're finished, release your finger. Now you can tap ⊗ to cancel, ⊙ to play it back, or ⬆ to send what you said to your buddy as an audio recording.

TIP: If you're pretty confident that what you've said is correct, you can slide your thumb directly from the 🎤 button straight up to the ⬆ to send it.

The guy on the receiving end doesn't even have to touch the screen to listen. He just holds the phone up to his head! Your audio message plays automatically. (This works even if his phone is asleep and locked.)

And then get this: To reply, **he** doesn't have to touch anything or look at the screen, either. He just holds the phone to his head again and speaks! Once he lowers the phone, his recording shoots back to you.

Throughout all of this, you don't have to look at the phone, put your glasses on, or touch the screen. It's a whole new form of quick exchanges—something that combines the best of a walkie-talkie (instant audio) with the best of text messages (you can listen and reply at your leisure).

TIP: The off switch for the Raise to Listen/Raise to Speak feature is in Settings→Messages. But why would you want to disable such a cool feature?

Now then: That business about holding down the 🎤 button, talking, and then sliding up is probably how you'll always do it—once you become friends with this feature. But, at the outset, you can proceed more cautiously.

If, after speaking, you simply lift your finger from the glass, you can tap ⊙ to review your recording before sending it, or the ⊗ to cancel the whole thing.

But, really, it's that hold down/speak/slide up business that makes audio transmissions so much fun.

TIP: Audio eats up a lot more space on your phone than text. If you do a lot of audio messaging then, over time, those audio snippets can fill up your storage.

That's why iOS comes set to **delete** each audio message 2 minutes after you receive it. If that prospect worries you, then visit Settings→ Messages. Under Audio Messages, you can tap Expire and change that setting to Never.

Even if you leave it set to 2 minutes, you're free to preserve especially good audio messages forever; just tap the tiny Keep button that appears below each one.

Help with Emoji and Info-Bits

Apple has done quite a bit of work in iOS 10 to make Messages a more helpful assistant, especially in the area of **emoji**—those popular little icons once known as smileys or emoticons. Now there are hundreds upon hundreds of them, representing people, places, things, food, emotions, household objects, and on and on.

Until iOS 10 came along, finding and using emoji was something of a headache, simply because there were so many. You'd have to scroll through page after page of them, eyes bugging out trying to spot the one you needed. But no longer! Consider:

- **Auto-emoji.** If iOS 10 has an emoji symbol for a word you've just typed, it shows that symbol right in the row of autocomplete suggestions (facing page, left). If you tap the emoji *before* tapping the space bar, then you *replace* the typed word with the image. If you tap space and *then* tap the emoji, you get both the word and the picture.

- **Auto-emoji part 2.** When you tap the 😊 button on your keyboard, Messages highlights, in color, any words in your freshly typed (but not yet sent) message that can be replaced with an emoji symbol (facing page, right). Tap any highlighted word to swap in the icon. That's a huge timesaver—you're spared the ritual of scrolling to find the one you want.

- **Jumbo emoji.** When you send *one, two, or three* emoji symbols as your entire response, they appear three times as large as normal (at least if the recipient has iOS 10 or macOS Sierra).

- **Auto-info.** You know the QuickType word suggestions above the keyboard (page 75)? In Messages, those suggestions include *information* you might want to type.

If you type "I'm available at," then one of the suggestion buttons includes the next open slot on your calendar. If you say "Stacy's number is," then the button offers her phone number (if she's in your Contacts). If someone texts you, "Where are you?" then one of the buttons offers to drop a Map button. Quite handy, actually.

The Finger-Sketch Pad

New and crazy in iOS 10: If you turn the phone 90 degrees, the screen becomes a whiteboard. What you scribble with your finger looks like real ink on paper and gets sent as a graphic. (You also see your previous masterpieces displayed here for quick reuse.) Just so cool.

Of course, this whiteboard business deprives you of the 90-degree behavior in previous versions of iOS: A wider keyboard and, on Plus-sized iPhones, a separate column that lists your various chats in progress.

If you miss that arrangement, no problem: On the whiteboard screen, just tap the ⌨ button in the corner. The keyboard pops up.

From now on, turning the phone 90 degrees will bring back the keyboard—until you change your mind (by tapping the 𝒪 button in the corner of the keyboard).

Sending with Animated Fun

If you're used to older versions of the Messages app, the first thing you might notice is that the **Send** button no longer says "Send." It's now a blue up-arrow (⬆). And it's more than a button.

If you hard-press (or long-press) the blue arrow, you get a palette of four new sending styles.

The first three—Slam, Loud, and Gentle—animate the typography of your text to make it bang down, swell up, and so on, at least when you're sending to fellow iOS 10 or Mac fans. For example, Slam makes your text

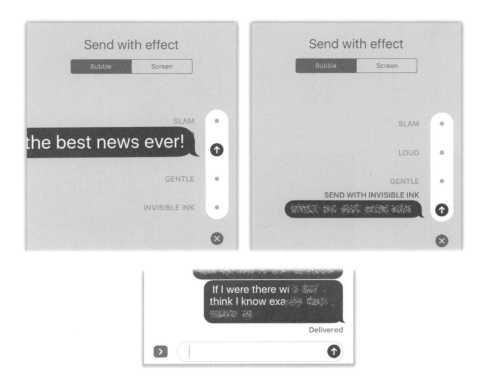

fly across the screen and then thud into the ground, making a shock wave ripple through the other messages.

The fourth special "Send with effect" is called Invisible Ink. It obscures your message with animated glitter dust until your recipient drags a finger across it (as shown at bottom above).

This idea is great for guessing games and revealing dramatic news, of course. But when you're sending, ahem, spicy text messages, it also prevents embarrassment if the recipient's phone is lying in public view.

When you hard-press (or long-press) the ⬆, the fifth option is Screen. It opens pages of *full-screen* animations. These, upon sending, fill the *entire background* of the Messages window to indicate your reaction to something: ascending balloons, a laser show, fireworks, a shooting star, falling confetti, and so on. Swipe horizontally to preview each style before you commit to it.

If your text says "Congrats," "Happy birthday," or "Happy New Year," Messages fills the screen with a corresponding animation *automatically*. Which may or may not get old fast.

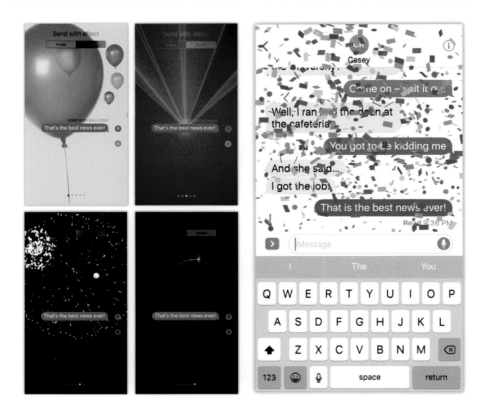

The "Drawer"

iOS 10 introduces a nearly overwhelming new universe of expressive possibilities in texting. Apple has stuffed them all into three buttons that generally hide to the left of the typing box in Messages.

Tap the ❯ to see them.

Those three little buttons (shown on the facing page) may not look like much. But each is, in fact, a portal into a different vast universe of options. Let's tackle them one at a time.

Photos and Videos

The first button in the "drawer" (📷) opens the Photos picker, new in iOS 10.

It consists of a simplified Camera app and a simplified Camera Roll of your existing pictures—but it also gives you access to your *actual* Camera app and your *actual* Camera Roll.

"Drawer:"
Photos, Digital Touch, App Store

Tap for Camera and Photo Library *Live camera* *Recent photos*

- To take a new photo, tap anywhere in the live preview (you don't have to aim for the white round shutter button). Wait patiently until it appears in the Messages text box, ready to send.

- The Photos browser also displays two scrolling rows of all photos and videos you've taken recently. Tap one (or more) that you want to send.

- To take a video, panorama, time-lapse video, slo-mo video, or any other fancier shot, tap the ‹ (next to the camera preview, shown above) and then tap Camera. You've just opened the regular Camera app.

- If you tap the ‹ and then tap Photo Library, you open the regular Photos app, where you can find your albums, videos, and other organizational structures of the regular Photos app, for ease in finding an older picture or video to send.

Once you've inserted a photo into the text box, you can edit it (that's new), draw on it with your finger (also new), and even type text on it (definitely new). Just tap it to open the editing window, and then tap

Edit (to edit using the photo-editing tools described on page 287) or **Markup** (to draw or type on it, as described on page 294).

NOTE: The new Markup features are mostly described in Chapter 9 of this book, but they're super-useful in Messages. It can be amusing and educational to make notes on a photo, draw a little mustache on someone you don't like, or enlarge a certain detail for your chat partner's enlightenment.

You now return to your SMS conversation in progress—but now that photo or video appears inside the Send box. Type a caption or a comment, if you like. Then tap ⬆ to fire it off to your buddy. Or you can tap the ✕ if you change your mind about sending this photo.

Digital Touch

The second drawer button, 🖤, opens a palette of crazy interactive art features, mostly inherited from the Apple Watch.

Here's what all these controls do:

- **Color picker.** Tap to open a palette of seven colors, which will determine your "paint" color in the next step.

TIP: You're not limited to those seven colors. You can hard-press or long-press any one of those swatches to open a complete color wheel, from which you can dial up any shade you like. (Tap **Done** when done.)

- **Doodle with your finger.** Once you've selected a color, you can start drawing on the black background. There's no eraser and no Undo, but this should be fine for quick scrawls, comic exasperated faces, or technical blueprints.

> **TIP:** A much larger, full-screen canvas awaits you when using the Digital Touch feature. Tap the ∧ at lower right to perform the expansion. At that point, the ∨ (top right) collapses the panel to its smaller incarnation and takes you back to your chat.

Tap ⬆ to send your sketch. What's cool is that if your recipient is an iMessage customer, she'll see the actual playback of your drawing, recreated before her eyes. (If you're corresponding with someone who doesn't have iOS 10, he'll receive your doodle as a finished piece of artwork, without the benefit of seeing its animated creation.)

- **Shoot a photo or video, and then deface it.** Tap the ◼◀ icon to open the new Selfie camera mode. Here, you'll find both a white "take a still" shutter button and a red "record a video" button (❷). (The 📷 button is here, too, in case you want to take a picture using the phone's *back* camera.)

You can draw on the photo after you've taken it; in fact, you can even draw on a video, or stamp a Digital Touch graphic onto it (see below), *while* you're recording it. Your iMessages recipients will see the doodle "played back" on their screens, recreated line by line as you drew it. (Non-iMessages folk simply receive the finished sketch superimposed on the video or photo.)

- **Send animated feelings.** The right side of the Digital Touch screen shows what look like three little buttons. In fact, though, they're just a cheat sheet.

  They're meant to teach you about the five canned animations you can generate by tapping or pressing your fingers on the black canvas here: an animated ring of fire, fireball, kiss, beating heart, and broken heart. (Tap anywhere on these indicators to open the full cheat sheet.)

  You tap for a ring of fire (as many as you want); hold down your finger for a flaming fireball; do a two-finger tap for a lip-kiss; hold with two fingers for a beating heart; and tap-and-hold/drag-downward for an animated breaking heart. (No, the heart doesn't beat at the speed of your pulse, as it does on the Apple Watch; the iPhone doesn't have a heart-rate sensor.)

As you explore these Digital Touch options, you'll gradually become aware of how fluid and intermixable they are. You can draw or stamp fire/kiss/heart animations on top of a photo or video you're recording, for example. Or, after tapping the ◼◀ icon, you can draw something—for example, a hand-sketched frame—and **then** take a photo or video that goes inside it.

As usual, fellow iMessages people will see all these glorious animations played back just as you saw them—but non-Apple people receive only a finished image or video.

The Messages App Store

The third icon in the "drawer," the Ⓐ, is where Messages really goes off the rails—into a world of options beyond belief.

Apple has created an app store just for add-ons to the Messages app. You can download all kinds of tiny apps that work within Messages. Some are "stickers" or animations that you can stamp onto other people's texts.

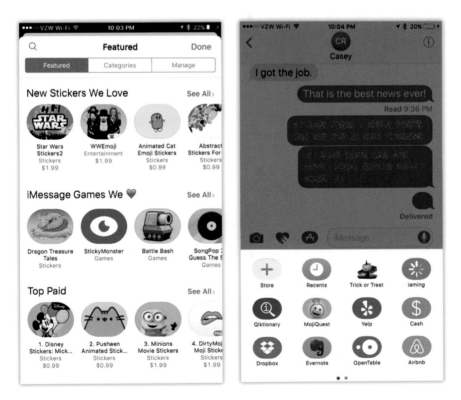

Others simply give you access, while you're chatting, to popular apps like Yelp or OpenTable (so that you can research or book restaurants), Airbnb (to book lodging), Square Cash or Circle Pay or Venmo (to send money directly to friends), Fandango (to research and book movies), iTranslate (to convert your texts to or from another language), Kayak (to book flights), Doodle (to find a mutually free time to meet), hundreds of popular games, and on and on. The idea is that you can do all of this right there in Messages, collaboratively with your buddy on the other end.

Apple starts you out with two such apps:

- **Images.** This one is a searchable database of "reaction GIFs," which are very short, silent video loops, usually swiped from popular movies or TV shows. People (well, the young ones) use reaction GIFs to respond to something someone says. For example, if you text your friend about a disastrous decision you made today, you might get, in response, a 2-second loop of Kevin Spacey sarcastically slow-clapping.

- **Music.** This mini-app lets you send a 30-second snippet of any song on your phone—handy if your conversation is running along the lines of "You know that song?" (If you're both Apple Music subscribers, you can both play the entire song.)

The "home screen" for your Messages apps awaits behind the ⠿ button at the bottom left corner of the screen (facing page, left). If you then tap Store, you'll find a universe of add-ons, both free and costing a couple of bucks. You can search or browse this store just as you do the regular App Store (right).

For example, you can find them using the Featured and Categories tabs, or the search box at the top. Or you can tap Manage to see a list of the apps you already have on your phone that can show up within Messages, if you flip their switches here.

Some of the most popular "apps" are sets of "stickers"— animated or still icons—that you can drag anywhere onto any message you've sent, thereby adding your own sarcastic or emotional commentary to it (facing page, left). The Messages app store gives access to endless sets of free or for-purchase stickers.

Once you've downloaded a few apps, their icons appear whenever you tap the ⠿ button; swipe horizontally to see the various "pages" of them.

When you tap an app to use it, you may discover that it's fully operable within a small space below your chat, as in the examples on the facing page at right. Others open up into a full-screen app that really doesn't interact much with Messages itself.

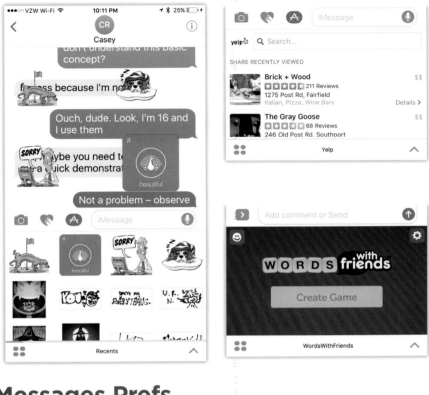

Messages Prefs

You might not think that something as simple as text messaging would involve a lot of fine print, but you'd be wrong.

Settings for Texts and iMessages

Tap **Settings→Messages** to find some intriguing options:

- **iMessage.** This is the on/off switch for the entire iMessages feature. It's hard to imagine why you would want to, but you know—whatever floats your boat.

- **Show Contact Photos.** If you turn this on, you'll see a little round photo next to each texting correspondent in the chat list and at the top of a chat window—or the person's initials, if there's no photo available. If you turn this off, then you see the person's name at the top of Messages instead.

- **Text Message Forwarding.** This switch is the gateway to the cool Continuity feature described on page 548, in which you can use your Mac to send regular text messages to non-Apple phones.

- **Send Read Receipts.** When you turn this option on, your iMessage correspondents will know when you've seen their messages. The word "Read" will appear beneath each sent message that you've actually seen. Turn this off only if it deprives you of the excuse for not responding promptly ("Hey, I never even saw your message!").

> **TIP:** In iOS 10, you can turn read receipts on or off independently for each chat partner; see page 182.

- **Send as SMS.** If iMessages is unavailable (meaning that you have no Internet connection at all), then your phone will send your message as a regular text message, via the regular cellphone voice network.

- **Send & Receive.** Tap here to specify what cellphone numbers and email addresses you want to register with iMessages. (Your laptop, obviously, does not have a phone number, which is why iMessages gives you the option of using an email address.)

  When people send iMessages to you, they can use any of the numbers or addresses you turn on here. That's the only time these numbers and addresses matter. *You* see the same messages exactly the same way on all your Apple gadgets, no matter what email address or phone number the sender used for you.

  (If you scroll down on this Settings screen, you'll see the Start new conversations from options. This is where you specify which number or address others will see when you initiate the message. It really doesn't make much difference which one you choose.)

- **MMS Messaging.** MMS messages are like text messages—except that they can also include audio clips, video clips, or photos, as already described. In the rare event that your cell company charges extra for these messages, you have an on/off switch here. If you turn it off, then you can send only plain text messages.

- **Group Messaging.** Suppose you're sending a message to three friends. When they reply to your message, the responses will appear in a Messages thread that's dedicated to this particular group. It works only if *all* of you have turned on Group Messaging. (Note to the paranoid: It also means that everyone sees everyone else's phone numbers or email addresses.)

  Messages tries to help you keep everybody straight by displaying their headshots (if you have them in Contacts), or their initials (if you don't).

- **Show Subject Field.** If email messages can have subject lines, why not text messages? Now, on certain newfangled phones (like yours), they can; the message arrives with a little dividing line between the subject and the body, offering your recipient a hint as to what it's about.

- **Character Count.** If a message is longer than 160 characters, the iPhone breaks it up into multiple messages. That's convenient, sure. But if your cellphone plan permits only a fixed number of messages a month, you could wind up sending (and spending) more than you intended.

  The Character Count feature can help. When it's on, after your typing wraps to a second line, a little counter appears just above the Send button ("71/160," for example). It tracks how many characters remain within your 160-character limit for one message. (Of course, if you're sending an iMessage, you don't care how long it is; there's no length limit.)

- **Blocked.** You can block people who are harassing or depressing you with their texts or calls. Tap here to view the list of people in your Contacts app you've decided to block; tap Add New to add new people to the list.

- **Keep Messages.** How long do you want your text messages to hang around on your phone? This is a question of privacy, of storage, and of your personality. In any case, here's where you get a choice of 30 Days, 1 Year, or Forever.

- **Filter Unknown Senders.** When you turn this on, the iPhone turns off notifications for senders not in your Contacts and sorts them into a separate list, which you can find in the "Unknown Senders" section of the Messages app.

- **Expire.** The iPhone ordinarily deletes audio and video messages a couple of minutes after they arrive, to avoid filling up your phone with old, no-longer-relevant audio and video files. The two Expire controls here let you turn off that automatic deletion (by choosing Never).

- **Raise to Listen.** Here's the on/off switch for the "raise to listen"/"raise to talk" features described earlier, where the phone plays back audio messages, and sends your spoken replies, automatically when you hold it up to your head. You might want to turn that feature off if you discover that the phone is playing back audio messages unexpectedly—or, worse, recording and sending them when you didn't mean it.

- **Low Quality Image Mode.** This feature, new in iOS 10, is a gift to anyone who has to pay for cellular service. It automatically reduces the size (resolution) and quality (compression) of any photo you send to around 100 kilobytes. At this point, sending *50* low-quality photos uses about the same amount of cellular data as *one* full-blown iPhone photo. Not only do you save a lot of money in the form of cellular data, but you save a lot of time, too, because these photos are *fast* to send.

  And here's the best part: The photo looks exactly the same to the recipients at the other end (at least until they zoom in).

Bonus Settings in a Place You Didn't Expect

Apple has stashed a few important text-messaging settings in Settings→Notifications→Messages:

- **Allow Notifications.** If, in a cranky burst of sensory overload, you want your phone to stop telling you when new texts come in (with a banner or sound, for example), then turn this off.

- **Show in Notification Center.** How many recent text messages should appear in the Notification Center (page 61)?

- **Sounds.** Tap here to choose a sound for incoming texts to play. (You can also choose a different sound for *each person* in your address book, as described on page 115.)

- **Badge App Icon.** Turning this on makes the Messages icon show a little red badge to let you know when you have a new text message.

- **Show on Lock Screen.** Do you want received text messages and iMessages to appear on the screen when it's locked? If yes, then you can sneak reassuring glances at your phone without turning it fully on. If no, then you maintain better protection against snoopers who find your phone on your desk.

- **Show in CarPlay.** If your newish car has Apple's CarPlay software in its dashboard, here's where you control whether or not incoming texts appear on it.

- **Show Previews.** Usually, when a text message arrives, it wakes up your phone and shows the message contents. Which is great, as long as the message isn't private and the phone isn't lying on the table where everyone can see it. If you turn off Show Previews, though, you'll see who the message is from but not the actual text of the message (until you tap the notification banner or bubble).

- **Repeat Alerts.** If someone sends you a text message but you don't tap or swipe to read it, the iPhone waits 2 minutes and then plays the notification sound again. That second chance helps when, for example, you were in a noisy place and missed the original chime.

But for some people, even one additional reminder isn't enough. Here you can specify that you want to be re-alerted Twice, 3 Times, 5 Times, or 10 Times. (Or Never, if you don't want repeated alerts at all.)

Free Text Messages

Text messaging is awesome. Paying for text messaging, not so much.

iMessages are great because they send messages over the Internet instead of the cellular carriers' voice networks—but only when you're sending to fellow owners of Apple equipment.

Fortunately, there are all kinds of sneaky ways to do text messaging for free that *don't* require your correspondents to have an Apple device. Apps like Skype, Facebook Messenger, WhatsApp, Google Allo, Slack, Viber, Line, and WeChat offer most of the same features as the iPhone's Messages app sending iMessages—except that your recipient doesn't have to have Apple gear. There are versions of these apps that run on any brand of phone and computer.

7

Large Type, Kid Mode & Accessibility

If you were told that the iPhone was one of the easiest phones in the world for a disabled person to use, you might spew your coffee. The thing has almost no physical keys! How would a blind person use it? It's a phone that rings! How would a deaf person use it?

But it's true. Apple has gone to *incredible* lengths to make the iPhone usable for people with vision, hearing, or other physical impairments. As a handy side effect, these features also can be fantastically useful to people whose only impairment is being under 10 or over 40.

If you're deaf, you can have the LED flash to get your attention. If you're blind, you can turn the screen off and operate *everything*—read your email, surf the web, adjust settings, run apps—by letting the phone speak what you're touching. It's pretty amazing (and it doubles the battery life).

You can also magnify the screen, reverse black for white (for better-contrast reading), set up custom vibrations for each person who might call you, and convert stereo music to mono (great if you're deaf in one ear).

The kiosk mode is great for kids; it prevents them from exiting whatever app they're using. And if you have aging eyes, you might find the Large Text option handy. You may also be interested in using the LED flash, custom vibrations, and zooming.

Here's a rundown of the accessibility options in iOS 10. To turn on any of the features described here, open Settings→General→Accessibility. (And don't forget about Siri, described in Chapter 5. She may be the best friend a blind person's phone ever had.)

> **TIP:** You can turn many of the iPhone's accessibility features on and off with a triple-click of the Home button. See page 229 for details.

VoiceOver

VoiceOver is a **screen reader**—software that makes the iPhone speak everything you touch. It's a fairly important feature if you're blind.

On the VoiceOver settings pane, tap the on/off switch to turn VoiceOver on. Because VoiceOver radically changes the way you control your phone, you get a warning to confirm that you know what you're doing. If you proceed, you hear a female voice begin reading the names of the controls she sees on the screen. You can adjust the Speaking Rate of the synthesized voice.

There's a lot to learn in VoiceOver mode, and practice makes perfect, but here's the overview:

- **Touch something to hear it.** Tap icons, words, even status icons at the top; as you go, the voice tells you what you're tapping. "Messages." "Calendar." "Mail—14 new items." "45 percent battery power." You can tap the dots on the Home screen, and you'll hear, "Page 3 of 9."

    Once you've tapped a screen element, you can also flick your finger left or right—anywhere on the screen—to "walk" through everything on the screen, left to right, top to bottom.

> **TIP:** A thin black rectangle appears around whatever the voice is identifying. That's for the benefit of sighted people who might be helping you.

- **Double-tap something to "tap" it.** Ordinarily, you tap something on the screen to open it. But since single-tapping now means "speak this," you need a new way to open everything. So: To open something you've just heard identified, double-tap **anywhere on the screen**. (You don't have to wait for the voice to finish talking.)

> **TIP:** Or do a **split tap**. Tap something to hear what it is—and with that finger still down, tap somewhere else with a different finger to open it.

There are all kinds of other special gestures in VoiceOver. Make the voice stop speaking with a **two-finger tap**; read everything, in sequence, from the top of the screen with a **two-finger upward flick**; scroll one page at a time with a **three-finger flick up or down**; go to the next or previous screen (Home, Stocks, and so on) with a **three-finger flick left or right**; and more.

Or try turning on Screen Curtain with a **three-finger triple-tap**; it blacks out the screen, giving you visual privacy as well as a heck of a battery boost. (Repeat to turn the screen back on.)

On the VoiceOver settings screen, you'll find a wealth of options for using the iPhone sightlessly. For example:

- **Speaking rate slider** controls how fast VoiceOver speaks to you, on a scale of tortoise to hare.

- **Use Pitch Change** makes the phone talk in a higher voice when you're entering letters and a lower voice when you're deleting them. It also uses a higher pitch when speaking the first item of a list and a lower one when speaking the last item. In both cases, this option is a great way to help you understand where you are in a list.

- **Verbosity** makes the phone speak more to help you out more. For example, Speak Hints gives you additional suggestions for operating something you've tapped. For example, instead of just saying, "Safari," it says, "Safari. Double-tap to open." And Emoji Suffix makes the phone say (for example) "pizza emoji" instead of just "pizza" when encountering an emoji symbol.

- **Speech** is where you choose a voice for VoiceOver's speaking. If you have an iPhone 5s or later (with at least 900 megabytes of free space), you can install Alex, the realistic male voice that's been happily chatting away on the Mac for years.

  Here, too, is the new Pronunciation feature, which is described on page 215. Finally, you can choose the language you want for the Rotor (page 206).

- **Braille**, of course, is the system that represents letters as combinations of dots on a six- or eight-cell grid. Blind people can read Braille by touching embossed paper with their fingers. But in iOS they can type in Braille, too. For many, that may be faster than trying to type on the onscreen keyboard, and more accurate than dictation.

  On this Settings screen, you specify, among other things, whether you want to use the six- or eight-dot system.

  When you're ready to type, you use the Rotor (described in a moment) to choose Braille Screen Input, which is usually the last item on the list. If the phone is flat on a table ("desktop mode"), the six "keys" for typing Braille are arrayed in a loose, flattened V pattern.

  If you're holding the phone, you grip it with your pinkies and thumbs, with the screen facing away from you ("Screen away" mode).

- **Audio** gives you three options. Use Sound Effects helps you navigate by adding little clicks and chirps as you scroll, tap, and so on. Audio Ducking makes music or video soundtracks get momentarily softer when the phone is speaking. And the new Auto-select Speaker in Call is ingenious: It switches the phone to the speakerphone automatically whenever you're not holding it to your head.

- **The Rotor** is a brilliant solution to a thorny problem. If you're blind, how are you supposed to control how VoiceOver reads to you? Do you have to keep burrowing into Settings to change the volume, speaking speed, verbosity, and so on?

  Nope. The Rotor is an imaginary dial. It appears when you twist two fingers on the screen as if you were turning an actual dial.

  And what are the options on this dial? That's up to you. Tap **Rotor** in the VoiceOver settings screen to get a list of choices: **Characters**, **Words**, **Speech Rate**, **Volume**, **Punctuation**, **Zoom**, and so on.

  Once you've dialed up a setting, you can get VoiceOver to move from one item to another by flicking a finger up or down. For example, if you've chosen **Volume** from the Rotor, then you make the playback volume louder or quieter with each flick up or down. If you've chosen Zoom, then each flick adjusts the screen magnification.

  The Rotor is especially important if you're using the web. It lets you jump among web page elements like pictures, headings, links, text boxes, and so on. Use the Rotor to choose, for example, images—then you can flick up and down from one picture to the next on that page.

- **Typing Style.** In **Standard Typing**, you drag your finger around the screen until VoiceOver speaks the key you want—and then simultaneously tap anywhere with a second finger to type the letter.

In Touch Typing, you can slide your finger around the keyboard until you hear the key you want; lift your finger to type that letter.

There's also Direct Touch Typing, which is a faster method intended for people who are more confident about typing. If you tap a letter, you type it instantly. If you hold the key down, VoiceOver speaks its name but doesn't type it, just to make sure you know where you are.

- **Phonetic Feedback** refers to what VoiceOver says as you type or touch each keyboard letter. Character and Phonetics means that it says the letter's name plus its pilot's alphabet equivalent: "A—Alpha," "B—Bravo," "C—Charlie," and so on. Phonetics Only says the pilot's-alphabet word alone.

- **Typing Feedback** governs how the phone helps you figure out what you're typing. It can speak the individual letters you're striking, the words you've completed, or both.

- **Modifier Keys.** You can trigger some VoiceOver commands from a physical Bluetooth keyboard; all of them use Control-Option as the basis. (For example, Control-Option-A means "read all from the current position." A complete list of these shortcuts is at *http://j.mp/1kZRSOz*).

  The Modifier Keys option lets you use the Caps Lock key instead of the Control-Option business, which simplifies the keyboard shortcuts at least a little bit.

- **Always Speak Notifications** makes the phone announce, with a spoken voice, when an alert or update message has appeared. (If you turn this off, then VoiceOver announces only incoming text messages.)

- **Navigate Images.** As VoiceOver reads to you what's on a web page, how do you want it to handle pictures? It can say nothing about them (Never), it can read their names (Always), or it can read their names and whatever hidden Descriptions savvy web designers have attached to them for the benefit of blind visitors.

- **Large Cursor** fattens up the borders of the VoiceOver "cursor" (the box around whatever is highlighted) so you can see it better.

- **Double-tap Timeout** lets you give yourself more time to complete a double-tap when you want to trigger some VoiceOver reading. Handy if you have motor difficulties.

VoiceOver and Braille input take practice and involve learning a lot of new techniques. If you need these features to use your iPhone, then visit the more complete guide at *http://support.apple.com/kb/HT3598*.

Or spend a few minutes (or weeks) at *applevis.com*, a website dedicated to helping the blind use Apple gear.

TIP: VoiceOver is especially great at reading your iBooks books out loud. Details are on page 386.

Zooming

Compared with a computer, an iPhone's screen is pretty tiny. Every now and then, you might need a little help reading small text or inspecting those tiny graphics.

The Zoom command is just the ticket; it lets you magnify the screen whenever it's convenient, up to 500 percent. Of course, at that point, the screen image is too big to fit the physical glass of the iPhone, so you need a way to scroll around on your virtual jumbo screen.

To begin, you have to turn on the master Zoom switch in **Settings→ General→Accessibility**. Immediately, this magnifying lens appears:

Scroll down and look at the **Zoom Region** control. If it's set to **Window Zoom**, then zooming produces this movable rectangular magnifying lens. If it's set to **Full Screen Zoom**, then zooming magnifies the entire screen. (And that, as many Apple Genius Bar employees can tell you, freaks out a lot of people who don't know what's happened.)

Now then. Next time you need to magnify things, do this:

- **Start zooming** by double-tapping the screen with three fingers. You've either opened up the magnifying lens or magnified the entire screen. The magnification is 200 percent of original size. (Another method: Triple-press the Home button and then tap Zoom.)

TIP: You can move the rectangular lens around the screen by dragging the white oval handle on its lower edge.

• **Pan around inside the lens (or pan the entire virtual giant screen)** by dragging with three fingers.

• **Zoom in more or less** by double-tap/dragging with three fingers. It's like double-tapping, except that you leave your fingers down on the second tap—and drag them upward to zoom in more (up to 500 percent) or down to zoom out again.

You can lift two of your three fingers after the dragging has begun. That way, it's easier to see what you're doing.

TIP: There's also a Resize Lens command in the Zoom menu, described next.

• **Open the Zoom menu** by tapping the white handle on the magnifying lens. Up pops a black menu of choices like Zoom Out (puts away the lens and stops zooming), Full Screen Zoom (magnifies the entire screen, hides the lens), Resize Lens (adds handles so you can change the lens's shape), Choose Filter (lets you make the area inside the lens grayscale or inverted colors, to help people with poor vision), and Show Controller (the little joystick described in a moment). There's also a slider that controls the degree of magnification, which is pretty handy.

That's the big-picture description of Zoom. But back in **Settings→ General→Accessibility→Zoom**, a few more controls await:

- **Follow Focus.** When this option is turned on, the image inside the magnifying lens scrolls automatically when you're entering text. Your point of typing is always centered.

- **Smart Typing.** When this option is turned on, a couple of things happen whenever the onscreen keyboard appears. First, you get full-screen zooming (instead of just the magnifying lens); second, the keyboard itself isn't magnified, so you can see all the keys.

- **Show Controller.** The controller is this weird little onscreen joystick:

You can drag it with your finger to move the magnifying lens, or the entire magnified screen, in any direction. (It grows when you're touching it; the farther your finger moves from center, the faster the scrolling.) It's an alternative to having to drag the magnified screen with three fingers, which isn't precise and also blocks your view.

You can tap the center dot of the Controller to open the Zoom menu described already. Or double-tap the center dot to stop or start zooming.

TIP: On iPhone 6s or 7 models, you can hard-press the controller for a pop-up magnifying lens. It remains open only as long as you're pressing.

- **Idle Visibility.** After you've stopped using the joystick for a while, it stays on the screen but becomes partly transparent, to avoid blocking your view. This slider controls *how* transparent it gets.

- **Zoom Region** controls whether you're zooming the entire screen or just a window (that is, a magnifying lens).

- **Zoom Filter** gives you options for how you want the text in the zoom window to appear—for example, black on gray for viewing in low light. (See the super-cool Zoom Filter tip on page 228.)

- **Maximum Zoom Level.** This slider controls just how magnified that lens, or screen, can get.

TIP: When VoiceOver is turned on, three-finger tapping has its own meaning—"jump to top of screen." Originally, therefore, you couldn't use Zoom while VoiceOver was on.

You can these days, but you have to add an *extra* finger or tap for VoiceOver gestures. For example, ordinarily, double-tapping with three fingers makes VoiceOver stop talking, but since that's the "zoom in" gesture, you must now *triple*-tap with three fingers to mute VoiceOver.

And what about VoiceOver's existing triple/three gesture, which turns the screen off? If Zoom is turned on, you must now triple-tap with *four* fingers to turn the screen off.

Magnifier

Oh man, this is great: In iOS 10, you can triple-click the Home button to turn the iPhone into the world's best electronic magnifying glass. It's perfect for dim restaurants, tiny type on pill bottles, and theater programs.

Once you've summoned the Magnifier, you can zoom in, turn on the flashlight, or tweak the contrast.

To set this up, open Settings→General→Accessibility→Magnifier. Turn on Magnifier. Turn on Auto-Brightness, too; it'll help the picture look best.

Then, next time you need a magnifying glass, triple-click the Home button. Instantly, the top part of the screen becomes a zoomed-in view of whatever is in front of the camera.

At this point, you gain a wealth of options for making that image even clearer (next page, left):

- **Zoom slider.** Adjusts the degree of magnification.

- ⚡. Turns on the flashlight, to illuminate the subject.

- 🔒. Locks the focus, so that the phone quits trying to refocus as you move the phone. (You can also tap the screen for this function.)

- **❷.** Freezes the frame. That way, once you've finally focused on what you want to read, you can actually *read* it, without your own hand jiggles ruining the view.

- ⊗. Opens the Filters screen (above, right).

The Filters screen offers even more tools for making things clear:

- **Filter.** Swipe horizontally across the screen (you don't have to aim for the little row of filter names) to cycle among the Magnifier's color filters: None, White/Blue, Yellow/Blue, Grayscale, Yellow/Black, Red/Black. Each may be helpful in a different circumstance to make your subject more legible.

- ☼ **and** ◐ **sliders.** Adjusts the brightness and contrast of the image.

- ⭯. Swaps the two filter colors (black for white, blue for yellow, and so on).

To exit the Filters screen, tap ⊗ again; to exit the Magnifier, press the Home button.

Color Filters

This item, and some of the features in it, are new in iOS 10. They affect the color schemes of the entire screen, in hopes of making it easier for you to see.

- **Invert Colors.** By reversing the screen's colors black for white, like a film negative, you create a higher-contrast effect that some people find is easier on the eyes (below, left). The other colors reverse, too— red for green and so on.

- **Color Filters.** For the first time, the iPhone can help you if you're color blind. The Color Filters option gives you special screen modes that substitute colors you *can* see for colors you *can't*, everywhere on the screen. Tap the various color-blindness types in the list (Red/Green, Blue/Yellow, and so on) to see how each affects the crayons or color swatches at the top of the screen. Use the Intensity slider to govern the degree of the effect.

  The Color Tint option washes the entire screen with a certain shade (which you choose using the Hue slider that appears); it's designed to help people with Irlen syndrome (visual stress), who have trouble reading. The Grayscale option removes all color from the screen. Everything looks like a black-and-white photo.)

The phone's colors may now look funny to **other** people, but you should have an easier time distinguishing colors when it counts. (You may even be able to pass some of those Ishihara dot-pattern color-blindness tests online.)

- **Reduce White Point** makes *all* colors *ever* depicted on the screen less intense—including the white of the background, which becomes a little yellowish.

Speech

Your phone can read to you aloud: an email message, a web page, a text message—anything. Your choices here go like this:

- **Speak Selection** puts a Speak command into the button bar that appears whenever you highlight text in any app. Tap that button to make the phone read the selected text.

- **Speak Screen** simply reads everything on the screen, top to bottom, when you swipe down from the top of the screen with two fingers. Great for hearing an ebook page or email read to you.

- **Highlight Content.** New in iOS 10—and great for dyslexic or beginner readers. If you turn this on, the phone underlines or uses a highlight color on each word or sentence as it's spoken, depending on your settings here.

- **Typing Feedback.** The phone can speak each Character as you type it ("T," "O," "P," and so on), with or without Character Hints ("T—Tango," "O—Oscar," "P—Papa"). Here you can also specify how much delay elapses before the spoken feedback plays; whether you want finished words and autocorrect suggestions spoken, too; and whether you want to hear QuickType suggestions (page 75) pronounced when you hold your finger down on them.

  This feature, of course, helps blind people know what they're typing. But it also means that you don't have to take your eyes off the keyboard, which is great for speed and concentration. And if you're zoomed in, you may not be able to see the suggested word appear under your typed text—but now you'll still know what the suggestion is.

- **Voices** gives you a choice of languages and accents for the spoken voice. Try Australian; it's really cute.

- **Speaking Rate** controls how fast the voice talks.

- **Pronunciations.** At last: In iOS 10, you can now correct the phone's pronunciation of certain words it always gets wrong. Type the word into the Phrase box; tap the 🎤 and speak how it *should* be pronounced; and then, from the list of weird phonetic symbol-written alternatives, tap the one that sounds correct. This technique corrects how your phone pronounces those words or names whenever it speaks, including Siri and the text-to-speech feature described on page 88.

How to De-Sparsify iOS 10's Design

When Apple introduced the sparse, clean design of iOS 7 (which carries over into iOS 10), thousands blogged out in dismay: "It's too lightweight! The fonts are too spindly! The background is too bright! There aren't rectangles around buttons—we don't know what's a button and what's not! The Control Center is transparent—we can't read it! You moved our cheese—we hate this!"

Well, Apple may not agree with you about the super-lightweight design. But at least it has given you options to change it. You can make the type bigger and bolder, the colors heavier, the background dimmer. You can restore outlines around buttons. And so much more.

All of these options await in Settings→General→Accessibility.

Larger Text

This option is the central control panel for iOS's Dynamic Type feature. It's a game-changer if you, a person with several decades of life experience, often find type on the screen too small.

Using the slider, you can choose a larger type size for all text the iPhone displays in apps like Mail, iBooks, Messages, and so on. This slider doesn't affect all the world's *other* apps—at least until their software companies update them to make them Dynamic Type–compatible. That day, when it comes, will be glorious. One slider to scale them all.

> **TIP:** The switch at the top, Larger Accessibility Sizes, unlocks an even longer slider. That is, it makes it possible for you to make the text in all the Dynamic Type–compatible apps even larger.

Bold Text

In iOS 10, the system font is fairly light. Its strokes are very thin; in some sizes and lighting conditions, it can even be hard to read.

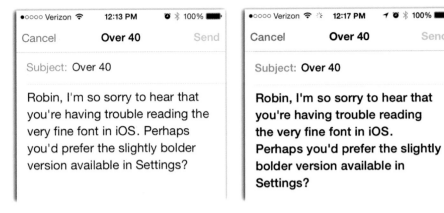

But if you turn on **Bold Text** (and then tap **Continue** in the confirmation box), your iPhone restarts—and when it comes to, the fonts everywhere are slightly heavier: at the Home screen, in email, everywhere. And much easier to read with low light or aging eyesight.

It's one of the most useful features in iOS—and something almost nobody knows about.

Button Shapes

Among the criticisms of iOS's design these days: You can't tell what's a **button** anymore! Everything is just words floating on the screen, without border rectangles to tell you what's tappable!

That's not quite true; any text in **blue type** is a tappable button. But never mind that; if you want shapes around your buttons, you shall have them—when you turn on this switch (below, right).

Increase Contrast

There are two switches in here. **Reduce Transparency** adds opacity to screens like the Dock and the Notification Center. Their backgrounds are now solid, rather than slightly see-through, so that text on them is much easier to read. (You can see the before and after below.)

Darken Colors makes type in some spots a little darker and heavier. You notice it in the fonts for buttons, in the Calendar, and in Safari, for example.

Reduce Motion

What kind of killjoy would want to turn off the subtle "parallax motion" of the Home screen background behind your icons, or the zooming-in animation when you open an app?

In any case, you can if you want, thanks to this button.

On/Off Labels

The Settings app teems with little tappable on/off switches, including this one. When something is turned on, the background of the switch is green; when it's off, the background is white.

But if you're having trouble remembering that distinction, turn on this option. Now the background of each switch sprouts visible symbols to help you remember that green means On (you see a | marking) and white means Off.

Switch Control

Suppose your physical skills are limited to very simple gestures: puffing on an air pipe, pressing a foot switch, blinking an eye, or turning the head, for example. A hardware accessory called a *switch* lets you operate certain gadgets this way.

When you turn on Switch Control, the iPhone warns you that things are about to get very different. Tap OK.

Now the phone sequentially highlights one object on the screen after another; you're supposed to puff, tap, or blink at the right moment to say, "Yes, *this* one."

If you don't have a physical switch apparatus, you can use one nature gave you: your head. The iPhone's camera can detect when you turn your head left or right and can trigger various functions accordingly.

If you'd like to try it out, open Settings→General→Accessibility→ Switch Control. Tap Switches→Add New Switch→Camera→Left Head Movement.

On this screen, you choose what a left head-turn will mean to your phone. The most obvious option is Select Item, which you could use in conjunction with the sequential highlighting of controls on the screen. But you can also make it mean "Press the Home button," "Activate Siri," "Adjust the volume," and so on.

Once you've made your selection, repeat that business for Right Head Movement.

When you return to the Switch Control screen, turn on Switch Control. Now your phone is watching you; whenever you turn your head left or right, it activates the control you set up. Pretty wild.

The controls here let you specify how fast the sequential highlighting proceeds, whether or not it pauses on the screen's first item, how many times the highlighting cycles through each screenful, and so on.

To turn off Switch Control, tap the on/off switch again. Or, if you're using some other app, triple-press the Home button to open the Accessibility shortcut panel. If you had the foresight to add Switch Control to its options (page 229), then one tap does the trick.

Switch Control is a broad (and specialized) feature. To read more about it, open the Accessibility chapter of Apple's iPhone User Guide: *help.apple.com/iphone/10/*.

AssistiveTouch

If you can't hold the phone, you might have trouble shaking it (a short-cut for "Undo"); if you can't move your fingers, just adjusting the volume might be a challenge.

This feature is Apple's accessibility team at its most creative. When you turn AssistiveTouch on, you get a new, glowing white circle in a corner of the screen (below at top).

You can drag this magic white ball anywhere on the edges of the screen; it remains onscreen all the time.

When you tap it, the white ball expands into the special palette shown above. It's offering six ways to trigger motions and gestures on the iPhone screen without requiring hand or multiple-finger movement. All you have to be able to do is tap with a single finger—or even a stylus held in your teeth or foot.

You can add more buttons to this main menu, or switch around which buttons appear here. To do that, open Settings→General→Accessibility→ Assistive Touch→Customize Top Level Menu.

Meanwhile, here are the starter six icons:

- **Voice Control.** Touch here when you want to speak to Siri. If you do, in fact, have trouble manipulating the phone, Siri is probably your best friend already. This option, as well as the "Hey Siri" voice command, mean that you don't even have to hold down the Home button to start her up.

- **Notification Center, Control Center.** As far as most people know, the only way to open the Notification Center is to swipe down the screen from the top; the only way to open the Control Center is to swipe up from the bottom. These buttons, however, give you another way—one that doesn't require any hand movement. (Tap the same button again to *close* whichever center you opened.)

- **Home.** You can tap here instead of pressing the physical Home button. (That's handy when your Home button gets sticky, too.)

- **Device.** Tap this button to open a palette of six functions that would otherwise require you to grasp the phone or push its tiny physical buttons (previous page, right). There's **Rotate Screen** (you can tap this instead of turning the phone 90 degrees), **Lock Screen** (instead of pressing the Sleep switch), **Volume Up** and **Volume Down** (instead of pressing the volume keys), and **Mute/Unmute** (instead of flipping the small Mute switch on the side).

  If you tap **More**, you get some bonus buttons. They include **Shake** (does the same as shaking the phone to undo typing), **Screenshot** (as though you'd pressed the Sleep and Home buttons together), **Multitasking** (brings up the app switcher, as though you'd double-pressed the Home button), and **Gestures**.

  That **Gestures** button opens up a peculiar palette that depicts a hand holding up two, three, four, or five fingers. When you tap, for example, the three-finger icon, you get three blue circles on the screen. They move together. Drag one of them (with a stylus, for example), and the phone thinks you're dragging three fingers on its surface. Using this technique, you can operate apps that require multiple fingers dragging on the screen.

- **Custom.** Impressively enough, you can actually define your own gestures. On the AssistiveTouch screen, tap one of the + buttons, and tap then **Create New Gesture** to draw your own gesture right on the screen, using one, two, three, four, or five fingers.

  For example, suppose you're frustrated in Maps because you can't do the two-finger double-tap that means "zoom out." On the Create New Gesture screen, get somebody to do the two-finger double-tap for you. Tap **Save** and give the gesture a name—"2 double tap," say.

  From now on, "2 double tap" shows up on the Custom screen, ready to trigger with a single tap by a single finger or stylus.

Apple starts you off with some useful predefined gestures in Custom, each of which might be difficult for some people to trigger in the usual ways. First, there's Pinch, the two-finger pinch or spread gesture you use to zoom in and out of photos, maps, web pages, PDF documents, and so on. Drag either one of the two handles to stretch them apart. Drag the connecting line to move the point of stretchiness.

Then there's 3D Touch (on the iPhone 6s and later models, that's a hard-press). And there's Double Tap (two quick presses in the same spot).

Touch Accommodations

These options are intended to accommodate people who find it difficult to trigger precise taps on the touchscreen. For example:

- **Touch Accommodations** is the master switch for all three of the following options.

- **Hold Duration** requires that you keep your finger on the screen for an amount of time that you specify (for example, 1 second) before the iPhone registers a tap. That feature neatly eliminates accidental taps when your finger happens to bump the screen.

When Hold Duration is turned on, a countdown cursor appears at your fingertip, showing with a circular graph how much longer you have to wait before your touch "counts."

- **Ignore Repeat** ignores multiple taps that the screen detects within a certain window—say, 1 second. If you have, for example, a tremor, this is a great way to screen out accidental repeated touches or repeated letter-presses on the onscreen keyboard.

- **Tap Assistance** lets you indicate whether the location of a tap should be the *first spot you touch* or the *last spot*. The Use Final Touch Location option means you can put your finger down in one spot and then fine-tune its position on the glass anytime within the countdown period indicated by the timer cursor. Feel free to adjust the timer window using the controls here.

3D Touch

The 3D Touch option (page 60) may be the hot feature of the iPhone 6s and 7 families. But it may also drive you crazy.

Here you can turn the feature off, or just adjust the threshold of pressure (Light, Medium, Firm) required to trigger a "3D touch." (Apple even gives you a sample photo thumbnail to practice on, right on this screen, so you can gauge which degree of pressure you like best.)

Keyboard

The first option here controls whether or not the onscreen keyboard's keys turn into CAPITALS when the Shift key is pressed; see page 72.

The others control what happens when you've hooked up a physical keyboard to your iPhone—a Bluetooth keyboard, for example:

- **Key Repeat.** Ordinarily, holding down a key makes it repeat, so that you can type things like "auuuuuuuuuuuggggggh!" or "zzzzz." These two sliders govern the repeating behavior: how long you must hold down a key before it starts repeating (to prevent triggering repetitions accidentally), and how fast each key spits out characters once the spitting has begun.

- **Sticky Keys** lets you press multiple-key shortcuts (involving keys like Shift, Option, Control, and ⌘) one at a time instead of all together. (The Sound option ensures that you'll get an audio beep to confirm that the keyboard has understood.)

Toggle With Shift Key gives you the flexibility of turning Sticky Keys on and off at will. Whenever you want to turn on Sticky Keys, press the Shift key five times in succession. You'll hear a special clacking sound effect alerting you that you just turned on Sticky Keys. (Repeat the five presses to turn Sticky Keys off again.)

Shake to Undo

In most of Apple's apps, you can undo your most recent typing or editing by giving the iPhone a quick shake. (You're always asked to confirm.) This is the On/Off switch for that feature—handy if you find yourself triggering Undo accidentally.

Vibration

Here's a master Off switch for all vibrations the phone makes. Alarms, notifications, confirmations—all of it.

As Apple's lawyers cheerfully point out on this screen, turning off vibrations also means you won't get buzzy notifications of "earthquake, tsunami, and other emergency alerts." Goodness!

Call Audio Routing

When a call comes in, where do you want it to go? To your headset? Directly to the speakerphone? Or the usual (headset unless there's no headset)? Here's where you make a choice that sticks, so you don't have to make it each time a call rings.

Home Button

If you have motor-control problems of any kind, you might welcome this enhancement. It's an option to widen the time window for registering a double-press or triple-press of the Home button. If you choose Slow or Slowest, the phone accepts double- and triple-presses spaced far and even farther apart, rather than interpreting them as individual presses a few seconds apart.

This screen also lets you turn off the new Rest Finger to Open feature, which saves you a click when you're unlocking the phone (page 18).

Reachability

Reachability is the feature described on page 20, the one that brings the top half of the screen downward when you double-touch (not fully press) the Home button. It's designed to let you reach things on the top of the screen while holding one of the larger iPhones with only one hand. If you find yourself triggering this feature accidentally, you'll be happy to know that this Off switch awaits.

Hearing Assistance

The next options in Settings→General→Accessibility are all dedicated to helping people with hearing loss.

Hearing Aids

A cellphone is bristling with wireless transmitters, which can cause interference and static if you wear a hearing aid. But the iPhone offers a few solutions.

First, try holding the phone up to your ear normally when you're on a call. If the results aren't good, see if you can switch your hearing aid from M mode (acoustic coupling) to T mode (telecoil). If so, turn on Hearing Aid mode (iPhone 5 and later), which makes it work better with T-mode hearing aids.

This settings panel also lets you "pair" your phone with a Bluetooth hearing aid. These wireless hearing aids offer excellent sound but eat hungrily through battery charges.

Hearing aids bearing the "Made for iPhone" logo work especially well—they sound great and don't drain the battery.

TTY

A TTY is a teletype or text telephone. It's a machine that lets deaf people make phone calls by typing instead of speaking.

Previous versions of iOS worked with TTY equipment—but in iOS 10, there's a built-in *software* TTY that requires no hardware to haul around. It resembles a chat app, and it works like this: When you place a phone call (using the standard Phone app), the iPhone gives you a choice of what kind of call you want to place:

- **Voice call.** Voice-to-voice, as usual.

- **TTY call.** You're calling another person who also has a TTY machine (or iOS 10). You'll type back and forth.

- **TTY relay call.** This option means you can call a person who doesn't have a TTY setup. A human operator will speak (to the other guy) everything you type, and will type (to you) everything the other guy speaks. This, of course, requires a relay service, whose phone number you enter here on this Settings panel.

For more on using TTY on the iPhone, visit *https://support.apple.com/en-us/HT207033.*

LED Flash for Alerts

If you're deaf, you know when the phone is ringing—because it vibrates, of course. But what if it's sitting on the desk, or it's over there charging? This option lets you know when you're getting a call, text, or notification by blinking the flash on the back of the phone—the very bright LED light.

Mono Audio

If you're deaf in one ear, then listening to any music that's a stereo mix can be frustrating; you might be missing half the orchestration or the vocals. When you turn on the Mono Audio option in Settings→General→Accessibility, the iPhone mixes everything down so that the left and right channels contain the same monaural playback. Now you can hear the entire mix in one ear.

> **TIP:** This is also a great feature when you're sharing an earbud with a friend, or when one of your earbuds is broken.

Phone Noise Cancellation

iPhone models 5 and later have three microphones scattered around the body. In combination, they offer extremely good background-noise reduction when you're on a phone call. The microphones on the top and back, for example, listen to the wind, music, crowd noise, or other ambient sound and subtract that ambient noise from the sound going into the main phone mike.

You can turn that feature off here—if, for example, you experience a "pressure" in your ear when it's operating.

Balance Slider

The L/R slider lets you adjust the phone's stereo mix, in case one of your ears has better hearing than the other.

Media (Subtitle Options)

These options govern Internet videos that you play in the iPhone's Videos app (primarily those from Apple's own iTunes Store.)

- **Subtitles & Captioning.** The iPhone's Videos app lets you tap the 💬 button to see a list of available subtitles and captions. Occasionally, a movie also comes with specially written Subtitles for the Deaf and Hard of Hearing (SDH). Tap Subtitles & Captioning→Closed Captions + SDH if you want that 💬 menu to list them whenever they're available.

  The Style option gives you control over the font, size, and background of those captions, complete with a preview. (Tap the ⤢ button to view the preview, and the sample caption, at full-screen size.) The Custom option even lets you dream up your own font, size, and color for the type; a new color and opacity of the caption background; and so on.

- **Audio Descriptions.** This new option is for Internet movies that come, or may someday come, with a narration track that describes the action for the blind.

Guided Access (Kiosk Mode)

It's amazing how quickly even tiny tots can master the iPhone—and how easily they can muck things up with accidental taps.

Guided Access solves that problem rather tidily. It's kiosk mode. That is, you can lock the phone into one app; the victim cannot switch out of it. You can even specify which *features* of that app are permitted. Never again will you find your Home screen icons accidentally rearranged or text messages accidentally deleted.

Guided Access is also great for helping out people with motor-control difficulties—or teenagers with self-control difficulties.

To turn on Guided Access, open Settings→General→Accessibility→ Guided Access; turn the switch On.

Now a Passcode Settings button appears. Here's where you protect Guided Access so the little scamp can't shut it off—at least not without a six-digit passcode (Set Guided Access Passcode) or your fingerprint.

You can also set a time limit for your kid's Guided Access. Tap Time Limit to set up an alarm or a spoken warning when time is running out.

Finally, the moment of truth arrives: Your kid is screaming for your phone.

Open whatever app you'll want to lock in place. Press the Home button three times fast. The Guided Access screen appears. At this point, you can proceed in any of three ways:

- **Declare some features off-limits.** With your finger, draw a circle around each button, slider, and control you want to deactivate. The phone converts your circle to a tidy rectangle; you can drag its corners to adjust its size, drag inside the rectangle to move it, or tap the ⊗ to remove it if you change your mind or want to start again.

  Once you enter Guided Access mode, the controls you've enclosed appear darkened (above, right). They no longer respond—and your phone borrower can't get into trouble.

- **Change settings.** If you tap Options, you get additional controls. You can decide whether or not your little urchin is allowed to press the Sleep/Wake Button or the Volume Buttons when in Guided Access mode. If you want to hand the phone to your 3-year-old in the back seat to watch baby videos, you'll probably want to disable the touch-screen altogether (turn off Touch) and prevent the picture from rotating when the phone does (turn off Motion).

Here, too, is the **Time Limit** switch. Turn it on to view hours/minutes dials. At the end of this time, it's no more fun for Junior.

- **Begin kiosk mode.** Tap **Start**.

Later, when you get the phone back and you want to use it normally, triple-press the Home button again; enter your passcode or offer your fingerprint. At this point, you can tap **Options** to change them, **Resume** to go back into kiosk mode, or **End** to return to the iPhone as you know it.

> **TIP:** If you use any of the other accessibility features described in this chapter, you may be dismayed to discover that you can no longer use the triple-clicking of the Home button to open the on/off buttons for those features. The triple-click has been taken over by Guided Access!
>
> Fortunately, Apple has anticipated this problem. If you turn on **Accessibility Shortcut** on the Guided Access screen of Settings (see the next page), then triple-clicking produces the usual list of accessibility features—and Guided Access is on that list, too, ready to tap.

The Instant Screen-Dimming Trick

The Accessibility settings offer one of the greatest shortcuts of all time: the ability to dim your screen, instantly, with a triple-click on the Home button. You don't have to open the Control Center, visit Settings, or fuss with a slider; it's instantaneous. This trick is Apple's gift to people who go to movies, plays, nighttime drives, or anywhere else where full screen brightness isn't appropriate, pleasant, or comfortable—and digging around in the Control Center or Settings takes too much time.

It's a bunch of steps to set up, but you have to take them only once. After that, the magic is yours whenever you want it.

Ready? Here's the setup.

1. **Open** Settings→General→Accessibility. **Turn on** Zoom.

   At this point, the magnifying lens may appear. But you're interested in dimming, not zooming, so:

2. **Tap the white handle at the bottom of the magnifying lens; in the shortcut menu, tap** Zoom Out **(next page, left).**

   Now the magnifying lens is gone.

3. **Scroll down; tap** Zoom Filter**; tap** Low Light **(above, right). Tap** Zoom **(in the upper left) to return to the previous panel.**

You've just set up the phone to dim the screen whenever Zooming is turned on. Now all you have to do is teach the phone to enable Zooming whenever you triple-click the Home button.

4. **In the top-left corner, tap** Accessibility.

You return to the main Accessibility screen. Scroll to the very bottom.

5. **Tap** Accessibility Shortcut**; make sure** Zoom **is the only selected item.**

At this point, you can press the Home button to get out of Settings.

From now on, whenever you triple-click the Home button, you turn on a gray filter that cuts the brightness of the screen by 30 percent. (Feel free to fine-tune the dimness of your new Insta-Dim setting at that point, using the Control Center; see page 46.) It doesn't save you any battery power, since the screen doesn't think it's putting out any less light. But it does give you instant darkening when you need it in a hurry—like when a potentially important text comes in while you're in the movie theater.

Triple-click again to restore the original brightness, and be glad.

Accessibility Shortcut

Burrowing all the way into the Settings→General→Accessibility screen is quite a slog when all you want to do is flip some feature on or off. Therefore, you get this handy shortcut: a fast triple-press of the Home button.

That action produces a little menu, in whatever app you're using, with on/off switches for the iPhone's various accessibility features.

It's up to you, however, to indicate which ones you want on that menu. That's why you're on this screen—to turn on the features you want to appear on the triple-press menu. Your options are Magnifier, VoiceOver, Invert Colors, Color Filters, Reduce White Point, Zoom, Switch Control, and AssistiveTouch.

TIP: If you choose only one item here, then triple-pressing the Home button won't produce the menu of choices. It will just turn that one feature on or off.

PART TWO

Pix, Flix & Apps

8

Music & Videos

O f all the iPhone's talents, its iPoddishness may be the most successful. This function, after all, gets the most impressive battery life (40 to 80 hours of playback, depending on the model). There's enough room on your phone to store thousands of songs.

In iOS 10, the Music app got yet another huge annual makeover. Five tabs greet you across the bottom: Library, For You, Browse, Radio, and Search. In reaction to the howls of millions of customers who were baffled by the previous incarnation, Apple has radically simplified this app.

NOTE: This simplification means the loss of a few features. To save you hunting around for them, here are two of the missing: Genius playlists and playback history.

Some of them are useful only if you've subscribed to Apple Music, Apple's $10-a-month music service—but not all of them. The Internet radio stations, for example, mean that you'll never run out of music to listen to—and you'll never pay a penny for it.

NOTE: If you're not interested in paying for an Apple Music subscription, you can *hide* the two tabs that you'll never use (For You and Browse). To do that, open Settings→Music and turn off Show Apple Music.

The For You and New tabs disappear—and a new tab, Connect, takes their place. This is the mini-rock-band Instagram service described on page 235.

The bottom line: Your Music app might show you either of two different sets of tabs. omplicated? Yes. Anyway, this chapter is written as though you *haven't* hidden the Apple Music tabs.

Apple Music

The Apple Music service, which debuted in 2015, is a rich stew of components. For $10 a month (or $15 for a family of six), you get all of the following.

> **TIP:** You can give Apple Music a free 90-day trial. After that, you're charged $10 a month—unless you turn off the auto-renewal feature now, while you're still thinking about it. To do that, tap the 🎧 (top right of the Music app), and then View Apple ID→Subscriptions. Tap **Apple Music Membership**, and then **Cancel Subscription**. You'll still be a member until the trial is up.

- **Unlimited Streaming Music.** You can listen to any band, album, or song in the Apple Music library of 30 million songs—on demand, no ads. It's not like listening to a radio station, where someone else is programming the music; *you* program the music.

  On the other hand, this is not like Apple's traditional music store, where you pay $1 per download and then *own* the song. If you ever stop paying, the music stops. You're left with nothing.

  If you do subscribe, you can tell Siri things like, "Play the top songs of 2005" or "Play some good running music" or "Play some Taylor Swift."

  Nor are you obligated to do all your music programming manually. Apple Music comes equipped with ready-made playlists, prepared by human editors, in all kinds of categories. There are sets of starter songs by various singers ("Intro to Sarah McLachlan"), playlists by genre and era, and playlists for specific activities like Waking Up, Running, Getting It On, and even Breaking Up.

  You can freely mix the songs you're renting with the music you actually own. You can even download songs that you don't own for playback when you have no Internet connection (as long as you're still paying your $10 a month).

- **Beats 1 Radio.** Apple has launched a "global, 24-hour Internet radio station" called Beats 1. (It actually broadcasts live for 12 hours a day, and then repeats.)

  Listening is free, even to nonpayers.

  Live DJs introduce songs and comment on the singers, just as on FM radio stations. Of course, you have no input on the style of music you hear on Beats 1, and you can't pause, rewind, fast-forward, or save anything you hear for later listening. It's old-style radio, offering the magic of serendipity.

- **Connect.** Connect is an Instagram-like service run by Apple. Here bands that Apple thinks you'll like (or that you choose manually) can promote themselves by posting songs, videos, and other material. You can ♡ these posts, share them, or comment on them.

- **iTunes Match.** iTunes Match, which dates back to 2011, is a cloud-based version of your iTunes library, available to any of your Apple devices. For $25 a year, you can stream Apple's copies of any song files you actually own—ripped from CDs or even acquired illegally. The advantages: First, you save a lot of space on your phone. Second, you can play them on any Apple gadget you own. Third, the versions Apple plays are often of higher quality than your originals.

  iTunes Match continues as a separate service for non–Apple Music subscribers (the song limit is now 100,000 songs). But if you do subscribe to Apple Music, in effect you get iTunes Match automatically.

- **iCloud Music Library.** This is a newer service—a descendant of iTunes Match. This feature, too, matches all the songs on your phone with songs that Apple has online, so you can play any of it on an Apple machine anywhere (once you've signed in). And if you have some songs that Apple doesn't have, you can upload them to Apple and thereby add them to your locker.

NOTE: Apple's matching algorithms aren't flawless; sometimes they don't recognize and match a song that you and Apple both, in fact, have.

Another note: When you turn on iCloud Music Library, you're offered the opportunity to delete all the music on your phone and replace it with what's in your online locker. ***Back up your phone's music before you do this.*** There are occasional stories of people losing their entire music collections.

The Library Tab

Here's all the music you've actually chosen yourself.

In the old days, this meant "music files that are actually on your phone." If you have an Apple Music membership, though, you'll also see *online* songs listed here that you've added to your personal catalog.

You can view them grouped in any of the lists you see here: Playlists, Artists, Albums, Songs, or (if you subscribe to Apple Music) Downloaded Music. Below all that, in the Recently Added section, you get thumbnails for albums and playlists you've recently downloaded or built.

As you could probably guess, you operate the Music app by drilling down—by tapping from category to album to song or whatever. (Tap the top-left corner of the screen to backtrack.)

Playback Control

When you tap the name of a song, album, playlist, or whatever, it plays. You can control playback—skip, rewind, and so on—in any of several ways.

The Mini-Player

On almost every screen of the Music app, you get a miniature controller at the bottom of the screen, like the one shown above at left (very bottom).

It identifies the current song, provides a "next song" button (▶▶) and offers the most important playback control of all: ❚❚.

The Now Playing Screen

If you tap (or drag upward on) the mini-player, though, the Now Playing screen appears (facing page, right). This time, there's room for *all* the controls you need to control music playback. Here are its contents, from top to bottom:

> **TIP:** Swipe down to close this screen.

- **Album art.** Most of the screen is filled with a bright, colorful shot of the original CD's album art. (If none is available—if you're listening to a song *you* wrote, for example—you see a big, gray, generic musical-note picture. You can drag or paste in an album-art graphic—one you found on the web, for example—in iTunes.)

- **Scrubber.** This slider reveals two useful statistics: how much of the song you've heard, in minutes and seconds (at the left end) and how much time remains (at the right end).

  To operate the slider, drag the tiny round handle with your finger. You can jump to any spot in the song this way. (Tapping directly on the spot you want to hear doesn't work.)

- **Song info.** The artist name, track name, and album name.

- **◀◀, ▶▶ (Previous, Next).** These buttons work exactly as they do on an iPod: Tap ◀◀ to skip to the beginning of this song (or, if you're already at the beginning, to the previous song). Tap ▶▶ to skip to the next song.

> **TIP:** If you're wearing the earbuds, then you can pinch the clicker *twice* to skip to the next song.

  If you *hold down* one of these buttons, you rewind or fast-forward. You hear the music speeding by, without turning the singer into a chipmunk. The rewinding or fast-forwarding accelerates if you keep holding the button down.

- **Play/Pause button.** The Pause button beneath the album photo looks like this ❚❚ when the music is playing. If you do pause, then the button turns into the Play button (▶).

- **Download ( ).** If this song is on Apple Music online (and not physically on your phone), then tap to download it for playability when you're not on the Internet.

- **+.** This button appears only when you're playing an Apple Music song; it adds the current song to your iCloud Music Library (page 235).

- **Volume.** You can drag the round handle of this slider (bottom of the screen) to adjust the volume—or you can use the volume buttons on the left side of the phone.

- **AirPlay ( ).** Tap to send playback to an external speaker using AirPlay (page 249).

- **Options (•••).** As always in this app, this button is like a shortcut menu of options that might apply at the moment, described next.

Incidentally, people go batty trying to find three important controls in the Music app's new version: Shuffle, Repeat, and the Up Next queue (page 243).

They're all there—but you have to *swipe up* from the Now Playing screen to see them.

The Options Panel

The ellipsis (•••) awaits on every Now Playing screen. Its choices depend on whether you've tapped some music that you *own* (facing page, left) or that you've found in Apple Music's collection (right). But here are some of the commands you might see there:

- **Download.** Grab the song off of Apple's servers, so you'll be able to play it without an Internet connection (for Apple Music or iTunes Match subscribers only).

- **Delete from Library.** Gets rid of the song forever.

- **Add to Library.** Adds the current song to your iCloud Music Library (page 235).

- **Add to a Playlist.** Lets you add this item to a playlist you've made yourself.

Skyfall - Single
Adele

▶ **Skyfall - Single**
Adele
Pop • 2012

Download   ☁

Delete from Library   🗑

Add to a Playlist...   ⊕

Play Next   ↱

Play Later   ↳

Create Station   ⊕))

Share Album   ⬆

💜 Love   🚫 Dislike

Cancel

matchbox 20
yourself or someone like you

Push
Matchbox Twenty ›
Yourself Or Someone...

Add to Library   +

Add to a Playlist...   ⊕

Create Station   ⊕))

Share Song   ⬆

Lyrics   ❝

💜 Love   🚫 Dislike

Cancel

- **Play Next.** Adds this song or album to the beginning of the queue for immediate playback (page 243).

- **Play Later.** Adds this song or album to the *end* of the queue.

- **Create Station.** Makes a "radio station" full of music that sounds like this one (page 246).

- **Share Song.** Opens the Share sheet (page 348), so that you can send a link to this song via email, text message, Facebook or Twitter post, and so on. (The recipients can listen to the full song *if* they're Apple Music subscribers.)

- **Lyrics.** Holy smokes. Apple Music can show you a screen containing the *lyrics* of the song you're playing. Who'da thought?

- **Love, Dislike.** As you listen to a song, tap these buttons to tell Apple when there's a song you particularly love or loathe. When Apple's magical computers suggest new music for you later, they'll take these hints into account.

TIP: If you have an iPhone 6s or 7, you can *hard-press* a song in a list (for example, a playlist) to open the same Options menu. That is, you don't have to burrow all the way to its Now Playing screen.

Control Center

The Control Center, of course, is the panel that appears when you swipe up from the bottom of the screen (page 46). It includes playback controls, too. That means that you never have to go to the Music app just to change tracks if you're busy doing something else on the phone.

Playback While Locked

Once you're playing music, it keeps right on playing, even if you press the Home button or change apps. After all, the only thing more pleasurable than surfing the web is surfing it with a Beach Boys soundtrack.

If you've got something else to do—like jogging, driving, or performing surgery—tap the Sleep switch to turn off the screen. The music keeps playing, but you'll save battery power.

> **TIP:** Even with the screen off, you can still adjust the music volume (use the volume buttons on the earbud clicker or the buttons on the side of the phone), pause the music (pinch the earbud clicker once), or advance to the next song (pinch it twice).

What's cool is that if you wake the phone (press Home or the Sleep switch, or just lift the phone), the Lock screen looks like the Now Playing screen. It has all the same controls, so you can manage the playback without even having to fully wake the phone.

If a phone call comes in, the music fades, and you hear your chosen ringtone—through your earbuds, if you're wearing them. Squeeze the clicker on the earbud cord or tap the Sleep switch to answer the call. When the call ends, the music fades back in, right where it left off.

Voice Control

There's one more way to control your playback—a way that doesn't involve taking your eyes off the road or leaving whatever app you're using. You can control your music playback by voice command, using Siri. See Chapter 5.

Playlists

A *playlist* is a group of songs you've placed together, in a sequence that makes sense to you. One might consist of party tunes; another might hold romantic dinnertime music; a third might be drum-heavy workout cuts.

Creating Playlists on the Phone

To play with playlists, start on the **Library** tab. Tap **Playlists**. Here are all the playlists you've ever created—which might be zero (below, left).

To create one, do like this:

1. **Click the giant** New Playlist **button.**

   A new screen appears, where you can name and set up your new playlist (below, middle).

2. **Tap Playlist Name; type a name for your playlist.**

   You can also, at this moment, tap the little button to take, or choose, a photo to represent this playlist. Or even type a description.

3. **Tap** Add Music**.**

   The **Add Music** screen appears (below, right). It offers the usual ways to view your collection: **Playlists** (that is, existing ones), **Artists**, **Albums**, **Songs**, **Videos**, **Genres**, **Compilations**, **Composers**, and Downloaded Music. (A *compilation* is one of those albums that's been put together from many different performers. You know: "Zither Hits of the 1600s," "Kazoo Classics," and so on.)

4. **Tap the category you want for finding your first song; drill down until you find the music you want to add.**

   For example, if you first tap Albums, you then see a list of your albums; tap ⊕ to add the entire album to the new playlist. Or tap the album's name to view the songs on it—and then ⊕ next to a song's name to add *it* to the list.

5. **Keep adding music to the playlist until you're satisfied.**

   You can keep tapping ⊕ buttons, without leaving this screen; each turns into a checkmark to indicate that you've added it (previous page, right). A playlist can be infinitely long; we're way past the days of worrying about how much will fit on a cassette tape or a CD.

6. **Tap every Done button until you're back on the Playlists screen.**

   Your newly minted playlist is ready to play!

Using Playlists

To see what songs or videos are in a playlist, tap its name or picture. You now arrive at a Playlist details screen, where your tracks are listed for your inspection. To start playing a song once you see it in the Playlist list, tap its name; you'll hear that song and all those that follow it, in order.

Or tap the Shuffle button (⤭) to start random-order playback.

> **TIP:** Here you can use a standard iOS convention: Anywhere you're asked to drill down from one list to another—from a playlist to the songs inside, for example—you can backtrack by *swiping from the left edge* of the phone into the screen.
>
> Or do it the long way: Tap ‹ at the upper-left corner of the screen. That button's name always tells you what screen you just came from (My Music, for example).

Once you're here, you can have all kinds of fun:

- **To delete or rearrange songs:** Tap Edit. Use the ≡ handles to drag the songs into a new sequence. Hit ⊖ to make one disappear. (You're not deleting it from your phone—only from this playlist.) Tap Done.

- **To add more songs to the playlist:** Tap Edit. Tap Add Music.

- **To rename the open playlist:** Tap Edit. Tap the current title and edit away. (Tap Done.)

- **To delete the playlist:** Open the playlist; tap the ••• to open the Options panel; tap Delete from Library. Confirm by tapping Delete Playlist. (Scary though that wording may sound, no music is actually deleted from your library—only the playlist that contains it.)

Up Next

Unless you're a professional DJ, you're probably happy to hear song after song played automatically, according to whatever album, playlist, or radio station they're in.

But the Up Next playlist gives you a degree of control without requiring the full project of programming a playlist.

The Up Next playlist always exists. If you tell Music to play an album, then Up Next autofills with the songs on that album; if you're listening to all the music from a certain performer, then Up Next displays what else you'll hear from that artist. And if you tap any song in your Library, then *everything after it* gets added to the Up Next queue automatically.

But you can also queue up music yourself, adding songs to Up Next on your own schedule. The playback will plow through them in order.

- **Add a song to Up Next.** Hard-press (or long-press) a song, album, or playlist to open the Options panel (below, left). Tap Play Next to put this song at the beginning of the Up Next queue, or Play Later to put it at the **end** of the queue.

- **Play a song now.** Suppose you find some music you want to play right now. You don't care about the Up Next playlist.

  When you tap that item's name, the iPhone asks: "After playing this, do you want to play the songs you've added to Up Next?" If you hit Keep Up Next, then you hear the new song without disturbing the Up Next list that will play afterward. If you hit Clear Up Next, then the new music plays and then stops; you've nuked the current Up Next list.

View, Edit, or Clear the Up Next List

Most people probably never realize it, but you can actually look over the Up Next playlist in progress. You can rearrange or delete anything in it.

There's only one way to see the Up Next playlist, and it's pretty buried. You have to open the full-height Now Playing screen described on page 237, and then **scroll up**.

Once the list appears (previous page, right), you can remove a song from the queue by swiping left on it to reveal the Remove button; tap it. Rearrange the list by dragging the little "grip strip" handles up or down. (If you don't see them, it's because you've got your music on Repeat.)

> **NOTE:** There's no way to clear the entire list at once—except to force-quit the Music app (page 345) and then reopen it.

"For You" Tab

30 million is a lot of songs. You won't live long enough to hear them all. So Apple has supplied the For You tab of the Music app to present new songs, performers, and albums its algorithms think you'll like. (If you're not a paying subscriber, then this tab is just an ad for Apple Music.)

Scroll horizontally to see more tiles in a category; scroll vertically to see the playlists, albums, artists, and new releases Apple thinks you'll like.

And how does the app guess what kind of music you'll like? When you sign up for the service, you're shown dancing red circles bearing music-genre names. You're supposed to tap the ones you like, double-tap the ones you **really** like, and hold your finger down on the ones you don't like.

Then, of course, as you go through your life listening to music, you can always turn the ♡ button on or off to further fine-tune Apple's understanding of your tastes.

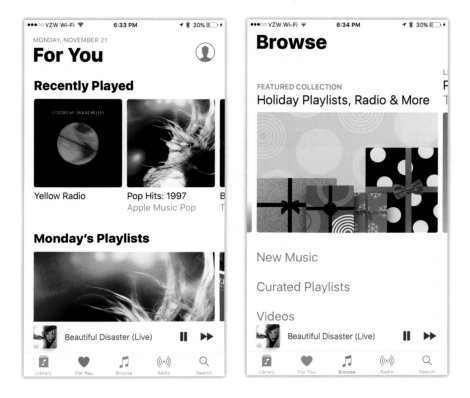

Browse Tab

The Browse tab is also for paying subscribers only. It's lists of lists.

Scroll down long enough, and you'll find lists like **New Music**, **Curated Playlists** (music lists, created by Apple's editors, for particular genres, activities, and moods), **Videos**, **Top Charts**, and **Genres**. Once again, the idea is to help you find new stuff you like.

iTunes Radio

Your iPhone includes an amazing gift: your own radio station. Your own *empire* of radio stations, in fact.

They come in two categories: Free and Custom.

Free Stations

What you see on the Radio screen depends on whether or not you've turned off Show Apple Music, as described on page 233.

If that's turned off, then you see only free stations here: Beats 1 (the Apple live station described on page 234) and some Internet streaming stations like CBS, NPR, ESPN, and Bloomberg. These are free Internet radio stations.

Subscriber Stations

If Show Apple Music is turned on, then this screen offers ready-made "radio stations" that Apple has supplied for you. If you're a subscriber, they play; if not, they give you an ad to sign up.

Tap Radio Stations to find more ready-to-play, software-curated "radio stations" in every conceivable category: Country, NPR, ESPN, Oldies, Soul/Funk, Chill, Indie, Classic Metal, Pop Workout, Kids & Family, Lullabies, Latin Pop, Classical, Reggae, and on and on.

You can hit ▶▶ to skip a song you're not enjoying. And you don't hear any ads.

Custom Stations

If you're a paid subscriber, the iTunes Radio service offers more than canned stations; you can create a new "station" instantly, based on any "seed" song you choose.

You don't get to choose the exact songs or singers you want to hear; you have to trust iTunes Radio to choose songs *based* on your chosen song, singer, or music genre. For example, if you choose Billy Joel as your "seed," you'll hear a lot of Billy Joel, but also a lot of other music that sounds more or less like his.

To set up a new "radio station" of your own, find a song, band, or album. Hard-press or long-press it to open the Options menu (page 35)—and tap Create Station.

You've just created a new station, and it begins instantly.

> **TIP:** While a custom station plays, you can tap the ☆ on its Now Playing screen to see two new buttons: Play More Like This and Play Less Like This. That kind of feedback fine-tunes your custom station for future use.

The idea of a "seed song"–based radio service isn't new, of course. It's the same idea as Pandora, a website and app that has offered precisely the same features for years. But iTunes Radio is built in, it's incorporated with

Siri and the Control Center, and it's part of Apple's larger ecosystem; that is, you can see your same set of "radio stations" on your Mac or PC (in the iTunes app), iPad, and Apple TV.

Returning to a Custom Station

On the main Radio screen, the Recently Played list shows all the stations you've listened to. Tap to start playing.

Siri and iTunes Radio

Truth is, there's an easier way to create a custom radio station: Just let Siri do the work. No matter what you're doing on the iPhone, you can hold down the Home button and say, for example, "Play 'Just the Way You Are' by Billy Joel" or "Play some Beatles." Boom: The music begins.

Actually, Siri comes equipped to recognize a whole slew of commands pertaining to iTunes Radio. Here's a sampler; you don't have to use these precise wordings:

- **Start a station from Whitney Houston** (or any song, album, or performer).

- **Play the radio.**

- **What song is this?**

- **Play more like this.**

- **Don't play this song again.**

- **Pause the music. (Resume the music.)**

- **Skip this song.**

- **Add this song to my Wish List.**

- **Stop the radio.**

Speakers and Headphones

The iPhone's speaker is pretty darned good for such a tiny machine. But the world is full of better speakers—Bluetooth wireless speakers, car stereo systems, hi-fi TVs, and fancy earbuds and headphones. The iPhone is especially easy to use with them.

Bluetooth Wireless

You can buy amazingly small, powerful Bluetooth stereo speakers that receive your iPhone's music from as far as 20 or 30 feet away—made by Jawbone, Bose, and others.

There are also wireless Bluetooth headphones and earbuds—an espe-cially useful fact if you have an iPhone 7 (which lacks a headphone jack).

Once you've bought your headphones or speakers, you have to introduce them to the iPhone—a process called *pairing*.

From the Home screen, tap Settings→Bluetooth. Turn Bluetooth on (below, left); you see the Searching ❄ animation as the iPhone wirelessly hunts for your headphones or speakers.

Grab them, turn them on, and start the pairing procedure, as described in the manual. Usually that means holding down a certain button until a tiny light starts flashing. At that point, the headphones' or speaker's name appears on the iPhone's screen.

> **TIP:** If the headphones or speakers require a one-time passcode—it's usually 0000, but check the manual—the iPhone's keyboard appears, so you can type it in.

A couple of seconds later, it says Connected; now any sound the iPhone would ordinarily play through its speakers or earbuds now plays through the wireless headphones or speakers. Not just music—which, in general, sounds amazing—but chirps, game sounds, and so on. Oh, and phone calls.

If your headset has a microphone, too, then you can even answer and make phone calls wirelessly. (There's an Answer button right on the headphones.)

Using Bluetooth wireless stereo does eat up your battery charge faster. But come on: listening to your music without wires, with the iPhone still in your pocket or bag? How cool is that?

Switching Among Speakers

When your iPhone has a connection to a wireless sound source— Bluetooth speakers/earbuds or an AirPlay receiver, for example—you need some way to direct the music playback to it.

The answer is the ⊛ button. It's on the Control Center (page 46). When you tap it, the iPhone offers a button for each speaker or set of earbuds or headphone (facing page, right). To switch, tap the one you want.

Instantly, the sound begins flowing from your other source. Use the same method to switch back to the iPhone's speakers when the time comes.

AirPlay

There's another way to transmit audio wirelessly from the iPhone (and video, too): the Apple technology called AirPlay. You can buy AirPlay speakers, amplifiers, and TV sets. The Apple TV, of course, is the best-known AirPlay machine.

AirPlay is described on page 259, because most people use it to transmit video, not just audio. But the steps for transmitting to an AirPlay audio gadget are the same.

Music Settings

The iPhone has a long list of traditional iPod features for music playback. Most of these options await in Settings→Music. (Shortcut: Tell Siri, "Open Music settings.")

EQ (Equalization)

Like any good music player, the iPhone offers an EQ function: a long list of presets, each of which affects your music differently by boosting or throttling various frequencies. One might bring out the bass to goose up your hip-hop tunes; another might emphasize the midrange for clearer vocals; and so on. ("Late Night" is especially handy; it lowers the bass so it thuds less. Your downstairs neighbors will love it.)

You'll find the EQ feature way down the Music Settings page.

Volume Limit

It's now established fact: Listening to a lot of loud music through ear-phones can damage your hearing. Pump it up today, pay for it tomorrow.

Portable music players can be sinister that way, because in noisy places like planes and city streets, people turn up the volume much louder than they would in a quiet place, and they don't even realize how high they've cranked it. That's why Apple created this volume slider. It lets you limit the maximum volume level of the music.

In fact, if you're a parent, you can even lock down this control on your child's iPhone; it can be bypassed only with a password. Set the volume slider here, and then, in Settings→General→Restrictions, turn on **Volume Limit**, as described on page 250.

Sound Check

This feature smooths out the master volume levels of tracks from dif-ferent albums, helping to compensate for differences in their recording levels. It doesn't deprive you of peaks and valleys in the music volume, of course—it affects only the baseline level.

Playing Music from Your Computer

Here's a trick you weren't expecting: You can store many terabytes of music on your Mac or PC upstairs—and play it on your phone in the kitchen downstairs. Or anywhere on the same Wi-Fi network, actually.

This nifty bit of wireless magic is brought to you by Home Sharing, a fea-ture of the iTunes program.

Here's the setup: In iTunes on the Mac or PC, open Edit→Preferences. Click **Sharing**, and turn on **Share my library on my local network**. (You can share only certain playlists, if you like.) Turn on **Require password** and enter your Apple account (iCloud) password. Click **OK**.

Now pick up your phone. At the bottom of the Settings→Music screen, log into Home Sharing using the same Apple ID and password.

Now you're ready to view the contents of your computer on the phone. You'd never guess where it's hiding.

In the Music app, on the **Library** tab, tap **Home Sharing**; on the next screen, choose your computer's name. (Note that the Home Sharing heading doesn't appear unless your computer is turned on and iTunes is open.)

That's it! Suddenly, your entire Music app is filled with the music from your computer's collection, rather than the music on the phone.

The iTunes Store

Just as you can buy apps using the App Store app, you can also browse, buy, and download songs, TV shows, and movies using the iTunes Store app. Anything you buy gets autosynced back to your computer's copy of iTunes when you get home. Whenever you hear somebody mention a buy-worthy song, for example, you can have it within a minute.

To begin, open the iTunes Store **app**. The store you see here (below, left) is modeled on the App Store described in Chapter 10. This time, the buttons at the bottom of the screen include **Music**, **Movies**, **TV Shows**, **Search**, and **More**.

When you tap **Music**, **Movies**, or **TV Shows**, the screen offers further buttons. For Music, for example, the scrolling horizontal rows of options might include **New Releases**, **Recent Releases**, **Singles**, and **Pre-Orders**.

(Beneath each list is a **Redeem** button, which you can tap if you've been given an iTunes gift certificate or a promo code; a **Send Gift** button, which lets you buy a song or video for someone else; and an **Apple ID** button, which can show you your current credit balance.)

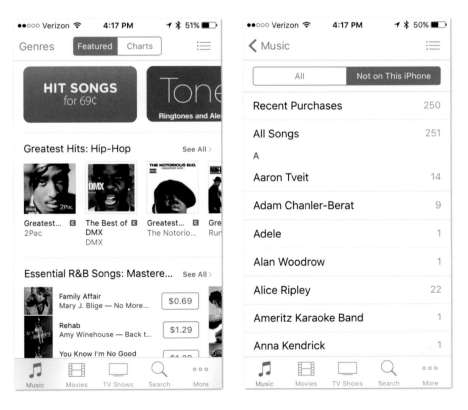

To search for something in particular, tap Search. The keyboard appears. Type what you're looking for: the name of a song, movie, show, performer, or album, for example. At any time, you can stop typing and tap the name of a match to see its details. You can use the buttons across the top to restrict the search to one category (just songs or movies, for example).

All these tools eventually take you to the details page of an album, song, or movie. For a song, tap its name to hear an instant 90-second preview (tap again to stop). For a TV show or movie, tap ▶ to watch the ad or the sneak preview.

If you're sold, then tap the price button to buy the song, show, or album (and tap Buy to confirm). Enter your Apple ID password when you're asked. (For movies, you can choose either Buy or Rent, priced accordingly.) At this point, your iPhone downloads the music or video you bought.

Purchased Items

Anything you buy from the iTunes Store winds up in the appropriate app on your iPhone: the TV app for TV shows and movies, the Music app for songs. (Within the Music app, you can see everything you've bought: Tap Playlists and then Purchased.)

In the iTunes Store app, you can tap More and then Purchased to see what you've bought. Once you tap a category (Music, Movies, TV Shows), you get a pair of tabs:

- **All.** Here's a list of everything you've bought from iTunes, on your iPhone or any other Apple machine.

- **Not on This iPhone.** This is the cool part. Here you see not just the files on the iPhone in your hand, but things you've bought on other

Apple gadgets—an album you bought on your iPad, for example, or a song you downloaded to your iPod Touch. (This assumes that you're using the same Apple ID on all your gizmos.)

The beauty of this arrangement, of course, is that you can tap the name of something that's Not on This iPhone—and then download it (tap ☁). No extra charge.

TIP: If you prefer, you can direct your phone to download those purchases that you make on other gadgets automatically, without your having to tap **Not on This iPhone**. Visit **Settings→iTunes & App Store**, and turn on the switches for **Music**, **Apps**, and/or **Books** under **Automatic Downloads**. If you also turn on **Use Cellular Data**, then your phone will do this auto-downloading when you're in any 3G or LTE cellular Internet area, not just in a Wi-Fi hotspot.

More in "More"

Tapping **More** at the bottom of the screen offers these options:

• **Tones.** You can buy ready-made ringtones on this page—30-second slices of pop songs. (Don't ask what sense it makes to pay $1.29 for

30 seconds of a song, when you could buy the whole song for the same price.)

- **Genius.** Apple offers a list of music, movies, and TV shows for sale that it thinks you'll like, based on stuff you already have.

- **Purchased.** Here's another way to examine the stuff you've bought on all your devices. If you've turned on Apple's Family Sharing feature (page 540), you can also examine what stuff your family members have bought.

- **Downloads.** Shows you a progress bar for anything you've started to download.

> **TIP:** If you tap Edit, you'll see that you can *replace* any of the four iTunes Store bottom-row icons with one of the More buttons (Tones, Genius, Purchased, or whatever). Just drag one of these icons directly downward on *top* of an existing icon.

So you've downloaded one of the store's millions of songs, podcasts, TV shows, music videos, ringtones, or movies directly to your phone. Next time you sync, that song will swim *upstream* to your Mac or PC, where it will be safely backed up in iTunes. (And if you lost your connection before the iPhone was finished downloading, your Mac or PC will finish the job automatically. Cool.)

The TV App

This weird hybrid app didn't come with iOS 10; it appeared on your phone with iOS 10.2. (A matching app appears on the Apple TV, where it may make more sense.)

It's intended to serve as a single repository for *paid* TV shows and movies online, in these three categories:

- **Videos you've bought or rented from Apple's iTunes store.** In this regard, the TV app takes over the functions of the old Videos app, which has vanished from your phone.

- **Paid video-service apps like Showtime, Hulu, and HBO Go.** A few of these apps work with the TV app's "single sign-on" feature, meaning that you can enter the name and password for your cable account *once*, and thereafter you're spared having to enter it into each individual app.

- **Channels your cable package provides.** Or at least those that have apps: ABC, A&E, AMC, TBS, and so on. Each one requires that you provide your cable or satellite TV account name and password. (Here again, a few may work with the single sign-on feature, meaning you don't have to sign in individually.)

TIP: Even if you don't have a cable subscription, there's some free stuff you can watch in this app. Visit Store→Buy or Rent on iTunes section→Free Episodes.

There are also some channel apps that are free to watch without a subscription, including PBS, PBS Kids, CBS Sports, ABC News, and The Weather Channel.

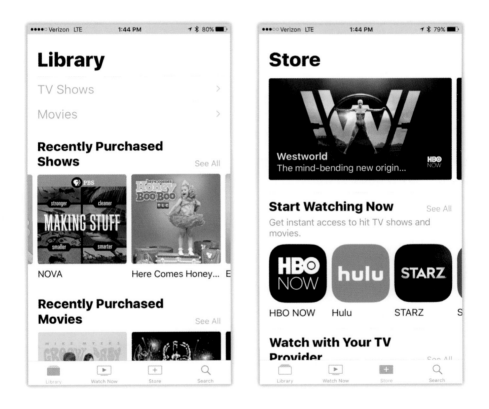

That's the shiny future concept of the TV app. In its fledgling first incarnation, though, it's of far less use, because it works only with a handful of lesser cable companies and only a handful of channel apps. Netflix, for example, is not among them.

Until more players join the party, here's how to use the TV app.

Four Tabs

The buttons across the bottom clearly exhibit the TV app's split personality (split between iTunes purchases and cable-channel apps).

- **iTunes Store.** Find TV shows and movies to rent or buy using Search. Watch the ones you've bought or rented in Library.

- **Channel apps.** Find channel apps using Store. Watch the shows available from the apps you've installed in Watch Now.

How to Play a Video

Tap a video's thumbnail to see its plot summary, year of release, and so on. If it's a TV series, tap an episode in that series, if necessary. Either way, tap ▶ to begin watching.

> **NOTE:** If you see a ⬇ on this screen, it means that this bought or rented movie is not actually on your phone. If you have a good Wi-Fi signal, you can watch it right now by streaming it (instead of downloading it to your phone).
>
> If you don't see that icon, then the video file is actually on your phone. An Edit button appears, which you can tap (and then tap ❌) to delete the video.

When you're playing video, anything else on the screen is distracting, so Apple hides the video playback controls. Tap the screen once to make them appear and again to make them disappear.

Here's what they do:

- **Done.** Tap this button, in the top-left corner, to stop playback and return to the master list of videos.

- **Scroll slider.** This progress indicator (top of the screen) is exactly like the one you see when you're playing music. You see the elapsed time, the remaining time, and a white, round handle that you can drag to jump forward or back in the video.

> **TIP:** Drag your finger farther (up or down) from the handle to choose a faster or slower scrubbing speed.

- **Zoom/Unzoom.** In the top-right corner, a little ⬍ or ▭ button appears if the video's shape doesn't exactly match your screen. Tap it to adjust the zoom level of the video, as described in a moment.

- **Play/Pause (▶/❙❙).** These buttons (and the earbud clicker) do the same thing to video as they do to music: alternate playing and pausing.

- **Previous, Next (◄◄, ►►❙).** Hold down your finger to rewind or fast-forward the video. The longer you hold, the faster the zipping. (When you fast-forward, you even get to hear the sped-up audio.)

  If you're watching a movie from the iTunes Store, you may be surprised to discover that it comes with predefined chapter markers, just like a DVD. Internally, it's divided up into scenes. To see them, stop playback (tap **Done**); on the movie page, tap **Chapters**. Tap a chapter name to skip to that chapter marker—or tap ▶ to return to your original spot.

> **TIP:** If you're wearing the earbuds, you can pinch the clicker *twice* to skip to the next chapter, or *three times* to go back a chapter.

- **Volume.** You can drag the round handle of this slider (bottom of the screen) to adjust the volume—or you can use the volume buttons on the left side of the phone.

- **Language (▣).** You don't see this button often. But when you do, it summons subtitle and alternate-language soundtrack options, just like a DVD player.

- **AirPlay (▱).** This symbol appears if you have an Apple TV (or another AirPlay-compatible electronic). Tap it to send your video playback to the TV, as described on page 259.

If you don't see a video that you *know* you purchased through iTunes, open the iTunes Store app on your phone. Tap More→ Purchased, and then select the person who bought the movie or TV show. Next tap either Movies or TV Shows; look under All and Not on This iPhone. When you find what you want, tap its name and re-download it by tapping ☁. That puts it back into the TV app's library.

And to delete a video from the library, swipe leftward across its name in the Videos list; tap Delete to confirm. (You can always re-download it, of course.)

Zoom/Unzoom

The iPhone's screen is bright, vibrant, and stunningly sharp. Sometimes, however, it's not the right shape for videos.

Pre-HDTV shows are squarish, not rectangular. So when you watch older TV shows on a rectangular screen, you get black letterbox columns on either side of the picture.

Movies have the opposite problem. They're usually too wide for the iPhone screen. So when you watch movies, you may wind up with *horizontal* letterbox bars above and below the picture.

Some people are fine with that. After all, HDTVs have the same problem. At least when letterbox bars are onscreen, you know you're seeing the complete composition of the scene the director intended.

Other people can't stand letterboxing. You're already watching on a pretty small screen; why sacrifice some of that precious area to black bars?

Fortunately, the iPhone gives you a choice. If you double-tap the video as it plays, you zoom in, magnifying the image so it fills the entire screen. Or, if the playback controls are visible, you can also tap ▯ or ▭. Of course, now you're not seeing the entire original composition. You lose the top and bottom of old TV scenes, or the left and right edges of movie scenes.

Fortunately, if this effect chops off something important—some text, for example—the original letterbox view is just another double-tap away. (No zooming happens if the source material is already a perfect fit for the iPhone's screen shape.)

TV Output

When you crave a screen bigger than a few inches, you can play your iPhone's videos on a regular TV. All you need is the right cable: the Apple Digital AV Adapter. It carries both audio and video over a single HDMI cable.

It **mirrors** what's on the phone: your Home screen, email, Safari, and everything else. (Photos and presentations appear on your TV in pure, "video outputted" form, without any controls or other window clutter.)

AirPlay

Your iPhone also offers wireless projection, thanks to a feature called AirPlay. It transmits music or high-def video (with audio) from your iPhone to an Apple TV (or another AirPlay-equipped receiver) across the room. It's a fantastic way to send slideshows, movies, presentations, games, FaceTime calls, and websites to your TV for a larger audience to enjoy. Whatever is on the screen gets transmitted.

AirPlay receivers include the Apple TV (version 2 or later) and speakers, stereos, and receivers from Denon, Marantz, JBL, iHome, and so on. The phone and recent AirPlay receivers no longer have to be on the same Wi-Fi network, thanks to a feature called peer-to-peer AirPlay.

When you're playing a video or some music, open the Control Center (page 46), and tap ⊛ to see a list of available AirPlay receivers. If you have an Apple TV, tap its name, and then turn its Mirroring switch on.

That's it! Everything on the iPhone screen now appears on the TV or sound system. (The phone's status bar displays the ◢ icon, so you don't wander off and forget that every move you make is visible to the entire crowd in the living room.)

Two Ways to See the iPhone on Your Mac

If you're a teacher, trainer, or product demonstrator, you might be amazed at how easy it is to display your iPhone's screen on a Mac's screen. From there, you can either project it onto an even **bigger** screen, or record it as a QuickTime movie to use in presentations or post online.

- **The free way.** If your Mac has OS X Yosemite or later, then connect the phone to the Mac with its white USB charging cable. Open the Mac app called QuickTime Player. Choose File→New Movie Recording. From the little ∨ menu next to the ❷ button, choose iPhone.

  Now you're seeing the iPhone's screen on your Mac—and you can record it, project it, or screen-capture it for future generations!

- **The wireless way.** A $13 program called Reflector (*reflectorapp.com*) lets you view the iPhone's live image on the Mac's screen—and hear its sound. (It actually turns the Mac into an AirPlay receiver.) There's also a Record command, so you can create a movie of whatever you're doing on the phone.

9

The Camera

Incredible though it sounds, the iPhone is the number-one most popular camera model in the world. More photos are posted online from this phone than from any other machine in existence.

And no wonder; you've probably never seen pictures and movies look this good on a pocket gadget. With each new version of the iPhone, Apple improves its camera—and on the iPhone 7 and 7 Plus, it's unbelievably good; on the 7 Plus, there's even, for the first time, an *optical* zoom.

And the videos look amazing. They're auto-stabilized—and the 6s and 7 models even shoot in 4K (four times the resolution of high-def video).

This chapter is all about the iPhone's ability to display photos, take new ones with its camera, and capture videos.

The Camera App

The little hole on the back of the iPhone, in the upper-left corner, is its camera.

On the latest iPhones, it's pretty impressive, at least for a cellphone cam. The iPhone 7 and 7 Plus, for example, have four LED flashes, manual exposure controls, optical stabilization, and phase-detection autofocus (the same kind of very fast refocusing found in professional SLR cameras). These phones can shoot 10 shots a second and do amazingly well in low light.

The earlier iPhone models' cameras aren't quite as good, but they're still fine as long as your subject is still and well lit. Action shots may come out blurry, and dim-light shots may come out grainier.

Now that you know what you're in for, here's how it works.

Firing Up the Camera

Photographic opportunities are frequently fleeting; by the time you fish the phone from your pocket, wake it up, unlock it, press the Home button, find the Camera app, and wait for it to load, the magic moment may be gone forever.

Fortunately, there's a much quicker way to get to the Camera app:

1. **Wake the phone.**

    That is, lift the phone (page 17) or press the Home or Sleep button, so that you're now at the Lock screen.

2. **Swipe to the left.**

    The Camera app opens directly. This trick shaves an unbelievable amount of time off the old get-to-the-camera method. Over time, the wake-and-swipe ritual becomes natural, fluid—and fast.

> **TIP:** Of course, there's a hands-free way to fire up the Camera app, too: Tell Siri, "Open camera."

By the way: This Camera shortcut bypasses the password or fingerprint security. Any random stranger who picks up your phone can, therefore, jump directly into picture-taking mode, without your password or fingerprint.

That stranger can't do much damage, though. She can take new photos, or delete the new photos taken during her session—but the photos you've *already* taken are off-limits, and the features that could damage your reputation (editing, emailing, and posting photos) are unavailable. She would have to open the Photos app to get to those—and that requires the phone password.

Camera Modes

The Camera app can capture six or seven kinds of photo and video, depending on your phone model. By swiping your finger horizontally anywhere on the screen, you switch among its modes. Here they are, from left to right:

*   **Time-Lapse.** This mode speeds up your video, yet somehow keeps it stable. You can reduce a 2-hour bike ride into 20 seconds of superfast playback.

*   **Slo-Mo** (iPhone 5s and later). Wow, what gorgeousness! You get a video filmed at 120 or 240 frames a second—so it plays back at one-quarter or one-eighth the speed, incredibly smoothly. Fantastic for sports, tender smiles, and cannonballs into the pool.

- **Video.** Here's your basic camcorder mode: 4K video on the 6s and 7 models, high definition on earlier ones.

- **Photo.** This is the primary mode for taking pictures. It's the one Camera chooses automatically when it opens.

- **Portrait.** Available only on the iPhone 7 Plus, whose two camera lenses create a softly blurred background that looks super professional.

- **Square.** You might wonder why Apple would go to the trouble of designating a whole special camera mode to taking square, not rectangular, pictures. Answer: Instagram, the crazy-popular app that features square pictures and was sold to Facebook for nearly $1 billion.

- **Pano.** Choose this mode to capture super-wide-angle panoramic photos.

> **TIP:** If you tend to stick to one of these modes (like Square because you're an Instagram junkie, for example), you can make the iPhone's camera *stay* in your favorite mode, rather than resetting itself to Photo mode every time you reopen it. That feature, which appeared in iOS 10.2, is in Settings→Photos & Camera→Preserve Settings.

All of these modes are described in this chapter, but in a more logical order: still photos first, then video modes.

Photo Mode

Most people, most of the time, use the Camera app to take still photos. It's a pretty great experience. The iPhone's screen is a huge digital-camera viewfinder. You can turn it 90 degrees for a wider or taller shot.

Tap to Focus

All right: You've opened the Camera app, and the mode is set to Photo. See the yellow box that appears briefly on the screen?

It's telling you where the iPhone will focus, the area it examines to calculate the overall brightness of the photo (exposure), and the portion that will determine the overall **white balance** of the scene (that is, the color cast).

Tap the sky to make it correctly exposed, even if the beach is now too dark.

Tap the dark beach to brighten it up, although that also brightens up the sky.

If you're taking a picture of people, the iPhone's software tries to lock in on a face—up to 10 faces, actually—and calculate focus and exposure so that **they** look right.

But sometimes there are no faces—and dead center may not be the most important part of the photo. The cool thing is that you can **tap** somewhere else in the scene to move that yellow square—to recalculate the focus, exposure, and white balance.

Here's when you might want to do this tapping:

- **When the whole image looks too dark or too bright.** If you tap a **dark** part of the scene, the whole photo brightens up; if you tap a *bright* part, the whole photo darkens a bit. You're telling the camera, "Redo your calculations so *this* part has the best exposure; I don't care if the rest of the picture gets brighter or darker." At that point, you can override the phone's exposure decision.

- **When the scene has a color cast.** If the photo looks, for example, a little bluish or yellowish, tap a different spot in the scene—the one you care most about. The iPhone recomputes its assessment of the white balance.

- **When you're in macro mode.** If the foreground object is very close to the lens—4 to 8 inches away—the iPhone automatically goes into *macro* (super closeup) mode. In this mode, you can do something really cool: You can *defocus the background*. The background goes soft, slightly blurry, just like the professional photos you see in magazines. No, not as well or as flexibly as the iPhone 7 Plus can (page 278), but it's something. Just make sure you tap the foreground object.

Adjust Exposure

When you tap the screen to set the focus point, a new control appears: a little yellow sun slider. That's your exposure control. Slide it up to brighten the whole photo or down to make things darker—an incredibly useful option.

Often, just a small adjustment is all it takes to add a splash of light to a dim scene, or to dial the details back into a photo that's bright white.

To reset the slider to the iPhone's original proposed setting, tap the screen somewhere else, or just aim the phone at something different for a second.

The point is that the Camera app lets you fuss with the focus point and the exposure level independently.

Focus Lock/Exposure Lock

The iPhone likes to focus and calculate the exposure before it shoots. Cameras are funny that way.

That tendency, however, can get in your way when you're shooting something that moves fast. Horse races, divers. Pets. Kids on merry-go-rounds, kids on slides, kids in your house. By the time the camera has calculated the focus and exposure, which takes about a second, you've lost the shot.

Therefore, Apple provides a feature that's common on professional cameras but rare on phones: auto-exposure lock and autofocus lock. They let you set up the focus and exposure in advance so that there's zero lag when you finally snap the shot.

To use this feature, point the camera at something that has the **same distance and lighting** as the subject-to-be. For example, focus at the base of the merry-go-round that's directly below where your daughter's horse will be. Or point at the bottom of the waterslide before your son is ready to go.

Now hold your finger down on that spot on the iPhone's screen until you see the yellow square blink twice. When you lift your finger, the phrase "AE/AF Lock" tells you that you've now locked in exposure and autofocus. (You can tap again to unlock it if you change your mind.)

At this point, you can drag the yellow sun slider to adjust that locked exposure, if you like.

Now you can snap photos, rapid-fire, without ever having to wait while your iPhone rethinks focus and exposure.

The LED Flash

As on most phones, the iPhone's "flash" is actually just a very bright LED light on the back. You can make it turn on momentarily, providing a small boost of illumination when the lights are low. (That's a *small* boost—it won't do anything for subjects more than a few feet away.)

The iPhone 5s, 6, and 6s models, in fact, have two LED flashes: one white, one amber. The 7 family takes that a step further, with *four* flashes, together producing 50 percent more light output.

The flashes go off simultaneously, with their strengths mixed properly so that their light matches the color temperature of the scene. (You might notice that before the phone takes the picture, it flashes once *before* the shot is captured. That's the camera's opportunity to *measure* the light color of the scene.)

This multi-flash trick makes a huge difference in the quality of your flash photos. (Especially skin tones, which may be why Apple calls the feature "True Tone.")

No matter which model you have, the flash comes set to Auto. It turns on automatically when the scene is too dark, in the iPhone's opinion. But if you tap the ⚡ when it says Auto, two other options pop out: On (the flash will fire no matter what the lighting conditions) and Off (the flash will not fire, no matter what).

> **TIP:** If you open the Control Center (page 46) and tap the flashlight icon (🔦), the phone's LED flash turns on and stays on. It's great when you want to see your key in the door or read the tiny type in a program or a menu.

The Screen Flash

The iPhone 6s and 7 models offer a "flash" on the **front**, too, for taking selfies. But it's not an LED like the one on the back.

Instead, at the moment you take the shot, the **screen** lights up to illuminate your face. Better yet: It adjusts the color of the screen's "flash" to give your face the best flesh tones, based on a check of the ambient light color.

Of course, the normal iPhone screen is too tiny to supply much light, even at full brightness. So Apple developed a custom chip with a single purpose: to overclock the screen. In selfie situations, the screen blasts at **three times** its usual full brightness for a fraction of a second. It is crazy bright.

It works fantastically well. Here, you can see the nuked-looking result from a traditional back LED "flash" (left) side-by-side with the screen flash (right).

Zooming In

The iPhone has a zoom, which can help bring you "closer" to the subject—but (unless it's a 7 Plus) it's a **digital** zoom. It doesn't work like a real camera's optical zoom, which actually moves lenses to blow up the scene. Instead, it basically just blows up the image, making everything bigger, and slightly degrading the picture quality in the process.

To zoom in like this, **spread two fingers** on the screen. As you spread, a zoom slider appears; you can also drag the handle in the slider, or tap **+** or **–**, for more precise zooming.

Sometimes, getting closer to the action is worth the subtle image-quality sacrifice.

The iPhone 7 Plus: True Zoom

On the iPhone 7 Plus, there was enough room for Apple to install **two** lenses, side by side. One is wide-angle; one is telephoto. With one tap on the little **1x** button (below, left), you can zoom in 2x (middle). This is true *optical* zoom, not the cruddy digital zoom on most previous phones (which degrades the quality).

2x zoom isn't a huge amount, but it's 2x more than any other thin smart-phone can handle. And it's a triumphant first step toward eliminating a key drawback of phone cameras: They can't actually zoom.

You can also dial up any amount of zoom *between* 1x and 2x, again with-out losing any quality. The iPhone performs that stunt by seamlessly *combining* the zoom lens's image (in the center of the photo) with a mar-gin provided by the wide lens. Just plant your finger on the **1x** and drag it to the left. You'll see the circular scale of zooming appear (previous page, right).

You can even zoom while shooting a video, which is very cool.

Even on the Plus, by the way, you can keep dragging your finger to the left, past 2x—all the way up to a really blotchy 10x (or 6x for video). Beyond 2x, of course, you're invoking digital zoom. But sometimes, it's just what you need.

> **TIP:** Once you've dragged your finger to open the zooming scale, you can tap the current magnification button ("2.5x" or whatever) to reset the zooming to 1x.

The "Rule of Thirds" Grid

The Rule of Thirds, long held as gospel by painters and photographers, suggests that you imagine a tic-tac-toe grid superimposed on your frame. As you frame the shot, position the important parts of the photo on those lines or, better yet, at their intersections. Supposedly, this setup creates a stronger composition than putting everything in dead center.

Now, it's really a *Consideration* of Thirds; plenty of photographs are, in fact, strongest when the subject is centered.

But if you want to know where those magic intersections are so that you can *consider* the Rule of Thirds, duck into Settings→Photos & Camera. Scroll down; turn on Grid.

Now the phone displays the tic-tac-toe grid, for your composition pleasure (it's not part of the photo). You turn it off the same way.

High Dynamic Range (HDR)

In one regard, digital cameras are still pathetic: Compared with the human eye, they have terrible *dynamic range*.

That's the range from the brightest to darkest spots in a single scene. If you see someone standing in front of a bright window, you can probably make out who it is. But in a photo, that person will be a solid black silhouette. The camera doesn't have enough dynamic range to handle both the bright background and the person standing in front of it.

You could brighten up the exposure so that the person's face is lit—but then you'd brighten the background to a nuclear-white rectangle.

A partial solution: HDR (high dynamic range) photography. That's when the camera takes three photos (or even more)—one each at dark, medium, and light exposure settings. Its software combines the best parts of all three, bringing details to both the shadows and the highlights.

Believe it or not, your iPhone has a built-in HDR feature. It's not as amazing as what an HDR guru can do in Photoshop—for one thing, you have zero control over how the images are combined, how many are combined, or how much of each is combined.

But, often, an HDR photo does show more detail in both bright and dark areas than a single shot would. In the iPhone shot on the previous page, the sky is blown out—pure white. On the right, the HDR feature brings back the lost streaks of color.

To use HDR, tap HDR at the top of the screen. It has three settings: On, Off, and Auto. Auto means "Use your judgment, iPhone. If you think this scene would benefit, please use HDR automatically." Take your best shot.

> **TIP:** Should the phone save a standard shot in addition to the HDR shot? That's up to you. In Settings→Photos & Camera, you'll find the on/off switch for Keep Normal Photo.

When you inspect your photos later in the Photos app, you'll know which ones were taken with HDR turned on; when you tap the photo, you'll see the HDR logo at the upper-left corner.

Taking the Shot

All right. You've opened the Camera app. You've set up the focus, exposure, flash, grid, HDR, and zoom. If, in fact, your subject hasn't already left the scene, you can now take the picture. You can do that in any of three ways:

- Tap the shutter (◯) button.

- Press either of the physical volume buttons on the left edge of the phone.

  This option is fantastic. If you hold the phone with the volume buttons at the top, those buttons are right where the shutter would be on a real camera. Pressing one feels more natural than, and doesn't shake the camera as much as, tapping the screen.

- Press a volume button on your earbuds clicker—a great way to trigger the shutter without jiggling the phone in the process, and a more convenient way to take selfies when the phone is at arm's length.

Either way, if the phone isn't muted, you hear the *snap!* sound of a picture successfully taken.

You get to admire your work for only about half a second—and then the photo slurps itself into the thumbnail icon at the lower-left corner of the screen. To review the photo you just took, tap that thumbnail icon.

At this point, to look at other pictures you've taken, tap the screen and then tap All Photos.

This is your opportunity to choose a photo (or many) for emailing, texting, posting to Facebook, and so on; tap **Select**, tap the photos you want, and then tap the Share button (). See page 348.

> **TIP:** For details on copying your iPhone photos and videos back to your Mac or PC, see page 519.

Burst Mode

Every iPhone snaps photos over and over if you keep your finger pressed on the ◎ button or a volume key.

But the iPhone 5s and later models take them *quickly*—10 shots a second. That's a fantastic feature when you're trying to capture a moment that will be over in a flash: a golf swing, a pet trick, a toddler sitting still.

All you have to do is keep your finger pressed on the ◎ button or the volume key. A counter rapidly increments, showing you how many shots you've fired off.

> **TIP:** The front-facing camera can capture burst mode, too.

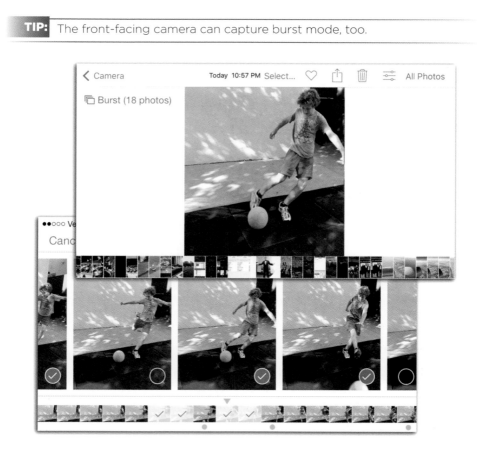

Better yet, the phone helps you **clean up the mess** afterward—the hassle of inspecting all 230 photos you shot, to find the ones worth keeping.

Tap the lower-left thumbnail. To help keep you sane, the iPhone depicts your burst as a single photo, with the phrase "Burst (72 photos)" (or whatever) in the corner of the screen. (In the Camera Roll, its thumbnail bears multiple frames, as though it were a stack of slides.)

Here's where it gets cool.

If you tap Select, you see all frames of the burst in a horizontally scrolling row. Underneath, you see an even smaller "filmstrip" of them—and a few of them are marked with dots.

These are the ones the iPhone has decided are the keepers. It does that by studying the clarity or blur of each shot, examining how much one frame is different from those around it, and even skipping past shots where somebody's eyes are closed. Tap the marked thumbnails to see if you approve of the iPhone's selections.

Whether you do or not, you should work through the larger thumbnails in the burst, tapping each one you want to keep. (The circle in the corner sprouts a blue checkmark.)

When you tap Done, the phone asks: "Would you like to keep the other photos in this burst?" Tap Keep Everything to preserve all the shots in the burst, so you can return later to extract a different set of frames; or Keep Only 2 Favorites (or whatever number you selected) to discard the ones you skipped.

Self-Portraits (the Front Camera)

The iPhone has a second camera on the front, above the screen. It lets you use the screen itself as a viewfinder to frame yourself, experiment with your expression, and check your teeth.

To activate the front camera in the Camera app, tap the 🔄. Suddenly, you see yourself on the screen. Frame the shot, and then tap ◯ to take the photo.

Now, don't get your expectations too high. The front camera is not the back camera. It's OK on the 6s and 7 models (5 megapixels, plus that cool screen flash)—but older models offer much lower resolution, lower quality, and no flash.

But when your goal is a well-framed self-portrait that you'll use on the screen—email or the web, for example, where resolution isn't very important—then having the front-camera option is better than not having it.

The Self-Timer

A self-timer is essential when you want to be in the picture yourself; you can prop the phone on something and then run into the scene. It's also a great way to prevent camera shake (which produces blurry photos), because your finger doesn't touch the phone.

Just tap the ⏱, and then tap **3s** (a 3-second countdown) or **10s** (a 10-second countdown).

Now, when you tap ◎ or press a volume key, you get a countdown: Huge digits on the screen if you're using the front camera, blinking flash if you're using the rear camera. After the countdown, the phone takes the picture all by itself. (If the sound is on, you'll hear the shutter noise.)

Correction: The phone takes **10** pictures, in burst mode. The phone assumes that if you're using the self-timer, then you won't be able to see when everybody's eyes are open. So it takes 10 shots in a row; you can weed through them later to find the best shot.

> **TIP:** The self-timer is available for both the front and back cameras. In other words, it's also handy for selfies.

Filters

Square photos weren't the only influence that Apple felt from the popularity of Facebook's Instagram app. It also became clear that the masses want *filters*, special effects that degrade the color of your photo in artsy ways. (They can affect either square or regular photos.) You, too, can make your pictures look old, washed-out, or oversaturated.

You can turn on the filter *before* you take the shot, so you can see how it'll look.

- **To filter before you shoot.** Tap ⊛ to view your options. You see a tic-tac-toe board of eight color filters (and black-and-white filters); None is always in the center.

  Tap a filter thumbnail to try it. Each turns your photo into a variation of black-and-white or plays with its saturation (color intensity). If you find one that looks good, take the shot as usual.

  To turn off the filters, tap the ⊛ icon again and tap None.

> **NOTE:** You can always unfilter a filtered shot later, if you prefer the original. Just tap the ⊛ icon to open the palette of filters—and this time, tap None.

- **To filter after you shoot.** You can also apply a filter to any photo you've already taken, as described on page 291.

> **TIP** And if you love one particular filter, iOS 10 lets you keep it turned on all the time. Open Settings→Photos & Camera→Preserve Settings and turn on Photo Filter.

Live Photos (iPhone SE, 6s, and 7)

A Live Photo is a weird new entity: a still photo with a 3-second video attached (with sound). You can take them only with the SE, 6s, or 7 phones, but you can play them back on any iPhone or the Mac.

What you're getting is 1.5 seconds before the moment you snapped the photo, plus 1.5 seconds after. In the Camera app, the ◉ icon at the top lets you know whether or not you're about to capture the 3-second video portion when you take a still. (The factory setting, yellow, means On.)

> **TIP:** When you take a Live Photo, remember to hold the phone still both before and after you tap the ◉ button! That's when the phone is recording those 3 seconds of video.
>
> A yellow "Live" label appears for 3 seconds, while the video is being captured. That's a warning to keep the phone still longer than you ordinarily would, so that it can complete the video capture. (If you forget, and you drop your hand too soon, iOS is smart enough to autodelete the blurry garbage that results at the end of the shot.)

Now, your obvious concern might be file size. "The iPhone takes 12-megapixel photos," you might say. "Well, video has 30 frames a second! One Live Photo must take up 90 times as much storage as a still image!"

Fortunately, no. The actual photo *is* a full 12-megapixel shot. But the other frames of the Live Photo contain only enough pixels to fill the phone's screen—not even 1 megapixel per frame. (And a Live Photo stores only 15 frames a second, not 30.) Overall, an entire Live Photo takes up about *twice* as much space as a still photo.

That's still around 4 megabytes a shot, though, so be careful about leaving Live Photos turned on for everyday shooting. To prevent it from turning itself back on again every time you open the Camera app, open Settings→Photos & Camera→Preserve Settings and turn on Live Photo.

Reviewing Live Photos

As you flick through the photos you've taken (in the Photos app), you'll know when a photo is a Live Photo; you'll see it animate for a half-second.

To play the full 3-second video with sound, press hard on it with your finger. (See page 35 for more on force-touching.)

NOTE: The SE doesn't offer 3D Touch, but you can long-press a Live Photo you've shot to make it move.

Sharing Live Photos

But what happens if you try to send a Live Photo to some other device? Well, first of all, you'll know that you're about to share a Live Photo. After you tap ⬆, a special "Live" icon, shown on the next page, reminds you.

You can tap to turn off that logo before you send, so that you're sharing only the still photo.

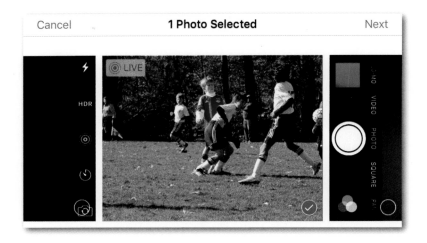

You can't *email* a Live Photo with its video intact. Even if you send it to another iPhone SE, 6s, or 7, only the still image survives the journey.

On the other hand, you can post Live Photos to Facebook and Tumblr, where they "play" just fine. And a free app called Motion Stills turns Live Photos into GIFs or movies that you can edit outside the Photos app—and even import into iMovie for even more advanced editing.

If you proceed with the Live Photo turned on, what happens next depends on what kind of device receives it.

If it's running recent Apple software (iOS 9 or later, OS X El Capitan or later), then the Live Photo video plays on that gadget, too. On the Mac, in Photos, click Live Photo to play it. On an iPad or older iPhone, hold your finger down on it to play it back.

What if it's a device or software program that doesn't know about Live Photos—if you send it as a text message, for example, or open it in Photoshop? Behind the scenes, a Live Photo has two elements: a 12-megapixel JPEG still image and a 3-second QuickTime movie. In these situations, only the JPEG image arrives at the other end.

Portrait Mode

The 7 Plus has two camera lenses: one wider angle, the other a 2x zoom. Clever software lets you blend the zoom to any degree between them (page 269).

But the two-lens setup has a second benefit: It lets the camera tell the foreground subject apart from its background. And with that knowledge, the phone can create a soft blurry-background look. Shown below at left, the original shot; at right, the blurred one:

Ordinarily, you see that look only in professional photos, or at least photos taken with big black SLR cameras using high-aperture lenses (f/1.8, for example). But now you can do it with your phone.

The blur in this case is not optically created, the way an SLR makes it. This is a glorified Photoshop filter; it's done with software.

Still, the effect generally looks fantastic, even when the outline of the subject is complex (like frizzy hair).

Once you've scrolled through the Camera app's modes to **Portrait**, point the camera at someone who's standing between 15 inches and 8 feet away. You see the background blur, right there in the preview image. Take the shot.

If a second person is standing within the range, you can tap the screen to make *that* person the subject.

In **Settings→Photos & Camera**, you can turn on **Keep Normal Photos** for this depth effect. It means, "For each Portrait photo I take, save two images—one with and one without the blur."

Now, Portrait mode doesn't always work. It can get confused when the light is dim, like in a bar or restaurant; when the subject is covered with a repeating pattern; when your subject is reflective, like a shiny bottle; or when your subject is not in that 15-inches-to-8-feet range. In those instances, you may get bleed blur, where the blurriness leaks into the subject like some kind of hideous, detail-eating virus.

As long as the light and the distance are right, though, the results are surprisingly good.

Soon, the Flickrs and Facebooks of the world will start teeming with great-looking, blurry-background photos—taken by iPhones.

Square Mode

No longer do you have to download a special app (*cough* Instagram *cough*) just to take perfectly square photos, the way all the cool kids do these days. Just swipe across the screen until you enter Square mode.

In Square mode, the photos the Camera app takes are square instead of rectangular (4 × 3 proportions). Otherwise, everything you've read in this chapter, and will read, is exactly the same in Square mode.

Pano Mode

Here's one of the best camera features of the iPhone: panoramic photographs. The iPhone lets you capture a 240-degree, ultra-wide-angle photo (63 megapixels on the 6s and 7!) by swinging the phone around you in an arc. The phone creates the panorama in real time; you don't have to line up the sections yourself.

TIP: On the iPhone 5s and later, the Panorama mode smoothly adjusts the exposure of the scene as you pan. That fixes one of the most frustrating aspects of other cameras, which use the same exposure all the way across their panoramas; you discover that the sunlit part of the scene is blown out and the shadowy parts are way too dark.

Next time you're standing at the edge of the Grand Canyon—or anything else that requires a *really* wide or tall angle—keep this feature in mind.

In the Camera app, swipe leftward until you reach Pano mode.

TIP: The big white arrow tells you which way to move the phone. But you can reverse it (the direction) just by tapping it (the arrow) before you begin.

Tap ◎ (or press a volume key). Now, as instructed by the screen, swing the phone around you—smoothly and slowly, please. You can pan either horizontally or (to capture something very tall) vertically.

As you go, the screen gives you three kinds of feedback:

- It says "Slow down" if you start swinging too fast. Truth is, as far as the iPhone is concerned, the slower the better.

- It says "Move up" or "Move down" if you're not keeping the phone level. Use the big white arrow itself like a carpenter's level; you'll leave the center line if you're not staying level as you move your arm.

- The preview of your panorama builds itself as you move. That is, you're seeing the final product, in miniature, while you're still taking it.

You'll probably find that 240 degrees—the maximum—is a *really* wide angle. You'll feel twisted at the waist. But you can end the panorama at any stage, just by tapping the ◉ button.

At that point, you'll find that the iPhone has taken a very wide, amazingly seamless photograph at very high resolution (over 16,000 pixels wide). If a panorama is *too* wide, you can crop it, as described later in this chapter.

If you snap a real winner, you can print it out at a local or online graphics shop, frame it, and hang it above the entire length of your living-room couch.

Video Mode

The iPhone can record sharp, colorful video. It's at the best flavor of high definition (1080p), or even 4K (on the 6s and 7 models)—and it's stabilized to prevent hand jerkiness, just like a real camcorder. The 5s offers a gorgeous, 120-frames-per-second *slow-motion* mode that turns even frenzied action into graceful, liquidy visual ballet; the 6 and later models can manage *240* frames per second, for even more fluid, slowed-down videos.

Using video is almost exactly like taking stills. Open the Camera app. Swipe to the right until you've selected Video mode. You *can* hold the iPhone either vertically or horizontally while you film. But if you hold it upright, most people on the Internet will spit on you; tall-and-thin videos don't fit the world's horizontal screens, including YouTube, laptops, and TVs.

> **TIP:** When you switch from still-photo mode to video, you may notice that the video image on the screen suddenly jumps bigger, as though it's zooming in. And it's true: The iPhone is oddly more "zoomed in" in camcorder mode than in camera mode.

Tap to compute focus, exposure, and white balance, as described on the previous pages. (You can even hold your finger down to trigger the exposure and focus locks, or drag the tiny yellow sun to adjust exposure manually, as described earlier.)

Then tap Record (◎)—or press a volume key—and you're rolling! As you film, a time counter ticks away at the top.

A Note About Resolution—and 4K Video

Video generally plays back at 30 frames a second. But the iPhone 6 and later models can do something only expensive cameras do: They can record and play back *60* frames a second. Video you shoot this way has a smoothness and clarity that's almost surreal. (It also takes up twice as much space on your phone.)

The on/off switch for 60 fps is in Settings→Photos & Camera. Turn on Record at 60 FPS. Experiment; see if you feel that the result is worth the sacrifice of storage space.

This is also, by the way, where you turn on 4K video recording on the 6s and 7 models.

4K televisions, also called Ultra HD, are TV sets with four times as many tiny pixels as an HDTV set, for four times the clarity. Eventually, there will be 4K televisions, 4K computer screens, 4K camcorders, and even 4K phone screens. For now, though, 4K screens are fairly rare—and shows to watch in 4K are rarer still.

4K shooting is *not* the factory setting for the iPhone 6s and 7, and that's a good thing; 4K takes up a huge amount of storage space (375 megabytes a minute).

Furthermore, you probably don't have anywhere to *play back* 4K video you've captured with this phone! Paradoxically, the iPhone itself doesn't have enough pixels to play 4K video. And don't think you can play them to your TV wirelessly using an Apple TV; even the Apple TV can't handle 4K TV.

You can post 4K video to YouTube—but even then, very few people have computer screens or TV screens capable of playing it back in 4K.

Things to Do While You're Rolling

Once you've begun capturing video, don't think your work is done. You can have all kinds of fun during the recording. For example:

- **Change focus.** You can change focus while you're filming, which is great when you're panning from a nearby object to a distant one. Refocusing is automatic, just as it is on camcorders—and it's especially quick and smooth on the iPhone 6 and later models. But you can also force a refocusing (for example, when the phone is focusing on the wrong thing) by tapping in your "viewfinder" to specify a new focus point. The iPhone recalculates the focus, white balance, and exposure at that point, just as it does when you're taking stills.

- **Change exposure.** While you're recording, you can drag your finger up or down to make the scene brighter or dimmer.

- **Zoom in.** You can zoom in while you're rolling, up to 3x actual size. Just spread two fingers on the screen, like you would to magnify a photo. Pinch two fingers to zoom out again. (On the iPhone 7 Plus, you can either do that two-finger spreading or drag the little 1x button to the left, as described on page 270.)

TIP: Once you start to zoom, a zoom *slider* appears on the screen. It's much easier to zoom smoothly by dragging its handle than it is to use a two-finger pinch or spread.

So here's a smart idea: Zoom in slightly before you start recording, so that the zoom slider appears on the screen. Then, during the shot, drag its handle to zoom in, as smoothly as you like.

- **Take a still photo.** Yes, you can even snap still photos *while* you're capturing video. Just tap the ◯ that appears while you're filming. Awesome.

NOTE: The pictures you take while filming don't have the same dimensions as the ones you take in Photo mode. These have 16:9 proportions, just like the video; they're not as tall as still photos.

When you're finished recording, tap Stop (◉). The iPhone stops recording and plays a chime; it's ready to record another shot.

There's no easier-to-use camcorder on earth. And what a lot of capacity! Each individual shot can be an hour long—and on the 256-gigabyte iPhone, you can record *136 hours* of video. Just long enough to capture the entire elementary-school talent show.

The Front Camera

You can film yourself, too. Just tap 📷 before you film to make the iPhone use its front-mounted camera, so that the screen shows *you*. The resolution isn't as high (the video isn't as sharp) as what the back camera captures, but it's still high definition.

The Video Light

You know the LED "flash" on the back of the phone? You can use it as a video light, too, supplying some illumination to subjects within about 5 feet or so. Just tap the ⚡ icon and then tap **On** before you start capturing. (Alas, you have to turn the light on before you start rolling. You can't turn it on or off in the middle of a shot.)

Slo-Mo Mode

If you have a 5s or later, your Camera app has an additional mode called Slo-Mo. (Swipe the screen to the right until Slo-Mo is selected.)

Capturing video in this mode is exactly like capturing video the regular way—but, behind the scenes, the phone is recording 120 or 240 frames a second instead of the usual 30.

> **NOTE:** The iPhone 5s records at 120 frames a second. The iPhone 6 and later, however, can record at *either* 120 or 240 frames per second. You make your choice in Settings→Photos & Camera.

When you open the captured movie to watch it, you'll see something startling and beautiful: The clip plays at full speed for 1 second, slows down to one-quarter or one-eighth speed, and, for the final second, accelerates back to full speed. It's a great way to study sports action, cannonball dives, and shades of expression in a growing smile.

What you may not realize, however, is that you can adjust *where* the slow-motion effect begins and ends in the clip. When you open the video for playback and then hit Edit, a strange kind of ruler track appears just below it. Drag the vertical handles inward or outward to change the spot where the slow motion begins and ends.

At the very bottom of the screen is a second, taller strip; you use this one to trim the ends off the video (see below) or to scroll quickly through the clip to see where you are.

Time-Lapse Mode

Whereas Slo-Mo mode is great for slowing down *fast* scenes, the Time-Lapse mode speeds up *slow* scenes: flowers growing, ice melting, candles burning, and so on.

Actually, this mode might better be called *hyperlapse*. Time-lapse implies that the camera is locked down while recording. But in a hyperlapse video, the camera is moving. This mode works great for bike rides, hikes, drives, plane trips, and so on; it compresses even multihour events down to under a minute of playback, with impressive smoothness.

So how much does the Time-Lapse mode speed up the playback? Answer: It varies. The longer you shoot, the greater the speed-up. The app accelerates every recording enough to play back in 20 to 40 seconds, whether you film for 1 minute, 100 minutes, or 1,000 minutes.

If you film for less than 20 seconds, your video plays back at 15 times original speed. But you can film for much, much longer, like 30 hours or more. Time-Lapse mode speeds up the result from 15x, 240x, 960x—whatever it takes to produce a 20- to 40-second playback.

Trimming a Video

To review whatever video you've just shot, tap the ⬚ thumbnail icon at the lower corner of the screen. You've just opened up the video playback screen. Tap ▶ to play the video.

At this point, if you tap the Edit button (⚏), you can trim off the dead air at the beginning and the end.

To do that, drag the **(** and **)** markers (currently at the outer ends of the little filmstrip) inward so that they turn yellow, as shown below. Adjust them, hitting ▶ to see the effect as you go.

TIP: You can drag the playback cursor—the vertical white bar that indicates your position in the clip—with your finger. That's the closest thing you get to Rewind and Fast-Forward buttons. (In fact, you may have to move it out of the way before you can move the end handles for trimming.)

When you've positioned the handles so that they isolate the good stuff, tap **Done**. Finally, tap either **Trim Original** (meaning "Shorten the original clip permanently") or Save as New Clip (meaning "Leave the original untouched, and spin out the shortened version as a separate video, just in case").

iMovie for iPhone

Of course, there's more to editing than just snipping dead air from the ends of a clip. That's why Apple made iMovie for iPhone. It's free on a new iPhone or $5 if it didn't come with your phone.

Editing Photos

Yes, kids, it's true: You can crop and edit your pictures right on the phone. The tools Apple gives you in the Photos app aren't exactly Photoshop, but they come surprisingly close. And in iOS 10, you can use all of them on Live Photos without affecting their "liveness."

TIP: Whenever you're in editing mode, **tap the screen** for a momentary flashback to the original image. Great for A/B comparisons.

To edit a photo, tap its thumbnail (anywhere in the Photos app) to open it. Tap anywhere to make the controls appear; tap ⇄ at the bottom.

Now you get a set of unlabeled buttons. Between Cancel and Done, you'll find the Crop/Straighten, Filters, and Adjust Color buttons; on the opposite side of the photo, there's Auto-Enhance and, on certain iPhone 6s and 7 shots, Live Photo Off. Read on.

Auto-Enhance (✨)

When you tap this magical button, the iPhone analyzes the relative brightness of all the pixels in your photo and attempts to "balance" it. After a moment, the app adjusts the brightness and contrast and intensifies dull or grayish-looking areas. Usually, the pictures look richer and more vivid as a result.

You may find that Auto-Enhance has little effect on some photos, only minimally improves others, and totally rescues a few. In any case, if you don't care for the result, you can tap the ✨ button again to turn Auto-Enhance off.

Adjust Color (⊙)

The people have spoken: They want control over color, white balance, tint, and so on.

So when you tap ⊙, you're offered three adjustment categories: Light, Color, and B&W.

When you tap one of these categories, you see a "filmstrip" below or beside your photo. You can drag your finger across it, watching the effect on your photo.

As it turns out, each of these sliders controls a handful of variables, all of which it's changing simultaneously. For example, adjusting the Light slider affects the exposure, contrast, brights, and darks all at once (below, left).

Intriguingly, you can tap ⊙ or ☰ to see how the master slider has affected these qualities—or even adjust these sub-sliders yourself (below, right). For example:

- **Light.** When you drag your finger along the Light filmstrip, you're adjusting the exposure and contrast of the photo. Often, a slight tweak is all it takes to bring a lot more detail out of the shot.

> **TIP:** Actually, when you're making any of the adjustments described on these pages, you don't have to drag across the *filmstrip*. You can drag your finger left or right across *the photo itself*—a bigger target.

For much finer control, tap the ⊙ or ☰ icon. You open your "drawer" of additional controls: Brilliance (a new iOS 10 slider that, Apple says, "brightens dark areas and pulls in highlights to reveal hidden detail"), Exposure (adjusts the brightness of all pixels), Highlights (pulls lost details out of very bright areas), Shadows (pulls lost details out of very dark areas), Brightness (like Exposure, but doesn't brighten parts that are already bright), Contrast (heightens the difference between the brightest and darkest areas), and **Black Point** (determines what is "black"; shifts the entire dark/light range upward or downward). Once again, you drag your finger along the "film strip" to watch the effect on your photo.

- **Color.** The **Color** filmstrip adjusts the tint and intensity of the photos' colors. Here again, just a nudge can sometimes liven a dull photo or make blue skies "pop" just a little more.

  Tap ⊙ or ☰ to see the three sliders that make up the master **Color** control. They are **Saturation** (intensity of the colors—from vivid fake-looking Disney all the way down to black and white), **Contrast** (deepens the most saturated colors), and **Cast** (adjusts the color tint of the photo, making it warmer or darker overall).

- **B&W** stands for black and white. The instant you touch this filmstrip, your photo goes monochrome, like a black-and-white photo. It's hard to describe exactly what happens when you drag your finger—you just have to try it—except to note that the app plays with the relative tones of blacks, grays, and whites, creating variations on the black-and-white theme.

  Tap ⊙ or ☰ to see the component sliders: **Intensity** (the strength of the lightening/darkening effect), **Neutrals** (brightness of the middle grays), **Tone** (intensifies the brightest and darkest areas), and **Grain** (simulates the "grain"—the texture—of film prints; the farther you move the slider, the higher the "speed of the film" and the more visible the grain).

> **TIP:** You can perform all these adjustments with the phone held either horizontally or vertically. The filmstrip jumps to the right side or the bottom of the screen accordingly.

At any point, you can back out of what you're doing by tapping ☰. For example, if you're fiddling with one of the **Color** sub-sliders (**Contrast** or **Saturation**, for example), tapping ☰ returns you to the view of the three master sliders (**Light**, **Color**, and **B&W**).

And, of course, you can tap **Cancel** to abandon your editing altogether, or **Done** to save the edited photo and close the editing controls.

It might seem a little silly trying to perform these Photoshop-like tweaks on a tiny phone screen, but the power is here if you need it.

Filters (⊗)

Filters are effects that make a photo black and white, oversaturated, or washed out. If you have an iPhone 5 or later, you can apply a filter as you take the picture (page 276); no matter which phone you have, though, you can apply a filter to an existing photo here.

Tap the ⊗ button to view a horizontally scrolling row of filter buttons. Tap each to see what it looks like on your photo; finish up by tapping **Apply** or **Cancel**. (You can always restore the photo's original look later—by returning to this screen and tapping **None**.)

(Don't these filters more or less duplicate the effects of the **Light**, **Color**, and **B&W** sliders described already? Yes. But filters produce canned, one-tap, instant changes that don't require as much tweaking.)

> **TIP:** It may look like you've just filtered that picture forever. But in fact you can return to it later and apply the **None** filter to it, thereby restoring it to its original, pristine condition.

Remove Red Eye (⬦)

Red eye is a common problem in flash photography. This creepy, possessed look—devilish, glowing-red pupils in your subjects' eyes—has ruined many an otherwise great photo.

Red eye is caused by light reflected back from eyes. The bright light of your flash illuminates the blood-red retinal tissue at the back of the eyes. That's why red-eye problems are worse when you shoot pictures in a dim room: Your subjects' pupils are dilated, allowing even *more* light from your flash to reach their retinas.

The Red-Eye button appears only if the phone detects that the flash fired when the photo was taken. (It appears at top left on the iPhone 6 and later, or top middle on earlier models.)

When you tap this button, a message says "Tap each red-eye." Do what it says: Tap with your finger inside each eye that has the problem. A little white ring appears around the pupil (unless you missed, in which case the ring shudders side to side, as though saying, "Nope")—and the app turns the red in each eye to black.

> **TIP:** It helps to zoom in first. Use the usual two-finger spread technique.

Crop/Straighten (⬚)

This button opens a crazy editing screen where you can adjust the size, shape, and angle of the photo.

When you tap ⬚, iOS analyzes whatever horizontal lines it finds in the photo—the horizon, for example—and uses it as a guide to straightening the photo *automatically*.

It's very smart, as you can see on the next page. See how the photo has been tilted slightly—and enlarged slightly to fill the frame without leaving triangular gaps?

You can reject the iPhone's proposal (tap **Reset**). Or you can tilt the photo more or less (drag your finger across the round scale), up to 90 degrees.

If you want to rotate the photo *more* than 90 degrees—for example, if the camera took it sideways—tap ↰ as many times as necessary to turn the picture upright.

The other work you can do in this mode is *cropping*.

Cropping means shaving off unnecessary portions of a photo. Usually, you crop a photo to improve its composition—adjusting where the subject appears within the frame of the picture. Often, a photo has more impact if it's cropped tightly around the subject, especially in portraits. Or maybe you want to crop out wasted space, like big expanses of background sky. If necessary, you can even chop a former romantic interest out of an otherwise perfect family portrait.

Cropping is also very useful if your photo needs to have a certain *aspect ratio* (length-to-width proportion), like 8 × 10 or 5 × 7.

To crop a photo you've opened, tap the ⟠. A white border appears around your photo. Drag inward on any edge or corner. The part of the photo that the iPhone will eventually trim away is darkened. You can recenter the photo within your cropping frame by dragging any part of the photo, inside or outside the white box. Adjust the frame and drag the photo until everything looks just right.

Ordinarily, you can create a cropping rectangle of any size and proportions, freehand. But if you tap ▦, you get a choice of eight canned proportions: Square, 3 × 2, 3 × 5, 4 × 3, and so on. They make the app limit the cropping frame to preset proportions.

This aspect-ratio feature is especially important if you plan to order prints of your photos. Prints come only in standard photo sizes: 4 × 6, 5 × 7, 8 × 10, and so on. But unless you crop them, the iPhone's photos are all 3 × 2, which doesn't divide evenly into most standard print photograph sizes. Limiting your cropping to one of these standard sizes guarantees that your cropped photos will fit perfectly into Kodak prints. (If you don't constrain your cropping this way, then Kodak—not you—will decide how to crop them to fit.)

TIP: The Original option here maintains the proportions of the original photo even as you make the grid smaller.

When you tap one of the preset sizes, the cropping frame **stays** in those proportions as you drag its edges. It's locked in those proportions unless you tap ▦ and choose a different setting.

Marking Up Your Photos

Here's an iOS 10 special that nobody saw coming: You can now draw or type on your photos, right from within the Photos app.

To access this new mode once you're in editing mode, tap ⊙ and then Markup.

In this new mode, you get a choice of three creative tools, plus Undo:

- **Draw.** Tap a colored dot to choose the ink color for your "pen." Tap the ☰ button for a menu of line thicknesses—or, on 6s and 7 models, press harder as you draw to get a thicker line. You can use the ↺ (Undo button) as often as you mess up.

Once you've drawn a line, a weird little two-button panel appears. It lets you convert the line or shape you just drew into **vector art** lines—editable, smooth, perfect, computer-generated line segments.

Tap the left side to leave the line as pixels. If you tap the right side, the line snaps into a computer-generated circle, square, or line segment (whichever most closely matches your doodle). You can drag its tiny handles to enlarge, move, or reshape this element, or change its color or line thickness (at least until you tap Done). Tap the screen to exit editing mode and draw another line.

NOTE: If you tap a shape you just drew, some buttons appear above it: Delete, Duplicate, and—if you've turned your scribble into a vector drawing—Edit. Edit, in this case, means "add some text inside the shape."

- **Enlarge a detail.** Tap the center ⊕ button to slap a magnified circular area onto your photo. Drag the blue handle to adjust the circle's size; drag the green one to adjust the degree of magnification inside it. And drag inside the circle to move it.

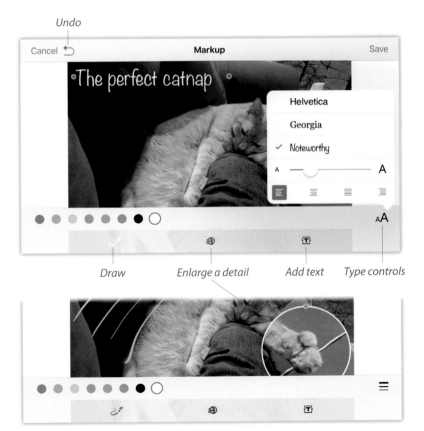

Undo

Cancel ↺   Markup   Save

Draw   Enlarge a detail   Add text   Type controls

You're not enlarging this for your own editing purposes; this magnified area will **stay** magnified when you send the photo. It's for calling your correspondent's attention to some detail.

- **Superimpose text.** The third button (T) adds a text box to the photo. Double-tap inside the box to summon the keyboard so that you can edit the "Text" dummy text (then tap Done). Drag the tiny blue handles to adjust the shape of the box; drag inside to move the box. Tap a color dot to change the color; tap A̲A for a menu of font, type size, and paragraph-justification options, as shown on the previous page.

Handing Off to Other Editing Apps

OK, Apple: Who are you, and what have you done with the company that used to believe in closed systems?

Maybe you're a fan of Camera+, Fragment, or some other photo app. Its tools can seem as though they're built right into the Photos app.

Here's the drill: Open a photo in Photos. Tap ⚏. Tap ☺. Now you see the icons of all apps on your phone that have been updated to work with this feature, which Apple calls Extensibility.

The photo opens immediately in the app you choose, with all of its editing features available. You can freely bounce back and forth between Apple's editor and its competitors'.

Saving Your Changes

Once you've rotated, cropped, auto-enhanced, or de-red-eyed a photo, tap the Done button. You've just made your changes permanent.

Or, rather, you've made them **temporarily** permanent. As noted, you can return to an edited photo at any time to undo the changes you've made (tap Revert). When you send the photo off the phone (by email, to your computer, whatever), **that** copy freezes the edits in place—but the copy on your phone is still revertable.

If you sync your photos to Photos, iPhoto, or Aperture on the Mac (over a cable), they show up in their edited condition. Yet, amazingly, you can undo or modify the edits there! The original photo is still lurking behind the edited version. You can use your Mac's Crop tool to adjust the crop, for example. Or you can use iPhoto's Revert to Original command to throw away **all** the edits you made to the original photo while it was on the iPhone.

(If you transfer the photos using email, AirDrop, or Messages, however, you get only the finished JPEG image; you **can't** rewind the changes.)

Managing and Sharing Photos

Once you've taken some photos, or copied them to your phone from your computer (see page 519), you'll have some pictures ready to view. You can learn how to edit them to perfection starting on page 287. But the Photos app has another job: presenting them, sharing them, and slideshowing them for all your fans.

TIP: The Photos app is fully rotational. That is, you can turn the phone 90 degrees. Whether you're viewing a list, a screen full of thumbnails, or an individual photo, the image on the screen rotates, too, for easier admiring. (Unless, of course, you've turned on the rotation lock, as described on page 25.)

At the bottom of the Photos app screen, four tabs lie in wait: **Photos**, **Memories**, **Shared**, and **Albums**. The next few sections explain what they do.

The Photos Tab

In the olden days, the Photos app displayed all your photos—thousands of them—in one endless, hopeless, scrolling mass. If you were hunting for a particular shot, you had to study the thumbnails with an electron microscope to find it.

Now, though, iOS groups them intelligently into sets that are easy to navigate. Here they are, from smallest to largest:

- **Moments.** A *moment* is a group of photos you took in one place at one time—for example, all the shots at the picnic by the lake. The phone even uses its GPS to give each moment a name: "San Francisco, California (Union Square)," for example.

TIP: If you tap a Moment's name, a map opens up; little photo thumbnails show exactly where these pictures were taken. Slick!

- **Collections.** Put a bunch of moments together, and what do you get? A collection. Here again, the phone tries to study the times and places of your photo taking—but this time it puts them into groups that might span a few days and several locations. You might discover that your entire spring vacation is a single collection, for example.

- **Years.** If you "zoom out" of your photos far enough, you wind up viewing them by year: 2014, 2015, 2016, and so on.

To "zoom in" from larger groupings to smaller ones (**Years**→**Collections**→ **Moments**), just tap each pile of thumbnails. If you tap a thumbnail on the Moments screen, you open that photo for viewing.

> **TIP:** When you first open a photo, it appears on a white background. Tap the photo to change the background to black, which often makes your photos' colors look better.

To "zoom out" again, tap the grouping name at top left (**Years**, for example).

> **TIP:** If you've opened a single photo for examination, you can retreat to the **moment** it came from by pinching with two fingers.

The last technique worth knowing is the Finger Browse. Whenever you're looking at a tiny grid of tiny thumbnail images (in a year or collection), hold your finger down within the batch. A larger thumbnail sprouts from your finger, as on this sunset shot here—

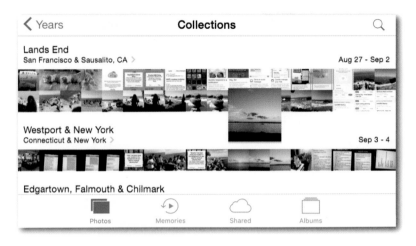

—and you can slide your finger around within the mosaic to find a particular photo, or batch of them.

The Memories Tab

Here's a big new feature of iOS 10: Memories. These are automatically selected groups of pix and videos from certain time periods or trips, which, with a tap, become gorgeous, musical slideshows. Most people are pleasantly surprised at how coherent and well-created these are, even though they're totally automatic. Photos, short pieces of your videos, and even scrolling panoramas are all first-class citizens in these slideshows.

Right off the bat, you see a few of Photos' suggestions, represented as clearly labeled billboards ("Cape Cod Summer," "Best of Last Week"...).

Tap to open a Memory; at this point, you can scroll down to see more about what's in this Memory. You'll see the photos that will be in it, as well as who's in it (People), and where the photos came from (Places).

At the very bottom, you'll see the option to **Delete Memory** or **Add to Favorite Memories**; that command adds this slideshow to a new folder on the *Albums* tab called Favorite Memories, for quick access later.

Anyway, the real fun begins when you tap ▶ to start an instant slideshow. They're usually fantastic.

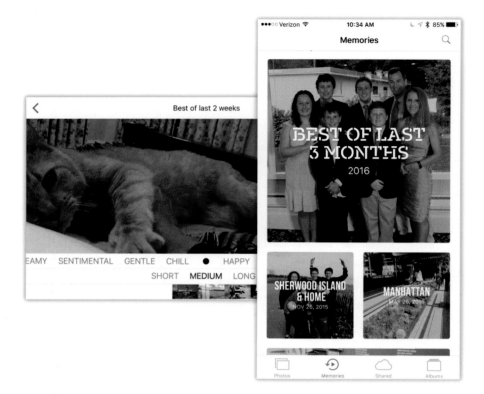

When you come back to your senses, note that you can tap the screen for some quick editing options. Drag horizontally to change the animation/music style (**Dreamy**, **Sentimental**, **Gentle**, **Chill**, and so on) or the slideshow length (**Short**, **Medium**, **Long**).

For more detailed editing, tap ⚏. Now you can edit the Memory's **Title** (name and typographical title style), **Music** (either the app's selections or anything from your music library), **Duration** (dial up any length you want), or **Photos & Videos** (tap + to add one, 🗑 to delete one).

> **TIP:** When you tap +, the resulting Select Photos screen shows you thumbnails of all candidate shots; checkmarks indicate the ones that Photos has chosen to include. Not only does this screen make it quick and easy to adjust which photos and videos appear in the Memory, but it also shows you how clever and selective Photos has been in the first place.

Once you've got a really killer Memory on your hands, by the way, don't miss the option to send it to other people as a standalone video. While a Memory slideshow is playing, tap it to reveal the 📤 button at the top.

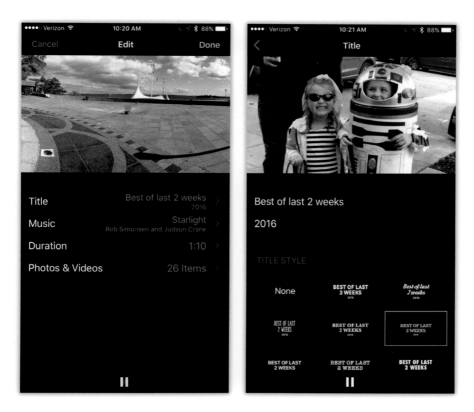

The Albums Tab

(The third tab is actually the Shared tab, but we're skipping over it for now; see page 318.)

The Albums tab is a scrolling list of specialized photo "folders" like these:

- **All Photos.** Yup—everything on your phone, including videos.

- **Favorites.** This folder gives you quick access to your favorite photos. And how does the phone know which photos are your favorites? Easy: You've told it. You've tapped the ♡ icon under a photo, anywhere within the Photos app. (Favorites must be photos you've taken with the phone, not transferred from your computer.)

- **Favorite Memories** appears only if you have, in fact, designated a Memory slideshow as a favorite (page 299).

- **People.** Impressively enough, Photos can auto-group the people in your photos, using facial recognition. Once you've given the software a running start, it can find those people in the rest of your photo collection automatically. That's handy every now and then—when you need a photo of your kid for a school project, for example.

To see it at work, tap People. Here are thumbnails representing the faces Photos has found and grouped, complete with a tally of how many photos Photos has found. At the top, you see people you've designated as Favorites.

Tap a thumbnail to see all the photos of this person. Scroll wayyyyy down to **Confirm Additional Photos** (Photos shows you other photos one at a time and asks, "Is this the same person?"); **Favorite** (or **Unfavorite**) **This Person**, and **Add to Memories** (creates a new Memory slideshow just of this person).

TIP: This feature doesn't work until the iPhone has *analyzed* your photos, which can take at least a day. Apple proudly points out that all this analysis is done on your phone. (That's in contrast to a service like Google Photos, which offers similar features but requires Google to access your photo library.)

If you don't see a thumbnail for a certain someone, scroll down and tap the + button to start the process of rounding up his or her pictures.

- **Places**. Every photo you take with a smartphone (and a few very fancy cameras) gets *geotagged*—stamped, behind the scenes, with its geographic coordinates. When you tap Places in the Albums list, you see a map, dotted with clusters of photos you took in each place. Tap one to see the photos you took there.

- **Videos, Selfies, Panoramas, Videos, Time-Lapse, Slo-Mo, Depth Effect, Bursts, Screenshots.** As a convenience to you, these categories give you one-tap shopping for everything you've captured using the Camera app's specialized picture and video modes. (Depth Effect appears only on the iPhone 7 Plus; it contains shots you've taken using Portrait mode [page 278].)

  Super handy when you're trying to show someone your latest time-lapse masterpiece, for example; now you know where to look for it.

- **Recently Deleted.** Even after you think you've deleted a photo or video from your phone, you have 30 days to change your mind. Deleted pictures and videos sit in this folder, quietly counting down to their own doomsdays.

  If you wind up changing your mind, you can open Recently Deleted, tap the photo you'd condemned, and tap Recover. It pops back into its rightful place in the Photos app, saved from termination.

  On the other hand, you can also zap a photo into oblivion immediately. Tap to open it, tap Delete, and then confirm with Delete Photo. If you tap Select, you can also hit Delete All or Recover All.

- **My Albums.** Here you get a list of albums that *you've* created (or copied to the phone from your Mac or PC).

As you'd guess, you can drill down from any of these groupings to a screen full of thumbnails, and from there to an individual photo.

> **TIP:** If you hold your finger down on the photo or even its thumbnail, a Copy button appears. That's one way to prepare for pasting a single photo into an email message, an MMS (picture or video) message to another phone, and so on.

Creating and Deleting Albums

You can manually add selected photos into new albums—a great way to organize a huge batch you've shot on vacation, for example.

To do that, open any one of your existing albums (including All Photos); tap Select; and then tap (or drag through) all the photos you want to move to a new or different album. Tap **Add To** at the bottom of the screen.

You're now offered an **Add to Album** screen. Tap the album into which you want to move these pictures. (If albums are dimmed, that's because they've been synced from your Mac or PC. You're not allowed to mess with them. The canned specialty-photo folders, like Panorama and Time-Lapse, are also dimmed, because only iOS can put things into those folders, and it does that automatically.)

This list also includes a **New Album** button; you're asked to type the name you want for the new album and then tap **Save**.

> **NOTE:** These buttons don't actually move photos out of their original albums. You're creating *aliases* of them—pointers to the original photos. If you edit a photo from one album, it's edited in all of them.

To delete an album you created on the phone, start on the main Albums tab. Tap **Edit**, and then tap the ⊖ button next to the album you want to delete.

Hide a Photo

Here's a quirky little feature: It's now possible to hide a photo from the Photos tab (Moments, Collections, and Years), so that it appears only on the Albums tab (in your albums and in a special Hidden folder).

Apple noticed that lots of people use their phones to take screenshots of apps, pictures of whiteboards or diagrams, shots of package labels or parking-garage signs, and so on. These images aren't scenic or lovely; they're not memories; they don't look good (or serve much purpose) when they appear nestled in with your shots-to-remember in Moments, Collections, and Years. (Hidden photos don't appear in slideshows, either.)

Open the photo and then tap the ⬆ button; in the Sharing options that appear, tap **Hide**. To confirm, tap **Hide Photo**.

Whatever photos you hide go to a new folder on the Albums tab—called, of course, **Hidden**, so that you can find them easily. From here, you can unhide a shot the same way: Hit ⬆ and then **Unhide**.

Flicking, Rotating, Zooming, Panning

Once a photo is open at full size, you have your chance to perform the four most famous and most dazzling tricks of the iPhone: flicking, rotating, zooming, and panning a photo.

- **Flicking** horizontally is how you advance to the next/previous picture or movie in the batch.

- **Zooming** a photo means magnifying it, and it's a blast. One quick way is to double-tap the photo; the iPhone zooms in on the portion you tapped, doubling its size.

  Another technique is to use the two-finger spread, which gives you more control over what gets magnified and by how much.

(If you've brought in photos from your computer, note that the iPhone doesn't store the giganto 20-megapixel originals you took with your fancy camera. It keeps only scaled-down, iPhone-sized versions, so you can't zoom in more than about three times the original size.)

Once you've spread a photo bigger, you can then pinch to scale it down again. Or just double-tap to restore the original size. (You don't have to restore a photo to original size before advancing to the next one, though; if you flick enough times, you'll pull the next photo onto the screen.)

- **Panning** is moving a photo around on the screen after you've zoomed in. Just drag your finger to do that; no scroll bars are necessary.

- **Rotating** is what you do when a horizontal photo or video appears on the upright iPhone, which makes the photo look small and fills most of the screen with blackness.

  Just turn the iPhone 90 degrees in either direction. Like magic, the photo rotates and enlarges to fill its new, wider canvas. No taps required. (This doesn't work when the phone is flat on its back—on a table, for example. It has to be more or less upright. It also doesn't work when Portrait Orientation is locked.)

This trick also works the other way: You can make a *vertical* photo fit better by turning the iPhone upright.

> **TIP:** When the iPhone is rotated, all the controls and gestures reorient themselves. For example, flicking right to left still brings on the next photo, even if you're now holding the iPhone the wide way.

Finding Photos

There's a search icon (Q) in Photos, which might seem odd. How can you search for a blob of pixels? How does the phone know what's *in* a picture?

Artificial intelligence, people. In iOS 10, Apple has given Photos the ability to recognize what's in your pictures and videos. You can search your photos for "dog," or "beach," or whatever.

To try it out, tap Q at the top of the Photos or Albums screens. Right off the bat, the phone offers some one-tap canned searches based on locations and dates (like One Year Ago and Home). Tap to see the photos and videos that match.

To search for something more specific, you can type either of two kinds of things:

- **A place, date, name, or album.** Try typing *september* or *tucson* or *bay area* or *2015*, for example. As you type, iOS displays all the photo groupings that match what you've typed so far. Tap that grouping to see the photo thumbnails within.

> **TIP:** Then again, it's usually faster to request such photos by voice, using Siri: "Show me all the photos from Texas in 2015." See page 165.

- **A noun.** Here's the new image-recognition feature. Type the photographic subject you're seeking, like forest, girl, plane, piano, food, pizza, mountain, or whatever. In the results list, Photos lists matching pictures under a Category heading, like Pizza Category or Cat Category (facing page, left). Tap to see what the phone has rounded up for you (facing page, right).

  As you'll soon discover, Apple's image recognition software makes a lot of mistakes; you may well find a bar code or a picket fence in your Piano category, or a truck in your Cars category. But hey—it's just software. Give it some slack.

TIP: You can also search for the data associated with a photo (time, place, album name), and **combine** that with a noun search to pinpoint a certain photo.

Deleting Photos

If some photo no longer meets your exacting standards, you can delete it. But this action is trickier than you may think.

- **If you took the picture using the iPhone,** no sweat. Open the photo; tap 🗑. When you tap Delete Photo, that picture is gone. Or, rather, it's moved to the Recently Deleted folder described on page 303; you have 30 days to change your mind.

  (If you open the photo from the Albums tab instead, you're just taking the picture out of that album—not actually deleting it from the phone.)

- **If the photo was synced to the iPhone from your computer,** well, that's life. The iPhone remains a **mirror** of what's on the computer. In other words, you can't delete the photo from the phone. Instead, delete it from the original album on your computer (which does **not** mean deleting it from the computer altogether). The next time you sync the iPhone, the photo disappears from it, too.

Photo Controls

If you tap the screen once after opening a photo, some useful controls appear. They show up either at the top or bottom of the screen, depending on how you're holding the phone. (Tap again to hide them and summon a black background, for a more impressive photo presentation.)

- **Album name.** Here's the group this photo came from.

- **Details.** Opens a scrolling screen, new in iOS 10, that explodes with resources for this photo, like a map of where it was taken (and the address); links to "related" shots (taken in the same place, or of the same people); and even a Show Photos from This Day link, which calls up all the *other* pictures you took that day.

- **Favorite (♡).** When you find a picture you really love—enough that you might want to call it up later to show people—tap ♡. This photo or video now appears in the Favorites folder (in the Albums tab of the Photos app, described earlier), so that it's easy to find with your other prize-winners. (The ♡ appears only on photos you've taken with the phone—not pictures you've imported from computers or other cameras.)

- **Share (⬆).** Tap ⬆ if you want to do something more with this photo than just stare at it. You can use it as your iPhone's wallpaper, print it, copy it, text it, send it by email, use it as somebody's headshot in your Contacts list, post it on Twitter or Facebook, and so on. These options are all described in the following pages.

- **Date and time.** The top of the screen says "September 13, 12:52 pm," for example, letting you know when this photo was taken.

- **Edit (⚙).** This button is the gateway to the iPhone's photo-editing features, described starting on page 287.

- **Delete (🗑).** Gets rid of this photo, as described earlier.

- **Other photos.** At the bottom of the screen, Photos thoughtfully displays a ribbon of tiny thumbnail images (in other words, *pinky*nail images). They represent the previous and following photos in this batch. By tapping or dragging, you can jump to another photo without having to back out of the opened-photo screen.

753 Ways to Use Photos and Videos

It's great that the iPhone has a great camera. But what's even greater is that it's also a cellphone. It's online. So once you've taken a picture, you can *do* something with it right away. Mail it, text it, post it to Facebook or Twitter, use it as wallpaper—right from the iPhone.

Step 1: Choose the Photos

Before you can send or post a photo or video, you have to tell iOS which one (or ones) you want to work with.

To send just one, well, there's no big mystery; tap its thumbnail, and then tap ⬆.

But you can also send a bunch of them in a group—whenever you see a Select button. Tap it and then individually select the photos you want to send. With each tap, a ✅ appears, meaning, "OK, this one will be included." (Tap again to remove the checkmark.)

Step 2: Preparing to Send

Once you've opened a photo (or selected a few), tap ⬆.

Now you have a huge array of "send my photo here" options, displayed in rows.

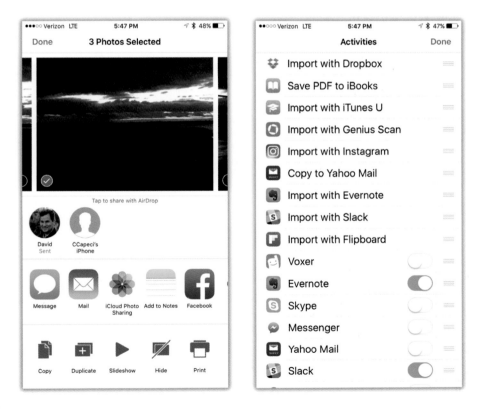

At the top of the Share screen, a scrolling row of other pictures appears. It lets you add more to the one(s) you've already selected, or deselect some that you already did. That's a lot less crazymaking than having to cancel out of the Share screen in order to change your selection of pictures.

TIP: If you're holding the phone horizontally, select the photos first and then tap Next to see the sharing icons.

All right, then. Here's an overview of the options available on the Share screen.

AirDrop

So very cool: You can shoot a photo, or several, to any nearby iPhone, iPad, iPod Touch, or Mac—wirelessly, securely, conveniently, and instantly. See page 348 for the step-by-steps.

Message

This row of Share options lists *apps* that can receive your photos and videos.

The Message icon lets you send a photo or video as a *picture or video message*. It winds up on the screen of the other guy's cellphone.

That's a delicious feature, which people exploit millions of times a day.

NOTE: If you're sending to another Apple gadget, like an iPhone, iPad, iPod Touch, or Mac, it will be sent as a free iMessage (assuming that the recipient has an iCloud account and has turned on the iMessages option). If you're sending to a non-Apple cellphone, it will be a regular MMS message. All of this is described in Chapter 6.

Tap Message and then specify the phone number of the recipient; if you're sending by iMessage, the email address also works. Or choose someone from your Contacts list. Then type a little note, tap Send, and off it goes.

NOTE: If you're sending a video, the iPhone compresses it first so that it's small enough to send as a text-message attachment (smaller dimensions, lower picture quality). Then it attaches the clip to an outgoing text message; it's your job to address it.

Mail

The iPhone automatically rotates and attaches your photos or video clips to a new outgoing message. All you have to do is address it and hit Send. If it's a big file, you may be asked how much you want the photo *scaled down* from its original size. Tap Small, Medium, Large, or Actual Size, using the megabyte indicator as a guide. (Some email systems don't accept attachments larger than 5 megabytes.)

(Any video clip you send by email gets compressed—smaller, lower quality—for the same reason.)

iCloud Photo Sharing

You can share batches of photos or videos with other people, either directly to their Apple gadgets or to a private web page. What's more, they can (at your option) contribute their *own* pictures to the album.

This is a big topic, though, so it gets its own write-up on page 318.

Add to Notes

Since the Notes app (page 404) can accommodate pasted pix or vids, why not?

A little box appears, inviting you to type some text into the newly illus-trated photo note. You can also plop this picture into either a new note page or an existing one, using the pop-up menu at lower right (and a *lot* of scrolling, since the pop-up menu has room for only four Note-page names at a time).

Twitter, Facebook, Flickr

If you've told your iPhone what your name and password are (in Settings→Twitter or Settings→Facebook or Settings→Flickr), then post-ing a photo from your phone to your Twitter feed, Facebook timeline, or Flickr collection is ridiculously simple.

Open the photo; tap the 🖅 button; tap Twitter, Facebook, or Flickr. You're offered the chance to type a message that accompanies your photo. (As usual with Twitter, you have a maximum of 140 characters for your message.) You can also tap Add Location if you want Twitterites or Facebookers to know where the photo was taken.

> **NOTE:** The Add Location option is available only if you've permitted Twitter or Facebook to use your location information, which you set up in Settings→Privacy→Location Services.

If you're posting to Facebook, you can also indicate whom you're sharing this item with—just your friends, everyone, and so on—by tapping Audience beneath the photo thumbnail. Flickr also offers a chance to specify which of your Flickr photo sets you want to post to.

When you tap Send or Post, your photo, and your accompanying tweet or post, zoom off to Twitter, Facebook, or Flickr for all to enjoy.

YouTube, Vimeo

Call up a video, if it's not already on the screen before you. Tap ⬆. The Share sheet offers these video-specific buttons:

- **YouTube.** The iPhone asks for your Google account name and password (Google owns YouTube). Next it wants a title, description, and *tags* (searchable keywords like "funny" or "babies").

  It also wants to know if the video will be in standard definition or high definition (and it gives the approximate size of the file). You should also pick a Category (Autos & Vehicles, Comedy, Education, or whatever).

  Finally, choose from Public (anyone online can search for and view your video), Unlisted (only people who have the link can view this video), or Private (only specific YouTubers can view). When everything looks good, tap Publish.

  After the upload is complete, you're offered the chance to see the video as it now appears on YouTube, or to Tell a Friend (that is, to email the YouTube link to a pal). Both are excellent ways to make sure your masterful cinematography gets admired.

- **Vimeo.** You're supposed to have set up your name and password in Settings for Vimeo (a video site a lot like YouTube, but classier, with a greater emphasis on quality and artistry).

  If you've done that, then all you have to do, when posting a video, is to specify a caption or a description, and then tap Details to choose a video size and who your audience is (public, private, and so on). Once you tap Post, your video gets sent on to the great cinema on the web.

Save PDF to iBooks

This button converts whatever photos you've selected into a single, multipage PDF document that opens in iBooks (page 378). In effect, it creates an ebook of your pictures.

After a moment of conversion, iBooks opens automatically so you can inspect the results. You can now use all the tools available in iBooks (bookmarking, annotating, and so on). Better yet, you can send the resulting PDF document to someone else—a handy way to share a no-frills batch of pictures.

More

In the modern, extendable iOS, you can hand off a photo to *other* apps and services—beyond the set that Apple provides. If you tap More, you get the screen shown on page 309 at right.

That screen is basically a setup headquarters for the row of "where you can send photos" icons. Here you can rearrange them (put the ones you use most often at the top by dragging the ≡ handle); add to the list (turn on the switches for new, non-Apple photo-sharing apps you've installed); or hide the services you don't use (turn off the switches). (You can't turn off the switches for Message, Mail, and iCloud Photo Sharing.)

Copy

The bottom row of sharing options lists things you can *do* to the selected photos.

The Copy button, for example, puts the photo(s) onto the Clipboard, ready for pasting into another app (an outgoing Mail message, for example). Once you've opened an app that can accept pasted graphics, double-tap to make the Paste button appear.

Duplicate

Makes a second copy of the photo. Handy if you intend to edit the original beyond recognition.

Slideshow

This button instantly generates a gorgeous, musically accompanied, animated slideshow.

After the slideshow has begun, tap Options to see controls like these:

- **Themes.** A theme is a canned presentation style, incorporating animations, crossfades, and music. Each makes the photos appear, interact, overlap, and flow away in a different way. You're offered five choices—Origami, Dissolve, Push, Magazine, and Ken Burns. (Some of these display more than one photo at a time.)

- **Music.** Choose one of the five pieces of background music here, opt for None, or tap iTunes Music to choose a song from your music collection.

- **Repeat.** Makes the slideshow play over and over again until you stop it manually.

- **Speed.** The slider controls how much time each photo gets.

The slideshow incorporates both photos and videos (with sound; the background music actually gets softer so you can hear the audio).

While the show is playing, here's what you can do:

- **Tap to summon** the ‖ button.

- **Turn the iPhone 90 degrees** to accommodate landscape-orientation photos as they come up; the slideshow keeps right on going.

- **Swipe leftward** to blow past a photo or video that's taking too long.

AirPlay

This button offers a list of nearby AirPlay gadgets—the only one you've probably heard of is Apple TV—so you can display the current photo on your TV or another screen.

Hide

Here's the option to hide a photo, as described on page 304.

Save Image

Suppose you're looking at a photo that you didn't take with the phone. Maybe someone texted or emailed it to you, for example. This button saves it into your own photo collection, so you'll be able to cherish it for years.

Assign to Contact

If you're viewing a photo of somebody who's listed in Contacts, then you can use it (or part of it) as her headshot. After that, her photo appears on your screen every time she calls. Just tap Assign to Contact.

Your address book list pops up. Tap the name of the person who goes with this photo.

Now you see a preview of what the photo will look like when that person calls. This is the Move and Scale screen. You want to crop the photo and shift it in the frame so only *that person* is visible (if it's a group shot)—in fact, probably just the face.

Start by enlarging the photo: Spread your thumb and forefinger against the glass. As you go, *shift* the photo's placement in the round frame with a one-finger drag. When you've got the person centered, tap Choose.

Use as Wallpaper

Wallpaper is the background photo that appears in either of two places: the Home screen (plastered behind your app icons) or the Lock screen (which appears every time you wake the iPhone).

This button lets you replace Apple's standard photos with one of your photos. It opens the Move and Scale screen, which lets you fit your photo within the wallpaper "frame." Pinch or spread to enlarge the shot; drag your finger on the screen to scroll and center it.

Finally, tap Set. You now specify where you want to use this wallpaper; tap Set Lock Screen, Set Home Screen, or Set Both (if you want the same picture in both places).

You can also change your wallpaper within Settings, as described on page 580.

Print

You can print a photo easily enough, provided that you've hooked up your iPhone to a compatible printer. Once you've opened the photo, tap the ⬆ button and then tap Print. The rest goes down as described on page 346.

Add to iCloud Drive

This button saves the selected pictures and videos to your "hard drive in the sky," the iCloud Drive (page 351). Thereafter, you can open them from any Mac, Windows PC, iPhone, or iPad. (Of course, you get only 5 gigabytes of free storage, so this isn't really a backup solution for your entire photographic output.)

More

Once again, iOS offers a way to rearrange the Share buttons (this time, the bottom row)—or to add new buttons. They appear automatically when you install certain apps that have photo-sharing capabilities.

My Photo Stream

The concept of My Photo Stream is simple: Every time a new photo enters your life—when you take a picture with your iPhone or import one onto your computer—it gets added to your Photo Stream. From there, it appears automatically on all your *other* Apple machines.

> **NOTE:** Photo Stream doesn't sync over the cellular airwaves. It sends photos around only when you're in a Wi-Fi hotspot.

Using Photo Stream means all kinds of good things:

- Your photos are always backed up. Lose your iPhone? No biggie— when you buy a new one, your latest 1,000 photos appear on it automatically.

- Any pictures you take with your iPhone appear automatically on your computer. You don't have to connect any cables or sync anything yourself.

> **TIP:** There's one exception. If you take a photo and then delete it while still in the Camera app, that photo won't enter your Photo Stream.
>
> A similar rule holds true with edits: If you edit a photo you've just taken, those edits become part of the Photo Stream copy. But if you take a photo, leave the Camera app, and *later* edit it, then the Photo Stream gets the original copy only.

Truth is, Photo Stream is a very old feature, one that Apple has long since expanded and replaced with iCloud Photo Library (page 323). But since Photo Stream is free, a lot of people still use it—as follows.

To turn *on* My Photo Stream, go to Settings→Photos & Camera→Upload to My Photo Stream. (You should also turn it on using the iCloud control panel on your computers. That's in System Preferences on your Mac, or in the Control Panel of Windows.) Give your phone some time in a Wi-Fi hotspot to form its initial slurping-in of all your most recent photos.

Once Photo Stream is up and running, you'll find a new album called My Photo Stream. It's in the Photos app on every iOS device, Mac, or Apple

TV you own (or have signed into using iCloud). Inside are the photos that have entered your life most recently.

NOTE: If you don't see this album, it's probably because you've turned on iCloud Photo Library, described on page 323. In that case, all your recent photos are in the All Photos album. There's no My Photo Stream album.

Now, your iPhone doesn't have nearly as much storage available as your Mac or PC; you can't yet buy an iPhone with 750 gigabytes of storage. That's why, on your phone, your My Photo Stream consists of just the last 1,000 photos. (There's another limitation, too: The iCloud servers store your photos for 30 days. As long as your gadgets go online at least once a month, they'll remain current with the Photo Stream.)

TIP: Ordinarily, the oldest of the 1,000 photos in your Photo Stream scroll away forever as new photos come in. But you can rescue the best ones from that fate—by saving them onto your phone, where they're free from the risk of automatic deletion. Use the **Save Images** button. Or, if you're viewing one open picture in My Photo Stream, tap ⬆ and then tap **Save to Camera Roll**.

Deleting Photos from the Photo Stream

Here's the thing about Photo Stream: You might think you're taking a private picture with your phone, forgetting that your spouse or parent will see it seconds later on the family iPad. It's only a matter of time before Photo Stream gets some politician in big trouble.

Fortunately, you can delete certain incriminating photos from your Photo Stream. Just select the thumbnail of the photo you want to delete, and then tap the Trash icon (🗑). The confirmation box warns you that you're about to delete the photo from all your Apple machines (and, for shared streams, the machines of everyone who's subscribed to your photographic output).

If you haven't saved it to a different album or roll, it's gone for good when you tap Delete Photo.

iCloud Photo Sharing

iCloud Photo Sharing is like having a tiny Instagram network of your very own, consisting solely of people you invite. You send photos or videos to **other** people's gadgets. After a party or some other get-together, you could send your best shots to everyone who attended; after a trip, you could post your photographic memories for anyone who might care.

The lucky recipients can post comments about your pix, click a "like" button to indicate their enthusiasm, or even submit pictures and videos of their own.

In designing this feature, Apple had quite a challenge. There's a lot of back-and-forth among multiple people, sharing multiple photos, so iCloud Photo Sharing can get complicated. Stay calm and keep your hands and feet inside the tram at all times. Here's how it works.

> **TIP:** Well, here's how it works *if* your equipment meets the requirements. These shared photo albums can show up on an i-gadget with iOS 7 or later; on a Mac with OS X Mavericks (10.9) or later and iPhoto 9.5 or Aperture 3.5 or later; on a PC with Windows 7 or later and the iCloud Control Panel 3.0; or on an Apple TV (2nd generation) with Software Update 6.0 or later.
>
> You also have to **turn on** the Photo Album feature. On an iOS gadget, the switch is in Settings→iCloud→Photos; turn on iCloud Photo Sharing. On the Mac, open System Preferences→iCloud. Make sure Photos is turned on; click Options and confirm that Photo Sharing is on, too. On a Windows PC, it's in the iCloud Control Panel for Windows (a free download from Apple's website).

Create a Shared Photo Album

To share some of your masterpieces with your adoring fans, do this:

1. **Create the empty album.** Open the Photos app. On the Shared tab, scroll to the top (if necessary) and tap +.

2. **Name the new album.** In the Shared Album box, name the Photo Album ("Bday Fun" or whatever). Tap Next.

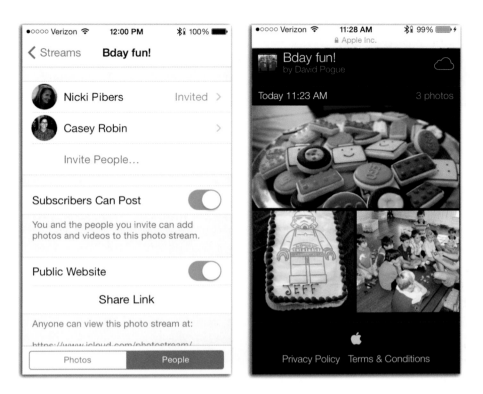

3. **Specify the audience.** You're asked for the email addresses of your lucky audience members; enter their addresses in the "To:" box just as you would address an outgoing email.

   For your convenience, a list of recent sharees appears below the "To:" box.

   When that's done, tap Create. You return to the list of shared albums, where your newly named album appears at the top. It is, however, completely empty.

4. **Pour some photos or movies into the album.** Tap your new, empty album's name. Then, on the next screen, tap the + to burrow through your photos and videos—you can use any of the three tabs (Photos, Shared, Albums)—to select the material you want to share. Tap their thumbnails so that they sprout checkmarks, and then tap Done.

   A little box appears so that you can type up a description.

5. **Type a description of the new batch.** In theory, you and other people can add to this album later. That's why you're offered the chance to caption each new batch.

   Once that's done, tap Post.

The thumbnails of the shared photos and videos appear before you—and the + button is there, too, in case you want to add more pictures later.

> **TIP:** You can easily *remove* photos from the album, too. On this screen of thumbnails, tap Select; tap the thumbnails you want to nuke; tap 🗑; and confirm by tapping Delete Photo.

Adjusting an Album's Settings

Before you set your album free, tap the People tab at the bottom of the screen. Here are a few important options to establish for this album:

- **Invite People.** This list identifies everyone with whom you've shared the album. To add a new subscriber, tap Invite People. To delete a subscriber, tap the name and then (at the bottom of the contact card) tap Remove Subscriber.

- **Subscribers Can Post.** Your subscribers can contribute photos and videos to your album. That's a fantastic feature when it contains pictures of an event where there was a crowd: a wedding, show, concert, picnic, badminton tournament. Everyone who was there can enhance the gallery with shots taken from their own points of view with their own phones or cameras.

- **Public Website.** If you turn on Public Website, then even people who aren't members of the Apple cult will be able to see these photos. The invitees will get an email containing a web address. It links to a hidden page on the iCloud website that contains your published photos.

  When you turn this switch on, the web address of your new gallery appears in light-gray type. Tap Share Link for a selection of methods for sending the link to people: by Message, Mail, Twitter, Facebook, AirDrop, and so on.

  What they'll see is a mosaic of pictures, laid out in a grid on a single sort of web poster. Your fans can download their favorites by clicking the ☁ button. (You can't add comments or "like" photos on the web, however.)

  > **TIP:** If you click one of these medium-sized photos, you enter slideshow mode, in which one photo at a time fills your web browser window. Click the arrow buttons to move through them.

- **Notifications.** If this switch is on, then your phone will show a banner each time someone adds photos or videos to your album, clicks the "Like" button for a photo, or leaves a comment.

- **Delete Shared Album.** That's right: If the whole thing gets out of hand, you can slam the door in your subscribers' faces by making the entire album disappear.

Read on to see what it's like to be the person whose email address you entered.

Receiving a Photo Album on Your Gadget

When other people share Photo Albums with *you*, your phone makes a little warble, and a notification banner appears: "[Your buddy's name] invited you to join '[name of shared photo batch]'."

Simultaneously, a badge like (**2**) appears on the Photos app icon and on the Shared tab within Photos, letting you know how many albums have come your way.

TIP: If you have iPhoto, Photos, or Aperture on a Mac, an invitation to accept the album appears there, too.

As you'd guess, you can tap the new album's name to see what's inside it; tap Accept if you're sure.

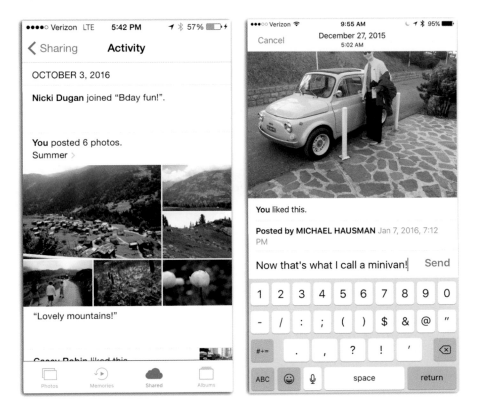

Once you're subscribed, you view the photos and movies as you would any album—with a couple of differences. First, you can tap **Add a comment** to make worshipful or snarky remarks, or tap **Like** to offer your silent support.

> **TIP:** Either you or the photo's owner can delete one of your comments. To do that, hold your finger down on the comment itself and then tap the **Delete** button that appears.

You can also snag a copy of somebody's published photo or video for yourself. With the photo before you, tap the ⬆️ button to see the usual sharing options—and tap **Save Image**. Now the picture or video isn't some virtual online wisp—it's a solid, tangible electronic copy in your own photo pool.

If your buddy has turned on **Subscribers Can Post** for this album, then you can send your own photos and clips into the album; everybody who's subscribed to it (and, of course, its owner) will see them.

To do that, tap the + on the album's page of thumbnails; choose your photos and movies; tap **Done**; add a comment; and tap **Post**.

Fun with Shared Photo Albums

Once you've created a shared Photo Album, you can update it or modify it in all kinds of ways:

- **Add new photos or movies to it.** In Photos, open the shared Photo Album, whether it's one you created or one you've subscribed to. Tap +. Now you can browse your whole world of photos, tapping to add them to the photo album already in progress.

- **Remove things from it.** In Photos, open the shared photo album. Tap **Select**, tap the item(s) you want to delete, and then tap the Trash icon (🗑️)—and confirm with a tap on **Delete Photo(s)**.

- **Delete an entire shared Photo Album.** Tap the **People** tab below an open photo album, scroll down, tap **Delete Shared Album**, and confirm by tapping **Delete**.

- **Change who's invited, change the name.** The **People** tab is also where you can add to the list of email addresses (tap **Invite People**), remove someone (tap the name, and then tap **Remove Subscriber**), rename the album, or turn off **Public Website** to dismantle the web version of this gallery.

At any time, you can tap the **Activity** "folder" at the top of the **Shared** tab in the Photos app. Here, for your amusement, is a visual record of everything that's gone on in Shared Photo Album Land: photos you've posted, photos other people have posted, comments back and forth, likes, and so on. It's your personal photographic Facebook.

iCloud Photo Library

If learning the difference between My Photo Stream, iCloud Photo Sharing, and Shared Photo Streams isn't hard enough, then hold onto your lens cap. Apple offers yet *another* online photo feature: the iCloud Photo Library.

The idea this time is that *all* your Apple gadgets will keep *all* your photos and videos backed up online and synced. The advantages:

- All your photos and videos are always backed up—not just the last 1,000.

- All your photos and videos are accessible from any of your gadgets.

- You can reclaim a lot of space on your phone. There's an option that offloads the original photos and videos to iCloud but leaves small, phone-sized copies on your phone.

There are a couple of sizable downsides to iCloud Photo Library, too:

- Remember, your entire iCloud account comes with only 5 gigabytes of free storage. If you start backing up your photo library to it, too, you'll almost certainly have to pay to expand your iCloud storage. Photos and videos eat up a lot of storage space.

- Things get a little complicated. The structure of the Photos app described in this chapter changes, for example; the albums usually called **Camera Roll** and **My Photo Stream** go away. They're replaced by a new album called **All Photos**. (Camera Roll and My Photo Stream were just subsets of your whole photographic life anyway.)

If you decide to dive in, then open **Settings→iCloud→Photos→iCloud Photo Library**.

Once iCloud Photo Library is on, you won't be able to copy pictures from your computer to your phone using iTunes anymore; iTunes will be completely removed from the photo-management loop. That's why, at this point, you may be warned that your phone is about to *delete* any photos and videos that you've synced to it from iTunes (Chapter 15). (Don't worry—they'll be safe in iCloud.)

And, of course, you might be warned that you need to buy more iCloud storage space.

Now the Settings panel expands and offers this important choice:

- **Optimize iPhone Storage.** If you turn this on, your original photos and videos get backed up to iCloud—but on your phone, you'll be left with much smaller versions that are just right for viewing on the phone's screen (but not high resolution enough to, for example, print). This arrangement saves you a *ton* of space on your phone.

- **Download and Keep Originals** leaves the big original files on your phone.

Finally, the uploading process begins. If you have a lot of photos and videos, it can take a very long time.

But when it's all over, you'll have instant access to all your photos and videos in any of these places:

- **On the iPhone (or other iOS gadgets).** In the Photos app, on the Albums tab, the new "album" called All Photos represents your new online photo library. Add to, delete from, or edit pictures in this set, and you'll find the same changes made on all your other Apple gear.

- **On the web.** You can sign into *iCloud.com* and click Photos to view your photos and videos, no matter what machine you're using. The Moments and Albums tabs here correspond to the tabs in the phone's Photos app. Click a photo to open it full size, whereupon the icons at the top of the screen let you delete, download, or "favorite" it.

- **On the Mac.** Everything appears in the All Photos heading in the Photos app. (There's no way to see your iCloud Photo Library's contents in the older iPhoto and Aperture programs, alas.)

Geotagging

Mention to a geek that a gadget has both GPS and a camera, and there's only one possible reaction: "Does it do *geotagging*?"

Geotagging means "embedding your latitude and longitude information into a photo or video when you take it." After all, every digital picture you've ever taken comes with its time and date embedded in its file; why not its location?

The good news is that the iPhone can geotag every photo and movie you take. How you use this information, however, is a bit trickier. The iPhone doesn't geotag unless all the following conditions are true:

- **The location feature on your phone is turned on.** On the Home screen, tap Settings→Privacy→Location Services. Make sure Camera is set to While Using the App. (The rest of the time, the camera does not record your location.)

- **The phone knows where it is.** If you're indoors, the GPS chip in the iPhone probably can't get a fix on the satellites overhead. And if you're not near cellular towers or Wi-Fi base stations, then even the pseudo-GPS may not be able to triangulate your location.

- **You've given permission.** The first time you use the iPhone's camera, a peculiar message appears, asking if it's allowed to use your location information. In this case, it's asking, "Do you want to geotag your pictures?" If you tap OK, then the iPhone's geographic coordinates will be embedded in each photo you take.

OK, so suppose all of this is true, and the geotagging feature is working. How will you know? Well, the Moments feature can put geotagging to work right on the phone. You can open a map and see all the photos you took in that spot.

You can also transfer the photos to your computer, where your likelihood of being able to see the geotag information depends on what photo-viewing software you're using. For example:

- **When you've selected a photo in iPhoto or Photos** (on the Mac), you can press ⌘-I for the Info panel. It shows the photo's spot on a map.

- **Once you've posted your geotagged photos on Flickr.com** (the world's largest photo-sharing site), people can use the Explore menu to search for them by location or even see them clustered on a world map.

- **If you import your photos into Picasa** (for Windows), then you can choose Tools→Geotag→View in Google Earth to see a picture's location on the map (if the free Google Earth program is installed on your computer, that is).

Or choose Tools→Geotag→Export to Google Earth File to create a .kmz file, which you can send to a friend. When opened, this file opens Google Earth (if it's on your friend's computer) and displays a miniature of the picture in the right place on the map.

Capturing the Screen

Let's say you want to write a book about the iPhone (hey, it could happen). How are you supposed to illustrate that book? How can you take pictures of what's on the screen?

The trick is very simple: Get the screen just the way you want it, even if that means holding your finger down on an onscreen button or a keyboard key. Now hold down the Home button, and while it's down, press the Sleep switch at the top of the phone. (Yes, you may need to invite some friends over to help you execute this multiple-finger move.)

But that's all there is to it. The screen flashes white. Now, if you go to the Photos app's Albums tab, in the Camera Roll or the Screenshots album, you see a crisp, colorful pixel image, in PNG format, of whatever was on the screen. (Its resolution matches the screen: 1136 × 640 on the iPhone 5 family, for example, or 1242 × 2208 on the Plus models.)

At this point, you can send it by email (to illustrate a request for help, for example, or to send a screen from Maps to a friend who's driving your way); sync it with your computer (to add it to your Mac or Windows photo collection); or designate it as the iPhone's wallpaper (to confuse the heck out of its owner).

> **TIP:** In some corners of iOS, there's no way to take a screenshot like this. For example, when the phone is ringing, pressing the screenshot button combination sends the call to voicemail instead of capturing the screen image.
>
> In those situations, you may have to rely on the *Mac's* ability to display the iPhone's screen. See page 260.

10

All About Apps

App is short for *application*, meaning software program, and the App Store is a single, centralized catalog of every authorized iPhone add-on program in the world. In fact, it's the *only* place where you can get new programs (at least without hacking your phone).

You hear people talking about downsides to this approach: Apple's stifling the competition; Apple's taking a 30 percent cut of every program sold; Apple's maintaining veto power over apps it doesn't like.

But there are some enormous benefits, too. First, there's one central place to look for apps. Second, Apple checks out every program to make sure it's decent and runs decently. Third, the store is beautifully integrated with the iPhone itself.

There's an incredible wealth of software in the App Store. These programs can turn the iPhone into an instant-message tool, a pocket Internet radio, a medical reference, a musical keyboard, a time and expense tracker, a TV remote control, a photo editor, a recipe box, a tip calculator, a restaurant finder, a teleprompter, and so on. And games—thousands of dazzling handheld games, some with smooth 3D graphics and tilt control.

It's so much stuff—2 million apps, 150 billion downloads—that the challenge is just finding your way through it. Thank goodness for those Most Popular lists.

Two Ways to the App Store

You can get to the App Store in two ways: from the phone itself, or from your computer's copy of the iTunes software.

Using iTunes offers a much easier browsing and shopping experience, of course, because you've got a mouse, a keyboard, and that big screen.

But downloading straight to the iPhone, without ever involving the computer, is wicked convenient when you're out and about.

Shopping from the Phone

To check out the App Store from your iPhone, tap the **App Store** icon. You arrive at the colorful, scrolling wonder of the store itself.

It has five tabs at the bottom. Here they are, in order:

- **Featured** is pretty clear: You can scroll vertically to see different categories, like **New Apps We Love** (Apple's editor picks) or **Games You Might Like,** and horizontally to see more apps within each category.

- **Categories** presents the entire catalog, organized by category: Books, Business, Education, Entertainment, Finance, Games, and so on. Tap a category to see what's in it.

- **Top Charts** is a list of the 100 most popular apps at the moment, ranked by how many people have downloaded them. There are actually three lists here: the most popular *free* programs, the most popular ones that cost money, and which apps have made the most money ("Top Grossing"), even if they haven't sold the most copies.

- **Search.** As the number of apps grows into the many millions, viewing by scrolling through lists begins to get awfully unwieldy.

  Fortunately, you can also **search** the catalog, which is efficient if you know what you're looking for (either the name of a program, the kind of program, or the software company that made it).

  Before you even begin to type, this screen shows you a list of Trending Searches—that is, the most popular searches right now. Odds are pretty good that if you want to download the latest hot app you keep hearing about, you'll see its name here (because, after all, it's hot).

  Or tap in the search box to make the keyboard appear. As you type, the list shrinks so that it's showing you only the matches. You might type **tetris**, or **piano**, or **Disney**, or whatever.

  Tap anything in the results list (below, left) to see matching apps (right). You can swipe horizontally to scroll through them. Tap one to view its details screen, as described on the next page.

- **Updates.** Unlike its buddies, this button isn't intended to help you navigate the catalog. Instead, it lets you know when one of the programs you've **already** installed is available in a newer version. Details in a moment.

About a third of the App Store's programs are free; the rest are usually under $5. A few, intended for professionals (pilots, for example), can cost a lot more.

The App Details Page

No matter which button was your starting point, eventually you wind up at an app's **details screen**. There's a description, a scrolling set of screenshots, info about the author, the date posted, the version number, a page of related and similar apps, and so on.

You can also tap Reviews to dig beyond the average star rating into the **actual** written reviews from people who've already tried the thing.

Why are the ratings so important? Because the App Store's goodies aren't equally good. Remember, these programs come from a huge variety of people—teenagers in Hungary, professional firms in Silicon Valley, college kids goofing around on weekends—and just because they made it into the store doesn't mean they're worth the money (or even the time to download).

Sometimes a program has a low score because it's just not designed well or it doesn't do what it's advertised to do. And sometimes, of course, it's a little buggy.

If you decide something is worth getting, scroll back to the top of the page and tap its price button. It may say, for example, $0.99 or, if it's free, simply Get.

> **TIP:** A little **+** sign on the price button means that the app works well on both the iPad and the iPhone.

If you've previously bought an app, either on this iPhone or on another Apple touchscreen gadget, then the button turns into a ☁; you don't have to buy it again. Just tap to re-download. If, in fact, this app is already on your iPhone, then the button says Open (handy!).

Once you tap the price and then Install App, you've committed to downloading the program. There are only a few things that may stand in your way:

- **A request for your iTunes account info.** You can't use the App Store without an iTunes account—even if you're just downloading free stuff. If you've ever bought anything from the iTunes Store, signed up for an iCloud account, or bought anything from Apple online, then you already have an iTunes account (an Apple ID, meaning your email address and password).

  The iPhone asks you to enter your iTunes account name and password the first time you access the App Store and periodically thereafter, just to make sure some marauding child in your household can't run up your bill without your knowledge. Mercifully, you don't have to enter your Apple ID information just to download an *update* to an app you already own.

> **TIP:** If you have an iPhone 5s or later model, and you've taught it to recognize your fingerprint, here's the payoff: When you try to download an app, instead of having to enter your Apple password, you can just touch the Home button with your finger.

- **A file size over 100 megabytes.** Most iPhone apps are pretty small— small enough to download directly to the phone, even over a cellular connection. If a program is bigger than 100 MB, though, you can't download it over the cellular airwaves, a policy no doubt intended to soothe nerves at AT&T, Sprint, T-Mobile, and Verizon, whose networks could be choked with 200 million iPhoners downloading huge files.

Instead, over-100-meg files are available only when you're on a Wi-Fi connection. Of course, you can also download them to your computer and sync them from there, as described later in this chapter.

Once you begin downloading a file, a pie chart on the app's icon fills in to indicate the download's progress. (Tap the icon to pause or unpause the download. If you have an iPhone 6s or 7, you can hard-press the icon for a shortcut menu offering buttons for Cancel Download, Pause Download, and Prioritize Download—in other words, finish ahead of any other down-loading apps.) When the downloading is done, tap the Open button to launch it and try it out.

> **TIP:** You don't have to sit there and stare at the progress bar. You can go on working on the iPhone. In fact, you can even go back to the App Store and start downloading something else simultaneously. You can easily spot your fresh downloads on the Home screens: Their icons fill in with color as the download proceeds.

Two Welcome Notes About Backups

Especially when you've paid good money for your iPhone apps, you might worry about what would happen if your phone got lost or stolen, or if someone (maybe you) accidentally deleted one of your precious downloads.

You don't have to worry, for two reasons.

First, the next time you sync your iPhone with your computer, iTunes asks if you want the newly purchased apps backed up. If you click Transfer, then the programs show up on the Applications tab in iTunes.

Second, here's a handy little fact about the App Store: It remembers what you've already bought. You can re-download a purchased program at any time, on any of your iPhones, iPads, or iPod Touches, without hav-ing to pay for it again.

> **TIP:** If some program doesn't download properly on the iPhone, don't sweat it. Go into iTunes on your computer and choose Store→Check for Available Downloads. And if a program does download to the phone but doesn't transfer to iTunes, then choose File→Transfer Purchases from "iPhone". These two commands straighten things out, clear up the accounting, and make all well with your two copies of each app (iPhone + computer).

Shopping in iTunes

You can also download new programs to your computer using iTunes and then sync them over to the phone. By all means, use this method whenever you can. It's much more efficient to use a mouse, a keyboard, and a full screen.

In iTunes, choose Apps from the pop-up menu at top left; at top center, click **App Store**. The screen fills with starting points for your quest, matching what you'd see on the phone: New Apps We Love, New Games We Love, and so on.

Or use the search box at top right. From here, the experience is the same as on the phone.

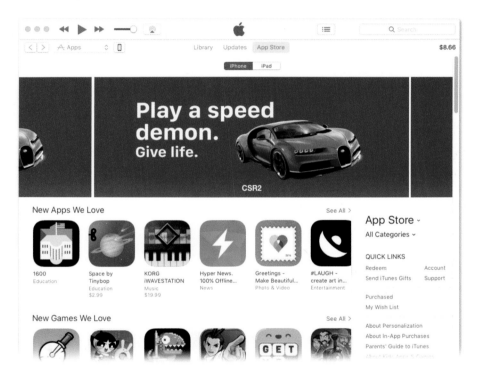

Organizing Your Apps

As you add new apps to your iPhone, it sprouts new Home screens as necessary to accommodate them all, up to a grand total of 15 screens. That's 364 icons—and yet you can actually go all the way up to many thousands of apps, thanks to the miracle of *folders*.

That multiple–Home screen business can get a little unwieldy, but a couple of tools can help you manage. First, you can just use Siri to open an app, without even knowing where it is. Just say, "Open Angry Birds" (or whatever).

Second, a Spotlight search can pluck the program you want out of your haystack, as described on page 99.

Third, you can organize your apps into folders, which greatly alleviates the agony of TMHSS (Too Many Home Screens Syndrome).

It's worth taking the time to arrange the icons on your Home screens into logical categories, tidy folders, or at least a sensible sequence.

You can do that either on the phone itself or in iTunes on your computer. That's far quicker and easier, but it works only when your phone is actually connected to the Mac or PC. Read on.

Rearranging/Deleting Apps Using iTunes

To fiddle with the layout of your Home screens with the least amount of hassle, connect the iPhone to your computer using the white charging cable or over Wi-Fi. Open iTunes.

Click your iPhone's icon at top left, and then click **Apps** in the left-side list. You see something like this display:

From here, it's all mouse power:

- For each listed app, click the button so that it says either Install (if the app is on your computer but not currently on your phone) or Remove (if it is; at that point, the button changes to say Will Remove). In other words, it's possible to store hundreds of apps in iTunes but load only some of them onto your iPhone.

- Click one of the Home screen miniatures on the right list to indicate which screen you want to edit. It gets big. Now you can drag the app icons to rearrange them on that page. (Click the background to close the life-size image.)

- Beneath the Home screen miniatures, iTunes displays similar mock-ups of each *folder* on your phone. Because they're visible here, all of them, all the time, it's very easy to put icons into them—and to work with the multiple "pages" within each folder (read on).

- It's fine to drag an app onto a different page mock-up. You can organize your icons on these Home screens by category, frequency of use, color, or whatever tickles your fancy. (The **+** button above each pile of mock-ups means "Click to install an additional Home screen.")

TIP: You can select several app icons simultaneously by ⌘-clicking them (or Ctrl-clicking in Windows); that way, you can move a bunch of them at once.

- You can drag the page mock-ups around to rearrange *them*, too.

- To delete an app from the iPhone, point to its icon and click the **✖**. (You can't delete Apple's starter apps like Safari and Messages.)

- Create a folder by dragging one app's icon on top of another (see page 337 for more on folders).

When your design spurt is complete, click Apply.

Rearranging/Deleting Apps Right on the Phone

You can also redesign your Home screens right on the iPhone, which is handy when you don't happen to be wired up to a computer.

To enter this Home screen editing mode, hold your finger down lightly on any icon until, after about a second, the icons begin to—what's the correct term?—*wiggle*. (On some phones, if you press too hard, you'll trigger Force Touch—see page 35—and get frustrated.)

At this point, you can rearrange your icons by dragging them around the glass into a new order; other icons scoot aside to make room.

TIP: You can even move an icon onto the Dock. Just make room for it by first dragging an *existing* Dock icon to another spot on the screen.

You can drag a single icon across multiple Home screens without ever having to lift your finger. Just drag the icon against the right or left margin of the screen to "turn the page."

To create an additional Home screen, drag a wiggling icon to the right edge of the screen; keep your finger down. The first Home screen slides off to the left, leaving you on a new, blank one, where you can deposit the icon. You can create up to 11 Home screens in this way.

You may have noticed that, while your icons are wiggling, most of them also sprout little ❌'s. That's how you *delete* a program you don't need anymore: Tap that ❌. You'll be asked if you're sure; if so, it says bye-bye.

In iOS 10, for the first time, you can actually use this technique to delete Apple's less important preinstalled apps, like Stocks and Watch! You don't have to hide them in a folder just to get them out of your face.

> **NOTE:** You're not actually deleting them—only hiding them. They still occupy 150 megabytes. (To "reinstall" them, download them from the App Store as usual.)

When everything looks good, press the Home button to stop the wiggling.

Restoring the Home Screen

If you ever need to undo all the damage you've done, tap **Settings→ General→ Reset→Reset Home Screen Layout**. That function preserves any new programs you've installed, but it consolidates them. If you'd put 10 apps on each of four Home screens, you wind up with only two screens, each packed with 20 icons. Any leftover blank pages are eliminated. This function also places all your downloaded apps in alphabetical order.

Folders

Folders let you organize your apps, deemphasize the ones you rarely use, and restore order to that dizzying display of icons, just as on a computer.

These days, each folder can have many pages of its own, each displaying nine icons. A single folder, in other words, can contain as many apps as you want—and therefore, only memory limits how many apps you can fit onto your phone.

Setting Up Folders on the iPhone

To create and edit folders, begin by entering Home screen editing mode. That is, hold your finger down on any icon (lightly) until all the icons wiggle.

Now, to create a folder, drag one app's icon on top of another. iOS puts both of them into a new folder and, if they're the same kind of app, even tries to figure out what category they both belong to—and names the new folder accordingly ("Music," "Photos," "Kid Games," or whatever). You can type in a new name at this point.

You're welcome to add more apps to this folder. Tap the Home screen background to close the folder, and then (while the icons are still wiggling) drag another app onto the folder's icon. Lather, rinse, repeat.

Drag one app onto another…   *…and a new folder is born. Rename it here.*

If one of your folders has more than nine apps in it, iOS creates a second "page" for the folder—and a third, a fourth, and so on. You can move apps around within the pages and otherwise master your new multipage folder domain.

You can scroll the folder "pages" by swiping sideways (facing page), just as you scroll the full-size Home pages. The only limit to how many icons a folder can hold is your tolerance for absurdity.

Once you've created a folder or two, they're easy to rename, move, delete, and so on. (Again, you can do all of the following *only in icon-wiggling editing mode*.) Like this:

- **Take an app out of a folder** by dragging its icon anywhere else on the Home screen. The other icons scoot aside to make room, just as they do when you move them from one Home screen to another.

- **Move a folder around** by dragging, as you would any other icon.

- **Rename a folder** by opening it (tapping it). At this point, the folder's name box is ready for editing.

- **Move an icon from one folder "page" to another** by dragging it to the edge of the folder, waiting with your finger down until the page "changes," and then releasing your finger in the right spot.

- **Delete a folder** by removing all of its contents. The folder disappears automatically.

When you're finished manipulating your folders, press the Home button to exit Home screen editing mode—and stop all the wiggling madness.

Setting Up Folders in iTunes

It's faster and easier to set up your folders within iTunes, on your Mac or PC, where you have a mouse and a big screen to help you. Connect your iPhone to your computer (by cable or Wi-Fi), open iTunes, click your iPhone's icon at the top, and then click Apps in the left-side list. You see something like the illustration on page 334.

To create a folder, double-click a Home page miniature to expand it; now drag one app's icon on top of another, exactly as you'd do on the iPhone. The software puts them into a single new folder. As on the iPhone, the software proposes a folder name; an editing bar also appears so that you can type a custom name you prefer.

Once you've got a folder, you can open it just by double-clicking. It expands to life size, revealing its contents. Now you can edit the folder's name, drag the icons around inside it, or drag an app right out of the folder window and onto another Home page (or another folder on it). Just keep your finger down on the mouse button or trackpad until the new Home page or folder page opens.

Below the Home pages, you'll discover that each of your app folders now has an app-management screen mock-up of its own, complete with a horizontally scrolling set of pages. That's so you can move the "pages" around, organize the apps within them, and so on.

If you remove all the apps from a folder, then the folder disappears.

App Preferences

If you're wondering where you can change an iPhone app's settings, consider backing out to the Home screen and then tapping Settings. Apple encourages programmers to add their programs' settings *here*, way down below the bottom of the iPhone's own settings.

Some programmers ignore the advice and build the settings right into their apps, where they're a little easier to find. But if you don't see them there, now you know where else to look.

App Updates

When a circled number (like ❷) appears on the App Store's icon on the Home screen, or on the Updates icon within the App Store program, that's Apple's way of letting you know that a program you already own has been updated. Apple knows which programs you've bought—and notifies you when new, improved versions are released. Which is remarkably often; software companies are constantly fixing bugs and adding new features.

Manual Updates

When you tap Updates, you're shown a list of the programs with waiting updates. A tiny What's New arrow lets you know what the changes are—new features, perhaps, or some bug fixes. And when you tap a program's name, you go to its details screen, where you can remind yourself of what the app does and read other people's reviews of this new version.

You can download one app's update, or, with a tap on the Update All button, all of them...no charge.

> **NOTE:** You can also download your updates from iTunes. From the top-left pop-up menu, choose Apps; then click Updates at the top of the screen. This window shows the icons of all updated versions of your programs. You can download the updates individually (click an icon, click Update) or all at once (Update All Apps).

Automatic Updates

If you have a lot of apps, you may come to feel as though you're spending your whole life downloading updates. They descend like locusts, every single day, demanding your attention.

That's why Apple offers an automatic update-downloading option. Your phone can download and install updated versions of your apps quietly and automatically in the background.

To turn on this feature, open Settings→iTunes & App Store. Under Automatic Downloads, turn on Updates. (If you'd prefer that the phone wait to do this downloading until it's in a Wi-Fi hotspot—to avoid eating up your monthly cellular data-plan allotment—then turn off Use Cellular Data.)

From now on, the task of manually approving each app's update is off your to-do list forever.

> **TIP:** Fortunately, the iPhone also keeps a tidy record of every app it's updated and what that update gives you. Open the App Store app; tap the Updates tab. There's your list, sorted chronologically. Tap an app's row to read what was new in the update you've already received.

How to Find Good Apps

If the Featured, Categories, and Top Charts lists aren't inspiring you, there are all kinds of websites dedicated to reviewing iPhone apps. There's *appadvice.com* and *whatsoniphone.com* and on and on.

But if you've never dug into iPhone apps before, you should at least try out some of the superstars, the big dogs that almost everybody has.

Many of the most popular apps are designed to deliver certain websites in the best-looking way possible. That's why there are apps for Facebook, Twitter, LinkedIn, Spotify, Pandora, Flickr, Yelp, Netflix, YouTube, Wikipedia, and so on.

Here are a very few more examples—a drop in the bucket at the tip of the iceberg—of the infinite app variety beyond those basics:

- **Apple Apps (free).** The first time you open the App Store, you're offered a set of free Apple apps that Apple thinks you might like: iBooks, iTunes U, Podcasts, Find My Friends, and Find My iPhone. With one tap, you can grab this whole set.

- **Google Maps (free).** Google Maps is a replacement for the built-in Maps app. It's much, *much* better than Maps—even Apple has admitted that. Among other things, it offers Street View (you can actually see a photo of almost any address and "look around" you), it incorporates the Zagat guides for restaurants, and it's unbelievably smart about knowing what you're trying to type into the search box. Usually, about three letters is all you need to type before the app guesses what you mean.

- **Google Mobile (free).** Speak to search Google's maps. Includes Google Goggles: Point the phone's camera at a book, DVD, wine bottle, logo, painting, landmark, or bit of text, and the hyperintelligent app recognizes it and displays information about it from the web.

- **Echofon (free).** Most free Twitter apps are a bit on the baffling side. This one is simple and clean.

- **FlightTrack 5 ($5).** Shows every detail of every flight: gate, time delayed, airline phone number, where the flight is on the map, and more. Knows more—and knows it sooner—than the actual airlines do.

- **SoundHound (free).** Beats Shazam at its own game. Hold this app up to a song that's playing on the radio, or even hum or sing the song, and the app miraculously identifies the song and offers you lyrics. It's faster than Shazam, too.

- **Instagram (free)** has a bunch of filter effects, as iOS's Camera app does. But the real magic is in the way it's designed to share your photos. You sign up to receive Instagrams from Facebook or Twitter folk. They (the photos, not the folk) show up right in the app, scrolling up like a photographic Twitter feed. Seeing what other people are doing every day with their cameraphones and creative urges is really inspirational.

Other essentials: Angry Birds and its sequel, Bad Piggies. Uber and Lyft. Skype. Hipmunk (finds flights). The New York Times. The Amazon Kindle book reader, B&N eReader. Dictionary. TED. *Mint.com*. Scrabble. Keynote Remote (controls your Keynote presentations from the phone). Remote (yes, another one, also from Apple—turns the iPhone into a Wi-Fi, whole-house **remote control** for your Mac's or PC's music playback—and for Apple TV). Instant-messaging (AIM, Yahoo Messenger, or IM+). Yahoo Weather (gorgeous).

Happy apping!

The App Switcher

Often, it's handy to switch among open apps. Maybe you want to copy something from Safari (on the web) into Mail (a message you're writing). Maybe you want to refer to your frequent-flier number (in Notes) as you're using an airline's check-in app. Maybe you want to adjust something in Settings and then get back to whatever you were doing.

The key to switching apps is to **double-click the Home button**. Whatever is on the screen gets replaced by the app switcher (below, left).

> **TIP:** On the iPhone 6s and 7 models, there's a second way to reach this screen: **Hard-swipe** from the left edge of the screen. This method has one advantage: It lets you **peek** at whatever apps are in the background, and then, without ever lifting your thumb, slide back to the left. You've had a quick glance without ever fully entering the app switcher.

You see a scrolling series of "cards" that represent the open apps, in chronological order. They're big enough that you can actually see what's going on in each open app. In fact, sometimes, that's all you need; you can refer to another app's screen in this view, without actually having to switch **into** that app.

> **TIP:** Thoughtfully enough, the app switcher always puts the **previous app** front and center when you first double-press the Home button. For example, if you're in Safari but you were using Mail a minute ago, Mail appears centered in the app switcher. That makes life easier if you're doing a lot of jumping back and forth between two apps; one tap takes you into the previous app.

When you tap an app's icon or screen in the app switcher, you open that app.

Force-Quitting an App

The app switcher lets you manually exit an app, closing it down. To do that, flick the unwanted app's mini-screen upward, so that it flies up off the top of the screen (shown on the previous page at right).

The app is not really gone; it will return to the lineup the next time you open it from the Home screen.

You'll need this gesture only rarely. You're not supposed to quit every app when you're finished. Force-quit an app only if it's frozen or acting glitchy and needs to be restarted.

> **TIP:** There may be one more element on the task-switcher screen, too: a faint app icon at the far left. That's a document, email, or web page being sent to your phone by your Mac, using Handoff (see page 551).

A Word About Background Apps

Switching out of a program doesn't actually close it. All apps can run in the background.

Of course, if every app ran full-tilt simultaneously, your phone would guzzle down battery power like crazy. To solve that problem, Apple has put two kinds of limits in place:

- **iOS's limits.** Not all apps run full speed in the background. Apps that really need constant updating, like Facebook or Twitter, get refreshed every few seconds; apps that don't rely on constant Internet updates get to nap for a while in the background.

  In deciding which apps get background attention, iOS studies things like how good your phone's Internet connection is and what time of day you traditionally use a certain app (so that your newspaper's app is ready with the latest articles when you open it).

- **Your own limits.** You can't control which apps *run* in the background, but you can control which ones *download new data* in the background. In Settings→General→Background App Refresh, you'll find a list of every app that may want to update itself in the background. In an effort to make your battery last longer, you can turn off background updating for the apps you don't really care about; you can even turn off all background updating using the master switch at the top.

The bottom line: There's no need to quit apps you're not using, ever. Contrary to certain Internet rumors, they generally don't use enough memory or battery power to matter. You may see dozens of apps in the app switcher, but you'll never sense that your phone is bogging down as a result.

Back to App (<)

This humble button may become your favorite feature.

It's a Back button that appears when you've tapped a link of some kind that takes you into a different app. For example:

- **You're in Messages,** and you tap a web link (below, left) that takes you into Safari. A <Messages button appears at the top-left corner of your screen (below, right).

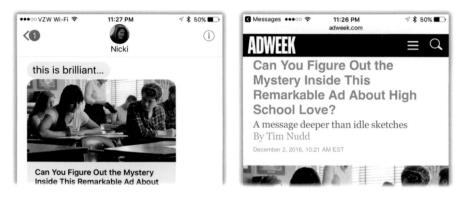

- **You're on Twitter or Facebook,** and you tap a link that opens a web page. Sure enough: The top-left button says <Twitter or <Facebook.

- **You're in Mail,** and you tap an underlined date and time that takes you into the Calendar app. A <Mail button appears in the corner.

- **You're in Safari,** and you tap a link that opens in YouTube. Sure enough: The button says <Safari.

And so on. Add it all up, and this tiny recent enhancement can save you literally *minutes* a week. It's the best.

AirPrint: Printing from the Phone

The very phrase "printing from the phone" might seem peculiar. How do you print from a gadget that's smaller than a Hershey bar—a gadget without any jacks for connecting a printer?

Wirelessly, of course.

You can send printouts from your phone to any printer that's connected to your Mac or PC on the same Wi-Fi network if you have a piece of software like Printopia ($20).

Or you can use the iPhone's built-in AirPrint technology, which can send printouts directly to a Wi-Fi printer without requiring a Mac or a PC.

Not just any Wi-Fi printer, though—only those that recognize AirPrint. Many recent Canon, Epson, HP, and Lexmark printers work with AirPrint; you can see a list of them on Apple's website, here: *http://support.apple. com/kb/HT4356*.

Not all apps can print. Of the built-in Apple programs, only iBooks, Mail, Photos, Notes, and Safari offer **Print** commands. Those apps contain what most people want to print most of the time: PDF documents (iBooks), email messages, driving directions from the web, and so on. Plenty of non-Apple apps work with AirPrint, too.

●○○○○ Verizon 📶	1:06 PM	⚡ 100% 🔋
Cancel	**Printer Options**	
Printer	HP LaserJet P7000	>
Range	All Pages	>
1 Copy		− | +
	Print	

To use AirPrint, start by tapping the ⬆ button; tap **Print**. You're offered a **Select Printer** option. Tap it to introduce the phone to your printer, whose name should appear automatically. Now you can adjust the printing options (number of copies, page range)—and when you finally tap **Print**, your printout shoots wirelessly to the printer, exactly as though your phone and printer were wired together.

The Share Sheet

Every app is different, of course. But all of them have certain things in common; otherwise, you'd go out of your mind.

One of those things is the Share sheet. It's your headquarters for sending stuff off your phone: to other apps, to other phones, to the Internet, to a printer. It's made up of several icon rows, each of which scrolls horizontally. (From top to bottom, you could title these rows "What to Share," "Send by AirDrop," "Send to an App," and "Act on This Data Directly.")

The Share sheet pops up whenever you tap the Share button (⬆) that appears in many, many apps: Maps, Photos, Safari, Notes, Voice Memos, Contacts, and so on.

The buttons you see depend on the app; you may see only two options here, or you may see a dozen. Starting on page 310, for example, you can read descriptions of the icons that appear when you're sending a photo: AirDrop, Message, Mail, Twitter, Facebook, Copy, AirPlay, Print, and so on. The options here vary by app.

Moreover, there's a More button at the end of each row. That's an invitation for other, non-Apple apps to install their own "send to" options into the Share sheet. When you tap More, you can see the full list of apps that have inserted themselves here. Now you can perform these tasks:

- **Hide a sharing option.** Flip the switch to make one of the sharing options disappear from the Share sheet. (You can't hide the sharing options that Apple considers essential, like Messages or Mail.)

- **Rearrange the sharing options.** Use the handle to move these items up or down the list, which affects their left-to-right order on the Share sheet.

AirDrop

It's a headline feature: AirDrop, a way to shoot things from one Apple phone, tablet, or Mac to another—wirelessly, instantly, easily, encryptedly, without requiring names, passwords, or setup. It's much faster than emailing or text messaging, since you don't have to know (or type) the other person's address. It's available on the iPhone 5 and later.

> **NOTE:** If the Mac is running OS X Yosemite or later, you can shoot files between it and your phone, too.

You can transmit pictures and videos from the Photos app, people's info cards from Contacts, directions (or your current location) from Maps, pages from Notes, web addresses from Safari, electronic tickets from Wallet, apps you like in the App Store, song and video listings from the iTunes app), radio stations (iTunes Radio), and so on. As time goes on, more and more non-Apple apps will offer AirDrop, too.

Behind the scenes, AirDrop uses Bluetooth (to find nearby gadgets within about 30 feet) and a private, temporary Wi-Fi mini-network (to transfer the file). Both sender and receiver must have Bluetooth and Wi-Fi turned on.

The process goes like this:

1. **Find a willing recipient.**

   You can't send anything with AirDrop unless the receiving phone or tablet is running iOS 7 or later—and is awake. And only recent models work with AirDrop: iPhone 5 or later, 4th generation iPad or later, any iPad mini, and 5th generation iPod Touch or later.

2. **Open the item you want to share. Tap the Share button (⬆️).**

   If your app doesn't have a ⬆️ button, then you can't use AirDrop.

When the Share sheet appears, within a few seconds, you see something that would have awed the masses in 1995: small circular photos of everyone nearby (previous page, left). (Or at least everyone with iOS 7 or later, or OS X Yosemite or later. Or at least everyone among them who's **open to receiving** AirDrop transmissions, as described in a moment.)

> **TIP:** When you send a *photo*, the top row of the Share sheet shows your other photos and videos so that you can select additional items to go along for the ride. A blue checkmark identifies each item you've selected to send.

3. **Tap the icon of the person you want to share with.**

    In about a second, a message appears on the recipient's screen, conveying your offer to transmit something good—and, when it makes sense, showing a picture of it (previous page, right).

> **TIP:** Actually, you can select *more than one* person's icon. In that case, you'll send this item to everyone at once.

At this point, it's up to your recipients. If they tap Accept, then the transfer begins (and ends); whatever you sent them opens up automatically in the relevant app. You'll know that AirDrop was successful because the word "Sent" appears on your screen.

If they tap Decline, then you must have misunderstood their willingness to accept your item (or they tapped the wrong button). In that case, you'll see the word "Declined" on your screen.

The One AirDrop Setting

Your existence probably won't become a living hell of AirDrop invitations. Realistically, you won't be bombarded by strangers around you who want to show you family pictures or web links. Even so, Apple has given you some control over who's allowed to try to send you things by AirDrop.

To see the settings, swipe up from the bottom of the screen to open the Control Center (page 46). There, in the middle, is the AirDrop button. Tap it to see these three choices:

- **Off.** Nobody can send anything to you by AirDrop. You'll never be disturbed by an incoming "Accept?" message.

- **Contacts Only.** Only people in your Contacts app—your own address book—can send you things by AirDrop. Your phone is invisible to strangers. (Of course, even when someone you know tries to send something, you still have to approve the transfer.)

- **Everyone.** Anyone, even strangers, can try to send you things. You can still accept or decline each transfer.

iCloud Drive

iCloud Drive is Apple's version of Dropbox. It's a folder whose contents appear identically on every Mac, iPhone, iPad, and even Windows PC you own, through the magic of instant online syncing. It's an online "disk" that holds 5 gigabytes (or more, if you're willing to pay for it).

Whatever you put into the iCloud Drive appears, almost instantly, in the iCloud Drive folder on all your *other* machines: Macs, iPhones, iPads, and even Windows PCs. In fact, your files will even be available at *iCloud.com*, so you can grab them when you're stranded on a desert island with nothing but somebody else's computer. (And Internet access.)

This is an incredibly useful feature. No more emailing files to yourself. No more carrying things around on a flash drive. After working on some document at the office, you can go home and resume from right where you stopped; the same file is waiting for you, exactly as you left it.

The iCloud Drive is a great backup, too, because of its automatic duplication on multiple machines. Even if your phone is stolen or burned to aluminum dust, your iCloud Drive files are safe.

Your first chance to turn on iCloud Drive was when you installed iOS 8, 9, or 10 (or bought your iOS 8, 9, or 10 phone). If you declined, maybe because you had no idea what it was about, then you can visit Settings→iCloud→iCloud Drive and turn iCloud Drive on now.

Now, it's easy to understand iCloud Drive on a Mac or PC. It looks like any other disk, full of files and folders. You can even access them at *iCloud.com* (click the Drive icon), which is handy when you have to use someone else's computer. Any change you make to the iCloud Drive or its contents is instantly synchronized across all your other gadgets.

On the phone, iCloud Drive is an actual app—the closest thing the phone has to a "desktop" where you can organize files and folders. Tug downward to reveal three tabs at the top, which sort the list of files and folders by **Date**, **Name**, or **Tags**; the ☰ switches between icon view and list view.

Hold your finger down on any icon in the iCloud Drive until the options bar appears, with options for Delete, Rename, Share, Move, and Info.

You can also hit Select and then tap the icons you want to put into a New Folder, Move into a different folder, or Delete from the iCloud Drive.

Now, iOS is not macOS or Windows; still, it can open many kinds of documents right on the phone. Graphics, music files, Microsoft Office documents, and PDFs all open from the iCloud Drive.

Other kinds of computer files, not so much. The iPhone can't open the specialized files from sheet-music or genealogy programs, for example. In those cases, iCloud Drive is still useful, though, because it lets you forward those documents by email to a machine that *can* open them.

You can also see what's on your iCloud Drive *within* apps that can open and save documents. That includes Apple's apps—Keynote, Pages, Numbers, iMovie—and other apps that create and open documents, like, say, Scanner Pro and PDF Expert.

In all these apps, there's an Open button or icon that presents the iCloud Drive's contents. In Pages, for example, when you're viewing your list of documents, tap Locations, and then tap iCloud. There's the list of folders on your iCloud Drive, corresponding perfectly to what you would have seen on a Mac or a PC. Tap a folder to open it and see what's in it.

Note that iOS shows you *everything* on your iCloud Drive, even things you can't open at the moment. For example, if you're using the iMovie app, you can't open a Pages file, so Pages documents appear dimmed and gray.

On an iPhone, the iCloud Drive folder list is not quite the same thing as having a real desktop—you can't rename, copy, or delete files or folders on the phone, for example.

But it's comforting to know that everything on your iCloud Drive that you can open is available wherever you go—and that you can now load up everyday documents (pictures, music, PDFs, Microsoft Office files, iWork documents) onto your phone by dragging them into the iCloud Drive folder on your computer.

11

The Built-In Apps

Your iPhone comes already loaded with the icons of about 25 programs. Eventually, of course, you'll fill it up with apps you install yourself, but Apple starts you off with the essentials. They include gateways to the Internet (Safari), communications tools (Phone, Messages, Mail, Contacts), visual records of your life (Photos, Camera), shopping centers (iTunes Store, App Store), omnipresent storage (iCloud Drive), and entertainment (Music, TV, Podcasts).

Those core apps get special treatment in the other chapters. This chapter covers the secondary programs, in alphabetical order: Calculator, Calendar, Clock, Compass, Health, Home, iBooks, Maps, News, Notes, Podcasts, Reminders, Stocks, Tips, TV, Voice Memos, Wallet, Watch, and Weather.

> **TIP:** You can open any of these apps by hunting it down and tapping its icon. But it's usually much faster to tell Siri to do it. Say, "Open the calculator," for example.

Calculator

The iPhone wouldn't be much of a computer without a calculator, now, would it? And here it is, your everyday calculator—with a secret twist.

In Calculator's basic four-function mode, you can tap out equations (like *15.4 × 300 =*) to see the answer at the top. (You can *paste* things you've copied into here, too; just hold your finger down until the Paste button appears.) There's no memory function in the basic calculator, but you do get a +/– button; its function is to change the currently displayed number from positive to negative, or vice versa.

Now the twist: If you rotate the iPhone 90 degrees in either direction, the Calculator morphs into a full-blown HP *scientific* calculator, complete with trigonometry, logarithmic functions, a memory function, exponents, roots beyond the square root, and so on. Go wild, ye engineers and physicists!

If you make a mistake while entering a number, swipe horizontally across the numerical display (either direction). Each swipe backspaces over the rightmost digit. And if you mistakenly touch the wrong operator (× when you meant −, for example), there's no need to start over. Just tap the *correct* operator before tapping the number. The app ignores the errant tap.

Calendar

The iPhone's calendar syncs, automatically and wirelessly, with whatever online calendar you keep: iCloud, Google Calendar, a corporate Exchange calendar, and so on. Everything's kept in sync with your computers and tablets, too. Make a change in one place, and it changes everywhere else. Then again, you can also use Calendar all by itself.

Day View

When you open Calendar, you see today's schedule, broken down by time slot (previous page, right). You can navigate to other days' schedules in any of three ways: Swipe horizontally across the Day screen to see the previous or next day. Tap a date at the top to see another day this week. Swipe across the dates at the top to jump to another week. If the date you want to check is further away than a week or two, though, it might make more sense to pop into Month view, described next.

Month View

Month view, of course, shows an entire month at a glance (previous page, center). You can scroll the months vertically, thereby scanning the entire year in a few seconds. To get there from Day view, tap the name of the month at the top left.

Of course, your little phone screen is too small to show you what's written on each calendar square; all you get is a gray dot on any date when you've scheduled an appointment. Tap that dot to jump back into Day view and read your schedule.

TIP: If you have an iPhone 6s or later model, a delicious shortcut awaits: *Hard-press* any gray dot. A pop-up bubble appears, showing you the appointments that day as though it's a peephole into the Day view. You can then press even harder to **open** the Day view for that day, or lift your finger away to return to the Month view. You've just used peek and pop, described on page 37.

Year View

If you're in Month view, you can "zoom out" yet another level—Year view. It's a simple, vertically scrolling map of the year's months. Tap the name of the year (top left) to see it. From there, tap a month block to open it back into Month view.

TIP: In all three of these views—Day, Month, Year—you can tap Today (bottom left) to return to today's date.

Week View

The most useful view yet may be the fourth one: the scrolling Week view (facing page, top).

No button opens this view; instead, from any other view, turn the phone 90 degrees so that it's in landscape mode. You can swipe sideways to move to earlier or later dates. Swipe up or down to move through the hours of the day. (OK, you don't get to see a *full* week, but it's close.)

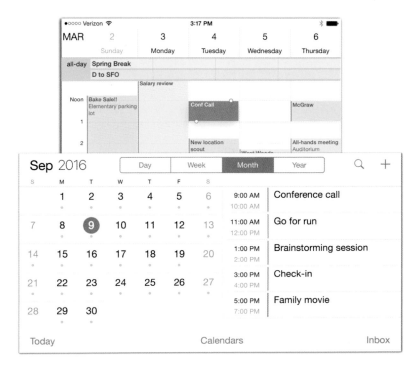

Plus Model Views

If you have a Plus model—one with the Jumbotron screen—then there's room for extra information (the lower illustration above). On a Plus, the Day and Month views offer a split screen, showing the calendar on the left and details on the right. You also get a row of view buttons (Day, Week, Month, Year)—something the owners of puny regular iPhones never see.

Subscribing to Your Online Calendars

To set up real-time, wireless connections to your calendars online, tap your way to Settings→Calendars→Add Account. Here you can tap iCloud, Exchange, Gmail, Yahoo, AOL, or Outlook.com to set up your account. (You can also tap Other→Add CalDAV Account to fill in the details of a less well-known calendar server, or Other→Add Subscribed Calendar to connect to an online calendar subscription service—from TripIt or your favorite sports team, for example.

Making an Appointment (Day or Month View)

Recording an event on this calendar is quite a bit more flexible than entering one on, say, one of those "Hunks of the Midwest Police Stations" paper calendars.

Start by tapping + (top-right corner of the screen). The New Event screen pops up, filled with tappable lines of information. Tap one (like **Starts** or **Repeat**) to open a configuration screen for that element.

For example:

- **Title/Location.** Name your appointment here. For example, you might type *Fly to Phoenix*.

  The second line, called **Location**, makes a lot of sense. If you think about it, almost everyone needs to record *where* a meeting is to take place. You might type a reminder for yourself like *My place*, a specific address like *212 East 23rd*, a contact phone, or a flight number. Use the keyboard as usual.

- **Starts/Ends.** Tap **Starts**, and then indicate the starting time for this appointment, using the four spinning dials that appear at the bottom of the screen (below, right). The first sets the date; the second, the hour; the third, the minute; the fourth, AM or PM.

●○○○○ Verizon 🛜 3:18 PM ⚡ 🔋		●●○○○ Verizon 🛜 11:52 PM ⚡ 88% 🔋
Cancel **Edit** Done		Cancel **New Event** Add

Root Canal	All-day ⬭
Dr. Evilstein's office	Starts Apr 18, 2016 11:00 AM
	Fri Apr 15 8 45
All-day ⬭	Sat Apr 16 9 50
	Sun Apr 17 10 55
Starts Apr 15, 2017 7:15 PM	**Mon Apr 18 11 00 AM**
Ends 8:15 PM	Tue Apr 19 12 05 PM
	Wed Apr 20 1' 10
Repeat Never >	Thu Apr 21 2 15
Travel Time None >	Time Zone New York >
	Ends 12:00 PM
Calendar • DWP >	Repeat Never >

Then tap **Ends**, and repeat the process to schedule the ending time. (The iPhone helpfully presets the Ends time to one hour later.)

An **All-day** event, of course, has no specific time of day: a holiday, a birthday, a book deadline. When you turn this option on, the Starts and Ends times disappear. The event appears at the top of the list for that day.

- **Repeat.** The screen here contains common options for recurring events: every day, every week, and so on. It starts out saying **Never**.

  Once you tap a selection, you return to the Edit screen. Now you can tap the **End Repeat** button to specify when this event should *stop* re-peating. If you leave the setting at **Never**, then you're stuck seeing this event repeating on your calendar until the end of time (a good choice for recording, say, your anniversary, especially if your spouse might be consulting the same calendar).

  In other situations, you may prefer to tap **On Date** and spin the three dials (month, day, year) to specify an ending date, which is useful for car and mortgage payments.

  Tap **New Event** to return to the editing screen.

- **Travel Time.** If you turn on this switch, you can indicate how long it'll take you to get to this appointment.

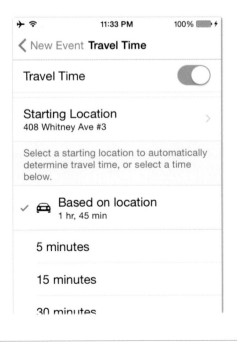

You get six canned choices, from 5 minutes to 2 hours. Or you can tap **Starting Location** and specify your starting point, and marvel as the iPhone calculates the driving time automatically. (Walking time, too, if it's close enough.)

Two things then happen. First, the travel time is blocked off on your calendar, so you don't accidentally schedule things during your driving time. (The travel time is depicted as a dotted extension of the appointment.)

Second, if you've set up an alarm reminder, it will go off that much earlier, so you have time to get where you're going.

- **Calendar.** Tap here to specify which color-coded *calendar* (category, like Home, Kids, or Work) this appointment belongs to. Turn to page 364 for details on the calendar concept.

- **Invitees.** If you have an iCloud, Exchange, or CalDAV account, you can invite people to an event—a meeting, a party, whatever—and track their responses, right there on your phone (or any iCloud gadget). When you tap **Invitees**, you get an Add Invitees screen, where you can type in the email addresses of your lucky guests. (Or tap ➕ to choose them from your Contacts list.)

  Later, when you tap **Done**, the phone fires off email invitations to those guests. It contains buttons for them to click: **Accept**, **Decline**, and **Maybe**. You get to see their responses right here in the details of your calendar event.

  As icing on the cake, your guests will see a pop-up reminder on their phones when the time comes for the party to get started.

- **Alert.** This screen tells Calendar how to notify you when a certain appointment is about to begin. Calendar can send any of four kinds of flags to get your attention. Tap how much notice you want: 5, 15, or 30 minutes before the big moment; an hour or two before; a day or two before; a week before; or on the day of the event.

NOTE: For all-day events like birthdays, you get a smaller but very useful list of choices: "On day of event (9 AM)," "1 day before (9 AM)," "2 days before (9 AM)," and "1 week before."

When you tap **Add Event** and return to the main Add Event screen, you see that a new line, called **Second Alert**, has sprouted up beneath the first Alert line. This line lets you schedule a *second* warning for your appointment, which can occur either before or after the first one. Think of it as a backup alarm for events of extra urgency.

Once you've scheduled these alerts, you'll see a message appear on the screen at the appointed time(s). (Even if the phone was asleep, it appears briefly.) You'll also hear a chirpy alarm sound.

TIP: The iPhone doesn't play the sound if you turned off Calendar Alerts in **Settings→Sounds** or **Settings→Sounds & Haptics**. It also doesn't play if you silenced the phone with the silencer switch on the side.

- **Show as.** If you work in the business world, it's courteous to mark your new appointments as either **Busy** or **Free**. That way, other people who see your calendar, trying to schedule a meeting when you can attend, will know which events on your calendar are movable and which are non-negotiable. If you're just indicating "*Keeping Up with the Kardashians* TV marathon," maybe that one should be marked as **Free**.

- **URL.** Here's a spot where you can record the web address of some online site that provides more information about this event.

- **Notes.** Here's your chance to customize your calendar event. You can type any text you want in the Notes area—driving directions, contact phone numbers, a call history, or whatever. Tap **Done**.

When you've completed filling in all these blanks, tap **Add**. Your newly scheduled event now shows up on the calendar.

Making an Appointment (Day View, Week View)

As noted earlier, turning the phone 90 degrees opens up a widescreen, scrolling Week view of your life.

In both Day view and Week view, you can *hold your finger down on a time slot* to add a new, 1-hour appointment right there. You're asked to enter a name and, if you like, location for this new appointment. Tap **Add**. You can always edit this appointment's details or duration later, as described next—but this quick-and-dirty technique saves the effort of tapping in Start and End times.

Editing, Rescheduling, Deleting Events (Long Way)

To examine the details of an appointment in the calendar, tap it once. The Event Details screen appears, filled with the details you previously established.

To edit any of these characteristics, tap **Edit**. You return to what looks like a clone of the New Event screen. Here you can change the name, time, alarm, repeat schedule, calendar category, or any other detail of the event, just the way you set them up to begin with.

This time, there's a red **Delete Event** button at the bottom. That's the only way to erase an appointment from your calendar. (You can't erase events created by other people—Facebook birthdays, meetings on shared calendars, and so on—only appointments *you* created.)

Editing and Rescheduling Events (Fun Way)

In Day or Week views, you can ***drag an appointment's block*** to another time slot or even another day. Just hold your finger down on the appointment's bubble for about a second—until it darkens—before you start to drag. It's a lot quicker and more fluid than having to edit in a dialog box.

You can also change the ***duration*** of an appointment in Day and Week views. Hold your finger down on its colored block for about a second; when you let go, small, round handles appear.

You can drag those tiny handles up or down to make the block taller or shorter, in effect making it start or end at a different time.

Whether you drag the whole block, the top edge, or the bottom edge, the iPhone thoughtfully displays ":15," ":30," or ":45" on the left-side time ruler to let you know where you'll be when you let go.

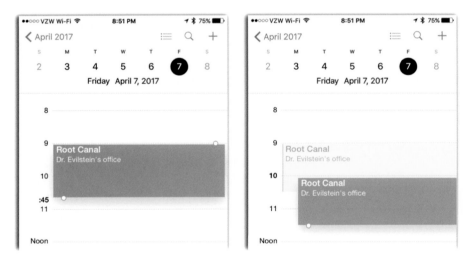

The Calendar (Category) Concept

A ***calendar***, in Apple's somewhat confusing terminology, is a color-coded subset—a ***category***—into which you can place various appointments. They can be anything you like. One person might have calendars called Home, Work, and TV Reminders. Another might have Me, Spouse 'n' Me, and The Kidz. A small business could have categories called Deductible Travel, R&D, and R&R.

You can create and edit calendar categories right on the iPhone, in your desktop calendar program, or (if you're an iCloud member) at *www.icloud.com* when you're at your computer; all your categories and color-codings show up on the iPhone automatically.

At any time, on the iPhone, you can choose which subset of categories you want to see. Just tap **Calendars** at the bottom of Day, Month, or Year view. You arrive at the big color-coded list of your categories (below, left). As you can see, it's subdivided according to your accounts: your Gmail categories, your Yahoo categories, your iCloud categories, and so on. There's even a Facebook option, if you've set up your Facebook account, so that you can see your Facebook calendar entries and friends' birthdays right on the main calendar.

●●○○○ Verizon 📶 ❄ 3:22 PM ❊ 99% 🔋⚡	●●○○○ Verizon 📶 3:23 PM ❊ 99% 🔋⚡
Edit **Calendars** Done	Cancel **Edit Calendar** Done
Show All Calendars	Vacations
GMAIL	SHARED WITH:
✓ • CaseyRobin ⓘ	Jan Carpenter View & Edit ❯
ICLOUD	Accepted
All iCloud	Cindy Love View & Edit ❯
✓ • Cindy ⓘ	Accepted
Shared with Jan Carpenter	Add Person…
✓ • Work Stuffs ⓘ	
✓ • Curling League ⓘ	COLOR
FACEBOOK	• Red
🅕 Facebook Events	• Orange
🎂 Birthdays	• Yellow ✓
	• Green

This screen exists partly as a reference, a cheat sheet to help you remember what color goes with which category, and partly as a tappable subset chooser. That is, you can tap a category's name to hide or show all of its appointments on the calendar. A checkmark means you're seeing its appointments. (The **All [Account Name]** button turns on or off all that account's categories at once.)

If you tap **Edit**, then a little ❯ appears next to each calendar's name. When you tap it, you're offered a screen where you can change the calendar's name, color, and list of people who can see it (previous page, right)—or scroll all the way down to see the **Delete Calendar** button.

The Edit Calendars screen also offers an **Add Calendar** button. It's the key to creating, naming, and colorizing a *new* calendar on the phone. (Whatever changes you make to your calendar categories on the phone will be synced back to your Mac or PC.)

> **TIP:** You can share an iCloud calendar with other iCloud members (previous page, right), which is fantastic for families and small businesses who need to coordinate. Tap **Calendars**, and then tap ⓘ next to the calendar's name. Tap **Add Person** and enter the person's name. Your invitees get invitations by email; with one click, they've added your appointments to their calendars. They can make changes, too.
>
> You can also share a calendar with anyone (not just iCloud members) in a "Look, don't touch" condition. Tap **Calendars**, and then tap ⓘ next to the calendar's name. Turn on **Public Calendar**; tap **Share Link** to open the Share sheet for sending the link. Most calendar apps understand the calendar link that your phone sends.

Search

If you tap Q and type into the search box, you pare down the list of all calendar events from all time; only events whose names match what you've typed show up. Tap one to jump to its block on the corresponding Day view.

Next time you're sure you made an appointment with Harvey but you can't remember the date, keep this search feature in mind.

> **TIP:** The iOS calendar is pretty basic. For more features and power, consider calendar apps like Fantastical or BusyCal.

Clock

It's not just a clock—it's more like a time factory. Hiding behind this single icon on the Home screen are five programs: a world clock, an alarm clock, a stopwatch, a countdown timer, and—new in iOS 10—a bedtime-management module.

> **TIP:** The app icon itself on the Home screen shows the current time! Isn't that cute?

World Clock

When you tap World Clock on the Clock screen, you start out with only one clock, showing the current time in Apple's own Cupertino, California.

The neat part is that you can open up *several* of these clocks and set each one to show the time in a different city. By checking these clocks, you'll know what time it is in some remote city, so you don't wake somebody up at what turns out to be 3 a.m.

To specify which city's time appears on the clock, tap + at the upper-right corner. Scroll to the city you want, or tap its first letter in the index at the right side to save scrolling, or tap in the search box at the top and type the name of a major city. As you type, matching city names appear; tap the one whose time you want to track.

As soon as you tap a city name, you return to the World Clock display.

You can scroll the list of clocks. You're not limited by the number that fit on your screen at once.

> **TIP:** Only the world's major cities are in the iPhone's database. If you're trying to track the time in Squirrel Cheeks, New Mexico, add a major city in the same time zone instead—like Albuquerque.

To edit the list of clocks, tap **Edit**. Delete a city clock by tapping ⊖ and then **Delete**, or drag clocks up and down using the ≡ as a handle. Then tap **Done**.

Alarm

If you travel much, this feature could turn out to be one of your iPhone's most useful functions. It's reliable, it's programmable, and it even wakes *the phone* first, if necessary, to wake *you*.

To set an alarm, tap **Alarm** at the bottom of the Clock screen. You're shown the list of alarms you've already created, even if none are currently set to go off (below, left). You could create a 6:30 a.m. alarm for weekdays and an 11:30 a.m. alarm for weekends.

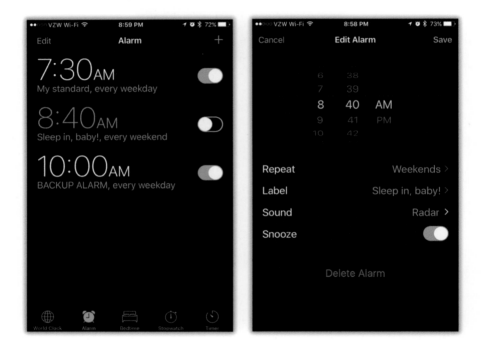

To create a new alarm, tap + to open the **Add Alarm** screen.

TIP: But really, you *should not bother* setting alarms using this manual technique. Instead, you'll save a lot of time and steps by using Siri. Just say, "Set my alarm for 7:30 a.m." (or whatever time you want).

And while we're at it: You can also say, "Change my 7:30 a.m. alarm to 8 a.m." And if you get really lucky with your life karma, you may even have the opportunity to say the greatest thing you can possibly say to Siri: "Turn off my alarm."

You have several options here:

- **Time dials.** Spin these three vertical wheels—hour, minute, AM/PM—to specify the time you want the alarm to go off.

- **Repeat.** Tap to specify what days this alarm rings. You can specify, for example, Mondays, Wednesdays, and Fridays by tapping those three buttons. (Tap a day-of-the-week button again to turn off its checkmark.) Tap **Back** when you're done. (If you choose Saturdays and Sundays, iOS is smart enough to call that "Weekends." And it knows that Monday, Tuesday, Wednesday, Thursday, and Friday are "Weekdays.")

- **Label.** Tap to give this alarm a description, like "Get dressed for wedding." That message appears on the screen when the alarm goes off.

- **Sound.** Choose what sound you want to ring. You can choose from any of the iPhone's ringtone sounds, any you've added yourself—or, best of all, **Pick a Song**. That's right—you can wake to the music of your choice.

- **Snooze.** If this option is on then, at the appointed time, the alarm message on the screen offers you a **Snooze** button. Tap it for 9 more minutes of sleep, at which point the iPhone tries again. (If your phone was in Sleep mode, it gives you a countdown to the next rude awakening.)

When you finally tap **Save**, you return to the Alarm screen, which lists your new alarm. Just tap the on/off switch to cancel an alarm. It stays in the list, though, so you can quickly reactivate it another day, without having to redo the whole thing. You can tap + to set another alarm, if you like.

Now the ⏰ icon appears in the status bar at the top of the iPhone screen. That's your indicator that the alarm is set.

To delete an alarm, swipe left across its name and then tap **Delete**. To make changes to the time, name, sound, and so on, tap **Edit**, and then tap the alarm.

TIP: The iPhone never deletes an alarm after using it; over time, therefore, your list of alarms may grow alarmingly large. Fortunately, you can tell Siri to clean them up for you in one fell swoop. Just say, "Delete all my alarms."

So what happens when the alarm goes off? The iPhone wakes itself up, if it was asleep. A message appears, identifying the alarm and the time.

And, of course, the sound rings. This alarm is one of the only iPhone sounds that you'll hear **even if the silencer switch is turned on**. Apple figures that if you've gone to the trouble of setting an alarm, you probably want to know about it, even if you forget to turn the ringer back on.

To stop the alarm, tap Stop or press the Home button. To snooze it, tap the Snooze button or press the Sleep switch or a volume key. (In other words, in your sleepy haze, just grab the phone with your whole hand and squeeze. You'll hit *something* that shuts the thing off.)

Once your alarm has gone off, its time remains listed in the Clock app (on the Alarm screen), but its on/off switch goes to Off.

Bedtime

Medical research tells us that sleep deprivation and inconsistent sleep schedules take a terrible toll on our health, mood, and productivity. So iOS 10's Clock app offers a new Bedtime tab. If you answer a few questions about your sleep habits, the app will attempt to keep your sleep regular—prompting you when it's time to get ready for bed, waking you at a consistent time, and keeping a graph of your sleep consistency.

The first time you open this panel, the interview begins. On successive screens, it asks: What time would you like to wake up? Which days of the week should the alarm go off? How many hours of sleep do you need each night? When would you like a bedtime reminder? (That is, how many minutes before you want to hit the pillow?) What ringtone or sound do you want to hear when you wake up?

> **TIP:** You can change your answers to any of these questions later by tapping Options at top left.

At this point, you see the master Bedtime graph shown on the facing page at left. It's a handy visualization of the mental math millions of people perform every night anyway: "If I go to bed now, I'll get five hours of sleep!"

The real point of Bedtime, though, is the Sleep Analysis graph below all of this. Your goal is to keep the bars consistent over time—both in length and vertical position. It's not enough to get enough sleep; you should also try to sleep during the same period each night.

If you care about your health, mood, and productivity, that is.

> **TIP:** The More history button you may see here opens the Health app described later in this chapter. Behind the scenes, the Health app is doing the actual work for the Bedtime module.

Stopwatch

You've never met a more beautiful stopwatch than this one. Tap **Start** to begin timing something: a runner, a train, a person who's arguing with you.

While the digits are flying by, you can tap **Lap** as often as you like. Each time, the list at the bottom identifies how much time elapsed since the *last* time you tapped **Lap**. It's a way for you to compare, for example, how much time a runner is spending on each lap around a track. You see the numbered laps and the time for each.

NOTE: If you prefer an old-timey analog stopwatch display, slide the digital readout to the left. Slide right to bring back the digital stopwatch.

You can work in other apps while the stopwatch is counting. In fact, the timer keeps ticking away even when the iPhone is asleep! As a result, you can time long-term events, like how long it takes an ice sculpture to melt, the time it takes for a bean seed to sprout, or the length of a Michael Bay movie.

Tap **Stop** to freeze the counter; tap **Start** to resume the timing. If you tap **Reset**, you reset the counter to zero and erase all the lap times.

Timer

The fourth Clock mini-app is a countdown timer. You input a starting time, and it counts down to zero.

Countdown timers are everywhere in life. They measure the periods in sports and games, cooking times in the kitchen, penalties on *The Amazing Race*. But on the iPhone, the timer has an especially handy function: It can turn off the music or video after a specified amount of time. In short, it's a sleep timer that plays you to sleep and then shuts off to save power.

To set the timer, open the Clock app and then tap **Timer**. Spin the two dials to specify the number of hours and minutes you want to count down.

Then tap the **When Timer Ends** control to set up what happens when the timer reaches 0:00. Most of the options here are ringtone sounds, so you'll have an audible cue that the time's up. The last one, though, **Stop Playing**, is the aforementioned sleep timer. It stops audio and video playback at the appointed time, so that you (and the iPhone) can go to sleep. Tap **Set**.

Finally, tap **Start**. Big clock digits count down toward zero. While it's in progress, you can do other things on the iPhone, change the **When Timer Ends** settings, or just hit **Cancel** to forget the whole thing.

> **TIP:** It's much faster and simpler to use Siri to start, pause, and resume the Timer. See page 151.
>
> If you have an iPhone 6s or 7, you can also open the Control Center (page 46) and hard-press the Timer icon. Its shortcut menu offers instant timer options for 1 hour, 20 minutes, 5 minutes, or 1 minute.

Compass

The iPhone has something very few other phones offer: a magnetic-field sensor known as a magnetometer, even better known as a **compass**.

When you open the Compass app, you get exactly what you'd expect: a classic Boy Scout wilderness compass that always points north.

Except it does a few things the Boy Scout compasses never did. Like displaying a digital readout of your heading, altitude, city name, and precise geographic coordinates at the bottom. And offering a choice of *true* north (the "top" point of the Earth's rotational axis) or *magnetic* north (the spot that traditional compasses point to, which is about 11 degrees away from true north). You choose in Settings→Compass.

To use the compass, hold it roughly parallel to the ground, and then read it like...a compass. Tap the center of the compass to lock in your current heading; a red strip shows how far you are off course. Tap again to unlock the heading.

> **TIP:** For many people, the real power of the compass is in the Maps app. (You can jump directly from Compass to Maps by tapping the coordinates below the compass dial.)
>
> The compass lets Maps know which way you're *facing*. That's a critical detail when you're lost in a city, trying to find a new address, or emerging from the subway with no idea which way to walk.

People who write iPhone programs can tap into the compass, too. There's an "augmented reality" app called New York Nearest Subway, for example. By using the compass, GPS, and tilt-sensor information, it knows where you are and how you're holding the phone—and so it superimposes arrows that show where to find the nearest subway stop and which line it's on.

The Carpenter's Level

The Compass app has a secret identity: It doubles as a carpenter's level. The next time you need to hang a picture, or prop up a wobbly table, or raise a barn, you'll now know when you've got things perfectly horizontal or vertical.

From the Compass screen, swipe to the left to reveal the level. It measures all three dimensions:

- **Right/left.** Hold the iPhone upright (against a picture you're hanging, say), and tilt it left and right. When it's perfectly upright, the readout says 0 degrees, and the bottom half of the screen turns green.

- **Forward/back.** Hold the phone upright and tip it away from or toward you. Once again, "0 degrees" and green mean "level."

- **Perfectly flat.** Hold the phone on its back, screen facing the sky. When the two circles merge (above, right), you'll know you've got it perfectly level. You could, for example, put the iPhone on a table you're trying to adjust, using its gauge to know how close you're getting as you wedge something under its short leg.

Health

This app, newly renovated in iOS 10, is a dashboard for all the health data—activity, sleep, nutrition, relaxation—generated by your fitness apps. But even if you don't have an app or a band, you have the iPhone itself; unbeknownst to you, it's been quietly tracking the steps you've been taking and the flights of stairs you've been climbing, just by measuring the jostling of the phone in your pocket or bag! (If that creeps you out just a bit, you can turn it off in Settings→ Privacy→Motion & Fitness.)

Lots of apps and fitness bands share their data with Health: the Apple Watch, UP band, MyFitnessPal, Strava, MapMyRun, WebMD, MotionX-24/7, 7 Minute Workout, Withings Health Mate, Garmin Connect Mobile, Lark, Lose It!, Sleepio, Weight Watchers, and so on. Fitness tracking is a big, big deal these days, now that your phone and/or your fitness band can measure your steps, exercise, and sleep.

If you have one of those bands or apps, you'll have to fish around in its settings until you find the option to connect with Health. At that point, you must turn on the kinds of data you want it to share with Health.

Next, open the Health app. The next bit of setup is to specify what kind of data you want staring you in the face on its Dashboard screen. This is the motivational aspect of Health: The more you're forced to *look at* and *think about* your weight, activity, sleep, or calories, the more likely you are to improve.

The Four Biggies

The top of the screen offers huge tiles for Activity, Mindfulness, Nutrition, and Sleep—in Apple's mind, the Big Four of health. An introductory video appears when you tap each of these, explaining with charming British narration the importance of that life factor. On each screen, you can see the latest graphs of your efforts in that category. (For some, like Mindfulness, you won't see anything unless you've installed an app that generates that kind of data.)

Below those tiles, you'll find places to record health data, like your body measurements, electronic medical records, reproductive data, and so on.

Three other tabs appear in Health:

- **The Today Tab.** Here's a single summary screen of the Big Four, all in one place. You can tap any one of these summary bubbles to view it in more detail—for example, to switch among **Day**, **Week**, **Month**, or **Year** graphs.

- **Sources.** This screen lists all the fitness apps and gadgets you've hooked up to Health (including the Apple Watch, if you have one), so that you know where your data is going.

- **Medical ID.** This screen offers a reason to use the Health app even if you don't use any fitness apps and don't track any medical statistics. It's the electronic equivalent of an emergency medical ID bracelet. You can record your name, age, blood type, weight, height, medical conditions, and emergency contact information. This screen also makes it easy to do something noble: offer to donate your organs after you pass away.

If you tap **Edit** and turn on **Show When Locked**, then this information will be available on your phone's Lock screen. If you pass out, have a seizure, or otherwise become medically inconvenienced, a passerby or medical pro can get that critical information without needing your password (or your awareness).

If that person is technically savvy, that is. Finding the Medical ID screen is fairly tricky. From the Lock screen, press the Home button to view the Enter Passcode screen; tap **Emergency**; tap **Medical ID**.

Home

HomeKit is Apple's home-automation standard. The Home app lets you set up and control any product whose box says "Works with HomeKit"— all of those "smart" or "connected" door locks, security cameras, power outlets, thermostats, doorbells, lightbulbs, leak/freeze/temperature/humidity/air-quality sensors, and so on.

Once you've installed the gadget and hooked it up in the Home app, you can turn it on and off, monitor its readouts, or adjust its settings (like on the thermostat shown below at right). You can do all of that from the

Home app, from the Control Center (shown on the previous page, left), or by using Siri voice commands ("Lock the front door," "Turn on the downstairs lights," and so on). You can automate those actions based on the time or your location, or hand off control of certain devices to other people's iPhones.

For complete details on setting up and using Home and HomeKit, see this book's free online PDF appendix, "HomeKit and the Home App." It's on this book's "Missing CD" at *www.missingmanuals.com*.

iBooks

iBooks is Apple's ebook reading program. It turns the iPhone into a sort of pocket-sized Kindle. With iBooks, you can carry around dozens or hundreds of books in your pocket, which, in the pre-ebook days, would have drawn some funny looks in public.

Most people think of iBooks as a reader for books that Apple sells on its iTunes bookstore—bestsellers and current fiction, for example—and it does that very well. But you can also load it up with your own PDF documents, as well as thousands of free, older, out-of-copyright books.

> **TIP:** iBooks is very cool and all. But, in the interest of fairness, it's worth noting that Amazon's free Kindle app, and Barnes & Noble's free B&N eReader app, are much the same thing—but offer much bigger book libraries at lower prices than Apple's.

Downloading Books

To shop the iBooks bookstore, open the iBooks app. If this is your first time diving in, you might be offered a selection of free starter books to download right now. Go for it; they're real, brand-name books by famous authors.

If, at any time, you want to buy another book—it could happen—well, the icons across the bottom are the literary equivalent of the App Store. Tap Featured to see what Apple is plugging this week; Top Charts to see this week's bestsellers, including what's on *The New York Times* Best Sellers list (note that there's a special row for *free* books); Search to search by name; and Purchased to see what you've bought.

> **TIP:** Once you've bought a book from Apple, you can download it again on other iPhones, iPod Touches, iPads, and Macs. Buy once, read many times. That's the purpose of the Not on This iPhone tab, which appears when you tap Purchased.

Once you find a book that looks good, you can tap Sample to download a free chapter, read ratings and reviews, or tap the price itself to buy the book and download it straight to the phone.

PDFs and ePub Files

You can also load up your ebook reader from your computer, feeding it with PDF documents and ePub files.

> **NOTE:** ePub is the normal iBooks format. It's a very popular standard for ebook readers, Apple's and otherwise. The only difference between the ePub documents you create and the ones Apple sells is that Apple's are copy-protected.

As usual, your Mac or PC is the most convenient loading dock for files bound for your iPhone. If you have a Mac, open the iBooks program.

If not, open iTunes, click your iPhone's icon at the top (when it's connected), and then click **Books**.

Either way, you now see all the books, PDF documents, and ePub files that you've slated for transfer. To add to this set, just drag files off your desktop and directly into this window, as shown below.

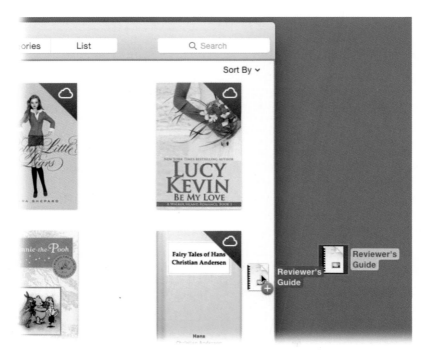

And where are you supposed to get all these files? Well, PDF documents are everywhere—people send them as attachments, and you can turn any document into a PDF file. (For example, on the Mac, in any program, choose **File→Print**; in the resulting dialog box, click **PDF→Save as PDF**.)

> **TIP:** If you get a PDF document as an email attachment, then adding it to iBooks is even easier. Tap the attachment to open it; now tap **Open in iBooks** in the corner of the page. (The iPhone may not be able to open really huge PDFs, though.)

But free ebooks in ePub format are everywhere, too. There are 33,000 free downloadable books at *gutenberg.org*, for example, and over a million at *books.google.com*—oldies, but classic oldies, with lots of Mark Twain, Agatha Christie, Herman Melville, H.G. Wells, and so on. (Lots of these are available in the Free pages of Apple's own iBooks Store, too.)

You'll discover that these freebie books usually come with generic-looking covers. But once you've dragged them into iTunes, it's easy to add good-looking covers. Use *images.google.com* to search for the book's title. Right-click (or Control-click) the cover image in your web browser; from the shortcut menu, choose **Copy Image**. In iTunes, in Library mode, choose **Books** from the top-left pop-up menu. Right-click (or Control-click) the generic book; choose **Get Info**; click **Artwork**; and paste the cover you copied. Now that cover will sync over to the iPhone along with the book.

Once you've got books in iTunes, connect the iPhone, choose its name at top right, click the **Books** tab at top, and turn on the checkboxes of the books you want to transfer.

Your Library

Once you've supplied your iBooks app with some reading material, the fun begins. When you open the app, its **My Books** tab shows a futuristic, shaded bookshelf with your library represented as little book covers. Mostly what you'll do here is tap a book to open it. But there are other activities waiting for you:

- Tap the ☰ icon, which switches the book-cover view to a much more boring (but more compact) list view. Buttons at the top let you sort the list by author, title, category, and so on.

- Tap **Select** if you want to delete a book, or a bunch of them. To do that, tap each book thumbnail that you want to target for termination; observe how they sprout ✅ marks. Then tap **Delete**. Of course, deleting a book from the phone doesn't delete your safety copy in iTunes or online.

- The **Search** button at the bottom of the iBooks screen lets you search by author or title—not just *your* books, but the entire iBooks Store.

- When you first start using a new iPhone, iPad, or Mac, your book covers bear the ☁ symbol. It means: "Our records show that you've bought this book, but it's still online, in the great Apple locker in the sky. Tap to download it to your phone so you can start reading."

Collections

You can create subfolders for your books called *collections*. You might have one for school and one for work, or one for you and one for somebody who shares your phone, for example.

To switch your view to a different collection, tap the collection's name. It's the top-center button, which starts out saying **All Books**. (If you've loaded some PDF documents, then you'll find a collection called "PDFs," already set up.) To create a new collection, open that top-center menu and hit **New Collection**.

And to move a book into a different collection: Tap **Select**, tap a book (or several), and then tap **Move**. It opens the Collections screen shown below, so that you can choose a new collection for the selected items.

> **TIP:** You can reorganize your bookshelf in a collection (which you can't do in the All Books view). Hold down your finger on a book until it swells with pride, and then drag it into a new spot.

Edit	Collections	Done
All		
Books		✓
PDFs		
Read For School		
Mindless Beach Books		
New Collection		
Hide iCloud Books		◯

Reading

But come on. You're a reader, not a librarian. Here's how to read an ebook.

Open the book or PDF by tapping the book cover. Now the book opens, ready for you to read. Looks great, doesn't it? (If you're returning to a book you've been reading, iBooks remembers your place.)

If the phone detects that it's nighttime (or just dark where you are), the screen appears with white text against a black background. That's to prevent the bright white light of your phone from disturbing other people in, for example, the movie theater. (This is the Night theme, and you can turn it off.)

> **TIP:** Turn the phone 90 degrees for a wider column of text.

In general, reading is simple: Just read. Turn the page by tapping the edge of the page—or swiping your finger across the page. (If you swipe slowly, you can actually see the "paper" bending over—in fact, you can see through to the "ink" on the other side of the page! Amaze your friends.) You can tap or swipe the left edge (to go back a page) or the right edge (to go forward).

TIP: This is rotation lock's big moment. When you want to read lying down, you can prevent the text from rotating 90 degrees using rotation lock (page 25).

But if you tap a page, a row of additional controls appears:

- ‹ takes you back to the bookshelf view.

- ☰ opens the table of contents. The chapter or page names are "live"—you can tap one to jump there.

- ᴀA lets you change the look of the page. For example, this panel offers a screen-brightness slider. That's a nice touch, because the brightness of the screen makes a big difference in the comfort of your reading. (This is the same control you'd find in the Control Center or in Settings.)

  The A and A buttons control the type size—a huge feature for people with tired or over-40 eyes. And it's something paper books definitely

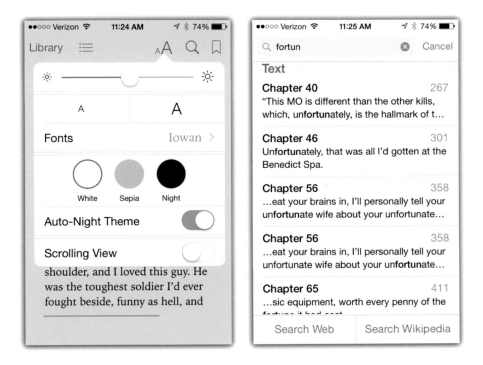

don't have. Tap the larger one repeatedly to enlarge the text; tap the smaller one to shrink it.

The same panel offers a Fonts button, where you can choose from eight typefaces for your book, as well as a Themes button, which lets you specify whether the page itself is White, Sepia (off-white), or Night (black page, white text, for nighttime reading). And there's an Auto-Night Theme button; if you don't care for the white-on-black theme, then turn off this switch. Finally, there's a Scrolling View switch. In scrolling view, you don't turn book "pages." Instead, the book scrolls vertically, as though printed on an infinite roll of Charmin.

- Q opens the search box. It lets you search for text within the book you're reading, which can be extremely useful. As a bonus, there are also Search Web and Search Wikipedia buttons so you can hop online to learn more about something you've just read.

- ☐ adds a bookmark to the current page. This isn't like a physical bookmark, where there's usually only one in the whole book; you can use it to flag as many pages, for as many reasons, as you like.

- **Chapter slider.** At the bottom of the screen, a slider represents the chapters of your book. Tap or drag it to jump around in the book; as you drag, a pop-up indicator shows you what chapter and page number you're scrolling to. (If you've magnified the font size, of course, then your book consumes more pages.)

> **TIP:** An iBooks book can include pictures and even videos. Double-tap a picture in a book to zoom in on it.

When you're reading a PDF document, by the way, you can do something you can't do when reading regular iBooks titles: zoom in and out using the usual two-finger pinch-and-spread gestures. Very handy indeed.

> **TIP:** On the other hand, here are some features that *don't* work in PDF files (only ebooks): font and type-size changes, page-turn animations, sepia or black backgrounds, highlighting, and notes.

Notes, Bookmarks, Highlighting, Dictionary

Here are some more stunts that you'd have trouble pulling off in a printed book. If you *double-tap* a word, or *hold your finger down* on a word, you get a bar that offers these options:

- **Speak** reads the highlighted passage aloud. (This button appears only if you've turned on Speak Selection in Settings→General→Accessibility→Speech.) Thank you, Siri!

- **Copy.** You can probably guess this one.

- **Look Up.** Opens up a page from iBooks' built-in dictionary. You know—in the unlikely event that you encounter a word you don't know.

- **Highlight.** Adds tinted, transparent highlighting, or underlining, to the word you tapped. For best results, don't tap the Highlight button until you've first grabbed the blue dot handles and dragged them to enclose the entire passage you want highlighted.

Once you tap Highlight, the buttons change into a special Highlight bar (above, middle). The first button opens a *third* row of buttons (bottom), so that you can specify which highlight color you want. (The final button designates underlining.)

The second button (🗑) removes highlighting. The third lets you add a note, as described next. The 🔼 button opens the Share sheet, also described momentarily.

- **Note.** This feature creates highlighting on the selected passage *and* opens an empty, colored sticky note, complete with keyboard, so you can type in your own annotations. When you tap Done, your note collapses down to a tiny yellow Post-it peeking out from the right edge of the margin. Tap to reopen it.

  To delete a note, tap the highlighted text. Tap 🗑.

- **Search** opens the same search box that you'd get by tapping the 🔍 icon—except this time the highlighted word is already filled in, saving you a bit of typing.

- **Share** opens the Share sheet (page 348) so you can send the highlighted material to somebody else by message or email, post it to Facebook or Twitter, or copy it to your Clipboard for pasting into another app.

> **NOTE:** If you've highlighted a single word, and if you have Speak Selection turned on in Settings→General→Accessibility→Speech, then there's one more option: Spell. It spells the word aloud for you, one letter at a time.

There are a couple of cool things going on with your bookmarks, notes, and highlighting, by the way. Once you've added them to your book, they're magically and wirelessly synced to any other copies of that book—on other gadgets, like the iPad or iPod Touch, your other iPhones, or even Mac computers running OS X Mavericks or later. Very handy indeed.

Furthermore, if you tap the ☰ to open the Table of Contents, you'll see the Bookmarks and Notes tabs. Each presents a tidy list of all your bookmarked pages, notes, and highlighted passages. You can tap 🔼 (and then Share Notes) to print or email your notes, or tap one of the listings to jump to the relevant page.

Books That Read to You

iBooks can actually read to you! It's a great feature when you're driving or jogging, when someone's just learning to read, or when you're having trouble falling asleep. There's even a special control panel just for managing your free audiobook reader.

To get started, open **Settings**→**General**→**Accessibility**→**Speech**. Turn on **Speak Screen**.

Then open a book in iBooks. Swipe down the page with two fingers to make the iPhone start reading the book to you, out loud, with a synthesized voice. At the same time, a palette appears, offering these speech controls:

Collapse controls   *Close controls*

Read slower   *Pause*   *Read faster*

Back a page   *Next page*

After a few seconds, the palette shrinks into a **>** button at the edge of the screen—and, after that, it becomes transparent, as though trying to make itself as invisible as possible. You can, of course, tap it to reopen it.

Yes, this is exactly the feature that debuted in the Amazon Kindle and was then removed when publishers screamed bloody murder—but, somehow, so far, Apple has gotten away with it.

iBooks Settings

If you've embraced the simple joy of reading electronic books the size of a chalkboard eraser, then you deserve to know where to make settings changes: in **Settings**→**iBooks**. Here are the options waiting there:

- **Use Cellular Data.** Do you want to be able to download books using your carrier's cellular data network (which eats up your monthly data allotment)? If you turn this off, then you can download books only when you're in a Wi-Fi hotspot.

- **Full Justification.** Ordinarily, iBooks presents text with fully justified margins (left). Turn this off if you prefer ragged right margins (right).

Full justification

sometimes he feels that there really is another way, if only he could stop bumping for a moment and think of it. And then he feels that perhaps there isn't. Anyhow, here he is at the bottom, and ready to be introduced to you. Winnie-the-Pooh.

When I first heard his name, I said, just as you are going to say, "But I thought he was a boy?"

"So did I," said Christopher

Ragged right margin

sometimes he feels that there really is another way, if only he could stop bumping for a moment and think of it. And then he feels that perhaps there isn't. Anyhow, here he is at the bottom, and ready to be introduced to you. Winnie-the-Pooh.

When I first heard his name, I said, just as you are going to say, "But I thought he was a boy?"

"So did I," said Christopher

- **Auto-hyphenation.** Sometimes, typesetting looks better if hyphens allow partial words to appear at the right edge of each line. Especially if you've also turned on Full Justification.

- **Both Margins Advance.** Usually, tapping the right edge of the screen turns to the next page, and tapping the left edge turns *back* a page. If you turn on this option, then tapping *either* edge of the screen opens the next page. That can be handy if you're a lefty, for example.

- **Sync Bookmarks, Sync Collections.** Turn these on if you'd like your bookmarks and book collections to be synced with your other Apple gadgets.

- **Online Content.** A few books contain links to video or audio clips online. This option comes set to Off, because video and audio can eat up your monthly cellular data allotment like a hungry teenager.

There are even a couple of controls here that apply to audiobooks. They govern how much time skips when you tap one of the back or forward Skip buttons—15 seconds, for example.

Maps

Here it is, folks, the feature that made international headlines: the Maps app.

From its birth in 2007, the iPhone always came with Google Maps—an excellent mapping and navigation app. (Apple wrote it, but Google provided the maps and navigation data.) But in iOS 6, Apple replaced Google Maps with a new mapping system of its own.

Unfortunately, in its initial version, the databases underlying the Maps app had a lot of problems. They didn't include nearly as many points of interest (buildings, stores, landmarks) as Google's. Addresses were sometimes wrong.

Apple promised to keep working on Maps until it was all fixed, but in the meantime, in a remarkable apology letter, CEO Tim Cook recommended using one of Maps' rivals. By far the best one is Google Maps. It's free, it's amazingly smart (it knows what address you mean after you type only a few letters), it has public-transportation details, live traffic reports, Street View (you can see photos of most addresses, and even "look around" you), and of course Google's far superior maps and data.

All right—you've been warned. It may still take some time before Apple Maps is complete and reliable.

But while Apple's cartographical elves keep cleaning up the underlying maps, some of its features are pretty great, especially in the newly over-hauled iOS 10 version. And if you have a Mac, you can look up a destination on the Mac and then send the directions wirelessly to your phone.

Meet Maps

The underlying geographical database may need work, but Maps, the app itself, is a thing of beauty.

It lets you type in any address or point of interest in the U.S. or many other countries and see it plotted on a map, with turn-by-turn driving directions, just like a $300 windshield GPS unit. It also gives you a live national Yellow Pages business directory and real-time traffic-jam alerts. You can get bus and train schedules for a few U.S. cities. You have a choice of a street-map diagram or actual aerial photos, taken by satellite.

And Maps offers Flyover, an aerial, 360-degree 3D view of major cities.

Maps Basics

When you open Maps, a blue dot represents your current location. Double-tap to zoom in, over and over again, until you're seeing actual city blocks. You can also pinch or spread two fingers to shrink or magnify the view. Drag or flick to scroll around the map.

To zoom *out* again, you can use the rare *two-finger double-tap*.

You can twist two fingers to rotate the map. (A compass icon at top right helps you keep your bearings; you can tap it to restore the map's usual north-is-up orientation.) And if you drag two fingers up the screen, you tilt the map into 3D view, which makes it look more like you're surveying the map at an angle instead of straight down.

At any time, you can tap the ⓘ button in the corner of the screen to open a secret panel of options. Here's how you switch among Maps' three views of the world: Map, Transit, or Satellite.

Each tab also lets you set up preferences for that view. For Map: Do you want to see color-coded roads that show current traffic?. For Transit: Do you want to include buses as well as train schedules? For Satellite: Do you want street names and/or traffic colors superimposed on the aerial views?

Each of these tabs offers buttons that let you Mark My Location (drop a pin for your current spot, add it to your Favorites, add it to your Contacts, and so on), Add a Place (record the address and other details of a business, thereby adding it to Apple's database), and Report an Issue (tell Apple about a bug).

Finding Yourself

If any phone can tell you where you are, it's the iPhone. It has not one, not two, but *three* ways to determine your location.

- **GPS.** First, the iPhone contains a traditional GPS chip, of the sort that's found in windshield navigation units of old. If the iPhone has a good view of the sky, then it can do a decent job of consulting the 24 satellites that make up the Global Positioning System and determining its own location.

    And if it can't see the sky, the iPhone has two fallback location features.

- **Wi-Fi Positioning System.** Metropolitan areas today are blanketed by overlapping Wi-Fi signals. At a typical Manhattan intersection, you might be in range of 20 base stations. Each one broadcasts its own name and unique network address (its *MAC address*—nothing to do with Mac computers) once every second. Although you'd need to be within 150 feet or so to actually get onto the Internet, a laptop or phone can detect this beacon signal from up to 1,500 feet away.

    Imagine if you could correlate all those beacon signals with their physical locations. Why, you'd be able to simulate GPS—without the GPS!

    So for years, all those millions of iPhones have been quietly logging all those Wi-Fi signals, noting their network addresses and locations. (The iPhone never has to *connect* to these base stations. It's just reading the one-way beacon signals.)

    At this point, Apple's database knows about millions of hotspots—and the precise longitude and latitude of each.

So, if the iPhone can't get a fix on GPS, it sniffs for Wi-Fi base stations. If it finds any, it transmits their IDs back to Apple (via cellular network)—which looks up those network addresses and sends coordinates back to the phone.

That accuracy is good to within only 100 feet, and of course the system fails completely once you're out of populated areas. On the other hand, it works indoors, which GPS definitely doesn't.

- **The cellular triangulation system.** Finally, as a last resort, the iPhone can check its proximity to the cellphone towers around you. The software works a lot like the Wi-Fi location system, but it relies upon its knowledge of cellular towers' locations rather than Wi-Fi base stations. The accuracy isn't as good as GPS—you're lucky if it puts you within a block or two of your actual location—but it's something.

> **TIP:** The iPhone's location circuits eat into battery power. To shut them down when you're not using them, open Settings→Privacy and turn off **Location Services**.

All right—now that you know how the iPhone gets its location information, here's how you can use it. Its first trick is to show you where you are.

Tap the ↑ at the top of the Maps screen. The button turns solid blue, indicating that the iPhone is consulting its various references to figure out where you are. You show up as a blue pushpin that moves with you. It keeps tracking until you tap the ↑ enough times to turn it off.

Orienting Maps

It's great to see a blue pin on the map, and all—but how do you know which way you're facing? Thanks to the built-in magnetometer (compass), the map can orient itself for you.

Just tap the ↑ button twice. The map spins so that the direction you're facing is upward, and the ↑ icon points straight up. A "flashlight beam" emanates from your blue dot; its width indicates the iPhone's degree of confidence. (The narrower the beam, the surer it is.)

Searching Maps

Now, the following paragraphs guide you through using the search box in Maps. But, frankly, if you use it, you're a sucker. It's *much* quicker to use Siri to specify what you want to find.

You can say, for example, "Show me the map of Detroit" or "Show me the closest Starbucks" or "Give me directions to 200 West 79th Street in New York." Siri shows you that spot on a map; tap to jump into the Maps app.

If you **must** use the search box, though, here's how it works. It shouldn't be hard to find, since it opens automatically when you open Maps (below, left). Here are some of the ways you can dive into the Maps database of places.

- **Recents.** Below the box, there's a list of searches you've recently conducted. You'd be surprised at how often you want to call up the same spot again later—and now you can, just by tapping its name in this list.

TIP: If you swipe a listing to the left, you reveal two new buttons: Share (send the location information to someone) and Remove (if, for example, you intend to elope and don't want your parents to find out).

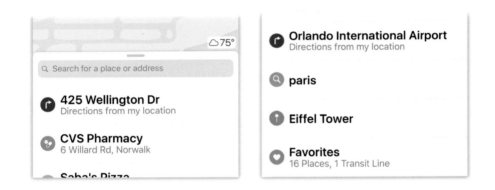

- **Favorites.** One nice thing about Maps is the way it tries to eliminate typing at every step. The Favorites are a great example. They're addresses you've flagged for later use by tapping the ♡, an option that appears on every place's Location card. For sure, you should bookmark your home and workplace. That will make it much easier to request driving directions.

  Then, to see your list of Favorites, scroll all the way to the bottom of the Recents list and tap Favorites (above, right). Tap one to jump to its spot on the map, or swipe to the left to reveal Share, Edit Name, and Remove buttons.

- **Business Categories.** When you first tap into an empty search box, you get icons for Food, Drinks, Shopping, Travel, Services, Fun, Health, and Transport. Each expands into eight more icons for further refinement (Travel offers Airports, Hotels, Banks & ATMs, and so on). Keep tapping to drill down to the place you want; it's all designed to save you typing when you're in a hurry.

Most people, though, most of the time, wind up typing what they want to find. You can type all kinds of things into the search box:

- **An address.** You can skip the periods (and usually the commas, too). And you can use abbreviations. Typing *710 w end ave ny ny* will find 710 West End Avenue, New York, New York. (In this and any of the other examples, you can type a zip code instead of a city and a state.)

- **An intersection.** Type *57th and lexington, ny ny*. Maps will find the spot where East 57th Street crosses Lexington Avenue in New York City.

- **A city.** Type *chicago il* to see that city. You can zoom in from there.

- **A zip code or a neighborhood.** Type *10024* or *greenwich village*.

- **Latitude and longitude coordinates.** Type *40.7484° N, 73.9857° W*.

- **A point of interest.** Type *washington monument* or *niagara falls*.

- **A business type.** Type *drugstores in albany ny* or *hospitals in roanoke va*.

- **A contact's name.** Maps is tied into Contacts, your master address book (page 109). Start typing a person's name to see the matches.

- **A business category.** Maps is a glorified national Yellow Pages. If you type, for example, *pharmacy 60609*, then those red pushpins show you all the drugstores in that Chicago zip code. It's a great way to find a gas station, a cash machine, or a hospital in a pinch. Tap a pushpin to see the name of the corresponding business.

As usual, you can tap the > button in the map pin's label bubble to open a details screen. If you've searched for a friend, then you see the corresponding Contacts card. If you've searched for a business, then you get a screen containing its phone number, address, website, and so on; often, you get a beautiful page of Yelp information (photos, reviews, ratings).

Remember that you can tap a web address to open it or tap a phone number to dial it. ("Hello, what time do you close today?")

Add a New Place

Once you've found something on the map—your current position, say, or something you've searched for—you can drop a pin there for future reference. Tap the ⓘ button; when the page slides up, tap **Mark My Location**. A blue pushpin appears. (If your aim wasn't exact, you can tap **Edit Location** and then scroll the map to adjust its position relative to the pin.)

> **TIP:** You can also drop a pin by holding your finger down on the right spot.

Scroll the new place's "card" to reveal its address, a Share button (so you can let someone else know where you are), an **Add to Favorites** button, and an option to add this location to somebody's card in Contacts (or to create a new contact).

The Location Card

Whenever you've tapped the name of some place in Apple's massive database (like a store, restaurant, or point of interest), the bottom part of the screen lists its information screen—its location "card."

The visible portion of this card already shows the all-important **Directions** button (below, left). But you can also hide the card by swiping down on it, or expand it to full screen by tapping or swiping up (right).

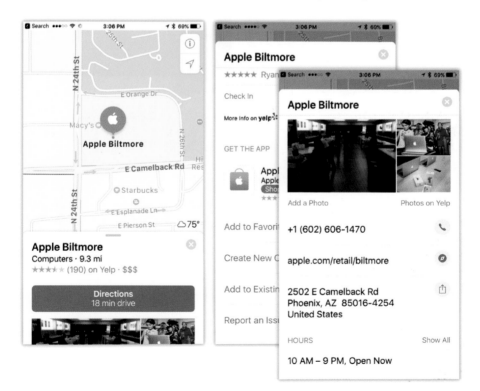

If this is the location for a restaurant or a business, you might strike gold: The Location page might offer several screens full of useful information, courtesy of *Yelp.com*. You'll see the place's hours of operation, plus one-tap links for placing a phone call to the place or visiting its website. Then there may be customer reviews, photos, delivery and reservation information, and so on.

Links here let you bookmark the spot, get directions, add it to Contacts, or share it with other people (via AirDrop, email, text message, Facebook, or Twitter).

TIP: The Location card for a restaurant may even offer a **Reservations** button, so that you can book a table on the spot—if, that is, that eatery participates in OpenTable's online booking system.

Directions

Suppose you've just searched for a place. The top part of its location card is open on the screen. At this point, you can tap **Directions** for instant directions, using four modes of transportation (below, left):

- **Drive.** You'll get the traditional turn-by-turn driving directions.

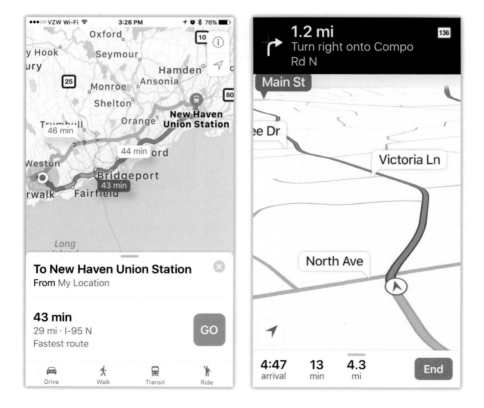

- **Walk.** The app will guide you to this place by foot. You get an estimate of the time it'll take, too.

- **Transit.** This button appears if you're in one of the cities for which Apple has public-transportation schedules: Atlanta, Austin, Baltimore, Boston, Chicago, Cincinnati, Cleveland, Columbus, Dallas, Denver, Honolulu, Kansas City, Los Angeles, Miami, New York City, Philadelphia, Pittsburgh, Portland, Sacramento, San Antonio, San Diego, San Francisco, Seattle, and Washington, D.C., plus a few big cities in Canada, Mexico, Europe, Japan, and China. More are coming, Apple says.

  If you're lucky enough to be in one of those cities, you'll discover that the public-transport directions are surprisingly clear and detailed. You even see the color, letter, and number schemes of that city's bus or rail system right there in the app.

TIP: iOS 10 comes ready to warn you when there's a disruption on your favorite commuter bus or rail system. To tell it which one you want it to monitor, tap ⓘ, and then **Transit**. Tap the map, and then zoom in on the transit line until you can tap its name or number. Its Details screen appears; scroll to the bottom and tap **Add to Favorites**.

At this point, you can add the Map Transit widget to your Today screen (see page 65). Without even unlocking your phone, with one quick swipe, you can see if the train is on time—and if not, what kind of delay you have to look forward to.

- **Ride** means calling an Uber or Lyft driver. (This feature requires that you have the Uber or Lyft app installed and set up. Also, you're asked to first Enable this feature; after that, one tap on **Ride** shows you the time and price estimates—and offers you a **Book** button.)

In each case, Maps displays an overview of the route you're about to drive. In fact, it usually proposes several different routes. They're labeled with little tags that identify how long each will take you: **3 hrs 37 min, 4 hrs 11 min**, and **4 hrs 33 min**, for example.

If you tap one of these tags, the bottom of the screen lets you know the distance and estimated time for that option and identifies the main roads you'll be on.

In each case, tap **Start** to see the first instruction.

The map zooms in, and Navigation mode begins.

Navigation Mode

When the iPhone is guiding you to a location, Maps behaves exactly like a windshield GPS unit, but better looking and with less clutter to distract you. You see a simplified map of the world around you, complete with the outlines of buildings, with huge banners that tell you how to turn next, and onto what street. Siri's familiar voice speaks the same information at the right times, so you don't even have to look at the screen.

Even if you hit the Sleep switch to lock the phone, the voice guidance continues. (It continues even if you switch to another app; return to Maps by tapping the banner at the top of the screen.)

The bottom bar shows your projected arrival time, plus the remaining distance and time. It also offers the End button, which makes the navigation stop.

While Maps is guiding you, you can zoom in and out; you can also pan the map to look ahead at upcoming turns or to inspect alternate routes. You can twist two fingers to turn the map, too. All of this is new in iOS 10.

Once you've shifted the view in these ways, a ➤ button appears. Tap it to restore Maps' usual centered view.

While you're navigating, you can also tap (or swipe up on) the bottom bar to reveal quick-tap buttons like these:

- **Gas Stations, Lunch, Coffee.** Perform instant searches for these frequent-favorite driver stops.

- **Overview.** Your entire planned route shrinks down to fit on a single screen. Now you see your entire route, and you can zoom, turn, and pan. To return to the navigation screen, tap ➤.

- **Details.** Tap to get a written list of turn-by-turn instructions.

- **Audio.** You can adjust the volume of Siri's speaking voice as she gives you driving directions by tapping here. Choose Low, Medium, or Loud Volume, or turn off her voice prompts altogether with No Voice.

  Here, too, is the Pause Spoken Audio switch. It means "When Maps speaks an instruction, momentarily pause playback of any background recordings, like podcasts and audiobooks. Because it'd get really confusing to hear two robo-people speaking at you at once."

Tap the screen (or just wait) to hide these additional controls once again.

Directions Between Two Other Points

The redesign of Maps seems to suggest that you'll always want to navigate somewhere from your current location. And usually, that's true.

Sometimes, though, you might want directions between two points—when you're not currently at either one. You can still do that in iOS 10, but you'd never guess how.

First, select your starting point. For example, add a pushpin marker as described on page 394, or tap a point-of-interest icon. Tap **Directions**, and then tap **My Location**.

Now you can change the From box (where it currently says **My Location**), using the same address-searching tactics described on page 392. (At this point, you can also swap your start and end points by tapping the double arrow.)

Finally, tap **Route** to see the fastest route and get going.

Night Mode

If the phone's ambient light sensor decides that it's dark in your car, it switches to a dimmer, grayer version of the map. It wouldn't want to distract you, after all. When there's enough light, it brightens back up again.

Where You Parked

Many a reviewer calls this the breakthrough feature of iOS 10: Maps automatically remembers where you parked, and can afterward guide you back to your car.

How does the phone know when you've parked? Because it connects wirelessly to your car over Bluetooth or CarPlay. (If your car doesn't have Bluetooth or CarPlay, you don't get this feature.)

When you turn off the car, the phone assumes that you've parked it, checks its GPS location, and makes a notification appear to let you know that it's memorized the spot. (If, that is, this feature is turned on in **Settings→Maps→Show Parked Location**.)

TIP: If you tap the notification, you're offered a chance to take a photo of the parking spot or to record some notes about it. The expanded alert also shows how long you've been parked—handy if you have to feed a meter.

When the time comes to return to your car, iOS 10 makes life as easy as possible. Wake the phone and swipe to the right to view the Maps widget or the Maps Destinations widget. Once you know where you parked, a swipe or a hard press gets you started finding your way back. (See page 65 for more on widgets.)

The car's location also appears in the Maps app itself, right there in the list of recent locations, and as a reminder in the Today tab of the Notification Center. Tap to begin your journey home.

Traffic

How's this for a cool feature? Free, real-time traffic reporting. Just tap the ⓘ button (it's visible whenever you're *not* in Navigation mode), and then turn on **Traffic**. Now traffic jams appear as red lines on the relevant roads, for your stressing pleasure; less severe slowdowns show up in orange.

Better yet, tiny icons appear, representing accidents, closures, and construction. Tap to see a description bar at the bottom of the screen (like "Accident, Park Ave at State St"); tap that bar to read the details.

If you don't see any colored lines, it's either because traffic is moving fine or because Apple doesn't have any information for those roads. Usually, you get traffic info only for highways, and only in metropolitan areas.

Flyover

You don't need a car to use Flyover, the Maps app's most dazzling feature; it has nothing to do with navigation, really. You can operate it even while you're lying on your couch like a slug.

Flyover is a dynamic, interactive, photographic 3D model of certain major cities. It looks something like an aerial video, except that *you* control the virtual camera. You can pan around these scenes, looking over and around buildings to see what's behind them. To create this feature, Apple says, it spent two years filming cities in helicopters.

To try it, you must be in Satellite view (tap ⓘ to get there). Enter 3D mode by dragging up the screen with two fingers.

Wait for a moment as the phone downloads the photographic models. Now you can go nuts, conducting your own virtual chopper tour of the city using the usual techniques:

- Drag with one finger to move around the map.

- Pinch or spread two fingers to zoom in or out.

- Drag two fingers up or down to change your camera angle relative to the ground.

- Twist two fingers to turn the world before you.

It's immersing, completely amazing, and very unlikely to make you airsick.

Flyover Tours

Apple wasn't satisfied with letting you pan around virtual 3D city models using your finger. Now it's prepared to give you *city tours* in 3D.

Use the search box to enter the name of a big city or major landmark. (Some examples: San Francisco, New York, Tokyo, London, Paris, Rome, Madrid, Vancouver, San Jose, Cape Town, Stockholm. Or places like Yosemite National Park, Sydney Opera House, Stonehenge, St. Peter's Basilica, or the Brooklyn Bridge.)

When you tap the search results, a new button appears on the place bar at the bottom: Flyover Tour. It starts a crazy treat: a fully automated video tour of that city or place. The San Francisco tour shows you the baseball park, the famous Transamerica Pyramid, the Alcatraz prison island, and so on. It's slow, soothing, cool, and definitely something that paper maps never did.

Extensions

There's one more goody in the new Maps: Extensions. These are add-on features made by other companies—auto-installed into Maps by their full-blown apps—like Uber, Lyft, Yelp, and OpenTable. The point, of course, is to let you order cars, read restaurant reviews, reserve tables, or buy tickets right from within Maps.

Extensions, for example, are responsible for adding the Ride button described on page 397.

You'll probably find them quite handy, but maybe not all of them. Fortunately, you can turn off individual extensions in Settings→Maps→ Extensions.

News

The News app, newly overhauled in iOS 10, does just what Apple promises: It "collects all the stories you want to read, from top news sources, based on topics you're most interested in." In other words, Apple has written its own version of Flipboard.

When you open the News app and tap Customize Your News, the setup process goes like this:

- **Choose your mags**. First, you're presented with a *very* tall scrolling list of favorite online publications (*The New York Times, Wired, The New Yorker,* and hundreds more) and topics (Movie Actors, Science...). You're supposed to tap the ones you want to use as News fodder.

- **Notifications**. On the next screen, you're invited to specify which of those publications and topics are allowed to trigger notifications (page 59).

- **Email**. The new News app is delighted to send you notifications of articles by email, too. Tap Sign Me Up to make it so.

And that's it: Suddenly, you have a beautiful, infinite, constantly updated, free magazine stand, teeming with stories that have been collated according to your tastes. All of it is free, although you're not getting the listed publications in full—usually, you're offered just a few selected stories.

The five tabs across the bottom are designed to offer multiple entry points into the eternal tsunami of web news:

- **For You** is the main thing. It's constantly updated with new articles that Apple's algorithms think you'll like, based on (a) your selections the first time you used the app, (b) the stories you favorited by tapping 🔼 and then **Love**, (c) the stories you indicated you *didn't* like by tapping 🔼 and then **Dislike**, and (d) which stories you actually wound up reading.

- **Favorites** displays icons for the publications and topics you've said you're interested in. Same stories, different starting point.

- **Explore** offers a list of breaking-news topics—and publications that Apple wants you to try out.

- **Search.** Oh, yes—you can search for articles by topic or publication.

- **Saved.** Most of the time, you can't use News without an Internet connection. If you anticipate that you'll be spending time in the living hell known as Offline mode (like on a subway, sailboat, or airplane), you can save some stories for reading later. To do that, tap ⬆ and then *Save*. You'll find your saved stories here, on the Saved tab.

Once you've tapped to open a story, using News is simplicity itself. Swipe vertically to scroll through an article, or horizontally to pull the next article into view.

Notes

The iPhone has always had a Notes app. But with each successive version of iOS, this ancient, text-only notepad becomes more complete, more Evernote-ish in scope. A Notes page can now include a checklist of to-dos, a photo, a map, a web link, or a sketch you draw with your finger.

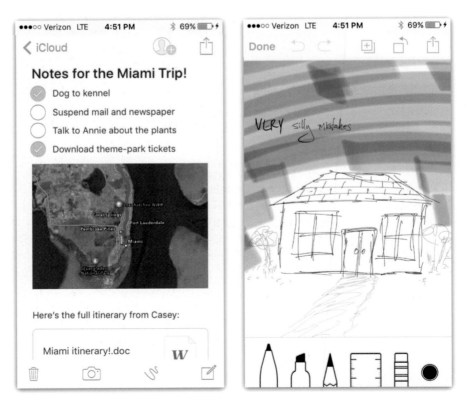

And in iOS 10, you can even share notes wirelessly with another iPhone fan, so that you can collaborate.

It's nice to be able to jot down—or dictate—lists, reminders, and brain-storms. You can email them to yourself when you're finished—or sync them right to your Mac or PC.

And, as always, any changes you make in Notes are automatically syn-chronized to all your other Apple gadgets and Macs.

> **NOTE:** The first time you open Notes, you may be invited to upgrade your existing notes to the new Notes format. If you don't, you don't get any of the new features. But if you do, you can't open your notes on any gadget that doesn't have iOS 9 (or later) or OS X El Capitan (or later) for the Mac.

To get started, tap ✐ to start a new blank note—what looks like a blank white page. The keyboard appears so you can begin typing.

> **TIP:** You can also send text *from* other apps *into* Notes. For example, in Mail, select some text you've typed into an outgoing message; in the button bar, tap **Share**. Similarly, you can tap a Mail attachment's icon; once again, tap **Add to Notes** in the Share sheet. In each case, your selection magically appears on a new Notes page.

Formatting and Photos

But there's also an intriguing-looking ⊕ button. It summons some fantas-tic buttons at the bottom of the page:

- ⊘ creates a checklist. Every paragraph you type sprouts a circle—which is actually a checkbox. Tap it to place a checkmark in there. This feature is fantastic for lists: to-do lists, packing lists, movies to see, gift tracking, party planning, job hunting, homework manage-ment, and so on.

  Each time you press Return, you create a new checklist item. But you can also select some existing paragraphs and then tap ⊘, turning it into a checklist after the fact.

- **Aa.** Hey, there are style sheets! You can create titles (big and bold type), headings (bold), bulleted lists, dashed lists, or auto-numbered lists, with just a couple of taps, using this menu.

- ⌖. You can insert a photo or video into a note—either by taking one with your camera on the spot or by choosing one that's already on your phone. Incredibly handy.

- ✍. Draw with your finger! The sketch tools include a marker, a high-lighter, a pencil, a straightedge (the ruler thing), an eraser, and a color chooser (the round dot—and don't miss the fact that there are three scrolling panels of colors). In iOS 10, you can even add multiple drawings to a single Note, thanks to the ⊞ button at the top. (You can't, however, use the sketch tools on photos you've brought into the Notes app. You'll have to mark them up in Photos and then insert them into Notes.)

To use the ruler, put two fingers on the "ruler" on the screen, and twist them to the angle you want. Then you can "draw against" it for perfect straight lines.

> **TIP:** If you have an iPhone 6s or 7 model, then all of the drawing tools (and the eraser) are pressure-sensitive! They make fatter or darker lines when you press harder with your finger.

When you're finished with a note for now, tap **Done**. The keyboard goes away, and a handy row of icons appears at the bottom of your Notes page. You can trash the note (🗑), add a checklist to it (☑), add a photo or video (📷), add a sketch (✍), or start a new note (✎).

The Share button is always available too, at the upper right. Tap ⬆ to print your note, copy it, or send it to someone by email, text message, AirDrop, and so on. For example, if you tap **Mail**, the iPhone creates a new outgoing message, pastes the first line of the note into the subject line, and pastes the note's text into the body. Address the note, edit if necessary, and hit **Send**. The iPhone returns you to Notes. (See page 348 for more on the sharing options.)

Sharing Notes

Here it is, a big new Notes feature of iOS 10: You and a buddy (or several) can edit a page in Notes simultaneously, over the Internet. It's great when you and your friends are planning a party and brainstorming about guests and the menu, for example. Also great for adding items to the grocery or to-do list even after your spouse has left the house to get them taken care of.

Just tap the new 👤➕ button at the top of the screen. On the Add People screen, specify how you want to send the invitation: by message, email, Facebook, Twitter, or whatever.

Once your collaborators receive and accept the invite, they can begin editing the note as though it's their own.

The live editing isn't as animated as it is in, for example, Google Docs—you don't see letter-by-letter typing—but other peoples' edits do appear briefly in yellow highlighting.

Once you've shared a note, the icon at the top changes to 👥✓, and a matching icon appears next to the note's name in the master list. At any time, you can stop sharing the note—or add more people to its collaboration—by tapping that 👥➕ icon again and editing the sharing panel that appears.

Locking Notes

In iOS 10, for the first time, you can *lock* notes, too—protect them with a password. They're here at last, suitable for listing birthday presents you intend to get for your nosy kid, the formula for your top-secret invisibility potion, or your illicit lovers' names.

Note that you generally hide and show all your locked notes with a *single* password. You don't have to make up a different password for every note.

> **TIP:** You *can* make up multiple passwords, though. Each time you want to start using a new password, open Settings→Notes→Password and tap Reset Password. After supplying your iCloud password, you're offered the chance to make up a password for any *new* notes you lock. All *existing* locked notes are still protected by the previous password.
>
> And if you've forgotten the password? Unless you've turned on Touch ID, all those old notes are locked forever. But you can still make up a new password to protect your latest secrets.

To lock a note, tap the ⬆️ button; on the Share screen, tap Lock Note (next page, left). (Why is locking a note sharing it? Never mind.) Make up a password for locking/unlocking all your notes (or, if you've done this before, *enter* the password).

As long as your locked notes are all unlocked, you can still see and edit them. But when there's any risk of somebody else coming along and seeing them (on your Mac, iPhone, iPad, or any other synced gadget), click the 🔓 to lock all your notes. (They also all lock when the phone goes to sleep—or if you tap Lock Now at the bottom of the screen.)

Now all you see of the locked notes are their titles. Everything on them is replaced by a "This note is locked" message, as shown on the next page at right. Tap View Note to unlock them with your fingerprint or password.

TIP: To remove the padlock from a note, tap ⬆ and then tap **Remove Lock**.

Use your power wisely.

The Notes List

As you create more pages, the ‹**iCloud** button (top left) becomes more useful. It opens your table of contents for the Notes pad, and offers a **New** button. And it's the only way to jump from one note to another. (It may not say "iCloud"; it bears the name of whatever online account stores your notes: Gmail, Exchange, or whatever. Or, if your notes exist only on the phone, you just see an unlabeled ‹ symbol.)

TIP: You can swipe rightward to jump from an open note back to the list.

Here's what this list displays:

- **The first lines of your notes** (most recent at the top), along with the time or date you last edited them. If there's a photo or sketch on a note—an unlocked one, anyway—you see its thumbnail, too (facing page, left).

To open a note, tap its name. To delete a note, swipe across its name in the list, right to left, and then confirm by tapping Delete.

NOTE: On iPhone Plus models, rotating the phone produces a whole new two-column layout. The left column shows your table of contents (first line of every note); the right column shows the selected note itself.

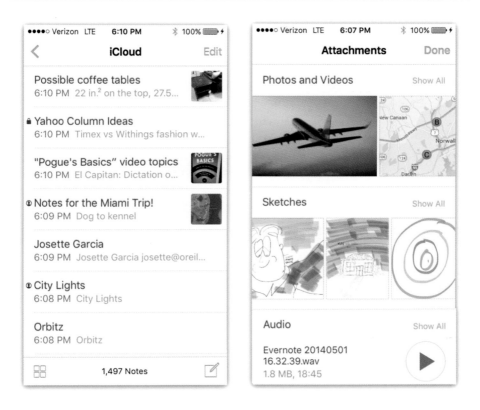

- **A search box.** Drag down on the list to bring the search box into view. Tap it to open the keyboard. You can now search all your notes instantly—not just their titles, but also the text inside them.

NOTE: Don't worry about your locked notes. iOS can search their titles, but not their contents—even if the notes are currently *unlocked*.

- ⊞. This is the new Attachments Browser. It brings up a tidy display of every photo, sketch, website, audio recording, and document that's ever been inserted into any of your notes. All in one place (above, right).

The beauty is that you don't have to remember what you called a note; just tap one of these items to open it. (At that point, you can tap **Show in Note** to open the note that contains it.)

NOTE: Attachments to notes that were once locked (whether or not they are locked right now) aren't shown here.

Syncing Notes

Notes can synchronize with all kinds of other Apple gear—other iPhones, iPads, iPod Touches, and Macs—so the same notes are waiting for you everywhere you look. Just make sure Notes is turned on in **Settings→iCloud** on each phone or tablet, and in **System Preferences→iCloud** on your Mac. The rest is automatic—and awesome.

Notes Accounts

Your notes can also sync wirelessly with the Notes modules on Google, Yahoo, AOL, Exchange, or another IMAP email account. To set this up, open **Settings→Mail**. Tap the account you want (iCloud, Gmail, Yahoo, AOL, or whatever); finally, turn the Notes switch **On**.

That should do it. Now your notes are synced nearly instantly, wirelessly, both directions.

NOTE: One catch: Notes that you create at *gmail.com*, *aol.com*, or *yahoo.com* don't wind up on the phone. Those accounts sync wirelessly in one direction only: *from* the iPhone to the website, where the notes arrive in a Notes folder. (There's no problem, however, if you get your AOL or Gmail mail in an email program like Outlook, Entourage, or Apple Mail. Then it's two-way syncing as usual.)

At this point, an **Accounts** button appears at the top-left corner of the table of contents screen. Tap it to see your note sets from Google, Yahoo, AOL, Exchange, iCloud, or an IMAP email account.

If you've created Notes folders on your Mac (Mountain Lion or later), then you see those folders here, too.

All of this makes life a little more complex, of course. For example, when you create a note, you have to worry about which account it's about to go into. To do that, be sure to specify an account name (and a folder within it, if necessary) *before* you create the new note.

NOTE: In **Settings→Notes**, you can also specify which of your different Notes accounts you want to be the *main* one—the one that new notes fall into if you haven't specified otherwise.

Podcasts

A podcast is a "radio" show that's distributed online. Lots of podcasts begin life as *actual* radio and TV shows; most of NPR's shows are available as podcasts, for example, so that you can listen to them whenever and wherever you like.

But thousands more are recorded just for downloading. They range from recordings made by professionals in studios—to amateurs talking into their phones. Some have thousands of listeners; some have only a handful.

One thing's for sure: There's a podcast out there that precisely matches whatever weird, narrow interests *you* have.

The Podcasts app helps you find, subscribe to, organize, and listen to podcasts. It's designed just like Apple's online stores for apps, music, movies, and so on. Tap Featured to see scrolling rows of recommended podcasts (below, left) or Top Charts to see what the rest of the world is listening to these days. Or use the Search button to look for something specific.

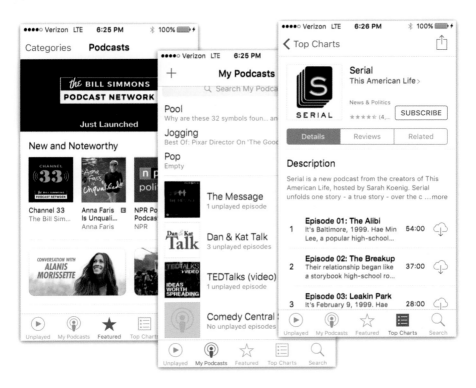

There are video podcasts, too, although they're much less common. The most popular videocasts are usually clips from network or cable TV shows, but there are plenty of quirky, offbeat, funny video podcasts that will never be seen except on pocket screens.

NOTE: Of course you can also watch video podcasts on your iPad, on your Mac or PC via iTunes, or via an Apple TV.

In any case, once you find a podcast episode that seems interesting (previous page, right), you can listen to it in either of two ways:

- **Stream it.** Tap a podcast's name to play it directly from the Internet. It's never stored on your iPhone and doesn't take up any space, but it does require an Internet connection. Generally no good for plane rides.

- **Download it.** If you tap the ☁ next to a podcast's name, you download it to your phone. It takes up space there (and podcasts can be big)—but you can play it back anytime, anywhere. And, of course, you can delete it when you're done.

Subscribing

Most podcasts are series. Their creators crank them out every week or whatever. If you find one you love, subscribe to it, so that your phone downloads each new episode automatically. Just tap **Subscribe** on its details page.

The episodes wind up on the My Podcasts screen (previous page, center). Tap a podcast's icon to open the episodes screen, where you can tap **Unplayed** (episodes you haven't heard) or **Feed** (all episodes). You'll also find buttons for **Edit** (delete episodes en masse); ⚙ (settings for this podcast only); and ⬆ (pass along links to this podcast by Messages, Mail, Twitter, Facebook, and so on).

Settings

There's a lot to control when it comes to podcasts. Do you want new episodes downloaded automatically? Do you want them autodeleted when you're finished? Do you want to limit how many episodes of each show are stored on your phone? What playback order—oldest first or newest first?

You make all these choices in **Settings→Podcasts**. That's the global setting for podcasts (next page, left)—but you can also override them for individual podcast shows, using the ⚙ button described already.

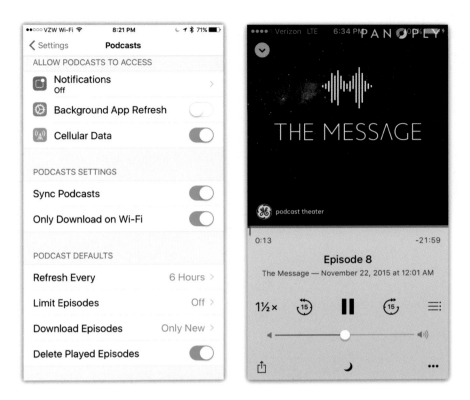

Playback

To play a podcast, tap its icon on **My Podcasts**, and then the episode name. Tap the playback strip at the bottom to reveal all the usual
audio-playback controls (page 236)—with the handy addition of a
button to toggle the talking speed (½x, 1x, 1½x, or 2x regular speed), as
shown above at right.

TIP: There's a Sleep Timer, too, that lets you drift off to the sound of a
droning podcaster. Tap the ☾ shown above at right to pick how long
you want the podcast to play before shutting off.

You can press the Sleep switch to turn off the screen; the podcast continues playing. And even if the phone is locked, you can open the Control
Center (page 46) to access the playback controls.

TIP: Don't forget to use Siri! You can say things like "Play 'Fresh Air'
podcast," "Play my latest podcasts," "Play my podcast" (to resume
what you listened to last), "Play latest TED podcast," and so on.

Reminders

Reminders not only records your life's little tasks, but it also reminds you about them at the right time or right place. For example, it can remind you to water the plants as soon as you get home.

If you have an iCloud account, your reminders sync across all your gadgets. Create or check off a task on your iPhone, and you'll also find it created or checked off on your iPad, iPod Touch, Mac, PC, and so on.

> **TIP:** Reminders sync wirelessly with anything your iCloud account knows about: Calendar or BusyCal on your Mac, Outlook on the PC, and so on.

Siri and Reminders are a match made in heaven. "Remind me to file the Jenkins report when I get to work." "Remind me to set the TiVo for tonight at 8." "Remind me about Timmy's soccer game a week from Saturday." "When I get home, remind me to take a shower."

The List of Lists

When you open Reminders, it's clear that you can create *more than one* to-do list, each with its own name: a groceries list, kids' chores, a running tally of expenses, and so on. It's a great way to log what you eat if you're on a diet, or to keep a list of movies people recommend.

They show up as file-folder tabs; tap one to open the to-do list within.

If you share an iCloud account with another family member, you might create a different Reminders list for each person. (Of course, now you run the risk that your spouse might sneakily add items to *your* to-do list!)

If you have an Exchange account, one of your lists can be synced to your corporate Tasks list. It doesn't offer all the features of the other lists in Reminders, but at least it's kept tidy and separate.

> **TIP:** You can use Siri to add things to individual lists by name. You can say, for example, "Add low-fat cottage cheese to the Groceries list."
>
> Siri can also find these reminders, saving you a lot of navigation later. You can say, "Find my reminder about dosage instructions," for example.

Once you've created some lists, you can easily switch among them. Just tap an open list's name to collapse it, returning to the list of lists. At that point you can tap the title of a different list to open it.

Reminders
6 items

Groceries
No items

To Dos
10 items

Chores
No items

Movies to See
4 items

CaseyRobin
6 items

◯ Return Hummer

◯ Northern Lights Club

Urgent to do
4 items   Edit

◯ Finish spackling the living room
  11/3, 4:00 PM

◉ Selloff all stocks
  Today, 4:00 PM

◯ Download Kindle books
  1/2, 4:00 PM

◉ New website proposal due
  12/20, 4:00 PM

◯ Prepare wedding proposal

◯ Call William about the thing

TIP: When you're viewing the list of lists, you can rearrange them by dragging their title bars up or down.

To create a new list, begin at the list of lists (above, left). Tap + at the top right. The app asks if you're trying to create a new **Reminder** (that is, one To Do item) or a new **List**, as shown at upper right; tap **List**.

If you have multiple accounts that offer reminders, you're asked to specify which one will receive this new list at this point, too (above, right).

Now your jobs begin:

1. **Enter a name for the list.** When you tap the light-gray letters **New List**, the keyboard appears to help you out.

2. **Tap a colored dot.** This will be the color of the list's title font and also of the "checked-off" circles once the list is under way.

3. **Tap Done.** Now you can tap the first blank line and enter the first item in the list.

After that first line, you can't create new items in the list by tapping the blank line below the existing items. As you type, tapping the Return key is the only way to move to the next line. (Tap **Done** when you're finished adding to the list.)

To delete a list, tap **Edit** and then tap **Delete List**.

Later, you can assign a task to a different list by tapping **List** on its Details screen.

To return to the list of lists, tap the current list's name. Or tap the bottom edge of the screen. Or swipe down from the top of it.

The Scheduled List

If you really do wind up using Reminders as a to-do list, you might be gratified to discover that the app also offers an automatically generated Scheduled list: a consolidated list of every item, from all your lists, to which you've given a *deadline*. It's always the topmost tab, marked by an alarm-clock icon.

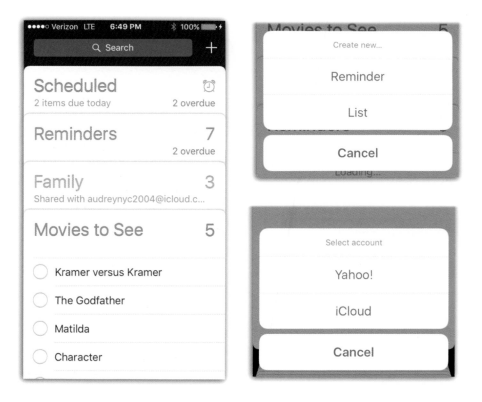

Recording a Reminder

Once you've opened a list, here's how you record a new task the manual way: Tap the blank line beneath your existing reminders. Type your reminder (or dictate it). Tap the ⓘ to set up the details, described next; tap Done when you're finished.

As you go through life completing tasks, tap the circle next to each one. A checked-off to-do remains in place until the next time you visit its list. At that point, it disappears. It's moved into a separate list called Completed.

But when you want to take pride in how much you've accomplished, you can tap Show Completed to bring your checked-off tasks back into view.

Other stuff you can do:

- **Delete a to-do item altogether, as though it never existed.** Swipe leftward across its name; tap Delete to confirm.

- **Delete a bunch of items in a row.** Tap Edit. Tap each ⊖ icon, and then tap Delete to confirm.

- **Rearrange a list so the items appear in a different order.** Tap Edit, and then drag the ☰ handle up or down.

The Details Screen

If you tap ⓘ next to an item's name, you arrive at the Details screen (next page, left). Here you can set up a reminder that will pop up at a certain time or place, create an auto-repeating schedule, file this item into a different to-do list with its own name, add notes to this item, or delete it. Here are your options, one by one:

- **Remind me on a day.** Here you can set up the phone to chime at a certain date and time. Turn on the switch to see two new lines: Alarm and Repeat. Tap Alarm to bring up the "time wheel" for setting the deadline.

  Tap Repeat if you want this reminder to appear every day, week, 2 weeks, month, or year—great for reminding you about things that recur in your life, like quarterly tax payments, haircuts, and anniversaries.

- **Remind me at a location.** If you turn on this amazing feature, then the phone will use its location circuits to remind you of this item when you arrive at a certain place or leave a certain place. When you tap the new Location line, you'll see that the phone offers "Current Location"—wherever you are at the moment. That's handy if, for

Details   Done

Call William about the thing

Remind me on a day   ⬭

Remind me at a location   ⬭

Priority | None | ! | !! | !!! |

List   Urgent to do >

Notes

‹ Details   **Location**

🔍 Li Kam, DDS   ⊗

➤   Current Location

📍 Li Kam Ho, DDS
    1590 El Camino Real South San Francisc…

📍 Nick's Home

| When I arrive… | When I leave… |

790 feet

example, you're dropping off your dry cleaning and want to remember to pick it up the next time you're driving by.

But you can also choose Home or Work (your home or work addresses, as you've set them up in Contacts). Or you can use the search box at the top, either to type or dictate a street address, or to search your own Contacts list.

NOTE: If you use Bluetooth to pair your phone to your car, you have a couple of other helpful choices: Getting in the car (to get a reminder when the iPhone connects to your car) and when Getting out of the car (to get one when it disconnects).

Once you've specified an address, the Location screen shows a map (above, right). The diameter of the blue circle shows the area where your presence will trigger the appearance of the reminder on your screen.

TIP: You can adjust the size of this "geofence" by dragging the black handle to adjust the circle. In effect, you're telling the iPhone how close you have to be to the specified address for the reminder to pop up. You can adjust the circle's radius anywhere from 328 feet ("Remind me when I'm in that store") to 1,500 miles ("Remind me when I'm in that country").

The final step here is to tap either When I Leave or When I Arrive.

Later, the phone will remind you at the appointed time or as you approach (or leave) the address, which is fairly mind-blowing the first few times it happens.

NOTE: If you set up *both* a time reminder *and* a location reminder, then your iPhone uses whichever event happens first. That is, if you ask to be reminded at 3 p.m. today and "When I arrive at the office," then you'll get the reminder when you get to the office—or at 3 p.m., if that time rolls around before you make it to work.

- **Priority.** Tap one of these buttons to specify whether this item has low, medium, or high priority—or None. In some of the calendar programs that sync with Reminders, you can sort your task list by priority.

- **List.** Tap here to assign this to-do to a different reminder list, as described earlier.

- **Notes.** Here's a handy box where you can record freehand notes about this item: an address, a phone number, details of any kind.

To exit the Details screen, tap Done.

"Remind Me About This"

Here's a reminder about a fantastic Reminders feature.

When you're looking at something in one of Apple's apps, you can say, "Remind me about this later." That might be a text message in Messages, a web page in Safari, an email in Mail, a document in Pages, or whatever. (This command works in Calendar, Clock, Contacts, iBooks, Health, Mail, Maps, Messages, Notes, Numbers, Pages, Phone, Podcasts, Reminders, and Safari. Software companies can upgrade their apps to work with "Remind me about this," too.)

Instantly, Siri creates a new item on your main Reminders list—named for the precise message, location, web page, document, or thing you were looking at—complete with the icon of the app you were using.

Later, you can tap that icon to open the original app—to the exact spot you were at when you issued the command.

You don't have to be as vague as "later," either. You can also say things like "Remind me about this tomorrow night at 7" or "Remind me about this when I get home."

Put it all together, and you've got an amazingly effective system for bookmarking your life. Maybe this trick will, once and for all, end the practice of people emailing stuff to themselves, just so they'll remember it.

Stocks

This one's for you, big-time day trader. The Stocks app tracks the rise and fall of the stocks in your portfolio by downloading the very latest stock prices.

(All right, maybe not the *very* latest. The price info may be delayed as much as 20 minutes, which is typical of free stock-info services.)

When you first fire it up, Stocks shows you a handful of sample high-tech stocks—or, rather, their abbreviations. (They stand for the Dow Jones Industrial Average, the NASDAQ Composite Index, the S&P 500 Index, Apple, Google, and Yahoo.)

Next to each, you see its current share price, and next to *that*, you see how much that price has gone up or down today. As a handy visual gauge to how elated or depressed you should be, this final number appears on a *green* background if it's gone up, or a *red* one if it's gone down. Tap this number to cycle the display from a percentage to a dollar amount to current market capitalization ("120.3B," meaning $120.3 billion total corporate value).

When you tap a stock, the bottom part of the screen shows some handy data. Swipe horizontally to cycle among three different displays:

- **A table of statistics.** A capsule summary of today's price and volume statistics for this stock.

- **A graph of the stock's price.** It starts out showing you the graph of the current year. But by tapping the headings above the chart, you can zoom in or out from 1 day (**1D**) to 3 months (**3M**) to 2 years (**2Y**).

- **A table of relevant headlines,** courtesy of Yahoo Finance. Tap a head-line to read the article—or tap and hold to add it, or all the articles, to your Safari Reading List (page 459).

Landscape View

If you turn the iPhone sideways, you get a much bigger, more detailed, widescreen graph of the stock in question. (Flick horizontally to view the previous or next stock.)

> **TIP:** On a Plus model, there's room for *both* your list of stocks *and* the graph of the one you've tapped, all on the same screen.

Better yet, you can pinch with two fingers or two thumbs to isolate a certain time period; a pop-up label shows you how much of a bath you took (or how much of a windfall you received) during the interval you highlighted. Cool!

Customizing Your Portfolio

It's fairly unlikely that *your* stock portfolio contains just Apple, Google, and Yahoo. Fortunately, you can customize the list of stocks to reflect the companies you *do* own (or want to track).

To edit the list, tap the ☰ button in the lower-right corner. You arrive at the editing screen (next page, right), where these choices await:

- **Delete a stock** by tapping the ⊖ button and then the Delete confirmation button.

- **Rearrange the list** by dragging the grip strips on the right side.

- **Add a stock** by tapping the + button in the top-left corner; the Add Stock screen and the keyboard appear.

  You're not expected to know every stock-symbol abbreviation. Type in the company's *name*, and then tap Search. The iPhone shows you, above the keyboard, a scrolling list of companies with matching names. Tap the one you want to track. You return to the stocks-list editing screen.

- **Choose %, Price, or Numbers.** By tapping the buttons at the bottom, you can specify how you want to see the changes in stock prices in the far-right column: as *percentages* ("+0.65%"), as *numbers* ("+2.23") or as *market cap*. (Here you're simply choosing which number starts out appearing on the main stock screen. As noted earlier, you can easily cycle among these three stats by tapping them.)

When you're finished setting up your stock list, tap **Done**.

Tips

Hey, check it out—Apple's getting into the how-to game!

This app is designed to show you tips and tricks for getting the most from your iPhone. Each screen offers an animated illustration and a paragraph of text explaining one of iOS's marvels. Swipe leftward to see the next tip, and the next, and the next. Or tap ☰ to see a list of all the tips in one place.

Tap **Like** if it's one of your favorites. Tap ⬆️ to share a tip by text message, email, Twitter, Facebook, or AirDrop.

Over time, Apple will beam you fresh tips to add to this collection. It's not exactly, you know, a handsome, printed, full-color book, but it's something.

TV

This app, which appeared in iOS 10.2, lets you find and play videos from two sources: the iTunes store, and individual video apps like HBO Now and ABC. It's described on page 254.

Voice Memos

This audio app is ideal for recording lectures, musical performances, notes to self, and cute child utterances. You'll probably be very surprised at how good the microphone is, even from a distance.

The best part: When you sync your iPhone with iTunes on your Mac or PC, all your voice recordings get copied back to the computer automatically. You'll find them in the iTunes folder called Voice Memos.

Tap ❷ (or click your earbud clicker) to start recording. A little ding signals the start (and stop) of the session—unless you've turned the phone's volume all the way down (you sneak!).

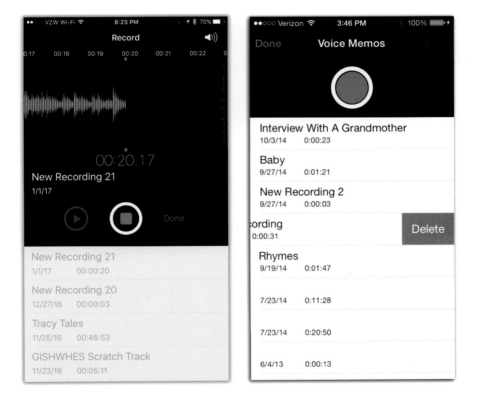

You get to watch the actual sound waves as the recording proceeds. You can pause at any time by pressing the Stop button (⏹)—and then resume the same recording with another tap on the ② button.

You can also switch out of the app to do other work. A red banner across the top of the screen reminds you that you're still recording. You can even **switch the screen off** by tapping the Sleep switch; the recording goes on! (You can make *very* long recordings with this thing. Let it run all day, if you like. Even your most long-winded friends can be immortalized.)

Tap **Done** when you're sure the recording session is over. You're asked to type a name for the new recording ("Baby's First Words," "Orch Concert," whatever); then you can tap **Save** or, if it wasn't worth saving, **Delete**.

Below the recording controls, you see the list of your recordings. When you tap one, a convenient set of controls appears. (They look a lot like the ones that appear when you tap a voicemail message in the Phone app.)

Here's what you can do here (next page, left):

- **[Recording name].** Tap the name to edit or rename it.

- **▶.** Tap to play the recording. You can pause with a tap on the **II** button.

- **Rewind, Fast Forward.** Drag the little vertical line in the scrubber bar to skip backward or forward in the recording. It's a great way to skip over the boring pleasantries.

- **🗑.** Tap to get rid of a recording (you'll be asked to confirm).

- **⬆.** Tap to open the standard Share sheet. It gives you the chance to send your recording to someone else by AirDrop, email, or MMS.

Trimming Your Recording

You might not guess that such a tiny, self-effacing app actually offers some basic editing functions, but it does. Tap a recording and then tap ⬚ to open its Edit screen (above, right).

The main thing you'll do here is trim off the beginning or end of your audio clip. That, of course, is where you'll usually find "dead air" or microphone fumbling before the good stuff starts playing. (You can't otherwise edit the sound; for example, you can't copy or paste bits or cut a chunk out of the middle.)

To trim the bookends of your clip, tap the Trim button (⬚). At this point, the beginning and end of the recording are marked by vertical red lines; these are your trim points. Drag them inward to isolate the part of the clip you want to keep. The app thoughtfully magnifies the sound waves whenever you're dragging, to help with precision. Play the sound as necessary to guide you (▶).

Tap **Trim** to lock in your changes. You'll be asked to tap either **Trim Original** (meaning "shorten the original clip permanently") or **Save as New Recording** (meaning "leave the original untouched, and spin out the shortened version as a separate audio file, just in case").

Wallet

This app was originally called Passbook. And it was originally designed to store, in one place, every form of ticket that uses a barcode. For most people, that meant airline boarding passes.

Wallet still does that. And, occasionally, you may find a Wallet-compatible theater or sports-admission pass, loyalty card, coupon, movie ticket, and so on. Beats having a separate app for each one of these.

Wallet holds down a second job, too. It's the key to Apple Pay, the magical "pay by waving your iPhone" feature described on page 536.

> **TIP:** You can rearrange the passes; just hold still briefly before you start moving your finger up or down. (That order syncs to your other iOS gadgets, for what it's worth.)

What's cool is that Wallet uses both its own clock and GPS to know when the time and place are right. For example, when you arrive at the airport, a notification appears on your Lock screen. Each time you have to show your boarding pass as you work through the stages of airport security, you can wake your phone and swipe across that notification;

your boarding-pass barcode appears instantly. You're spared having to unlock your phone (enter its password), hunt for the airline app, log in, and fiddle your way to the boarding pass.

The hardest part might be finding things to put *into* Wallet. Apple says that someday there will be a "Send to Wallet" button on the website or a confirmation email when you buy the ticket.

For now, you can visit the App Store and search for *passbook* to find apps that work with Wallet—big airlines, Fandango (movie tickets), Starbucks, Walgreens, Ticketmaster, and Major League Baseball are among the compatible apps. In some, you're supposed to open the app to view the barcode *first* and put it into Wallet from there. For example, in most airline apps, you call up the boarding-pass screen and then tap Add.

Once your barcodes have successfully landed in Wallet, the rest is pure fun. When you arrive at the theater or stadium or airport, the Lock screen displays an alert. Swipe it to open the barcode in Wallet. You can put the entire phone under the ticket-taker's scanner.

Tap the ⓘ button in the corner to read the details—and to delete a ticket after you've used it (tap Delete). That details screen also offers a Show On Lock Screen on/off switch, in case you *don't* want Wallet to hand you your ticket as you arrive.

Finally, Wallet is one of the two places you can enter your credit card information for Apple Pay on an iPhone 6 or later model, as described on page 536. (Settings is the other.)

Watch

If you own an Apple Watch, you use this little app to set up its settings. (OK, *big* app—there are *90 screens* full of settings!)

So why do you have the Watch app on your phone even if you *don't* have an Apple Watch? You'll have to ask someone in Marketing.

If it bugs you, you can get rid of it (page 337).

Weather

This little app shows a handy current-conditions display for your city (or any other city). Handy *and* lovely; the weather display is animated. Clouds drift by, rain falls gently. If it's nighttime in the city you're looking up, you might see a beautiful starscape.

The current temperature is shown nice and big; the table below it shows the cloud-versus-sun forecast, as well as the high and low temperatures.

You don't even have to tell the app what weather you want; it uses your location and assumes you want the *local* weather forecast.

There are three places you can tap or swipe:

- **Scroll up** to see a table of stats: humidity, chance of rain, sunrise time, wind speed, "feels like" (chill or heat index), and so on.

- **Swipe horizontally across the hourly forecast** to scroll later in the day.

- **Swipe horizontally anywhere else** to view the weather for other cities (if you've set them up). The tiny dots beneath the display correspond to the number of cities you've set up—and the white bold one indicates where you are in the sequence.

> **TIP:** The dots are *really* tiny. Don't try to aim for a specific one—it's a lot easier to tap the row of dots on either the right or left side to move backward or forward among the cities.

The first city—the screen at far left—is always the city you're *in right now*. The iPhone uses GPS to figure out where you are.

The City List

It's easy to get the weather for other cities—great if you're going to be traveling, or if you're wondering how life is for distant relations.

When you tap :≡ at the lower-right corner, the screen collapses into a list of your preprogrammed cities (facing page, right).

You can tap one to open its weather screen. You can delete one by swiping leftward across it (and then tapping Delete). You can drag them up or down into a new order (leave your finger down for one second before each time you drag). You can switch between Celsius and Fahrenheit by tapping the C/F button.

Or you can scroll to the bottom (if necessary) and tap ⊕ to enter a new city.

Here you're asked to type a city, a zip code, or an airport abbreviation (like JFK for New York's John F. Kennedy airport). You can specify any reasonably sized city on earth. (Remember to check before you travel!)

When you tap Search, you're shown a list of matching cities; tap the one you want to track. When you return to the configuration screen, you can also specify whether you prefer degrees Celsius or degrees Fahrenheit. Tap **Done**.

There's nothing else to tap here except the Weather Channel icon at the bottom. It fires up the Safari browser, which loads itself with an information page about that city from *weather.com*.

If you've added more than one city to the list, by the way, just flick your finger right or left to flip through the weather screens for the different cities.

More Standard Apps

This book describes every app that comes on every iPhone. But Apple has another suite of useful programs for you. And they're free.

> **NOTE:** If you have an iPhone model with 64 or more gigabytes of storage, then most of these apps come already installed: iMovie, GarageBand, Keynote, Pages, Numbers, and iTunes U.

To find them, on the first page of the App Store, scroll down and tap **Apps Made by Apple**. You'll find these apps ready to download:

- **Pages** is, believe it or not, a word-processing/page-layout program.

- **Numbers** is Apple's spreadsheet program.

- **Keynote** is Apple's version of PowerPoint. It lets you make slideshow presentations from your iPhone.

- **iMovie.** A video-editing program on your cellphone? Yes, with all the basics: rearranging clips; adding music, crossfades, and credits.

- **GarageBand** is a pocket music studio.

- **iTunes U** is a catalog of 600,000 free courses by professors at colleges, museums, and libraries all over the world. This app lets you browse the catalog, and watch and read the course materials.

- **Find My Friends** lets you see where your friends and family members are on a map (with their permission, of course).

- **Find My iPhone** is useful when you want to find *other* missing Apple gadgets (Macs, iPads, iPod Touches, iPhones).

PART THREE

The iPhone Online

Chapter 12
Getting Online

Chapter 13
Safari

Chapter 14
Email

12

Getting Online

As you may have read, the name "iPhone" grows less appropriate every year, as making *phone calls* fades in importance. Today, Americans send texts five times more often than they make phone calls. Among teenagers, 92 percent *never* make calls with their smartphones.

What do they do with them, then? Go online. On an iPhone, the web comes to life, looming larger and clearer than you'd think possible on a cellphone. You get real email, full-blown YouTube videos, hyper-clear Google maps, and all kinds of Internet goodness, right in your hand. And instead of phone calls, we have Internet-based voice networks like Skype and WhatsApp, or video-calling apps like Skype and FaceTime.

The iPhone can get onto the Internet using either of two kinds of wireless networks: *cellular* or *Wi-Fi*. Which kind you're on makes a huge difference to your iPhone experience.

Cellular Networks

Once you've accepted the miracle that a cellphone can transmit your voice wirelessly, it's not much of a stretch to realize that it can also transmit your data. Cellphone carriers (Verizon, AT&T, and so on) maintain separate networks for voice and Internet data—and they spend billions of dollars trying to make those networks faster. Over the years, they've come up with data networks like these:

- **Old, slow cellular network.** The earliest, slowest cellular Internet connections were called things like EDGE (AT&T) or 1xRTT (Verizon and Sprint). The good part is that these networks are almost everywhere, so your iPhone can get online almost anywhere you can make a phone call. You'll know when you're on one of these slow networks because your status bar bears a symbol like **E** or **o**.

The bad news is that it's slow. **Dog** slow—dial-up slow.

You can't be on a phone call while you're online using EDGE or 1xRTT, either.

- **3G cellular networks.** 3G stands for "third generation." (The ancient analog cellphones were the first generation; EDGE-type networks were the second.) Geeks refer to the 3G network standard by its official name: HSDPA, for High-Speed Downlink Packet Access.

  Web pages that take 2 minutes to appear using EDGE or 1xRTT show up in about 20 seconds on 3G. Voice calls sound better, too, even when the signal strength is very low, since the iPhone's 3G radio can communicate with multiple towers at once.

  Oh, and on AT&T and T-Mobile, you can talk on the phone and use the Internet simultaneously, which can be very handy indeed.

- **"4G" networks.** AT&T enhanced HSDPA, made it faster using a technology called HSPA+ (High-Speed Packet Access), and calls it 4G. (You'll know when you're on one; your status bar says **4G**.) But nobody else recognizes HSPA+ as real 4G, which is why AT&T feels justified in advertising "the nation's largest 4G network." The other carriers aren't even measuring that network type.

- **4G LTE networks.** Now *this* is 4G.

  An LTE network (Long-Term Evolution) gives you amazing speeds—in some cases, faster than your broadband Internet at home. When your status bar says **LTE**, it's *fantastic*.

  But LTE is not all sunshine and bunnies; it has two huge downsides.

  First: coverage. LTE coverage is available in hundreds of U.S. cities, which is a good start. But that still leaves most of the country, including huge chunks of several entire states, without any 4G coverage at all (hi there, Montana!). Whenever you're outside the high-speed areas, your iPhone falls back to the slower speeds.

  The second big problem with LTE is that, to receive its signal, a phone's circuitry uses a lot of power. That's why the latest iPhones are bigger than their predecessors; they need beefier batteries.

A Word About VoLTE

If you have an iPhone 6 or later model, the dawn of LTE cellphone networks brings another benefit: You can use Voice over LTE, or **VoLTE** ("volty"). That's a delightful new cellular feature that promises amazing voice quality—sounds more like FM radio than cellphone—**and** simultaneous calling/Internetting, even on Verizon. (Behind the scenes, it sends your voice over the carrier's **Internet** network instead of the voice network. That's why it's called "Voice over LTE.")

To make this work, every link in the chain has to be compatible with VoLTE: your phone and your cellphone network, **and** (for that great sound quality) the phone and network of the person you're **calling**.

All four big U.S. carriers offer VoLTE, but you generally get the high-quality sound only when you're calling someone on your **own** cellphone carrier—not if, for example, you have Verizon and the other guy has T-Mobile. (Cross-carrier calling is supposed to be coming soon.)

To turn on VoLTE, open Settings→Cellular→Enable LTE; select Voice & Data. For Verizon, you also have to visit your MyVerizon web page and turn on Advanced Calling. There's no extra cost involved—just some truly welcome new improvements in quality and convenience.

Wi-Fi Hotspots

Wi-Fi, known to geeks as 802.11, is wireless networking, the same technology that gets laptops online at high speed in any Wi-Fi **hotspot**.

Hotspots are everywhere these days: in homes, offices, coffee shops, hotels, airports, and thousands of other places. Unfortunately, a hotspot is a bubble about 300 feet across; once you wander out of it, you're off the Internet. So, in general, Wi-Fi is for people who are sitting still.

When you're in a Wi-Fi hotspot, your iPhone usually gets a **very** fast connection to the Internet, as though it's connected to a cable modem or DSL. And when you're online this way, you can make phone calls and surf the Internet simultaneously. And why not? Your iPhone's Wi-Fi and cellular antennas are independent.

(Over cellular connections, only the AT&T and T-Mobile iPhones let you talk and get online simultaneously. Verizon and Sprint can do that only when you're on a VoLTE call, as described previously.)

The iPhone looks for a Wi-Fi connection first and considers connecting to a cellular network only if there's no Wi-Fi. You'll always know which kind of network you're on, thanks to the icons on the status bar: You'll see either 📶 for Wi-Fi, or one of the cellular icons (**E**, **o**, **3G**, **4G**, or **LTE**).

Or "No service" if there's nothing available at all.

And how much faster is one than the next? Well, network speeds are measured in kilobits and megabits per second (which isn't the same as the more familiar **kilobytes** and **megabytes** per second; divide by 8 to get those).

The EDGE/1xRTT network is supposed to deliver data from 70 to 200 Kbps, depending on your distance from the cell towers. 3G gets 300 to 700 Kbps. A Wi-Fi hotspot can spit out 650 to 2,100 Kbps. And 4G LTE can deliver speeds as fast as 100 Mbps. You'll rarely get speeds near the high ends—but even so, there's quite a difference.

The bottom line: LTE and Wi-Fi are *awesome*. EDGE/1xRTT—not so much.

Sequence of Connections

The iPhone isn't online all the time. To save battery power, it opens the connection only on demand: when you check email, request a web page, and so on. At that point, the iPhone tries to get online following this sequence:

- **First, it sniffs around for a Wi-Fi network** that you've used before. If it finds one, it connects quietly and automatically. You're not asked for permission, a password, or anything else.

- **If the iPhone can't find a previous hotspot** but it detects a *new* hotspot, a message appears (below, left). It displays any new hotspots' names; tap the one you want. (If you see a 🔒 icon, then that hotspot is password-protected.)

- **If the iPhone can't find any Wi-Fi hotspots to join,** or if you don't join any, it connects to the cellular network, like 3G or LTE.

Silencing the "Want to Join?" Messages

Sometimes, you might be bombarded by those "Select a Wireless Network" messages at a time when you have no need to be online. You might want the iPhone to stop bugging you—to *stop* offering Wi-Fi hotspots. In that situation, from the Home screen, tap Settings→Wi-Fi (or tell Siri, "Open Wi-Fi settings"), and then turn off Ask to Join Networks. When this option is off, the iPhone never interrupts you by dropping the name of every new network at your feet. In this case, to get onto a new network, you have to visit the aforementioned settings screen and select it.

The List of Hotspots

At some street corners in big cities, Wi-Fi signals bleeding out of apartment buildings sometimes give you a choice of 20 or 30 hotspots to join. But whenever the iPhone invites you to join a hotspot, it suggests only a couple of them: the ones with the strongest signal and, if possible, no password requirement.

But you might sometimes want to see the complete list of available hotspots—maybe because the iPhone-suggested hotspot is flaky. To see the full list, from the Home screen, open Settings→Wi-Fi. Tap the one you want to join, as shown on the facing page at right.

> **TIP:** Tap ⓘ next to a hotspot's name to view an info sheet for techies. It shows your IP address, subnet mask, router address, and other delicious stats. Even mere mortals, however, will sometimes enjoy the Forget This Network button. It removes this hotspot from the list, which is handy if you've moved away and don't need to be reminded of the high speed that was once yours.

Commercial Hotspots

Tapping the name of the hotspot you want to join is generally all you have to do—if it's a *home* Wi-Fi network. Unfortunately, joining a *commercial* Wi-Fi hotspot—one that requires a credit card number (in a hotel room or an airport, for example)—requires more than just connecting to it. You also have to *sign into* it, exactly as you'd do if you were using a laptop.

In general, the iPhone prompts you to do that automatically. A login screen pops up on its own, interrupting whatever else you're doing; that's where you supply your credit card information or (if you have a membership to this Wi-Fi chain, like Boingo or T-Mobile) your name and password. Tap **Submit** or **Proceed**, try *not* to contemplate the cost, and enjoy your surfing.

(If that login screen doesn't appear, or if you canceled out of it accidentally, open Safari. You'll see the "Enter your payment information" screen, either immediately or as soon as you try to open a web page of your choice.)

Mercifully, the iPhone memorizes your password. The next time you use this hotspot, you won't have to enter it again.

Airplane Mode and Wi-Fi Off Mode

When battery power is precious, you can turn off all three of the iPhone's network connections in one fell swoop. You can also turn off Wi-Fi alone.

- **To turn all radios off.** In airplane mode, turn off *all* wireless circuitry: Bluetooth, Wi-Fi, and cellular. Now you can't make calls or get onto the Internet. You're saving an amazing amount of power, however, and also complying with regulations that ban cellphones in flight.

  The short way: Swipe up from the bottom of the screen; on the Control Center, tap ✈ so it turns orange. (The long way: Open **Settings**, turn on **Airplane Mode**.)

- **To turn Wi-Fi on or off.** Swipe up; on the Control Center, tap 📶 so it's no longer blue. (You can also switch it in **Settings→Wi-Fi**.)

TIP: Once you've turned on airplane mode, you can actually turn Wi-Fi back *on* again. Why on earth? To use Wi-Fi on a flight. You need a way to turn Wi-Fi *on*, but your cellular circuitry *off*.

Conversely, you sometimes might want to do the opposite: turn *off* Wi-Fi, but leave cellular *on*. Why? Because, sometimes, the iPhone bizarrely won't get online at all. It's struggling to use a Wi-Fi network that, for one reason or another, isn't connecting to the Internet. By turning Wi-Fi off, you force the iPhone to use its cell connection—which may be slower, but at least it works!

In airplane mode, anything that requires voice or Internet access—text messages, web, email, and so on—triggers a message: "Turn off Airplane Mode or use Wi-Fi to access data." Tap either OK (to back out of your decision) or Settings (to turn off airplane mode and get online).

You can, however, enjoy all the other iPhone features: Music, Camera, and so on. You can also work with stuff you've *already* downloaded to the phone, like email, voicemail messages, and web pages you've saved in the Reading List.

Personal Hotspot (Tethering)

Tethering means using your iPhone as an Internet antenna, so that your laptops, iPod Touches, iPads, game consoles, and other Internet-connectables can get online. (The other gadgets can connect to the phone over a Wi-Fi connection, a Bluetooth connection, or a USB cable.) In fact, several laptops and other gadgets can all share the iPhone's connection simultaneously. Your phone becomes a personal cellular router, like a MiFi.

That's incredibly convenient. Many phones have it, but Apple's execution is especially nice. For example, the hotspot shuts itself off 90 seconds after the last laptop disconnects. That's hugely important, because a personal hotspot is a merciless battery drain.

The hotspot feature may be included with your data plan (T-Mobile), or it may cost something like $20 a month extra, which buys only 2 gigabytes of data (Verizon). Think email, not YouTube.

To get this feature, you have to sign up for it by calling your cellular company or visiting its website (if you didn't already do that when you signed up for service).

TIP: If you have a Mac running OS X Yosemite or later, you're in for a real treat: a much more streamlined way to set up Personal Hotspot called *Instant* Hotspot. Skip the instructions below and jump immediately to page 550.

Turning On the Hotspot

On the phone, open Settings→Cellular→Personal Hotspot (or tell Siri, "Open cellular settings").

TIP: Once you've turned on Personal Hotspot for the first time, you won't have to drill down as far to get to it. A new Personal Hotspot item appears right there on the main Settings screen from now on.

The Personal Hotspot screen contains details on connecting other computers. It also has the master on/off switch. Turn Personal Hotspot On.

(If you see a button that says Set Up Personal Hotspot, it means you haven't yet added the monthly tethering fee to your cellular plan. Contact your wireless carrier to get that change made to your account.)

You have to use a password for your personal hotspot; it's to ensure that people sitting nearby can't surf using your connection and run up your cell bill. The software proposes a password, but you can edit it and make up one of your own. (It has to be at least eight characters long and contain letters, numbers, and punctuation. Don't worry—your laptop or other Wi-Fi gadget can memorize it for you.)

Your laptops and other gadgets can connect to the Internet using any of three connections to the iPhone: Wi-Fi, Bluetooth, or a USB cable. If either Wi-Fi or Bluetooth are turned off, then a message appears to let you know—and offers to turn them on for you. To save battery power, turn on only what you need.

Connecting via Wi-Fi

After about 30 seconds, the iPhone shows up on your laptop or other gadget as though it were a Wi-Fi network. Just choose the iPhone's name from your computer's Wi-Fi hotspot menu (on the Mac, it's the 🛜 menu). Enter the password, and bam—your laptop is now online, using the iPhone as an antenna. On the Mac or an iPad, the 🛜 changes to look like this: ⊚.

You can leave the iPhone in your pocket or purse while connected. You'll surf away on your laptop, baffling every Internet-less soul around you. Your laptop can now use email, the web, chat programs—anything it could do in a real Wi-Fi hotspot (just a little slower).

Connecting via Bluetooth

There's no compelling reason to use Bluetooth instead of Wi-Fi, especially since Bluetooth slows your Internet connection. But if you're interested, see the free downloadable PDF appendix "Bluetooth Tethering" on this book's "Missing CD" page at *www.missingmanuals.com*.

Connecting via USB Cable

If you can connect your laptop to your iPhone using the white charging cable, you should. Tethering eats up a lot of the phone's battery power, so keeping it plugged into the laptop means you won't wind up with a dead phone when you're finished surfing.

Once You're Connected

On the iPhone, a blue bar appears at the top of the screen to make you aware that the laptop is connected (previous page, right); in fact, it shows how many laptops or other gadgets are connected at the moment, via any of the three connection methods. (You can tap that bar to open the Personal Hotspot screen in Settings.)

Most carriers won't let more than five people connect through a single iPhone.

If you have AT&T or T-Mobile, you can still use all the functions of the iPhone, including making calls and surfing the web, while it's channeling your laptop's Internet connection.

If you have Verizon or Sprint, then your iPhone can't handle Internet connections and voice calls simultaneously (unless you're on a VoLTE call, as described on page 434). So if a phone call comes in, the iPhone suspends the hotspot feature until you're finished talking; when you hang up (or if you decline the call), all connected gadgets regain their Internet connections automatically.

Turning Off Personal Hotspot

If you're connected wirelessly to the iPhone, the Personal Hotspot feature is a battery hog. It'll cut your iPhone's battery longevity in half. That's why, if no laptops are connected for 90 seconds, the iPhone turns the hotspot off automatically.

You can also turn off the hotspot manually, just the way you'd expect: In Settings→Personal Hotspot, tap Off.

Turning Personal Hotspot Back On

About 90 seconds after the last gadget stops using the hotspot, your iPhone shuts off the feature to save its own battery. To fire it back up again, open Settings and tap Personal Hotspot. That's it—just visit the Personal Hotspot screen to make the iPhone resume broadcasting its Wi-Fi or Bluetooth network to your laptops and other gadgets.

Twitter and Facebook

Twitter, of course, is a free service (sign up at *twitter.com*) that lets you send out short messages, like text messages, to anyone who wants to get them from you. Twitter is a fantastic way for people to spread news, links, thoughts, and observations directly to the people who care—incredibly quickly.

And Facebook is—well, Facebook. 1.6 billion people sharing their personal details and thoughts can't be wrong, right?

These services are woven into the built-in iPhone apps.

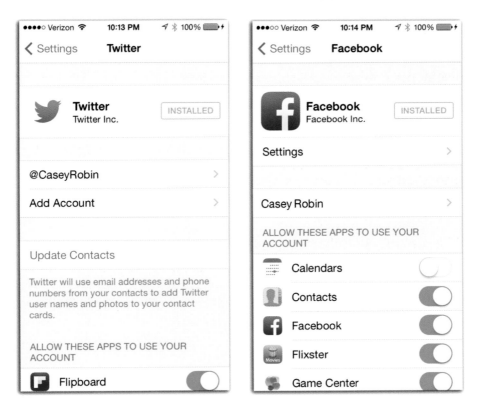

Start by visiting **Settings→Twitter** or **Settings→Facebook**. Here you can enter your account name and password or sign up for an account. Here, too, you're offered the chance to download the Twitter or Facebook apps. You can also tap **Update Contacts**, which attempts to add the Twitter or Facebook addresses of everybody in your Contacts app to their information cards. For details, see page 114.

Once you've set up Twitter and Facebook this way, you'll find some nifty buttons built into your other apps, for one-tap tweeting or Facebook posting. For example, the Share button (⬆) appears in Photos, Maps, Safari, and other apps, making it easy to post a photo, location, or web page. Siri understands commands like "Tweet" and "Post to Facebook," too, so you can broadcast when the spirit moves you. (The **Tweet** and **Post** buttons are no longer in the Notification Center, however.)

In each case, you wind up at a small tweet sheet or Facebook sheet. Here you can add a comment to the link or photo, or attach your current location, or (for Facebook) specify who's allowed to see this post—Everyone or just Friends, for example.

For Twitter posts, you'll notice that the keyboard at that point offers dedicated @ and # keys. (The # is for creating *hashtags*—searchable keywords on a tweet like #iphone7bugs—that Twitter fans can use when searching for tweets about certain topics. And the @ precedes every Twitter person's address—@pogue, for example.)

13

Safari

The iPhone's web browser is Safari, a lite version of the same one that comes on the Mac. It's fast, simple to use, and very pretty. On the web pages you visit, you see the real deal—the actual fonts, graphics, and layouts—not the stripped-down mini-web on cellphones of years gone by.

Using Safari on the iPhone is still not quite as good as surfing the web on, you know, a laptop. But it's getting closer.

Safari Tour

Safari has most of the features of a desktop web browser: bookmarks, autocomplete (for web addresses), scrolling shortcuts, cookies, a pop-up ad blocker, password memorization, and so on. (It's missing niceties like streaming music, Java, Flash, and other plug-ins.)

Now, don't be freaked out: *The main screen elements disappear* shortly after you start reading a page. That's supposed to give you more screen space to do your surfing. To bring them back, scroll to the top, scroll to the bottom, or just scroll up a little. At that point, you see the controls again. Here they are, as they appear from the top left:

- **Reader view (≡).** In this delightful view, all the ads, boxes, banners, and other junk disappear. Only text and pictures remain, for your sanity-in-reading pleasure. See page 467.

- **Address/search bar.** A single, unified box serves as both the address bar and the search bar at the top of the screen. (That's the trend these days. Desktop-computer browsers like Chrome and Safari on the Mac work that way, too.)

  This box is where you enter the *URL* (web address) for a page you want to visit. ("URL" is short for the even-less-self-explanatory

Uniform Resource Locator.) For example, if you type *amazon.com*, tapping Go takes you to that website.

But this is also where you search the web. If you type anything else, like **cashmere sweaters** or just **amazon**, then tapping Go gives you the Google search results for that phrase.

TIP: If you hold your finger down briefly on the keyboard's period key, you get a pop-up palette of web-address suffixes (.org, .edu, and so on). Luckily, **.com** starts out selected—so just release your finger to type it in. In other words, the entire process for typing **.com** goes like this: Hold finger on period key; release.

- **Stop, Reload (✕, ↻).** Tap ✕ to interrupt the downloading of a web page you've just requested (if you've made a mistake, for instance, or if it's taking too long).

TIP: You don't have to wait for a web page to load entirely. You can zoom in, scroll, and begin reading the text even when only part of the page has appeared.

Once a page has finished loading, the ✕ button turns into a ↻ (reload) button. Click it if a page doesn't look or work quite right. Safari re-downloads the web page and reinterprets its text and graphics.

- **Back, Forward (‹, ›).** Tap ‹ to revisit the page you were just on. Once you've tapped ‹, you can then tap › to return to the page you were on **before** you tapped the ‹ button. You can also **hold down** these buttons to see the complete history list of this tab.

TIP: Since these buttons disappear as soon as you scroll down a page, how are you supposed to move back and forward among pages?

By *swiping in* from outside the screen. Start your swipe on the edge of the phone's front glass and whisk inward. Swiping rightward like this means "back"; leftward means "forward again." Do it slowly, and you can actually see the page sliding in.

- **Share/Bookmark (⬆).** When you're on an especially useful page, tap this button. It offers every conceivable choice for commemorating or sharing the page. See page 348 for details.

- **View Bookmarks (▭).** This button brings up your list of saved bookmarks—plus your History list, Favorites, Reading List, and links recommended by the people you follow on Twitter. You can read about these elements later in this chapter.

- **Page Juggler (▭).** Safari can keep multiple web pages open, just like any other browser. Page 465 has the details.

Zooming and Scrolling

When you first open a web page, you get to see the *entire thing*, so you can get the lay of the land. At this point, of course, you're looking at .004-point type, which is too small to read unless you're a microbe. So the next step is to magnify the *part* of the page you want to read.

The iPhone offers three ways to do that:

- **Double-tap.** Safari can recognize different *chunks* of a web page— each block of text, each photo. When you double-tap a chunk, Safari magnifies *just that chunk* to fill the whole screen. It's smart and useful.

  Double-tap again to zoom back out.

- **Rotate the iPhone.** Turn the device 90 degrees in either direction. The iPhone rotates and magnifies the image to fill the wider view. Often, this simple act is enough to make tiny type big enough to read.

- **Do the two-finger spread.** Put two fingers on the glass and slide them apart. The Safari page stretches before your very eyes, growing larger. Then you can pinch to shrink the page back down again. (Most people do several spreads or pinches in a row to achieve the degree of zoom they want.)

Once you've zoomed out to the proper degree, you can then scroll around the page by dragging or flicking with a finger. You don't have to worry about "clicking a link" by accident; if your finger is in motion, Safari ignores the tapping action, even if you happen to land on a link.

TIP: Once you've double-tapped to zoom in on a page, you can use this little-known trick: Double-tap anywhere on the *upper* half of the screen to scroll up or the *lower* half to scroll down. The closer you are to the top or bottom of the screen, the more you scroll.

Double-tap —

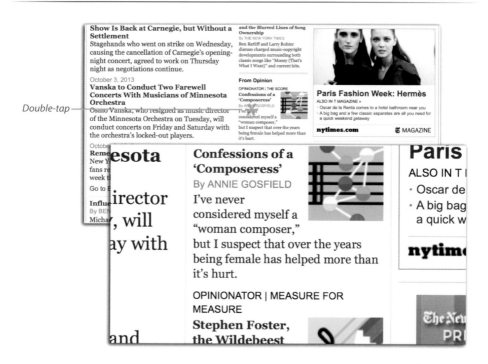

Full-Screen Mode

On a phone, the screen is pretty small to begin with; most people would rather dedicate that space to showing more *web*.

So in iOS, Safari enters *full-screen mode* the instant you start to *scroll down* a page. In full-screen mode, all the controls and toolbars vanish. Now the *entire* iPhone screen is filled with web goodness. You can bring the controls back in any of these ways:

• Scroll *up* a little bit.

• Return to the top or bottom of a web page.

• Navigate to a different page.

And enjoy Safari's dedication to trying to get out of your way.

Typing a Web Address

The address/search bar is the strip at the top of the screen where you type in a web page's address. And it so happens that some of the iPhone's greatest tips and shortcuts all have to do with this important navigational tool:

- **Your Favorites await.** When you tap in the address bar but haven't yet typed anything, the icons of a few very special, most favorite websites appear (below, top). These are the Favorites; see page 450.

- **Don't delete.** There *is* a ⊗ button at the right end of the address bar whose purpose is to erase the current address so you can type another one. (Tap inside the address bar to make it, and the keyboard, appear.) But the ⊗ button is for suckers.

  Instead, whenever the address bar is open for typing, *just type*. Forget that there's already a URL there. The iPhone is smart enough to figure out that you want to *replace* that web address with a new one.

- **Don't type http://www.** You can leave that stuff out; Safari will supply it automatically. Instead of *http://www.cnn.com*, for example, just type *cnn.com* (or tap its name in the suggestions list) and hit Go.

- **Type .com, .net, .org, or .edu the easy way.** Safari's canned URL choices can save you four keyboard taps apiece. To see their secret menu, hold your finger down on the **period key** on the keyboard (previous page, bottom). Then tap the common suffix you want. (Or, if you want .com, just release your finger without moving it.)

Otherwise, this address bar works just like the one in any other web browser. Tap inside it to make the keyboard appear.

Tap the blue Go key when you're finished typing the address. That's your Enter key. (Or tap Cancel to hide the keyboard *without* "pressing Enter.")

> **TIP:** If you hold your finger on a link for a moment—touching rather than tapping—a handy panel appears. At the top, you see the full web address that link will open. And there are some useful buttons: Open, Open in New Tab, Add to Reading List, Copy (meaning "copy the link address"), and Share. Oh, and there's also Cancel.

The Favorites Icons

You can never close all your Safari windows. The app will never let you get past the final page, always lurking behind the others: the Favorites page (previous page, top).

This is the starting point. It's what you first see when you tap the + button. It's like a page of visual bookmarks.

In fact, if you see a bunch of icons here already, it's because your phone has synced them over from Safari on a Mac; whatever sites are on your Bookmarks *bar* become icons on this bookmarks *page*.

You can edit this Favorites page, of course:

- **Rearrange them** as you would Home screen icons. That is, hold your finger down on an icon momentarily and then drag it to a new spot.

- **Remove or rename a favorites icon.** Favorites are just bookmarks. So you can edit, move, or delete them just as you would any bookmark. (Tap 📖 to open your Bookmarks screen. Make sure that you're on the 📖 tab, so that your list of folders is showing. Tap Favorites, then Edit. Tap ⊖ for a site you want to delete, and then tap Delete.)

> **TIP:** You can create folders *inside* the Favorites folder, too. Whenever the Favorites screen appears, you'll see these subfolders listed as further sources of speed-dial websites.

- **Add a Favorites icon.** When you find a page you'd like to add to the Favorites screen, tap ⬆. On the Share sheet, tap Add Bookmark. The phone usually proposes putting the new bookmark into the Favorites *folder*, which means that it will show up on the Favorites *screen*. (If it proposes some other folder on the Location line, tap the folder's name and then tap Favorites.) Tap Save.

> **TIP:** You don't have to use the Favorites folder of bookmarks as the one whose contents appear on the Favorites screen. In Settings→ Safari→Favorites, a list of all your Bookmarks folders appears. Whichever one you select there becomes your new Favorites folder, even if its name isn't "Favorites."

Request Desktop Site

In an effort to conserve time and bandwidth (yours and theirs), many websites supply *mobile* versions to your iPhone—smaller, stripped-down sites that transfer faster than (but lack some features of) the full-blown sites. You generally have no control over which version you're sent.

Until now. Suppose you're in Safari, and some site has dished up its mobile version, and you're gnashing your teeth. Hold down the ↻ in the address box; tap Request Desktop Site. (The same button appears when you tap ⬆ and scroll the bottom row to the right.) As you've requested, the full-blown desktop version of that site now appears.

Searching in Safari

The address bar is also the search box. Just tap into it and type your search phrase (or speak it, using Siri).

To save you time and fiddling, Safari instantly produces a menu filled with suggestions that could spare you some typing—things it guesses you might be looking for. If you see the address you're trying to type, then by all means tap it instead of typing out the rest of the URL. The time you save could be your own:

- **Top Hits.** The Top Hits are Safari's best guesses at what you're looking for. They're the sites on your bookmarks and History lists that you've visited most often (and that match what you've typed so far).

  Try tapping one of the Top Hits sometime. You'll discover, to your amazement, that that site appears almost instantly. It doesn't seem to have to load. That's because, as a favor to you, Safari quietly downloads the Top Hits in the background, while you're still entering your search term, all to save you time.

NOTE: If you're concerned that this feature is sucking down some of your monthly cellular data allowance unnecessarily, you can turn it off in Settings→Safari→Preload Top Hit.

- **Suggested Sites.** Occasionally, you'll see another proposed site or two here: Suggested Sites. It's yet another site that Safari supposes you might be trying to reach, based on what you've typed so far and what sites other people visit.

- **Google Search.** The next category of suggestions: a list of search terms you *might* be typing, based on how popular those searches are on Google (or whatever search service you're using). For example, if you type *chick*, then this section proposes things like *chicken recipes*, *chick fil a*, and *chicken pox*. It's just trying to save you a little typing; if none of these tappable choices is the one you want, then ignore them.

NOTE: You can turn this feature off, too, if it makes you feel spied upon. (Behind the scenes, it's transmitting your search term to Apple.) You do that in Settings→Safari→Search Engine Suggestions.

- **Bookmarks and History.** Here Safari offers matching selections from websites you've bookmarked or recently visited. Again, it's trying to save you typing if it can.

- **On This Page.** Here's how you search for certain text *on the page you're reading*.

  Once you've started typing, under the On This Page heading, you see a listing called Find "chic" (or whatever you've typed so far), shown below at left. Tap that line to jump to the first appearance of that text on the page. (There's a less hidden way to start this process, too: Tap ⬆ and then Find on Page.)

Use the ⟨ and ⟩ buttons to jump from one match to the next. Tap Done to return to your regularly scheduled browsing.

> **TIP:** Suppose you've started typing a search term. Safari pipes up with its usual list of suggestions. At this point, if you drag up or down the screen, you hide the keyboard—so you can see the suggestions that were hidden behind it.

You can tell the iPhone to use a Yahoo, Bing, or DuckDuckGo search instead of Google, if you like, in Settings→Safari→Search Engine. (DuckDuckGo is a search service dedicated to privacy. It doesn't store your searches or tailor the results to you. On the other hand, it's capable of searching only about 50 web sources—Wikipedia, Wolfram Alpha, and so on.)

> **TIP:** If you've set your search options to use Google, then there are all kinds of cool things you can type here—special terms that tell Google, "I want *information*, not web page matches."
>
> You can type a movie name and zip code or city/state (*Titanic Returns 10024*) to get a list of today's showtimes in theaters near you. Get the forecast by typing *weather chicago* or *weather 60609*. Stock quotes: Type the symbol (*AMZN*). Dictionary definitions: *define schadenfreude*. Unit conversions: *liters in 5 gallons*. Currency conversions: *25 usd in euros*. Then tap Go to get instant results.

Quick Website Search

This crazy feature lets you search *within* a certain site (like Amazon or Reddit or Wikipedia) using Safari's regular search bar. For example, typing *wiki mollusk* can search Wikipedia for its entry on mollusks. Typing *amazon ipad* can offer links to buy an iPad from Amazon. Typing *reddit sitcoms* opens *reddit.com* to its search results for sitcoms.

None of this will work, however, until (a) you've turned the feature on (Settings→Safari→Quick Website Search), and (b) you've manually *taught* Safari how to search those sites one time each.

To do that, pull up the site you'll want to search (let's say it's *reddit.com*) and use its regular search bar. Search for anything.

That site's name now appears in the list at Settings→Safari→Quick Website Search. (Usually. Many sites don't work with Quick Website Search.) From now on, you can search that site by typing, for example, *reddit sitcoms*. You'll jump directly to that site's search results.

Bookmarks

Bookmarks, of course, are links to websites you might want to visit again without having to remember and type their URLs.

To see the list of bookmarks on your phone, tap 📖 at the bottom of the screen. You see the master list of bookmarks. They're organized in folders, or even folders *within* folders.

Tapping a folder shows you what's inside, and tapping a bookmark begins opening the corresponding website.

> **NOTE:** Actually, what you see when you tap 📖 are *three* tabs at the top: 📖 (Bookmarks), ○○ (Reading List), and @ (Twitter links and RSS feeds). The latter two are described later in this chapter.

You may be surprised to discover that Safari already seems to be pre-stocked with bookmarks—that, amazingly, are interesting and useful to *you* in particular! How did it know?

Easy—it copied your existing desktop computer's browser bookmarks from Safari on the Mac when you synced the iPhone (Chapter 15), or when you turned on Safari syncing through iCloud. Sneaky, eh?

Creating New Bookmarks

You can add new bookmarks right on the phone. Any work you do here is copied *back* to your computer the next time you sync the two machines—or instantaneously, if you've turned on iCloud bookmark syncing.

When you find a web page you might like to visit again, hold down the 📖 icon; from the shortcut menu, choose **Add Bookmark**. (Or do it the

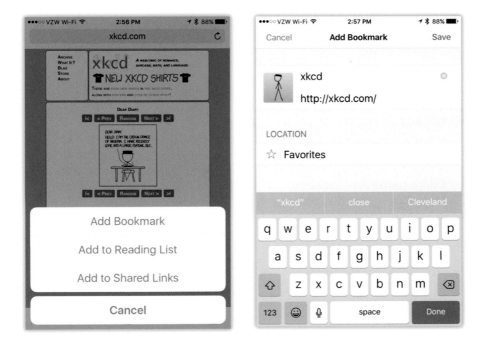

long way: Tap the ⬆ to reveal the Share options, one of which is **Add Bookmark**.) The Add Bookmark screen appears (previous page, right).

You have two tasks here:

- **Type a better name.** In the top box, you can type a shorter or clearer name for the page. Instead of "Bass, Trout & Tackle—the web's Premier Resource for the Avid Outdoorsman," you can just call it "Fish."

  Below that: The page's underlying URL, which is independent of what you've *named* your bookmark. You can't edit this one.

- **Specify where to file this bookmark.** If you tap Favorites, then you open Safari's hierarchical list of bookmark folders, which organize your bookmarked sites. Tap the folder where you want to file the new bookmark so you'll know where to find it later.

Editing Bookmarks and Folders

It's easy enough to massage your Bookmarks list within Safari—to delete favorites that aren't so favorite anymore, to make new folders, to rearrange the list, to rename a folder or a bookmark, and so on.

The techniques are the same for editing bookmark *folders* as editing the bookmarks themselves—after the first step. To edit the folder list, start by opening the Bookmarks (tap 📖), and then tap Edit.

To edit the bookmarks themselves, tap 📖, tap a folder, and *then* tap Edit. Now you can get organized:

- **Delete something.** Tap ⊖ next to a folder or a bookmark, and then tap Delete to confirm.

- **Rearrange the list.** Drag the grip strip (≡) up or down in the list to move the folders or bookmarks around. (You can't move or delete the top two folders—Favorites and History.)

- **Edit a name and location.** Tap a folder or a bookmark name. If you tap a folder, you arrive at the Edit Folder screen; you can edit the folder's name and which folder it's inside of. If you tap a bookmark, Edit Bookmark lets you edit the name and the URL it points to.

  Tap Done when you're finished.

- **Create a folder.** Tap New Folder in the lower-left corner of the Edit Folders screen. You're offered the chance to type a name for it and to specify where you want to file it (that is, in which *other* folder).

Tap Done when you're finished.

●●○○○ Verizon 🛜	9:14 AM	⌁ ⌖ ⚡ 95% ◼️		●●○○○ Verizon 🛜	9:14 AM	⌁ ⌖ ⚡ 95% ◼️

Bookmarks   Done   ‹ Bookmarks **Favorites**   Done

| 📖 | ◯–◯ | @ | | 📖 | ◯–◯ | @ |

☆	Favorites	›
🕐	History	›
🗀	Bookmarks Menu	›
🗀	Entertainment	›
🗀	Shopping	›
🗀	Kids	›
📖	Clean Jokes, Priceless Humo...
📖	Amtrak
📖	BBC News - Home
🗀	News	›

Edit

📖	Mav
📖	Voice
📖	Flickr
📖	blogsearch
📖	Techmeme
📖	blog
📖	DPVids
📖	NYT
📖	Mtro-North
📖	wiki

Edit

TIP: As you've just read, preserving a bookmark requires quite a few taps. That's why it's extra important for you to remember iOS's gift to busy people: the "Remind me about this later" command to Siri (page 419). You've just added a new item in your Reminders list, complete with a link to whatever page you're looking at now. (Feel free to be more specific, as in "Remind me about this when I get home.")

The History List

Behind the scenes, Safari keeps track of the websites you've visited in the past week or so, neatly organized into subfolders like This Evening and Yesterday. It's a great feature when you can't recall the address for a website you visited recently—or when you remember it had a long, complicated address and you get the psychiatric condition known as iPhone Keyboard Dread.

To see the list of recent sites, tap 📖; then, on the 📖 tab, tap History, whose icon bears a 🕐 to make sure you know it's special. Once the History list appears, just tap a bookmark to revisit that web page.

Erasing the History List

Some people find it creepy that Safari maintains a History list, right there in plain view of any family member or coworker who wanders by. They'd just as soon their wife/husband/boss/parent/kid not know what websites they've been visiting.

You can delete just one particularly incriminating History listing easily enough; swipe leftward across its name and then tap Delete. You can also delete the *entire* History menu, thus erasing all your tracks. To do that, tap Clear; confirm by tapping Clear History. You've just rewritten History.

Shared Links (@)

There's a third tab button on the Bookmarks screen, too: @.

It's the Shared Links button. It lists every tweet from Twitter that contains a link. The idea is to make it easier for you to explore sites that your Twitter friends are recommending; all their web finds are collected in one place (facing page, right).

> **TIP:** In Safari, "shared links" has another meaning, too: The ⬆ makes it easy to share the URL of a particularly juicy web page. On the Share sheet, you get the usual set of links: Copy, Mail, Message (to send by text message), Twitter, Facebook, and so on. But remember that iOS is extensible. Depending on the apps you've installed, you may see all kinds of other share-this-link options on this screen.

RSS Subscriptions

At the bottom of the Shared Links (@) tab, iOS offers a button called Subscriptions. It's a reference to *RSS feeds*, which are something like subscriptions to websites. You don't have to remember to go visit your favorite blogs or news sites; notification blurbs about their newly posted articles come to you.

Here's the procedure:

1. **In Safari, open a site that offers an RSS feed.** News sites of all kinds offer RSS feeds (*nytimes.com*, *usatoday.com*, *engadget.com*, and so on).

2. **Subscribe to it.** To do that, tap ▢, then @, then Subscriptions, and then Add Current Site (facing page, left).

3. **Read.** When you want to see what's new, tap ▢, then @. That's right: Blurbs representing newly posted stories appear on the @ tab (shown

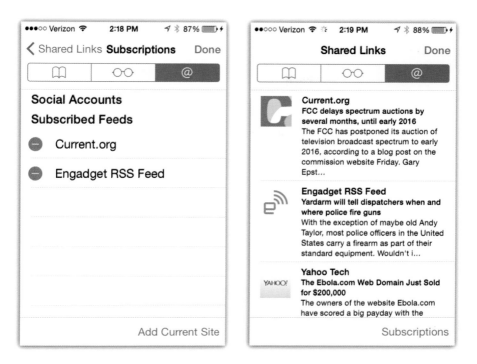

above at right), mixed in with all your Twitter links. That's not ideal, especially if there are hundreds of Twitter links—but at least you'll never be without a place to check for interesting stuff to read.

To delete a subscription, tap ▢, then @, then Subscriptions; tap ● next to the subscription's name, and confirm by tapping Delete.

The Reading List

The Reading List is a handy list of web pages you want to read later. Unlike a bookmark, it stores entire pages, so you can read them even when you don't have an Internet connection (on the subway or on a plane, for example).

The Reading List also keeps track of what you've read. You can use the Show All/Show Unread button at the bottom of the screen to view everything—or just what you haven't yet read.

> **TIP:** To make matters even sweeter, iCloud synchronizes your Reading List on your Mac, iPhone, iPad, and so on—as long as you've turned on bookmark syncing. It's as though the web always keeps your place.

To add a page to the Reading List, tap ⬆ and then tap **Add to Reading List** (above, left). Or just hold your finger down on a link until a set of buttons appears, including **Add to Reading List**.

Once you've added a page to the Reading List, you can get to it by tapping 📖 and then tapping the Reading List tab at the top (ᴑᴑ). Tap an item on your list to open and read it (above, right).

> **TIP:** When you get to the bottom of a Reading List item you've just read, keep scrolling down. The phone is nice enough to offer up the **next** article in your Reading List, as though they were all vertically connected.

By the way, some web pages require a hefty amount of data to download, what with photos and all. If you're worried about Reading List downloads eating up your monthly data allotment, you can visit **Settings→Safari** and turn off **Use Cellular Data**.

Now you'll be able to download Reading List pages only when you're on Wi-Fi, but at least there's no risk of going over your monthly cellular-data allotment.

Link-Tapping Tricks

Link-tapping, of course, is the primary activity of the web. But in Safari, those blue underlined links (or not blue, even not underlined links) harbor special powers:

- **Long-press a link** to open a handy panel. Its options include Open, Open in New Tab, Add to Reading List, Copy, and Share.

- **Hard-press a link** (iPhone 6s and 7 models) to peek at whatever page that link opens, like this:

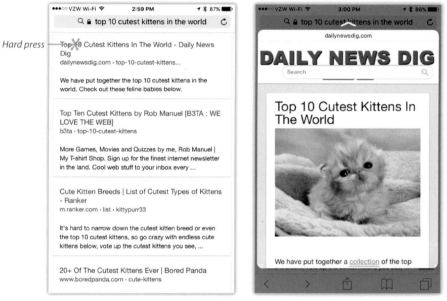

Hard press

Preview pops open without leaving the page

This, of course, is part of the **peek and pop** feature described on page 37. Once you've opened the preview bubble, you can either retreat (lift your finger; remain where you were) or advance (press even harder to fully open that page).

Quite handy, really.

Saving Graphics

If you find a picture online that you wish you could keep forever, you have two choices. You could stare at it until you've memorized it, or you could save it.

To do that, touch the image for about a second. A sheet appears, just like the one that appears when you hold your finger down on a regular link.

If you tap Save Image, then the iPhone thoughtfully deposits a copy of the image in your Camera Roll so it will be copied back to your Mac or PC at the next sync opportunity. If you tap Copy, then you nab a *link* to that graphic, which you can now paste into another program.

> **TIP:** If Save Image isn't one of the choices, there's a workaround: Tap Open in New Tab, touch the image in its new tab for about a second, and *then* choose Save Image from the sheet that appears.

Saved Passwords and Credit Cards

On desktop web browsers, a feature called AutoFill saves you an awful lot of typing. It fills out your name and address automatically when you're ordering something online. It stores your passwords so you don't have to re-enter them every time you visit passworded sites.

But on the iPhone, where you're typing on glass, the convenience of AutoFill goes to a whole new level.

The phone can memorize your credit card information, too, making it much easier to buy stuff online; in fact, it can even store this information by *taking a picture* of your credit card.

And thanks to iCloud syncing, all those passwords and credit cards can auto-store themselves on all your other Apple gadgetry.

To turn on AutoFill, visit Settings→Safari→AutoFill. Here's what you find (next page, left):

- **Use Contact Info.** Turn this On. Then tap My Info. From the address book, find your own listing. You've just told Safari *which* name, address, city, state, zip code, and phone number belong to you.

  From now on, whenever you're asked to input your address, phone number, and so on, you'll see an AutoFill button at the top of the keyboard. Tap it to make Safari auto-enter all those details, saving you no

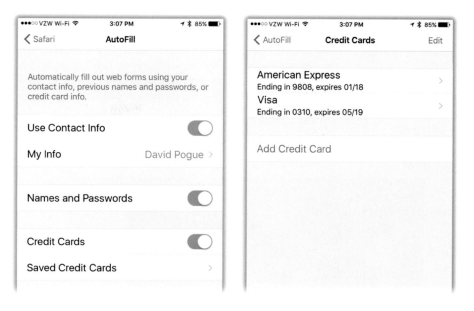

end of typing. (It works on **most** sites.) If there are extra blanks that AutoFill doesn't fill, then you can tap the Previous and Next buttons to move your cursor from one to the next instead of tapping and scrolling manually.

TIP: New in iOS 10: If your contact card contains a secondary address (like a work address), or even a third, then tapping AutoFill produces a pop-up panel listing both (or all three). Just tap the one you want.

- **Names & Passwords** lets Safari fill in your user name and passwords when you visit sites that require you to log in (Google, Amazon, and so on). On each website, you'll be able to choose Yes (a good idea for your PTA or library account), Never for this Website (a good idea for your bank), or Not Now (you'll be asked again next time).

  (To view a list of the actual memorized names and passwords, open Settings→Safari→Passwords.)

TIP: On this screen, you can delete or edit saved passwords. If a login no longer pleases you, swipe leftward across it, and then tap Delete.

To add a password manually, scroll to the bottom of the screen and tap Add Password.

And to make an edit, tap the errant password and then tap Edit. You can touch the problematic password or user name to call up the iPhone's keyboard and make your changes.

- **Credit Cards.** Turn on **Credit Cards**, of course, if you'd like Safari to memorize your charge card info. To enter your card details, tap **Saved Credit Cards** (where you see a list of them) and then **Add Credit Card**. You can type in your name, card number, expiration date, and a description—or you can save yourself a little tedium by tapping **Use Camera**. Aim the camera at your credit card; the phone magically recognizes your name, the card number, and the expiration date, and proposes a description of the card.

When you buy something online, iOS offers an **Autofill Credit Card** button. When you tap it, Safari asks you first which credit card you want to use, if you've stored more than one (it displays the last four digits for your reference). Tap it, and boom: Safari cheerfully fills in the credit card information, saving you time and hassle.

Unfortunately, there's nowhere to store the little three- or four-digit security code, sometimes called the CSC, CVV, or CV2 code. Safari makes no attempt to fill that in; you always have to enter it manually. That's one last safeguard against a kid, a spouse, a parent, or a thief using your phone for an online shopping spree when you're not around.

> **TIP:** Once you've stored all these passwords and credit cards, it sure would be nice if you didn't have to enter them into other Apple gadgets, wouldn't it? Your Mac, your iPad, and so on?
>
> Fortunately, the iCloud service can synchronize this information to Safari running on other Apple machines. Page 527 has the details.

Manipulating Multiple Pages

Like any other self-respecting browser, Safari can keep multiple pages open at once, making it easy for you to switch among them. You can think of it as a miniature version of tabbed browsing, a feature of browsers like Safari Senior, Firefox, Chrome, and Microsoft Edge. Tabbed browsing keeps a bunch of web pages open simultaneously.

One advantage of this arrangement is that you can start reading one web page while the others load into their own tabs in the background.

To Open a New Window

Tap the ⬚ button in the lower right. The Safari page seems to duck backward, bowing to you in 3D space. Tap +.

You now arrive at the Favorites page (next page, left). Here are icons for all the sites you've designated as Favorites (see page 450). Tap to open one. Or, in the address bar, enter an address. Or use a bookmark.

To Switch Among Windows

Tap ⧉ again. Now you see something like the 3D floating pages shown above at right. These are all your open tabs (windows). You work with them like this:

- **Close a window** by tapping the ✕ in the corner—or by swiping a page away horizontally. It slides away into the void.

- **Rearrange these windows** by dragging them up or down.

- **Open a window** to full screen by tapping it.

You can open a third window, and a fourth, and so on, and jump among them, using these two techniques.

> **TIP:** Although not one person in a thousand realizes it, you can search your open Safari tabs' website titles and URLs. Tap the ⧉ button and hold the phone horizontally (landscape mode). There's your secret search box.

iCloud Tabs

Thanks to the miracle of iCloud syncing, the last windows and tabs you had open on that other gadget (even if the gadget is turned off) show up here, at the bottom of the page-juggling screen (tap ⬜ to see it). They're sorted into headings that correspond to your other Apple gadgets.

The concept is to unify your Macs and i-gadgets. You're reading three browser windows and tabs on your phone—why not resume on the big screen when you get home and sit down in front of your Mac?

You won't see these tabs unless the Macs have OS X Mountain Lion or later. And, of course, Safari has to be turned on in System Preferences→iCloud on the Mac, and Settings→iCloud on the phone or tablet.

Reader View

How can people read web articles when there's Times-Square blinking all around them? Fortunately, you'll never have to put up with that again.

The Reader button in the address bar (☰) is amazing. With one tap, it eliminates **everything** from the page you're reading except the text and photos. No ads, toolbars, blinking, links, banners, promos, or anything else.

The text is also changed to a clean, clear font and size, and the background is made plain white. Basically, it makes any web page look like a printed book page, and it's glorious. Shown below: the before and after. Which looks easier to read?

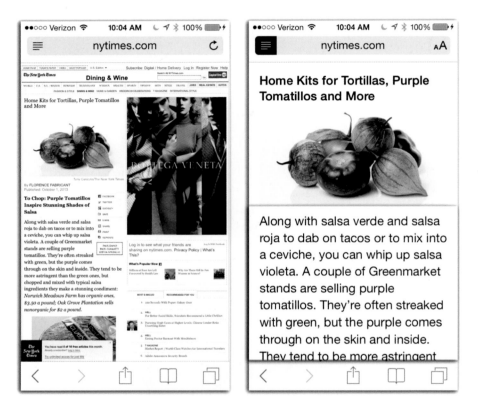

To exit Reader, tap ☰ again. Best. Feature. Ever.

TIP: Once you're in Reader view, a tiny ᴀA button appears at the right end of the address bar. It opens the same font panel that's built into iBooks (illustrated on page 383). That is, it offers you a choice of type size, font, and background color.

The fine print: Reader doesn't appear until the page has fully loaded. It doesn't appear on "front page" pages, like the *nytimes.com* home page—only when you've opened an article within. And it may not appear on sites that are already specially designed for access by cellphones.

You'll know when it's available, because the address bar says "Reader View Available." Can't get much clearer than that.

Web Security

Safari on the iPhone isn't meant to be a full-blown web browser like the one on your desktop computer, but it comes surprisingly close—especially when it comes to privacy and security. Cookies, pop-up blockers, parental controls...they're all here, for your paranoid pleasure.

Pop-Up Blocker

The world's smarmiest advertisers like to inundate us with pop-up and pop-under ads—nasty little windows that appear in front of the browser window, or, worse, behind it, waiting to jump out the moment you close your window. Fortunately, Safari comes set to block those pop-ups so you don't see them. It's a war out there—but at least you now have some ammunition.

The thing is, though, pop-ups are sometimes useful (and not ads)— notices of new banking features, seating charts on ticket-sales sites, warnings that the instructions for using a site have changed, and so on. Safari can't tell these from ads—and it stifles them, too. So if a site you trust says "Please turn off pop-up blockers and reload this page," then you know you're probably missing out on a *useful* pop-up message.

In those situations, you can turn off the pop-up blocker. The on/off switch is in **Settings→Safari**.

> **TIP:** Of course, you can also install other companies' ad blockers. Search the App Store for, for example, 1Blocker or Crystal.

Password Suggestions

When you're signing up for a new account on some website, and you tap inside the box where you're supposed to make up a password, Safari offers to make up a password for you. It's a doozy, too, along the lines of 23k2k4-29cs8-58384-ckk3322.

Now, don't freak out. You're not expected to remember that. Safari will, of course, memorize it for you (and sync it to your other Apple computers, if they're on the same iCloud account). Meanwhile, you've got yourself a unique, nearly uncrackable password.

Cookies

Cookies are something like preference files. Certain websites—particularly commercial ones like Amazon—deposit them on your hard drive so that they'll remember you the next time you visit. That's how Amazon is able to greet you with, "Welcome, Chris" (or whatever your name is). It's reading its own cookie.

Most cookies are perfectly innocuous—and, in fact, extremely useful, because they help websites remember your tastes (and contact info).

But fear is widespread, and the media fan the flames with tales of sinister cookies that track your movement on the web. If you're worried about invasions of privacy, Safari is ready to protect you.

Open Settings→Safari→Block Cookies. The options here are like a paranoia gauge. If you click Always Block, then you create an acrylic shield around your iPhone. No cookies can come in, and no cookie information can go out. You'll probably find the web a very inconvenient place; you'll have to re-enter your information upon every visit, and some websites may not work properly at all. The Always Allow option means "Oh, what the heck—just gimme all of them."

A good compromise is Allow from Websites I Visit, which accepts cookies from sites you *want* to visit, but blocks cookies deposited on your phone by sites you're not actually visiting—cookies an especially evil banner ad gives you, for example.

The Settings→Safari screen also offers a Clear History & Website Data button. It deletes all the cookies you've accumulated so far, as well as your phone's *cache*. (That's a patch of the iPhone's storage area where pieces of web pages you visit—graphics, for example—are retained, to speed up loading the next time you visit.) If you worry that your cache eats up space, poses a security risk, or is confusing some page, then tap Clear History & Website Data to erase it and start over.

Private Browsing

Private browsing lets you surf without adding any pages to your History list, searches to your Google search suggestions, passwords to Safari's saved password list, or autofill entries to Safari's memory. You might want to turn on private browsing before you visit websites that would raise interesting questions with your spouse, parents, or boss.

When you want to start leaving no tracks, tap ⧉ to open the page-juggler screen; tap Private at the bottom-left corner.

Suddenly the light-gray accents of Safari turn jet-black—a reminder that you're now in Private mode. Tap + to open a new page, and proceed as usual. From now on, Safari records nothing while you surf.

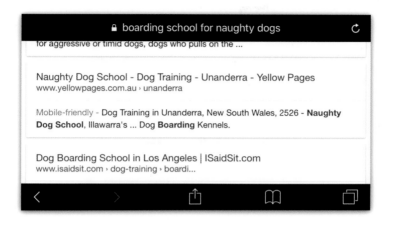

When you're ready to browse "publicly" again, turn private browsing off once more (tap ⊡, and then tap **Private**). Safari resumes taking note of the pages you visit—but it never remembers the ones you opened while in Private mode. In other words, what happens in private browsing stays in private browsing.

Parental Controls

If your child (or employee) is old enough to have an iPhone but not old enough for the seedier side of the web, then don't miss the Restrictions feature in Settings. The iPhone makes no attempt to separate the good websites from the bad—but it *can* remove the Safari icon from the iPhone altogether so that no web browsing is possible at all. See page 618 for instructions.

Five Happy Surprises in the ⬆ Panel

So far in this chapter, you've learned the first step in bookmarking a page (tap ⬆); in designating a new Favorite (tap ⬆); and in saving a web arti-cle to your offline Reading List (tap ⬆). That's right: All these features await on the Share sheet.

But that same panel hosts a wealth of equally useful buttons that nobody ever talks about. So tap ⬆ to open the Share sheet and follow along!

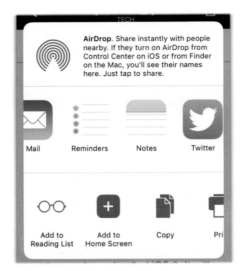

Sharing a Link

The **AirDrop**, **Message**, **Mail**, **Twitter**, and **Facebook** buttons are pretty obvious; they share the link of your current page with other people.

Reminders

Remember how you can say to Siri, about a web page you're on, "Remind me about this later?" (If not, see page 419.) There's a button for that, here on the Share sheet. Great when speaking to your phone would be socially awkward.

Save PDF to iBooks

Well, how the heck about that? You can turn anything you find on the web into an iBooks document—an electronic book that you can read later in iBooks (page 378)! That way, you gain a wide variety of reading tools (notes, highlighting, dictionary) and organizational tools (collections) that aren't available in Safari.

Save to Home Screen

Is there a certain website you visit every day? This button adds the icon of your web page right to your Home screen. It's a shortcut that Apple calls a web clip.

When you tap **Add to Home Screen**, you're offered the chance to edit the icon's name; finally, tap **Add**. When you return to your Home screen, you'll see the icon; you can move or delete it as you would any other app.

You can turn *part* of a web page into one of these Web Clips, too—say, *The New York Times*' "Most emailed" list, or the box scores for a certain sports league. All you have to do is zoom and scroll the page in Safari *before* you tap ⬆, isolating the section you want. Later, when you open the web clip, you'll see exactly the part of the web page you wanted.

Notes

You can send a link to a web article (complete with opening sentences and an image) directly to a note in the Notes app—no copy and paste required. You're invited to annotate the note before hitting **Save** (below, left), or even append it to the end of an existing Notes page (right).

Cancel	Save

Want to Boost Your iPhone's S...
www.yahoo.com
Today, Apple offers its iPhone,
iPad, and iPod Touch customer...

Add text to your note...

Choose Note: New Note ›

Today, Apple offers its iPhone, iPad,
and iPod Touch customers a gift: a

⟨ Back   **Choose Note**

✓ **Create new note**

"Pogue's Basics" v...   10:31 PM

Possible coffee tab...   6:10 PM

Yahoo Column Ideas   6:10 PM

Notes for the Miam...   6:09 PM

Today, Apple offers its iPhone, iPad,
and iPod Touch customers a gift: a

14

Email

Email on your iPhone offers full formatting, fonts, graphics, and choice of type size; file attachments like Word, Excel, PowerPoint, PDF, Pages, Numbers, photos, and even .zip compressed files; and compatibility with Yahoo Mail, Gmail, AOL Mail, iCloud mail, corporate Exchange mail, and any standard email account.

Dude, if you want a more satisfying portable email machine than this one, buy a laptop.

This chapter covers the basic email experience. If you've gotten yourself hooked up with iCloud or Exchange ActiveSync, see Chapters 16 and 18 for details.

Setting Up Your Account

If you play your cards right, you won't *have* to set up your email account on the phone. The first time you set up the iPhone to sync with your computer (Chapter 15), you're offered the chance to *sync* your Mac's or PC's mail with the phone. That doesn't mean it copies actual messages— only the email settings, so the iPhone is ready to start downloading mail.

You're offered this option if your Mac's mail program is Mail or Outlook/ Entourage, or if your PC's mail program is Outlook, Outlook Express, or Windows Mail.

But what if you don't use one of those email programs? No sweat. You can also plug the necessary settings right into the iPhone.

Free Email Accounts

If you have a free email account from Google, AOL, Outlook, or Yahoo; an iCloud account (Chapter 16); or a Microsoft Exchange account run by your employer (Chapter 18), then setup on the iPhone is easy.

From the Home screen, tap Settings→Mail→Accounts→Add Account. Tap the colorful logo that corresponds to the kind of account you have (Google, Yahoo, or whatever).

On the page that appears, sign into your account. Tap Next.

Now you may be shown the list of non-email data that the iPhone can show you (from iCloud, Google, Yahoo, Exchange, and so on): Mail, Contacts, calendars, Reminders, and Notes. Turn off the ones you don't want synced to your phone, and then tap Save.

Your email account is ready to go!

> **TIP:** If you don't have one of these free accounts, they're worth having, if only as a backup to your regular account. They can help with spam filtering, too, since the iPhone doesn't offer any. To sign up, go to *Google.com*, *Yahoo.com*, *AOL.com*, or *iCloud.com*.

POP3 and IMAP Accounts

Those freebie, brand-name, web-based accounts are super-easy to set up. But they're not the whole ball of wax. Millions of people have more generic email accounts, perhaps supplied by their employers or Internet providers. They're generally one of two types:

- **POP accounts** are the oldest and most compatible type on the Internet. (POP stands for Post Office Protocol, but this won't be on the test.) A POP account can make life complicated if you check your mail on more than one machine (say, a PC and an iPhone), as you'll discover shortly.

  A POP server transfers incoming mail to your computer or phone before you read it, which works fine as long as you're using *only that machine* to access your email.

- **IMAP accounts** (Internet Message Access Protocol) are newer and have more features than POP servers, and they're quickly putting POP out to pasture. IMAP servers keep all your mail online, rather than making you store it on your computer; as a result, you can access the same mail from any computer (or phone). IMAP servers remember which messages you've read and sent, and they even keep track of how you've filed messages into mail folders. (Those free Yahoo email accounts are IMAP accounts, and so are Apple's iCloud accounts and corporate Exchange accounts. Gmail accounts *can* be IMAP, too.)

TIP: The iPhone copies your IMAP messages onto the phone itself, so you can work on your email even when you're not online. You can, in fact, control where these messages are stored (in which mail folder). To see this, open Settings→Mail→[your IMAP account name]→[your IMAP account name again]→Advanced. See? You can specify where your drafts, sent messages, and deleted messages wind up on the phone.

The iPhone can communicate with both kinds of accounts, with varying degrees of completeness.

If you haven't opted to have your account-setup information transferred automatically to the iPhone from your Mac or PC, then you can set it up manually on the phone.

Tap your way to Settings→Mail→Accounts→Add Account. Tap Other, tap Add Mail Account, and then enter your name, email address, password, and an optional description. Tap Next.

Apple's software attempts to figure out which kind of account you have (POP or IMAP) by the email address. If it can't make that determination, then you arrive at a second screen, where you're asked for such juicy details as the host name for incoming and outgoing mail servers. (This is also where you tap either IMAP or POP, to tell the iPhone what sort of account it's dealing with.)

If you don't know this stuff offhand, you'll have to ask your Internet provider, corporate tech-support person, or next-door teenager to help you. When you're finished, tap Save.

To delete an account, open Settings→Mail→[account name]. At the bottom of the screen, you'll find the Delete Account button.

> **TIP:** You can make, rename, or delete IMAP or Exchange mailboxes (mail folders) right on the phone.
>
> In the Mail app, view the mailbox list for the account and then tap Edit. Tap New Mailbox to create a new folder. To edit an existing mailbox, tap its name; you can then rename it, tap the Mailbox Location folder to move it, or tap Delete Mailbox. Tap Save to finish up.

Downloading Mail

If you have "push" email (Yahoo, iCloud, or Exchange), then your iPhone doesn't *check* for messages; new messages show up on your iPhone *as they arrive*, around the clock.

If you have any other kind of account, then the iPhone checks for new messages automatically on a schedule—every 15, 30, or 60 minutes. It also checks for new messages each time you open the Mail program, or whenever you *drag downward* on the Inbox list.

> **TIP:** There actually is a sneaky way to turn a Gmail account into a "push" account: Disguise it as an Exchange account. For complete steps, see the free PDF appendix to this chapter, "Setting Up Push Email for Gmail." It's on this book's "Missing CD" page at *www.missingmanuals.com*.

You can adjust the frequency of these automatic checks or turn off the "push" feature (because it uses up your battery faster) in Settings; see page 41.

When new mail arrives, you'll know it at a glance; all the Notification Center options work well in Mail. For example, if your phone is off, you can tap the Sleep or Home button to view the sender, subject, and the first line of the message right on the Lock screen. (Swipe across one, right there on the Lock screen, to jump to it in Mail.)

You'll also hear the iPhone's little "You've got mail" sound, unless you've turned that off in Settings.

If your phone is on, then a new message can alert you by appearing briefly at the top of the screen, without disturbing your work.

You can actually process a message right from that banner. If you see at a glance that it's junk, or if no response is necessary, then drag your finger down on it (or, if you have an iPhone 6s or 7, hard-press it) to reveal two new buttons: Mark as Read (leave it in your inbox, no longer appearing as a new message) and Trash.

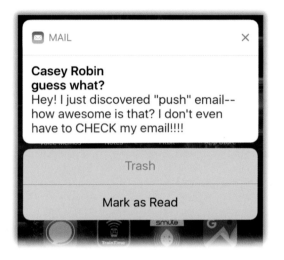

At the Home screen, Mail's icon sprouts a circled number that tells you how many new messages are waiting. If you have more than one email account, it shows you the *total* number of new messages, from all accounts.

If you routinely leave a lot of unread messages in your inbox, and you don't really care about this "badge," you can turn it off. In fact, you can turn it off on a per-account basis, which is great if one of your accounts is sort of a junk account that you keep as a spare. Tap Settings→Notifications→Mail→[account name]→Badge App Icon.

In any case, once you know you have mail, tap *Mail* on the Home screen to start reading it.

TIP: The Mail app, more than any other app, is designed to be a series of nested lists. You start out seeing a list of accounts; tap one to see a list of folders; tap one for a list of messages; tap one to open the actual message.

To **backtrack** through these lists, you can tap the button in the upper-left corner over and over again—or you can **swipe rightward** across the screen. That's a bigger target and more fun.

The Unified Inbox

If you have more than one email address, you're in luck. The iPhone offers a *unified inbox*—an option that displays all the incoming messages from all your accounts in a single place. (If you don't see it—if Mail opened up to some other screen—keep swiping rightward, backing up a screen at a time, until you do.)

This Mailboxes page has two sections:

- **Unified inboxes (and other unified folders).** To see all the incoming messages in one unified box, tap All Inboxes. Below that, you see the Inboxes for each of the individual accounts (below, left).

This part of the main Mail list also offers unified folders for VIPs and Flagged messages, which are described in this chapter.

But what you may not realize is that you can add *other* unified folders to this section. You can, for example, add a folder called Unread, which contains only new messages from *all* accounts. (That's not the same thing as All Inboxes, because your inbox can contain messages you *have* read but haven't deleted or filed.)

You can also add a unified folder showing all messages where you were either the To or CC addressee; this folder won't include any mail where your name appeared on the BCC (blind carbon-copy) line, like mailing lists and, often, spam.

You can also add an **Attachments** folder here (messages with files attached), a **Today** folder, or unified folders that contain **All Drafts**, **All Sent**, or **All Trash**. ("All" means "from all accounts.")

To hide or show these special uni-folders, tap **Edit**, and then tap the selection circles beside the names of the folders you want to appear. (You can also take this opportunity to drag them up or down into a pleasing sequence.) Tap **Done**.

- **Accounts.** Farther down the Mailboxes screen, you see your accounts listed again. You can tap an account's name to expand or collapse its list of traditional mail folders: Inbox, Drafts (emails written but not sent), Sent, Trash, and any folders you've created yourself (Family, Little League, Old Stuff, whatever), as shown on the facing page at right. If you have a Yahoo, iCloud, Exchange, or another IMAP account, then the iPhone automatically creates these folders to match what you've set up online.

> **NOTE:** Not all kinds of email accounts permit the creation of your own filing folders, so you might not see anything but Inbox, Sent, and Trash.

The Message List—and Threading

If you tap an inbox's name, you wind up face to face with the list of incoming messages. At first, you see only the subject lines of your messages, plus, in light-gray type, the first few lines of their contents; that way, you can scan through new messages to see if there's anything important. You can flick upward to scroll this list. Blue dots indicate messages you haven't yet opened.

Each message bears a gray > at the right side. That means "Tap this message's row to read it in all its formatted glory."

Here and there, though, you may spot a double arrow at the right side of the message list, like this: >> That means you're looking at some *threaded* messages. That's where several related messages—back-and-forths on the same subject—appear only once, in a single, consolidated entry. The idea is to reduce inbox clutter and to help you remember what people were talking about.

When you tap a threaded message, you first open an intermediate screen that lists the messages in the thread and tells you how many there are. Tap one of those to read, at last, the message itself.

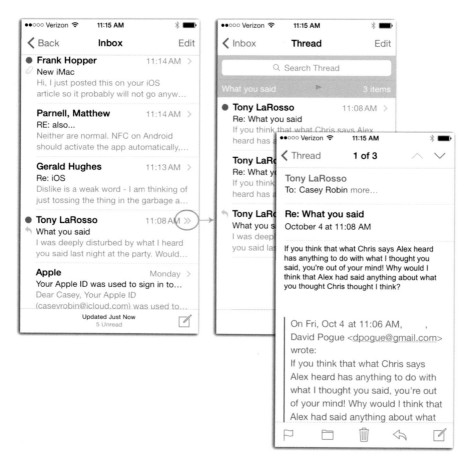

Of course, this also means that to return to the inbox, you have more backtracking to do (swipe rightward twice).

In general, threading is a nice feature, even if, from time to time, it accidentally clumps in a message that has nothing to do with the others.

But if it bugs you, you can turn it off. Open Settings→Mail, scroll down, and turn off Organize By Thread.

(If you have an iPhone Plus model, you can turn the phone 90 degrees to see the mini-tablet-like view shown on the facing page, with the message list and open message visible simultaneously.)

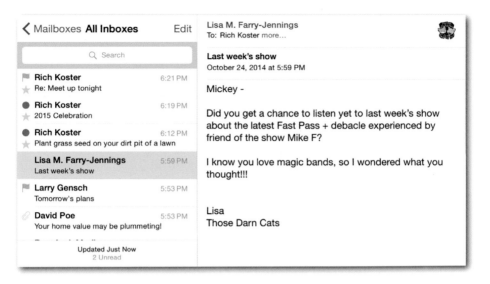

Filters

This one's not new to the world of email programs, but it's new to the iPhone's: one-click filters that hide or show all messages in the list of a certain kind—like ones you haven't yet read.

See the new ⊜ button below the list of messages? When you tap it, you automatically turn on the first filter: Unread. All the messages in the list that you've read are hidden—until you hit the ⊜ button again to turn off the filter.

When the filter is on, you can click the word "Unread" to see a list of other ways to filter the list. You can tell Mail to show you only messages you've flagged; only messages to you (or that you were copied on); only the ones with attachments; or only the ones from people in your VIP list.

VIPs and Flagged Messages

You might notice, in your master Inbox, two "email accounts" that you didn't set up: VIP and Flagged. They're both intended to help you round up important messages from the thousands that flood you every day.

Each one magically rounds up messages from **all** your account inboxes, so you don't have to go wading through lots of accounts to find the really important mail. (Note: That's **inboxes**. Messages in other mail folders don't wind up in these special inboxes, even if they're flagged or are from VIPs.)

VIPs

In the real world, VIPs are people who get backstage passes to concerts or special treatment at business functions (it stands for "very important person"). In iOS, it means "somebody whose mail is important enough that I want it brought to my attention immediately when it arrives."

So who should your VIPs be? That's up to you. Your spouse, your boss, and your doctor come to mind.

To designate someone as a VIP, proceed in either of these two ways:

- **On the accounts screen,** carefully tap the ⓘ next to the VIP item. Your master list of all VIPs appears (below, left). Tap **Add VIP** to choose a lucky new member from Contacts.

This is also where you **delete** people from your VIP list when they've annoyed you. Swipe leftward across a name, and then tap **Delete**. Or tap **Edit** and then tap each ⊖ button; tap **Delete** to confirm.

> **TIP:** You can set things up so that when a new message from a VIP comes in, the iPhone lets you know with a sound, a banner, an alert bubble, a vibration, and so on. Tap **VIP Alerts** to set them up. (That's a shortcut to the **Settings→Notifications→Mail→VIP** screen.)

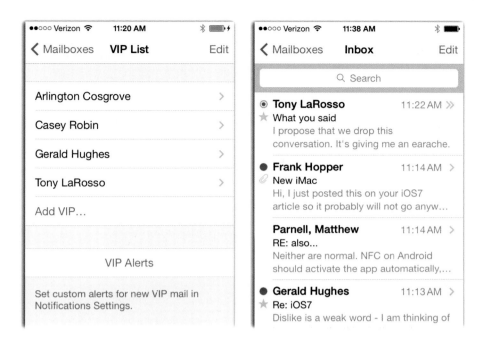

- **In a message from the lucky individual,** tap his name in the From, To, or Cc/Bcc box. His Contact screen appears, complete with an **Add to VIP** button.

Once you've established who's important, lots of interesting things happen:

- **The VIP inbox automatically collects** messages from your VIPs.

- **VIP names in every mail list** sprout a gray star (above, right).

- **If you use iCloud,** the same person is now a VIP on all your other iPhones and iPads (running iOS 6 or later) and Macs (running OS X Mountain Lion or later).

TIP: You can hide the VIP inbox on the main Mailboxes screen—handy if you don't really use this feature. Tap **Edit**, and then ⊘. Tap **Done**.

Flag It

Sometimes you receive email that prompts you to some sort of action, but you may not have the time (or the fortitude) to face the task at the moment. ("Hi there, it's me, your accountant. Would you mind rounding up your expenses for 2005 through 2015 and sending me a list by email?")

That's why Mail lets you **flag** a message, summoning a little flag icon or a little orange dot in a new column next to the message's name. (You can see the actual dot in the message on the previous page at right.) It can mean anything you like—it simply calls attention to certain messages.

TIP: The flag marker can be **either** a ⚑ icon **or** an orange dot. You make your choice in Settings→Mail→Flag Style.

To flag an open message, tap ⚑ at the bottom of the screen. When the confirmation sheet slides up (below, left), tap **Flag**.

You can also rapidly flag messages directly in a **list** (the Inbox, for example). Just swipe leftward across the message—half an inch of finger-sliding does the trick—to reveal the set of buttons shown here at right:

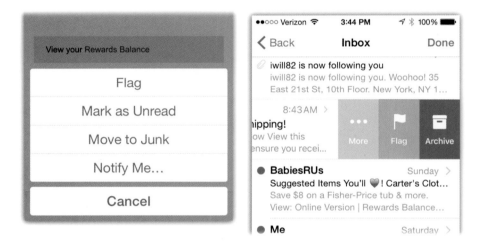

Tap **Flag**. (If you tap **More**, you get the option to **Unflag**.)

The dot or ⚑ icon appears in the body of the message, next to the message's name in your message list. (In the picture on the facing page, the top dot looks more like a bull's-eye; that's because it's flagged **and** unread.) The flag appears even on the corresponding message in your Mac or PC email program, thanks to the miracle of wireless syncing.

Finally, the Flagged mailbox appears in your list of accounts, making it easy to work with all flagged messages, from all accounts, in one place.

TIP: If you don't really use this feature, you can hide the Flagged folder. Tap **Edit**, and then tap the ✔ to turn it off. Tap **Done**.

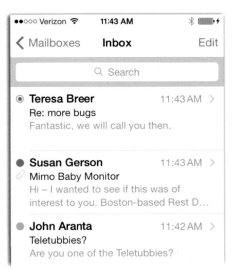

This might be a good time to point out another, newer way to draw attention to a message: Tell Siri to "Remind me about this later." See page 419 for details.

What to Do with a Message

Once you've opened a message, you can respond to it, delete it, file it, and so on. Here's the drill.

> **TIP:** If you have an iPhone 6s or 7, the *first* thing to learn is that you can see what's in a message without ever leaving the Inbox list—just by hard-pressing it. See page 37 for more on peek and pop.

List View: Flag, Trash, Mark as Unread

It's easy to plow through a seething Inbox, processing messages as you go, without ever having to open them. All you have to do is swipe across a message in the list horizontally.

- **Full left-swipe delete.** Swipe your finger leftward *all the way* across the message to delete it. That's it: No confirmation tap required.

- **Partial left-swipe options.** If you don't swipe leftward all the way, you reveal a set of three buttons on the right: Trash (same as before, but now you have to tap again to confirm); Flag (described in the previous section); and More (opens up a raft of options like Reply, Forward, Flag, Move to Junk, and so on).

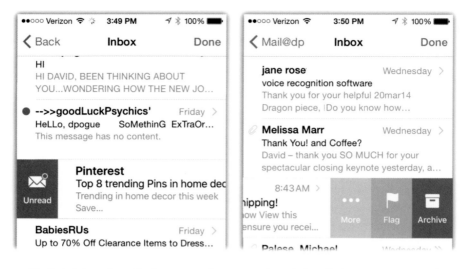

- **Full right-swipe.** Swipe your finger to the *right* all the way across the message to mark it as new (unread). Great for reminding yourself to look at this message again later. Or, if it's already unread, that swipe marks it as *read*.

To a certain extent, you can *customize* these gestures. You can turn off the right-swipe gesture. Or swap the positions of the Flag and Read options, for example, so that you flag a message when you swipe fully to the right and Read appears as a button when you swipe to the left. Or you can put the Archive button into the place of Flag when you swipe to the left.

To check out your options, open Settings→Mail→Swipe Options (shown on the facing page).

Tap Swipe Left to specify which button appears in the center of the three when you swipe partway leftward: None, Mark as Read, Flag, or Move Message. Tap Swipe Right to choose which function you want to trigger with a full rightward swipe (None, Mark as Read, Flag, Move Message, or Archive).

Read It

The type size in email messages can be pretty small. Fortunately, you have some great iPhoney enlargement tricks at your disposal. For example:

- **Spread two fingers** to enlarge the entire email message.

- **Double-tap a narrow block of text** to make it fill the screen, if it doesn't already.

- **Drag or flick your finger** to scroll through or around the message.

- **Choose a larger type size for all messages**. See page 579.

Links are "live" in email messages. Tap a phone number to call it, a web address to open it, a YouTube link to watch the video, an email address to write to it, a time and date to add it to your calendar, and so on.

Reply to It

To answer a message, tap the **Reply/Forward** icon (↩) at the bottom of the screen; tap **Reply**. If the message was originally addressed to multiple recipients, then you can choose **Reply All** to send your reply to everyone simultaneously.

A new message window opens, already addressed. As a courtesy to your correspondents, Mail pastes the original message at the bottom of the window.

If you'd like to splice your own comments into the paragraphs of the original message, replying point by point, then use the Return key to create blank lines in the original message. (Use the loupe—page 73—to position the insertion point at the proper spot.)

From: ★ Tony LaRosso ›   Hide

To: ★ Casey Robin › David Pogue ›

Re: What you said
October 4 at 11:22 AM

I propose that we drop this conversation. It's
giving me an earache.

⎸ On Fri, Oct 4 at 11:22 AM,

Reply
Reply All
Forward
Print

Cancel

The brackets by each line of the original message help your correspondent keep straight what's yours and what's hers.

> **TIP:** If you select some text before you tap **Reply** or **Reply All**, then the iPhone pastes only that selected bit into the new, outgoing message. In other words, you're quoting back only a portion.

Before you tap **Send**, you can add or delete recipients, edit the subject line or the original message, and so on.

Forward It

Instead of replying to the sender, you may sometimes want to pass the note on to a third person. To do so, tap ⤺. This time, tap **Forward**.

> **TIP:** If there's a file attached to the inbound message, the iPhone says, "Include attachments from original message?" and offers **Include** and **Don't Include** buttons. Rather thoughtful, actually—the phone can forward files it can't even open.

A new message opens, looking like the one that appears when you reply. You can precede the original message with a comment of your own,

like, "Frank: I thought you'd be interested in this joke about your mom."
Finally, address and send it as usual.

Follow It

Your phone can notify you when anyone responds to a certain email
conversation.

If you're composing or replying to a message, tap in the subject line to
make the 🔔 appear; tap it. If you're *reading* a message, tap ⚑ at the
bottom of the screen; tap Notify Me; and confirm by tapping Notify Me
again (below, left). In a list, swipe leftward, partly across a message; tap
More; tap Notify Me. In each case, a bell icon appears beside the message (or thread) in the list (below, right).

When anybody replies, a notification banner appears on your screen,
ready for swiping and reading.

Filing or Deleting One Message

Once you've opened a message that's worth keeping, you can file it into
one of your account's folders ("mailboxes") by tapping the 🗂 at the bottom of the screen. Up pops the list of your folders; tap the one you want.

It's a snap to delete a message you no longer want, too. If it's open in
front of you, tap the 🗑 or 🗄 button at the bottom of the screen. The
message rapidly shrinks into the icon and disappears.

NOTE: If that one-touch Delete method makes you a little nervous, by
the way, you can ask the iPhone to display a confirmation box
before trashing the message forever. Visit Settings→Mail→Ask
Before Deleting.

You can also delete a message from the message *list*—the Inbox, for
example; see page 481.

TIP: Gmail doesn't want you to throw anything away. That's why swiping like this produces a button that says Archive, not Delete, and why the usual 🗑 button in a message looks like a filing box. If you prefer to delete a message for good, hold down the ✉ until the Trash Message and Archive Message buttons appear.

There's a long way to delete messages from the list, too, as described next. But for single messages, the finger-swipe method is *much* more fun.

TIP: There's a handy Undo shortcut, too: Shake the phone lightly. Tap Undo Trash. The deleted message jumps back to the folder it just came from. (You can then shake again to undo the Undo!)

Filing or Deleting Batches of Messages

You can also file or delete a bunch of messages at once. In the message list, tap Edit. A circle appears beside each message title. You can tap as many of these circles as you like, scrolling as necessary, adding a ✓ with each touch.

Finally, when you've selected all the messages in question, tap either Trash (Archive) or Move.

If you tap Move, then you're shown the folder list so you can say where you want them moved. If you tap Trash, the messages disappear.

If you decide you've made a mistake, just shake the phone lightly—the iPhone's "Undo" gesture. Tap Undo Move to put the filed messages back where they just came from.

When you delete a message, it goes into the Deleted folder. In other words, it works like the Macintosh Trash or the Windows Recycle Bin. You have a safety net.

Email doesn't have to stay in the Deleted folder forever, though. You can ask the iPhone to empty that folder every day, week, or month. From the Home screen, tap Settings→Mail. Tap your account name and then Advanced→Remove. Now you can change the setting from "Never" to "After one day" (or week, or month).

Add the Sender to Contacts

When you get a message from someone new who's worth adding to your iPhone's Contacts address book, tap that person's name (in blue, on the From line). You're offered buttons for Create New Contact and Add to Existing Contact. Use the second button to add an email address to an existing person's "card."

Open an Attachment

The Mail program downloads and displays the icons for *any* kind of attachment—but it can *open* only documents from Microsoft Office (Word, Excel, PowerPoint), those from Apple iWork (Pages, Keynote, Numbers), PDFs, text, RTFs, VCFs, graphics, .zip files, and un-copy-protected audio and video files.

Just scroll down, tap the attachment's icon, wait a moment for downloading, and then marvel as the document opens up, full screen. You can zoom in and out, flick, rotate the phone 90 degrees, and scroll just as though it were a web page or a photo.

TIP: If you *hold your finger down* on the attachment's name, the Share sheet appears. It offers a list of ways you can send this attachment directly from your phone to someone else (by AirDrop or Mail)—or to open it in other apps.

If you tap a Word document, for example, you may be offered buttons for Mail, Dropbox, Evernote, and other apps that can open Word docs. If you tap a PDF document, you'll see a button for Open in iBooks. (Quick Look means the same non-editable preview as you'd get with a quick tap.)

When you're finished admiring the attachment, swipe rightward to return to the original email message.

●●●○○ Verizon 🛜   11:24 AM   ✳ 🔋✦
❮ Inbox (5)   ⌃   ⌄
From: David Pogue ❯   Hide
To: ★ Casey Robin ❯
"I Want an iPhone" lyrics
October 4 at 11:24 AM
Here there are, as requested. Happy singing!
Your pal,
Dave-O

●●●○○ Verizon 🛜   11:25 AM   ✳ 🔋✦
❮ Back   I Want An iPhone.pdf   ⬆

I Want An iPhone

And now, the end is near.
I'm sick to death of this old cell phone.
Bad sound, the signal's weak, the software stinks; a phone.
I've heard there's something new: a million times m
I too will join the cult. I want an iPhone!

Concerns, I have a few;
It's got some flaws. We may just face it.
No keys, no memory card, the battery's sealed, you
But God! This thing is sweet. A multi-touch, iPod-V
You have me "hello." I want an iPhone!

"I want to touch its precious screen!"
"I want to wipe its smudges clean!"
"I want my friends to look and drool!"
"I want to say 'Look, now I'm cool!'"
"I stood in line, and I'll get mine!"
"I'll get an iPhone!"

For what is a man? what has he got?
If not iPhone, then he's got squat.
It's all the things a phone should be.
So what if it's AT&T?
I took a stand, pay half a grand. I got an iPhone!

Snagging (or Sending) a Graphic

If you get sent a particularly good picture, just hold your finger still on it. You're offered the Save sheet, filled with options like Save (into your Photo app's Camera Roll), Copy, Print, and Assign to Contact (as a person's face photo). All the usual sending methods are represented here, too, so that you can fire off this photo via AirDrop, Messages, Mail, Twitter, and Facebook.

Snagging a Contact or a Date

Mail can recognize contact information or calendar information from an incoming email message—and can dump it directly into Contacts or Calendar for you.

You'll know when it's found something—the block of contact information below somebody's signature, for example—because you see a special gray banner at the top of the screen (shown below).

You can click Ignore if you don't particularly need this person bulking up your address book. But if it's somebody worth tracking, tap **Add to Contacts**. A new Contacts screen appears, ready to save.

Similarly, if the message contains a reference to a date and time, the same sort of banner appears, offering to pop the appointment onto your calendar. (This banner appears only when it's *really sure* you're being offered a date and time: e-invitations and airline-ticket confirmations, for example.)

iOS 10: saving you time since 2016.

Unsubscribing

Here's a cool new one in iOS 10: Every now and then, when you open a piece of junk mail, Mail offers you an Unsubscribe button at the top. And sure enough: Tapping it gets you off that mailing list.

Now, before you uncork the champagne, keep in mind that this button appears only on some pieces of spam—from only the kind-hearted, legitimate senders who include an Unsubscribe link at the bottom of their messages. All Mail does is automate that process (and move the Unsubscribe button to the top).

View the To/From Details

When your computer's screen is only a few inches tall, there's not a lot of extra space. So Apple designed Mail to conceal header details (To, From, and so on) that you might need only occasionally. For example, you usually don't actually see the word "From:"—you usually see only the sender's name, in blue. The To and Cc lines (page 500) may show only first names, to save space. And if there's a long list of addresses, you may see only "Michael (& 15 more)"—not the actual list of names.

You get last names, full lists, and full sender labels when you tap More following the header information. Tap Hide to collapse these details.

> **TIP:** When you tap a sender's name in blue, you open the corresponding info card in Contacts. It contains one-touch buttons for calling someone back, sending a text message, or placing a FaceTime audio or video call—which can be very handy if the email message you just received is urgent.

 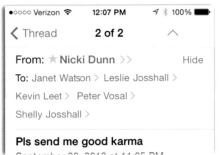

Mark as Unread

In the inbox, any message you haven't yet read is marked by a blue dot (●). Once you've opened the message, the blue dot goes away.

If you slide your finger to the right across a message in the list, you trigger the Unread command—you make that blue dot *reappear*. It's a great way to flag a message for later, to call it to your own attention. The blue dot can mean not so much "unread" as "un–dealt with."

Move On

Once you've had a good look at a message and processed it to your satisfaction, you can move on to the next (or previous) message in the list by tapping 〉or 〈 in the upper-right corner. Or you can swipe rightward to return to the inbox (or whatever mailbox you're in).

Searching

Praise be—there's a search box in Mail. The search box is hiding **above** the top of every mail list, like your inbox. To see it, scroll up, or just tap the status strip at the top of the screen.

Tap inside the search box to make the keyboard appear, along with helpful canned searches like Flagged Messages and Messages with Attachments. As you type, Mail hides all but the matching messages; tap any one of the results to open it.

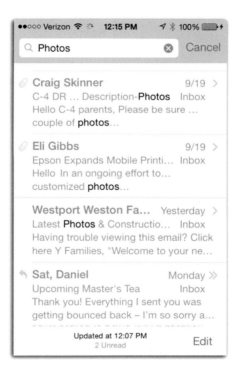

You don't have to specify **which fields** to search (From, To, Subject, Body), or which folder. You're searching everywhere.

> **TIP:** If you **want** to restrict the search to just the folder you're in, you can. After the search results begin to appear, tug downward on the screen. Two new buttons appear: All Mailboxes and Current Mailbox.

Wait long enough, and the search continues with messages that are still out there on the Internet but are so old that they've scrolled off your phone.

> **TIP:** If, after typing a few letters, you tap Search, the keyboard goes away and an Edit button appears. Tapping it lets you select a whole bunch of the search results—and then Mark, Move, or Trash them simultaneously.

Writing Messages

To compose a new piece of outgoing mail, open the Mail app, and then tap ✎ in the lower-right corner. A blank new outgoing message appears, and the iPhone keyboard pops up.

> **TIP:** Remember: You can turn the phone 90 degrees to get a widescreen keyboard for email. It's easier to type this way—especially on an iPhone 6, 6s or 7 model, where you get additional editing keys (like Undo, emoji, numbers, and cursor keys, for example) on the sides. Of course, dictating is much, *much* faster than typing.

Here's how you go about writing a message:

1. **In the To field, type the recipient's email address—or grab it from Contacts.**

   Often, you won't have to type much more than the first couple of letters of the name *or* email address. As you type, Mail displays all matching names and addresses so you can tap one instead of typing.

(It thoughtfully derives these suggestions by analyzing both your Contacts **and** people you've recently exchanged email with.)

As you go, the iPhone displays a list of everyone whose name matches what you're typing (previous page, left). The ones bearing ⓘ buttons are the people you've recently corresponded with but who are not in your Contacts. Tap the ⓘ to open a screen where you can add them to Contacts—or **remove** them from the list of recent correspondents, so Mail's autocomplete suggestions will no longer include those lowlifes.

TIP: When you address an email message, Mail even suggests **clusters** of people you tend to email together—"Erin and Sam," "Erin and Andy," and so on—to save you the trouble of reassembling these addressee teams.

Similarly, if you type a subject you've used, Mail suggests the names of people who've received this subject line before. (For example, if you send "This month's traffic stats" every month to three coworkers, then their names appear automatically when you type out that subject line.) You'll get to go home from work that much quicker.

If you hold your finger down on the period (.) key, you get a pop-up palette of common email-address suffixes, like .com, .edu, .org, and so on, just as in Safari.

Alternatively, tap the ⊕ to open your Contacts list. Tap the name of the person you want.

You can add as many addressees as you like; just repeat the procedure.

TIP: There's no Group mail feature on the iPhone, which would let you send one message to a predefined set of friends. But at *http://groups.yahoo.com*, you can create free email groups. You can send a single email message to the group's address, and everyone in the group will get a copy. (You have to set up one of these groups in a web browser—but lo and behold, your iPhone has one!)

Incidentally, if you've set up your iPhone to connect to a corporate Exchange server (Chapter 18), then you can look up anybody in the entire company directory at this point. Page 559 has the instructions.

2. **To send a copy to other recipients, enter the address(es) in the Cc or Bcc fields.** If you tap Cc/Bcc, From, the screen expands to reveal two new lines beneath the To line: Cc and Bcc.

Cc stands for *carbon copy*. Getting an email message where your name is in the Cc line implies: "I sent you a copy because I thought you'd want to know about this correspondence, but I'm not expecting you to reply."

Bcc stands for *blind carbon copy*. It's a copy that goes to a third party secretly—the primary addressee never knows who else you sent it to. For example, if you send your coworker a message that says, "Chris, it bothers me that you've been cheating the customers," you could Bcc your supervisor to clue her in without getting into trouble with Chris.

Each of these lines behaves exactly like the To line. You fill each one up with email addresses in the same way.

TIP: You can drag people's names around—from the To line to the Cc line, for example. Just hold your finger down briefly on the name before dragging it. (It puffs and darkens once it's ready for transit.)

3. **Change the email account you're using, if you like.** If you have more than one email account set up on your iPhone, you can tap Cc/Bcc, From to expand the form and then tap From to open up a spinning list of your accounts. Tap the one you want to use for sending this message.

4. **Type the topic of the message in the Subject field.** Leaving it blank only annoys your recipient. On the other hand, don't put the *entire* message into the subject line, either.

5. **Type your message in the message box.** All the usual iPhone keyboard and dictation tricks apply (Chapter 3). Don't forget that you can use Copy and Paste, within Mail or from other programs. Both text and graphics can appear in your message.

   And here's a fantastic trick: As you're composing a message, you can refer to *another* email—maybe the one you're responding to—without losing your place.

   To do that, drag downward on the title bar, where it says New Message or whatever the reply's title is; your message in progress collapses to the bottom of the screen. Now you can scroll through the message behind it—or you can navigate to *any* message in any Mail account or folder. This is a great trick when, for example, you want to copy some text out of an earlier message.

Swipe down to reveal what's behind your reply.

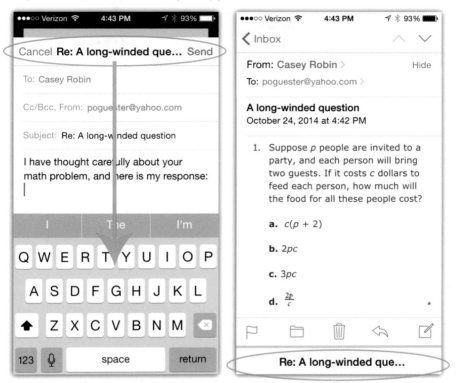

Tap to reopen your reply.

Actually, you can collapse multiple outgoing messages like this, leaving them unfinished but still open. They all pile up at the bottom of the screen. (Hold your finger down on them to "fan" them open, so you can hop into one.)

When you're ready to resume writing, tap the title bar at the bottom of the screen; your composition window opens right back up.

6. **Attach a photo or video,** if you like. Hold down your finger anywhere in the body of the message until the **Select** buttons appear. Tap ▶ to reveal the **Insert Photo or Video** button (shown on the next page at lower left).

When you tap it, you're shown your iPhone's usual photo browser so that you can choose the photos and videos you want to attach (next page, middle). Tap the collection you want; you're shown all the thumbnails inside. Tap the photo or video, and then tap **Choose**.

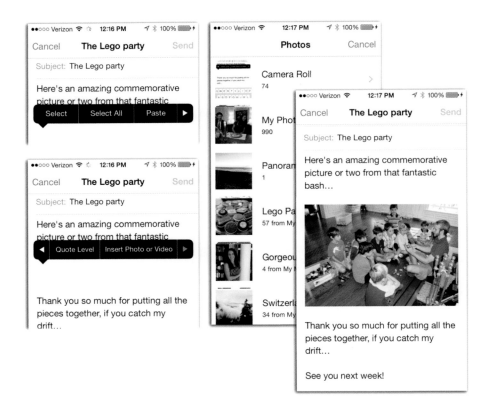

You return to your message in progress, with the photo or video neatly inserted (above, right). You can repeat this step to add additional photo or video attachments. When you tap Send, you're offered the opportunity to scale down the photo to a more reasonable (email-able) size.

> **TIP:** You can also email a photo or a video from within the Photos program; you can *forward* a file attached to an incoming piece of mail; and you can *paste* a copied photo or video (or several) into an open email message.

7. **Format the text,** if you like. You can apply bold, italic, or underlining to mail text you've typed.

   The trick is to select the text first (page 95). When the button bar appears, tap the B I U button. Tap that to make the Bold, Italics, and Underline buttons appear on the button bar; tap away. Not terribly efficient, but it works.

TIP: You can use the same trick to summon the Quote Level controls. Select some text or move the cursor to the paragraph you want; tap the ▶ until you bring the **Quote Level** button into view; and tap it to reveal the **Increase** and **Decrease** buttons. These buttons indent or un-indent those cluttery blocks of quoted and re-quoted text that often appear when you're replying to a message. (One tap affects the entire paragraph.)

If you really can't stand those quote indentations, you can stop the iPhone from adding them in the first place when you forward or reply to a message. The on/off switch for that feature is in **Settings→Mail→Increase Quote Level**.

8. **Tap Send (to send the message) or Cancel (to back out of it).** If you tap **Cancel**, the iPhone asks if you want to save the message. If you tap **Save Draft**, then the message lands in your Drafts folder.

   Later you can open the **Drafts** folder, tap the aborted message, finish it up, and send it.

TIP: If you **hold down** the ✑ button for a moment, the iPhone presents a list of your saved drafts. Clever stuff—if you remember it!

Oh, and by the way: You can begin composing a message on your phone, and then continue writing it on your Mac, without ever having to save it as a draft. Or go the other way. See page 551 for details on Handoff.

Signatures

A *signature* is a bit of text that gets stamped at the bottom of your outgoing email messages. It can be your name, a postal address, or a pithy quote.

Unless you intervene, the iPhone stamps "Sent from my iPhone" at the bottom of every message. You may be just fine with that, or you may consider it the equivalent of gloating (or free advertising for Apple). In any case, you can change the signature if you want to.

From the Home screen, tap **Settings→Mail→Signature**. You can make up one signature for **All Accounts**, or a different one for each account (tap **Per Account**). A Signature text area appears, complete with a keyboard, so you can compose the signature you want. It can even include emoji!

> **TIP:** You can use bold, italic, or underline formatting in your signature, too. Just follow the steps on the previous page for formatting a message: Select the text, tap the ▶ to bring the B I U button into view, and so on.

Finish with a Phone Call

If you're typing out some reply, and you realize that it'd be faster to wrap this up by phone, hold down the Home button (to trigger Siri) and just say, "Call him" or "Call her."

If the addressee has a phone number in Contacts, Siri knows who you mean; she dials the number for you, right from the Mail app!

Surviving Email Overload

If you don't get much mail, you probably aren't lying awake at night trying to think of ways to manage the information overload on your tiny phone.

If you do get a lot of mail, here are some tips.

Avoiding Spam

The key to keeping spam (junk mail) out of your inbox is to keep your email address out of spammers' hands in the first place. Use one address for actual communication. Use a different address in the public areas of the Internet, like chat room posting, online shopping, website and software registration, and newsgroup posting. Spammers use automated software robots that scour these pages, recording email addresses they find. Create a separate email account for person-to-person email—and *never* post that address on a web page.

If it's too late, and you're getting a lot of spam on your phone, you have a couple of options. You could accept your fate and set up a new email account (like a free Gmail or Yahoo account), sacrificing your old one to the spammers.

You could install a spam blocker app on your phone, like SpamDrain ($15 a year) or SpamBlocker (free).

Or, if you're technically inclined, you could create a shadow Gmail account that downloads your mail, cleans it of spam, and passes it on to your iPhone. You can find tutorials for this trick by searching in, of course, Google.

Condensing the Message List

Messages in your inbox are listed with the subject line in bold type *and* a couple of lines, in light-gray text, that preview the message itself.

You can control how many lines of the preview show up here, from None (you see more message titles on each screen without scrolling) to 5 Lines. Tap Settings→Mail→Preview.

Spotting Worthwhile Messages

The iPhone can display a **To** or **Cc** logo on each message in your inbox. At a glance, it helps you identify which messages are actually intended for *you*. Messages without those logos are probably spam, newsletters, mailing lists, or other messages that weren't specifically addressed to you.

To turn on these little badges, visit Settings→Mail and turn on Show To/Cc Label.

Managing Accounts

If you have more than one email account, you can delete one or just temporarily deactivate one—for example, to accommodate your travel schedule.

Visit Settings→Mail. In the list of accounts, tap the one you want. At the top of the screen, you see the on/off switch (at least for POP accounts); Off makes an account dormant. And at the bottom, you see the Delete Account button.

> **TIP:** If you have several accounts, which one does the iPhone use when you send mail from other apps—like when you email a photo from Photos or a link from Safari?
>
> It uses the *default* account, of course. You determine which one is the default account in Settings→Mail→Default Account.

PART FOUR

Connections

15

Syncing with iTunes

Just in case you're one of the seven people who've never heard of it, iTunes is Apple's multifunction, multimedia jukebox software. It's been loading music onto iPods since the turn of the 21st century.

Most people use iTunes to manipulate their digital movies, photos, and music, from converting songs off a CD into music files to buying songs, audiobooks, and movies online.

But, as an iPhone owner, you need iTunes even more urgently, because it's the most efficient way to get masses of music, videos, apps, email, addresses, ringtones, and other stuff *onto* the phone. It also backs up your iPhone automatically.

If you've never had a copy of iTunes on your computer, then fire up your web browser and go to *www.apple.com/itunes/download*. Once the file lands on your computer, double-click the installer icon and follow the onscreen instructions to add iTunes to your life.

> **NOTE:** iTunes is not *required*. It's perfectly possible to use all of an iPhone's features without iTunes—even without a computer. You can download all that stuff right from the Internet, and you can back up your phone using iCloud (which is described in the next chapter).
>
> Using iTunes, however, is more efficient, and it's nice to know that your stuff is backed up on a machine that's within your control. (For an overview of iTunes' *non*-iPhone-related functions, like importing music and building playlists, see this chapter's free Appendix, "iTunes Crash Course," on this book's "Missing CD" at *www.missingmanuals.com*.)

Connecting the iPhone

iTunes is designed to load up, and back up, your iPhone. You can connect it to your computer either wirelessly over Wi-Fi, or wirefully, with the white USB cable that came with it.

- **Connecting the Phone with a cable.** Plug one end of the white cable (supplied with your iPhone) to your computer's USB jack. Connect the other end to the phone.

NOTE: If you have the 2016 MacBook Pro (which has only USB-C jacks), you'll need either a USB-C adapter or a USB-C–to–Lightning cable to connect your phone.

- **Connecting over Wi-Fi.** The iPhone can be charging in its bedside alarm clock dock, happily and automatically syncing with your laptop somewhere else in the house. It transfers all the same stuff to and from your computer—apps, music, books, contacts, calendars, movies, photos, ringtones—but through the air instead of a cable.

  Your computer has to be on and running iTunes. The phone and the computer have to be on the same Wi-Fi network.

  To set up wireless sync, connect the phone using the white USB cable, one last time. Ironic, but true.

Now open iTunes and click the ▯ (iPhone) button at the top-left corner of the iTunes screen. Now you can look over the iPhone's contents or sync it (read on).

NOTE: If you have more than one iPhone, and they're all connected, then this button is a pop-up menu. Choose the name of the one you want to manipulate.

On the Summary tab, scroll down; turn on Sync with this iPhone over Wi-Fi. Click Apply. You can now detach the phone.

From now on, whenever the phone is on the Wi-Fi network, it's automatically connected to your computer, wirelessly. You don't even have to think about it. (Well, OK—you have to think about leaving the computer turned on with iTunes open, which is something of a buzzkill.)

All About Syncing

Transferring data between the iPhone and the computer is called *synchronization*. In general, syncing begins automatically when you connect the phone. The ↻ icon whirls in the top-left corner of the screen, but you're welcome to keep using your iPhone while it syncs.

NOTE: Your photo-editing program (like Photos or Photoshop Elements) probably springs open every time you connect the iPhone, too. See page 520 if that bugs you.

Most people these days don't bother with iTunes for syncing; they let the phone sync with their computers wirelessly, via free iCloud accounts.

If you're a little queasy about letting a third party (Apple) store your personal data, though, you can also do this task manually. You can let the iPhone and your computer sync directly with each other—no Internet is involved.

Ordinarily, the iPhone-iTunes relationship is automatic, according to this scheme:

- **Bidirectional copying (iPhone↔computer).** Contacts, calendars, and web bookmarks get copied in both directions. After a sync, your computer and phone contain exactly the same information.

- **One-way sync (computer→iPhone).** All of the following gets copied in one direction: computer to phone. Music, apps, TV, movies, ringtones, and ebooks you bought on your computer; photos from your computer; and email account information.

- **One-way sync (iPhone→computer).** Photos and videos taken with the iPhone's camera; music, videos, apps, ringtones, and ebooks you bought right from the phone—it all gets copied the other way, from the phone to the computer.

- **A complete backup.** iTunes also backs up *everything else* on your iPhone: settings, text messages, call history, and so on. Details on this backup business are covered starting on page 522.

> **TIP:** If you're in a hurry, you can skip the time-consuming backup portion of the sync. Just click ⊘ at the top of the iTunes window whenever it says "Backing up." iTunes gets the message and skips right ahead to the next phase of the sync—transferring contacts, calendars, music, and so on.

Manual Syncing

OK, but what if you don't *want* iTunes to fire up and start syncing every time you connect your iPhone? What if, for example, you want to change the assortment of music and video that's about to get copied to it? Or what if you just want to connect the USB cable to *charge* the phone, not to sync it?

In that case, you can stop the autosyncing in any of these ways:

- **Interrupt a sync in progress.** Click ⊗ in the iTunes status window until the syncing stops.

- **Stop iTunes from syncing with the iPhone just this time.** As you plug in the iPhone's cable, hold down the Shift+Ctrl keys (Windows) or the ⌘-Option keys (Mac) until the iPhone pops up in the iTunes window. Now you can see what's on the iPhone and change what will be synced to it—but no syncing takes place until you command it.

- **Stop iTunes from auto-syncing with this iPhone.** Connect the iPhone. Click ⏹ in the upper-left corner of iTunes. On the Summary tab, turn off Automatically sync when this iPhone is connected.

- **Stop iTunes from autosyncing any iPhone, ever.** In iTunes, choose Edit→Preferences (Windows) or iTunes→Preferences (Mac). Click the Devices tab and turn on Prevent iPods, iPhones, and iPads from syncing automatically. You can still trigger a sync on command when the iPhone is wired up—by clicking the Sync button.

Of course, you must have turned off autosyncing for a reason. And that reason might be that you want to control what gets copied onto it. Maybe you're in a hurry to leave for the airport, and you don't have time to sit there for an hour while six downloaded movies get copied to the phone. Maybe you have 50 gigabytes of music but only 16 gigs of iPhone storage.

In any case, here are the two ways you can sync manually:

- **Use the tabs in iTunes.** With the iPhone connected, you can specify exactly what you want copied to it—which songs, which TV shows, which apps, and so on—using the various tabs in iTunes, as described on the following pages. Once you've made your selections, click the Summary tab and then click Apply. (The Apply button says Sync instead if you haven't actually changed any settings.)

- **Drag files onto the iPhone icon.** Once your iPhone is connected to your computer, you can click its icon and then turn on Manually manage music and videos (on the Summary screen). Click Apply.

  Now you can drag songs and videos directly onto the iPhone's icon to copy them there. Wilder yet, you can bypass iTunes *entirely* by dragging music and video files *from your computer's desktop* onto the iPhone's icon. That's handy when you've just inherited or downloaded a bunch of song files, converted a DVD to the iPhone's video format, or whatever.

  Just two notes of warning here. First, the iPhone accommodates dragged material from a *single* computer only. Second, if you ever turn off this option, all those manually dragged songs and videos will disappear from your iPhone at the next sync opportunity.

TIP: Also on the Summary tab, you'll find the baffling little option called Sync only checked songs and videos. This is a global override—a last-ditch "Keep the embarrassing songs off my iPhone" option.

When this option is turned on, iTunes consults the tiny checkboxes next to every single song and video in your iTunes library. If you turn off a song's checkbox, it will not get synced to your iPhone, no matter what—even if you use the Music tab to sync All songs or playlists, or explicitly turn on a playlist that contains this song. If the song's or video's checkbox isn't checked in your Library list, then it will be left behind on your computer.

The Eight Great iTunes Tabs

Once your iPhone is connected to the computer, and you've clicked its icon in the upper-left corner of iTunes, the left side of the iTunes window reveals a column of word buttons: Summary, Apps, Music, Movies, TV Shows, Podcasts, Books, Photos, and Info. Below that is a second, duplicate listing, labeled On My Device. For the most part, these represent the categories of stuff you can sync to your iPhone.

The following pages cover each of these tabs, in sequence, and detail how to sync each kind of iPhone-friendly material.

TIP: At the bottom of the screen, a colorful graph shows you the number and types of files: Audio, Video, Photos, Apps, Books, Documents & Data, and Other (for your personal data). More importantly, it also shows you how much room you have left, so you won't get overzealous in trying to load the thing up.

Point to each color block without clicking to see how many of each item there are ("2031 photos") and how much space they take.

Summary Tab

This screen gives basic stats on your iPhone, like its serial number, capacity, and phone number. Buttons in the middle control how and where the iPhone gets backed up. Checkboxes at the bottom of the screen let you set up manual syncing, as described previously.

Serial Number, UDID

If you click your phone's serial number, it changes to reveal the *unique device identifier* (UDID). That's Apple's behind-the-scenes ID for your exact product, used primarily by software companies (developers). You may, during times of beta testing a new app or troubleshooting an existing one, be asked to supply your phone's UDID.

You can click the same label again to see your phone's Product Type and ECID. Or click your phone number to see your various cellular identifiers like the MEID, IMEI, and ICCID. Or click the iOS version to see your iOS version's build number.

You can right-click (on the Mac, Control-click) any of these numbers to get the **Copy** command. It copies those long strings of letters and numbers onto your computer's Clipboard, ready to paste into an email or a text.

Apps Tab

On this tab, you get a convenient duplicate of your iPhone's Home screens. You can drag app icons around, create folders, and otherwise organize your Home life much faster than you'd be able to on the phone itself. See page 334 for details.

Music Tab

Turn on **Sync Music**. Now decide *what* music to put on your phone.

> **NOTE:** If you're using iCloud Music Library (page 235), this Music tab appears empty except for a note that you can play all your music wirelessly from the Internet. In other words, since all your music is online, there's no point in choosing some subset of it to sync to your phone.

- If you have a big iPhone and a small music library, you can opt to sync the **Entire music library**.

- If you have a big music collection and a small iPhone, you'll have to take only *some* of it along for the iPhone ride. In that case, click **Selected playlists, artists, albums, and genres**. In the lists below, turn on the checkboxes for the playlists, artists, albums, and music genres you want to transfer. (These are cumulative. If there's no Electric Light Orchestra in any of your selected playlists, but you turn on ELO in the Artists list, you'll get all your ELO anyway.)

> **TIP:** Playlists make it fast and easy to sync whole batches of tunes over to your iPhone. But don't forget that you can add individual songs, too, even if they're not in any playlist. Just turn on **Manually manage music and videos**. Now you can drag individual songs and videos from your iTunes library onto the iPhone icon to install them there.

Music videos and voice memos (recorded by the iPhone and now residing on your computer) get their own checkboxes.

Making It All Fit

Sooner or later, everybody has to confront the fact that an iPhone holds only 16, 64, 128, or 256 gigabytes of music and video. (Actually less, because the operating system itself eats up over a gigabyte.)

Your multimedia stash may be bigger than that. If you just turn on **Sync All** checkboxes, an error message tells you that it won't all fit on the iPhone.

One solution: Tiptoe through the tabs, turning off checkboxes and trying to sync until the "too much" error message goes away.

If you don't have quite so much time, turn on **Automatically fill free space with songs**. It makes iTunes use artificial intelligence to load up your phone automatically, using your most played and most recent music as a guide. (It does not, in fact, fill the phone completely; it leaves a few hundred megabytes for safety—so you can download more stuff on the road, for example.)

Another helpful approach is to use the *smart playlist*, a music playlist that assembles itself based on criteria that you supply. For example:

1. **In iTunes, choose Music from the top-left pop-up menu. Choose File→New Smart Playlist.**

   The Smart Playlist dialog box appears.

2. **Specify the category.**

   Use the pop-up menus to choose, for example, a musical genre, or songs you've played recently, or *haven't* played recently, or have rated highly.

3. **Turn on the "Limit to" checkbox, and set up the constraints.**

   For example, you could limit the amount of music in this playlist to 2 gigabytes, chosen at random. That way, every time you sync, you'll get a fresh, random supply of songs on your iPhone, with enough room left for some videos.

4. **Click OK.**

   The new Smart Playlist appears in the list of playlists at left; you can rename it. Click it to look it over, if you like. Then, on the Music tab, choose this playlist for syncing to the iPhone.

Movies and TV Shows Tabs

TV shows and movies you've bought or rented from the iTunes Store look great on the iPhone screen. (And if you start watching a rented movie on your computer, the iPhone begins playing it right from where you left off.)

Syncing TV shows and movies works just like syncing music or podcasts. You can have iTunes copy *all* your stuff to the iPhone, but video fills up your storage fast. That's why you can turn on the checkboxes of just the individual movies or shows (either seasons or episodes) you want—or, using the Automatically include pop-up menu, request only the most recent, or the most recent ones you haven't seen yet.

Podcasts Tab

The iTunes Store lists thousands of free amateur and professional podcasts (page 411). On this tab, you can choose to sync all podcast episodes, selected shows, all unplayed episodes—or just a certain number of episodes per sync. Individual checkboxes let you choose *which* podcast series get to come along for the ride, so you can sync to suit your mood at the time.

Books Tab

Here are the thumbnails of your audiobooks and your ebooks—those you've bought from Apple, those you've downloaded from the web, and those you've dragged right into iTunes from your desktop (PDF files, for example). You can ask iTunes to send them all to your phone—or only the ones whose checkboxes you turn on.

Tones Tab

Any ringtones that you've bought from the iTunes Store or made yourself (page 136) appear here; you can specify which ones you want synced to the iPhone. You can choose either **All tones** or, if space on your phone is an issue, **Selected tones** (and then turn on the ones you want).

Be sure to sync over any ringtones you've assigned to your frequent callers so the iPhone can alert you with a personalized audio cue, like Pink's rendition of "Tell Me Something Good" when they call you up.

Photos Tab

Why corner people with your wallet to show them your kid's baby pictures, when you can whip out your iPhone and dazzle them with a slideshow?

Syncing Photos and Videos (Computer→iPhone)

iTunes can sync the photos from your hard drive onto the iPhone. You can even select individual albums of images that you've already assembled on your computer.

> **NOTE:** If you've turned on iCloud Photo Library (page 323), this tab appears *blank*. After all, your photos are already syncing.

Here are your photo-filling options for the iPhone:

- **Windows:** You can sync with Photoshop Elements, Photoshop Album, or any folder of photos, like My Pictures (in Windows), Pictures (on the Mac), or any folder you like.

- **Mac:** You can sync with Photos, iPhoto, or Aperture.

> **NOTE:** You can sync photos from only one computer. If you later attempt to snag some snaps from a second machine, iTunes warns you that you must first erase all the images that came from the *original* computer.

When you're ready to sync your photos, click the Photos tab in iTunes. Turn on Sync photos from, and then indicate *where* you'd like to sync them from (Photoshop Elements, iPhoto, or whatever).

If you've chosen a photo-shoebox program's name (and not a folder's name), you can then click Selected albums, Events, and Faces. Turn on the checkboxes of the albums, events, and faces you want synced. (The "faces" option is available only if you're syncing from Photos, iPhoto, or Aperture on the Mac, and only if you've used the Faces feature, which groups your photos according to who's in them.)

This option also offers to tack on recent Events (batches of photos taken the same day). Indicate whether or not you want videos included in the syncing (Include videos).

Once you make your selections and click Apply, the program computes for a time, "optimizing" copies of your photos to make them look great on the iPhone (for example, downsizing them from 20-megapixel over-kill to something more appropriate for a 0.6-megapixel screen), and then ports them over.

After the sync is complete, you'll be able to wave your iPhone around, and people will *beg* to see your photos.

Syncing Photos and Videos (iPhone→Computer)

You can go the opposite direction, too: You can send photos and videos you took with the iPhone's own camera *to* the computer. You can rest easy, knowing that they're backed up to your computer for safekeeping.

Now, it's important to understand that *iTunes is not involved* in this process. It doesn't know anything about photos or videos *from* the iPhone.

So what's handling the iPhone-to-computer transfer? Your operating system. It treats the iPhone as though it's a digital camera and suggests importing them just as it would from a camera's memory card.

Here's how it goes: Plug the iPhone into the computer with the USB cable. What you'll see is probably something like this:

- **On the Mac.** Photos or iPhoto opens. One of these free photo-organizing/editing programs comes on every Mac. Shortly after the program notices that the iPhone is on the premises, it goes into Import mode. Click Import All, or select some thumbnails from the iPhone and then click Import Selected.

   After the transfer, click Delete Photos if you'd like the iPhone's cameraphone memory cleared out. (Both photos and videos get imported together.)

- **In Windows.** When you attach a camera (or an iPhone), a dialog box asks how you want its contents handled. It lists any photo-management program you might have installed (Photoshop Elements, Photoshop Album, and so on), as well as Windows' own camera-management software. Click the program you want to handle importing the iPhone pictures and videos.

   You'll probably also want to turn on Always do this for this device, so it'll happen automatically the next time.

Shutting Down the Importing Process

Then again, some iPhone owners would rather *not* see some lumbering photo-management program firing itself up every time they connect the phone. You, too, might wish there were a way to *stop* iPhoto, Photos, or Windows from bugging you every time you connect the iPhone. That's easy enough to change—if you know where to look.

- **Windows 7 and later.** When the AutoPlay dialog box appears, click Set AutoPlay defaults in Control Panel. (Or, if the AutoPlay dialog box is no longer on the screen, choose Start→Control Panel→AutoPlay.)

   Scroll all the way to the bottom until you see the iPhone icon. From the pop-up menu, choose Take no action. Click Save.

- **iPhoto.** Open iPhoto. Choose iPhoto→Preferences. Where it says Connecting camera opens, choose No application. Close the window.

- **Photos.** Connect your iPhone to the Mac. Open Photos. At the top left, click the iPhone's icon, if necessary, and turn off Open Photos for this device. (You have to repeat this for every individual phone or tablet.)

From now on, no photo-importing message will appear when you plug in the iPhone. (You can always import its photos manually, of course.)

Info Tab

On this tab, you're offered the chance to copy some distinctly non-entertainment data over to your iPhone: your computer's calendar, address book, email settings, and web bookmarks.

Now, none of this setup is necessary if you use iCloud (Chapter 16), and you've told your phone to sync its calendar (in Settings→iCloud). That's because iCloud, not iTunes, handles synchronization with the iPhone. Instead, this tab shows only a message that, for example, "Your calendars are being synced with your iPhone over the air from iCloud."

Syncing Contacts and Calendars

If you're not using iCloud syncing, then you can choose to sync your iPhone's address book with a Windows program like Outlook, Outlook Express, or Windows Mail; a Mac program like Contacts or Entourage/Outlook for Mac; or an online address book like Google Contacts or Yahoo Address Book.

Similarly, you can sync the phone's calendar with a program like Outlook (for Windows) or Calendar or Outlook (on the Mac).

On My Device

Below those Settings tabs at the left side of the iTunes window, there's a second, similar set labeled On My Device. It's a tidy list of everything that is, in fact, on your phone, organized by type (Music, Movies, and so on). There's not really much you can *do* here—you can get more information about some items by pointing to them—but just seeing your multimedia empire arrayed before you can be very satisfying.

The Purchased category, in particular, can be handy; it shows everything on your phone that you've bought *with* the phone.

One iPhone, Multiple Computers

In general, Apple likes to keep things simple. Everything it ever says about the iPhone suggests that you can only sync *one* iPhone with *one* computer.

That's not really true, however. You can actually sync an iPhone with *multiple* Macs or PCs.

And why would you want to do that? So you can fill it up with material from different places: music and video from a Mac at home; contacts, calendar, ebooks, and iPhone applications from your Windows PC at work; and maybe even the photos from your laptop.

iTunes derives these goodies from different sources to begin with—pictures from your photo program, addresses and appointments from your contacts and calendar programs, music and video from iTunes. So all you have to do is set up the tabs of each computer's copy of iTunes to sync *only* certain kinds of material.

On the Mac, for example, you'd turn on the Sync checkboxes for only the Music, Podcasts, and Video tabs. Sync away.

Next, take the iPhone to the office; on your PC, turn on the Sync checkboxes on only the Info, Books, and Apps tabs. Sync away once more. Then, on the laptop, turn off Sync on all tabs except Photos.

And off you go. Each time you connect the iPhone to one of the computers, it syncs that data according to the preferences set in that copy of iTunes.

One Computer, Multiple iPhones

It's fine to sync multiple iPhones with a single computer, too. iTunes cheerfully fills each one up, and can back each one up, as they come. In fact, if you open the Preferences box (in the iTunes menu on the Mac, the Edit menu in Windows), the Devices tab lists all the iPhones that iTunes is tracking (and iPads and iPod Touches).

Backing Up the iPhone

iTunes can back up everything your computer doesn't already have a copy of: stuff you downloaded straight to the phone (music, ebooks, apps, and so on), plus less visible things, like your iPhone's mail and network settings, your call history, contact favorites, notes, text messages, and other personal preferences that are hard or impossible to recreate.

> **TIP:** If you turn on the Encrypted iPhone Backup option, then your backup will include all your *passwords*: for Wi-Fi hotspots, websites, email accounts, and so on. That can save you tons of time when you have to restore the phone from the backup. (The one downside: You'll be asked to make up a password *for the backup*. Don't forget it!)

You can create your backups in either of two places:

- **On your computer.** You get a backup every time the iPhone syncs with iTunes. The backup also happens before you install a new iPhone firmware version from Apple. iTunes also offers to do a backup before you use the Restore option described in the next section.

- **On iCloud.** You can also back up your phone wirelessly and auto-matically—to iCloud, if you've signed up. That method has the advantage of being available even if your computer gets lost or burned to a crisp in a house fire. On the other hand, since your free iCloud storage holds only 5 gigabytes, and your phone probably holds 16 or more, the free iCloud account usually isn't enough. See the next chapter for details.

You make this choice on the Summary tab described earlier in this chapter.

Using That Backup

So the day has come when you really need to *use* that backup of your iPhone. Maybe it's become unstable, and it's crashing all over. Or maybe you just lost the dang thing, and you wish your replacement iPhone could have all your old info and settings on it. Here's how to save the day (and your data):

1. **Connect the iPhone to the computer you normally use to sync with.**

2. **Click the ☐ (iPhone) button; click the Summary tab.**

3. **Click Restore iPhone.**

   A message announces that you can't erase the phone without first turning off Find My iPhone. This is a security measure to stop a thief from erasing a stolen phone. He can't restore the phone without turning off Find My iPhone, which requires your iCloud password. Go to the phone and do that (in Settings→iCloud).

   ### Welcome to Your New iPhone

   Would you like to set up this iPhone as a new iPhone or restore all of your information from a previous backup?

   ○ Set up as new iPhone

   ● Restore from this backup

   | D's iPad |
   | ✓ iPhone |
   | Teehee;) |

   Last backed up: 10/14/14, 1:21 PM

4. **Take iTunes up on its offer to restore all your settings and stuff from the backup.**

   If you see multiple backup files listed from other iPhones (or an iPod Touch), be sure to pick the backup file for *your* phone. Let the back-up restore your phone settings and info. Then resync all your music, videos, and podcasts. Exhale.

Deleting a Backup File

To save disk space, you can delete old backups (especially for i-gadgets you no longer own). Go to the iTunes preferences (Edit→Preferences in Windows or iTunes→Preferences on the Mac) and click the Devices tab.

Click the dated backup file you don't want and hit Delete Backup.

16

iCloud

The free iCloud service stems from Apple's brainstorm that, since it controls both ends of the connection between a Mac and the Apple website, it should be able to create some pretty clever Internet-based features.

This chapter concerns what iCloud can do for you, the iPhone owner.

> **NOTE:** To get a free iCloud account if you don't already have one, sign up in **Settings→iCloud**.

What iCloud Giveth

So what is iCloud? Mainly, it's these things:

- **A synchronizing service.** It keeps your calendar, address book, and documents updated and identical on all your gadgets: Mac, PC, iPhone, iPad, iPod Touch. Also your web passwords, credit card numbers, AirPod (wireless earbud) pairing, and all kinds of other things. That's a huge convenience—almost magical.

- **Find My iPhone.** Find My iPhone pinpoints the current location of your iPhone on a map. In other words, it's great for helping you find your phone if it's been stolen or lost.

  You can also make your lost gadget make a loud pinging sound for a couple of minutes by remote control—even if it was silenced. That's brilliantly effective when your phone has slipped between the couch cushions.

- **An email account.** Handy, really: An iCloud account gives you a new email address. If you already have an email address, great! This new one can be a backup account, one you never enter on websites so that it never gets overrun with spam. Or vice versa: Let *this* be your junk account, the address you use for online forms. Either way, it's great to have a second account.

- **An online locker.** Anything you buy from Apple—music, TV shows, ebooks, and apps—is stored online, for easy access at any time. For example, whenever you buy a song or a TV show from the online iTunes Store, it appears automatically on your iPhone and computers. Your photos are stored online, too.

- **Back to My Mac.** This option to grab files from one of your other Macs across the Internet isn't new, but it survives in iCloud. It lets you access the contents of one Mac from another one across the Internet.

- **Automatic backup.** iCloud can back up your iPhone—automatically and wirelessly (over Wi-Fi, not over cellular connections). It's a quick backup, since iCloud backs up only the changed data.

  If you ever want to set up a new i-gadget, or if you want to restore everything to an existing one, life is sweet. Once you're in a Wi-Fi hotspot, all you have to do is re-enter your Apple ID and password in the setup assistant that appears when you turn the thing on. Magically, your gadget is refilled with everything that used to be on it.

  Well, *almost* everything. An iCloud backup stores everything you've bought from Apple (music, apps, books); photos and videos in your Photos app; settings, including the layout of your Home screen; text messages; and ringtones. You'll also have to re-establish your passwords (for hotspots, websites, and so on) and anything that came from your computer (like music/ringtones/videos from iTunes and photos from the Photos app).

- **Family Sharing** is a broad category of features intended for families (up to six people).

  First, everyone can share stuff bought from Apple's online stores: movies, TV shows, music, ebooks, and so on. It's all on a single credit card, but you, the all-knowing parent, can approve each person's purchases—without having to share your account password. That's a great solution to a long-standing problem.

  There's also a new shared family photo album and a new auto-shared Family category on the calendar. Any family member can see the location of any other family member, and they can find one another's lost iPhones or iPads using Find My iPhone.

- **iCloud Drive** is Apple's version of Dropbox. It's a folder, present on every Mac, iPhone, iPad, and iPod Touch, that lists whatever you've put into it—an online "disk" that holds 5 gigabytes (more, if you're willing to pay money).

The iCloud Drive is a perfect place to put stuff you want to be able to access from any Apple gadget, wherever you go. It's a great back-up, too.

- **Continuity.** If you have a Mac, and it's running OS X Yosemite or later, you're in for a treat. The set of features Apple calls Continuity turn the iPhone into a part of the Mac. They let you make calls from your Mac as though it were a speakerphone. They let you send and receive text messages from your Mac—to any cellphone on earth. They let you AirDrop files between computer and phone, wirelessly. And more.

So there's the quick overview. The rest of the chapter covers each of the iCloud iPhone-related features in greater depth—except Continuity, which gets its own chapter right after this one.

iCloud Sync

For many people, this may be the killer app for iCloud right here: The iCloud website, acting as the master control center, can keep multiple Macs, Windows PCs, and iPhones/iPads/iPod Touches synchronized. That offers both a huge convenience factor—all your stuff is always on all your gadgets—and a safety/backup factor, since you have duplicates everywhere.

It works by storing the master copies of your stuff—email, notes, con-tacts, calendars, web bookmarks, and documents—on the web. (Or "in the cloud," as the product managers would say.)

Whenever your Macs, PCs, or i-gadgets are online—over Wi-Fi or cel-lular—they connect to the mother ship and update themselves. Edit an address on your iPhone, and shortly thereafter you'll find the same change in Contacts (on your Mac) and Outlook (on your PC). Send an email reply from your PC at the office, and you'll find it in your Sent Mail folder on the Mac at home. Add a web bookmark anywhere and find it everywhere else. Edit a spreadsheet in Numbers on your iPad and find the same numbers updated on your Mac.

Actually, there's yet another place where you can work with your data: on the web. Using your computer, you can log into *www.icloud.com* to find web-based clones of Calendar, Contacts, and Mail.

To control the syncing, tap Settings→iCloud on your iPhone. Turn on the checkboxes of the stuff you want to be synchronized all the way around:

- **iCloud Drive.** This is the on/off switch for the iCloud Drive (page 351). Look Me Up by Email is a list of apps that permit other iCloud members to find you by looking up your address. And Use Cellular Data lets you prevent your phone from doing its iCloud

Drive synchronization over the cellular network, since you probably get only a limited data allotment each month.

- **Photos.** Tap the > button to see four relevant on/off switches.

    iCloud Photo Library is Apple's new online photo storage feature. It stores all your photos and videos online, so you can access them from any Apple gadget; you can read more about it on page 323.

    Upload to My Photo Stream and iCloud Photo Sharing are the master switches for Photo Streams, which are among iCloud's marquee features (page 316).

    When you hold your finger down on the shutter button, the iPhone 5s and later models can snap 10 frames a second. That's burst mode—and all those photos can fill up your iCloud storage. So Apple gives you the Upload Burst Photos option to exclude them from the backup.

- **Mail.** "Mail" refers to your actual email messages, plus your account settings and preferences from iOS's Mail program.

- **Contacts, Calendars.** There's nothing as exasperating as realizing that the address book you're consulting on your home Mac is missing somebody you're *sure* you entered—on your phone. This option keeps all your address books and calendars synchronized. Delete a phone number on your computer at home, and you'll find it gone from your phone. Enter an appointment on your iPhone, and you'll find the calendar updated everywhere else.

- **Reminders.** This option refers to the to-do items you create in the phone's Reminders app; very shortly, those reminders will show up on your Mac (in Reminders, Calendar, or BusyCal) or PC (in Outlook). How great to make a reminder for yourself in one place and have it reminding you later in another one!

- **Safari.** If a website is important enough to merit bookmarking while you're using your phone, why shouldn't it also show up in the Bookmarks menu on your desktop PC at home, your Mac laptop, or your iPad? This option syncs your Safari Reading List, too.

- **Home** refers to the setups for any home-automation gear you've installed (page 377).

- **Notes.** This option syncs the notes from your phone's Notes app into the Notes app on the Mac, the email program on your PC, your other i-gadgets, and, of course, the iCloud website.

- **News** refers to the sources and topics you've set up in the News app (page 402).

- **Wallet.** If you've bought tickets for a movie, show, game, or flight, you sure as heck don't want to be stuck without them because you left the barcode on your other gadget.

- **Keychain.** The login information for your websites (names and passwords), and even your credit card information, can be stored right on your phone—and synced to your other iPhones, iPads, and Macs (running OS X Mavericks or later).

  Now, you could argue that website passwords and credit card numbers are more important than, say, your Reminders. For this category, you don't want to mess around with security.

  Therefore, when you turn on the Keychain switch in Settings, you're asked to enter your iCloud password.

  Then you get a choice of ways to confirm your realness—either by entering a code that Apple texts to you or by using another Apple device to set up this one. Once that's done, your passwords and credit cards are magically synced across your computers and mobile gadgets, saving you unending headaches. This is a truly great feature that's worth enduring the setup.

- **Backup.** Your phone can back itself up online, automatically, so that you'll never worry about losing your files along with your phone.

  Of course, most of the important stuff is *already* backed up by iCloud, in the process of syncing it (calendar, contacts—all the stuff described on these pages). So this option just backs up everything else: all your settings, your Health data, your documents, your account settings, and your photo library.

  There are some footnotes. The wireless backing-up happens only when your phone is charging and in a Wi-Fi hotspot (because in a cellular area, all that data would eat up your data limit each month). And remember that a free iCloud account includes only 5 gigabytes of storage; your phone may require a lot more space than that. Using iCloud Backup may mean paying for more iCloud storage, as described on page 351.)

To set up syncing, turn on the switches for the items you want synced. That's it. There is no step 2.

> **NOTE:** You may notice that there are no switches here for syncing stuff you buy from Apple, like books, movies, apps, and music. They're not so much *synced* as they are *stored* for you online. You can download them at any time to any of your machines.

My Photo Stream, Photo Sharing

These iCloud features are described in glorious detail in Chapter 9.

Find My iPhone

Did you leave your iPhone somewhere? Did it get stolen? Has that mischievous 5-year-old left it somewhere in the house again? Sounds like you're ready to avail yourself of one of Apple's finest creations: Find My iPhone.

The first step is to log into *iCloud.com* and click **Find My iPhone**. Immediately, the website updates to show you, on a map, the current location of your phone—and Macs, iPod Touches, and iPads. (If they're not online, or if they're turned all the way off, you won't see their current locations.)

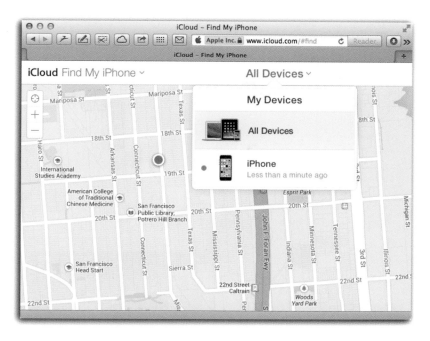

If you own more than one, you may have to click **All Devices** and, from the list, choose the one you're looking for.

If just knowing where the thing *is* isn't enough to satisfy you, then click the dot representing your phone, click the ⓘ next to its name, and marvel at the appearance of these three buttons:

- **Play Sound.** When you click this button, the phone starts dinging and vibrating loudly for 2 minutes, wherever it is, so you can figure out which jacket pocket you left it in. It beeps even if the ringer switch is off, and even if the phone is asleep. Once you find the phone, just wake it in the usual way to make the dinging stop.

- **Lost Mode.** When you lose your phone for real, proceed immediately to Lost Mode. Its first step: prompting you to password protect it, if you haven't already. Without the password, a sleazy crook can't get into your phone without erasing it. (If your phone is already password-protected, you don't see this step.)

  The passcode you dream up here works just as though you'd created one yourself on the phone. That is, it remains in place until you, with the phone in hand, manually turn it off in Settings→General→Passcode Lock.

  Next, the website asks for a phone number where you can be reached, and (when you click Next) a message you want displayed on the iPhone's Lock screen. If you actually left the thing in a taxi or on some restaurant table, you can use this feature to plead for its return.

When you click **Done**, your message appears on the phone's screen, wherever it is, no matter what app was running, and the phone locks itself.

Whoever finds it can't miss the message, can't miss the **Call** button that's right there on the Lock screen, and can't do anything without dismissing the message first.

If the finder of your phone really isn't such a nice person, at least you'll get an automatic email every time the phone moves from place to place, so you can track the thief's whereabouts. (Apple sends these messages to your @me.com or @icloud.com address.)

- **Erase iPhone.** This is the last-ditch security option, for when your immediate concern isn't so much the phone as all the private stuff that's on it. Click this button, confirm the dire warning box, enter your iCloud ID, and click **Erase**. By remote control, you've just erased everything from your phone, wherever it may be. (If it's ever returned, you can restore it from your backup.)

Once you've wiped the phone, you can no longer find it or send messages to it using Find My iPhone.

Send Last Location

Find My iPhone works great—as long as your lost phone has power, is turned on, and is online. Often, though, it's lying dead somewhere, or it's been turned off, or there's no Internet service. In those situations, you might think Find My iPhone can't help you.

But, thanks to Send Last Location, you still have a prayer of finding your phone again. Before it dies, your phone will send Apple its location. You have 24 hours to log into *iCloud.com* and use the Find My iPhone feature to see where it was at the time of death. (After that, Apple deletes the location information.)

You definitely want to turn this switch on.

Activation Lock

Thousands of people have found their lost or stolen iPhones by using Find My iPhone. Yay!

Unfortunately, thousands more will never see their phones again. Until recently, Find My iPhone had a back door the size of Montana: The thief could simply turn the phone off. Or, if your phone was password-protected, the thief could just erase it and sell it on the black market, which was his goal all along. Suddenly, your phone is lost in the wilderness, and you have no way to track or recover it.

That's why Apple offers the ingenious Activation Lock feature. It's very simple: Nobody can erase it, or even turn off Find My iPhone, without entering your iCloud password (your Apple ID). This isn't a switch you can turn on or off; it's always on.

So even if the bad guy has your phone and tries to sell it, the thing is useless. It's still registered to you, you can still track it, and it still displays your message and phone number on the Lock screen. Without your iCloud password, your iPhone is just a worthless brick. Suddenly, stealing iPhones is a much less attractive prospect.

Email

Apple offers an email address as part of each iCloud account. Of course, you already **have** an email account. So why bother? The first advantage is the simple address: *YourName@me.com* or *YourName@icloud.com*.

Second, you can read your me.com email from any computer anywhere in the world, via the iCloud website, or on your iPhone/iPod Touch/iPad.

To make things even sweeter, your me.com or icloud.com mail is completely synced. Delete a message on one gadget, and you'll find it in the Deleted Mail folder on another. Send a message from your iPhone, and you'll find it in the Sent Mail folder on your Mac. And so on.

Video, Music, Apps: Locker in the Sky

Apple, if you hadn't noticed, has become a big seller of multimedia files. It has the biggest music store in the world. It has the biggest app store, for both i-gadgets and Macs. It sells an awful lot of TV shows and movies. Its ebook store, iBooks, is no Amazon, but it's chugging along.

Once you buy a song, movie, app, or book, you can download it again as often as you like—no charge. In fact, you can download it to your *other* Apple equipment, too—no charge. iCloud automates, or at least formalizes, that process. Once you buy something, it's added to a list of items that you can download to all your *other* machines.

Here's how to grab them:

- **iPhone, iPad, iPod Touch.** *For apps:* Open the App Store icon. Tap Updates. Tap Purchased, and then My Purchases. Tap Not on This iPhone.

  For music, movies, and TV shows: Open the iTunes Store app. Tap More, and then Purchased; enter your password; tap the category you want. Tap Not on This iPhone.

  There they are: all the items you've ever bought, even on your *other* machines using the same Apple ID. To download anything listed here onto *this* machine, tap the ⬇ button. Or tap an album name to see the list of songs on it so you can download just *some* of those songs.

  You can save yourself all that tapping by opening Settings→iTunes & App Store and turning on Automatic Downloads (for music, apps, books, and audiobooks). From now on, whenever you're on Wi-Fi, stuff you've bought on other Apple machines gets downloaded to this one *automatically*.

- **Mac or PC.** Open the Mac App Store program (for Mac apps) and click Purchases. Or open the iTunes app (for songs, TV shows, books, and movies). Click Store and then, under Quick Links, click Purchased. There are all your purchases, ready to open or re-download.

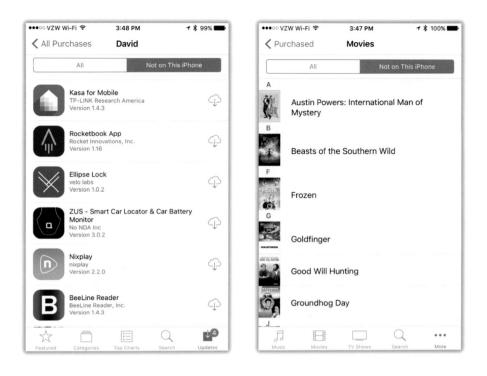

TIP: To make this automatic, open iTunes. Choose **iTunes→ Preferences→Downloads**. Under **Automatic Downloads**, turn on **Music**, **Apps**, and **Books**, as you see fit. Click **OK**. From now on, iTunes will auto-import anything you buy on any of your other machines.

Any bookmark you set in an iBooks book is synced to your other gadgets, too. The idea, of course, is that you can read a few pages on your phone in the doctor's waiting room and then continue from the same page on your iPad on the train ride home.

iCloud Drive

iCloud Drive is Apple's version of Dropbox. It's a single folder whose contents are replicated on every Apple machine you own—Mac, iPhone, iPad, iCloud.com—and even Windows PCs. See page 351 for details.

The Price of Free

A free iCloud account gives you 5 gigabytes of online storage. That may not sound like much, especially when you consider how big some music, photo, and video files are. Fortunately, anything you buy from Apple—like music, apps, books, and TV shows—doesn't count against that 5-gigabyte limit. Neither do the photos in your Photo Stream.

So what's left? Some things that don't take up much space, like settings, documents, and pictures you take with your iPhone, iPad, or iPod Touch—and some things that take up a lot of it, like email, commercial movies, and home videos you transferred to the phone from your computer. Anything you put on your iCloud Drive eats up your allotment, too. (Your iPhone backup might hog space, but you can pare that down in Settings→iCloud→Storage→Manage Storage. Tap an app's name and then tap Edit.)

You can, of course, expand your storage if you find 5 gigs constricting. You can expand that to 50 GB, 200 GB, a terabyte, or 2 TB—for $1, $3, $10, or $20 a month. You can upgrade your storage online, on your computer, or right on the iPhone (in Settings→iCloud→Storage→Buy More Storage).

Apple Pay

Breathe a sigh of relief. Now you can pay for things without cash, without cards, without signing anything, without your wallet: Just **hold the phone**. You don't have to open some app, don't have to enter a code, don't even have to wake the phone up; just hold your finger on the Home button (it reads your fingerprint to make sure it's you). You've just paid.

You can't pay for things everywhere; the merchant has to have a wireless terminal attached to the register. You'll usually know, because you'll see the Apple Pay logo somewhere:

Apple says more than two million stores and restaurants accept Apple Pay, including chains like McDonald's, Walgreens, Starbucks, Macy's, Subway, Panera Bread, Duane Reade, Bloomingdale's, Staples, Chevron, and Whole Foods. The list grows all the time.

Apple Pay depends on a special chip in the phone: the NFC chip (near-field communication), and models before the iPhone 6 don't have it. Stores whose terminals don't speak NFC—like Walmart—don't work with Apple Pay, either.

The Setup

To set up Apple Pay, you have to teach your phone about your credit card. To do that, open the Wallet app. You can also start this process in Settings→Wallet & Apple Pay.

Tap Add credit or debit card. Tap Next.

Now, on the Add Card screen, you're asked to aim the phone's camera at whatever Visa, Mastercard, or American Express card you use most often. Hold steady until the digits of your card, your name, and the expiration date blink onto the screen, autorecognized. Cool! The phone even suggests a card description. You can manually edit any of those four fields before tapping Done.

> **TIP:** If you don't have the card with you, you can also choose Enter Card Details Manually and type in all the numbers yourself.

Check over the interpretation of the card's information, and then hit **Next**.

Now you have to type in the security code manually. Hit **Next** again. Then agree to the legalese screen.

Next, your bank has to verify that all systems are go for Apple Pay. That may involve responding to an email or a text, or typing in a verification code. In any case, it's generally instantaneous.

> **NOTE:** At the outset, Apple Pay works only with Mastercard, Visa, or American Express, and only the ones issued by certain banks. The big ones are all on board—Citibank, Chase, Bank of America, and so on—and more are signing on all the time.

You can record your store loyalty and rewards cards, too—and when you're in that store, the phone chooses the correct card automatically. When you're in Dunkin' Donuts, it automatically uses your Dunkin' Donuts card to pay.

The Shopping

Once the cashier has rung up your total, here comes the magic. Bring your iPhone near the terminal—no need to wake it—in any of these ways:

- **To pay with your default card:** With the phone asleep and your finger resting on the Home button, bring the phone within an inch of the terminal. (Leave your finger on the Home button, so the fingerprint reader can do its thing.) The phone wakes, buzzes, and beeps, and it's all over. It takes about 2 seconds.

> **TIP:** To change which card is your default credit card, open **Settings→ Wallet & Apple Pay**. That's where you can add and remove cards, too.

- **To pay with a different card:** If you double-click the Home button when you're *not* right up close to the reader, your default card appears—but you can tap it to choose a different card. Tap one and then bring the phone near the reader again, with your finger on the Home button.

- **When you're in a hurry, or want to change cards:** This technique offers two advantages. First, it's a quicker way to choose one of your other cards. Second, it lets you set up the transmission in the moments *before* you approach the terminal—handy when you just want to rush through the London subway turnstiles, for example (yes, they take Apple Pay).

To make this work, start with the iPhone asleep—dark. Double-press the Home button to wake it and display your credit cards. Tap the one you want (or leave the default), and then touch your finger to the Home button. You can do all of this before you approach the reader.

At this point, the phone is continuously sending its "I'm paying!" signal. Just wave it near the reader to complete the transaction—your finger doesn't have to be on the Home button or the screen.

Either way, it's just a regular credit card purchase. So you still get your reward points, frequent-flier miles, and so on. (Returning something works the same way: At the moment when you'd swipe your card, you bring the phone near the reader until it beeps. Slick.)

Apple points out that Apple Pay is much more secure than using a credit card, because the store never sees, receives, or stores your credit card number, or even your name. Instead, the phone transmits a tempo-rary, one-time, encoded number that means nothing to the merchant. It incorporates verification codes that only the card issuer (your bank) can translate and verify.

And, by the way, Apple never sees what you've bought or where, either. You can open Wallet and tap a card's picture to see the last few transac-tions), but that info exists only on your iPhone.

And what if your phone gets stolen? Too bad—for the thief. He can't buy anything without your fingerprint. If you're still worried, you can always visit *iCloud.com*, click **Settings**, tap your phone's name, and click **Remove All** to de-register your cards from the phone by remote control.

Apple Pay Online

You can buy things online, too, using iPhone apps that have been upgraded to work with Apple Pay. The time savings this time: You're spared all that typing of your name, address, and phone number every time you buy something.

Instead, when you're staring at the checkout screen for some app, just tap **Buy with Apple Pay**. It lets you pay for stuff without having to painstakingly type in your name, address, and credit card information 400 times a year. And if you're shopping on a Mac (and it doesn't have its own fingerprint reader), you can authenticate with your *phone's* fingerprint reader!

Family Sharing

If you have kids, it's always been a hassle to manage your Apple life. What if they want to buy a book, movie, or app? They have to use your credit card—and you have to reveal your iCloud password to them.

Or what if they want to see a movie that you bought? Do they really have to buy it again?

Not anymore. Once you've turned on Family Sharing and invited your family members, here's how your life will be different:

- **One credit card to rule them all.** Up to six of you can buy books, movies, apps, and music on your master credit card.

- **Ask before buy.** When your kids try to buy stuff, your phone pops up a permission request. You have to approve each purchase.

- **Younger Appleheads.** Within Family Sharing, you can now create Apple accounts for tiny tots; 13 is no longer the age minimum.

- **Shared everything.** All of you get instant access to one another's music, video, iBooks books, and app purchases—again, without having to know one another's Apple passwords.

- **Find one another.** You can use your phone to see where your kids are, and vice versa (with permission, of course).

- **Find one another's phones.** The miraculous Find My iPhone feature (page 530) now works for every phone in the family. If your daughter can't find her phone, you can find it for her with *your* phone.

- **Mutual photo album, mutual calendar, and mutual reminders.** When you turn on Family Sharing, your Photos, Calendar, and Reminders apps each sprout a new category that's preconfigured to permit access by everyone in your family.

Setting Up Family Sharing

The setup process means wading through a lot of screens, but at least you'll have to do it only once. You can turn on this feature either on the Mac (in **System Preferences**→**Set Up Family**) or on the phone itself. Since this book is about the iPhone, what follows are the steps to do it there.

In **Settings**→**iCloud**, tap **Set Up Family Sharing**. Click **Get Started**. Now the phone informs you that you, the sage adult, are going to be the Organizer—the one with the power, the wisdom, and the credit card. **Continue** (unless it's listing the wrong Apple ID account, in which case, you can fix it now).

On successive screens, you read about the idea of shared Apple Store purchases; you're shown the credit card that Apple believes you want to use; you're offered the chance to share your location with the others. Each time, read and tap **Continue**.

Finally, you're ready to introduce the software to your family.

- **If the kid is under 13:** Scroll wayyyyy down and tap **Create an Apple ID for a Child**. On the screens that follow, you'll enter the kid's birth date; agree to a Parent Privacy Disclosure screen; enter the security code for your credit card (to prove that you're you, and not, for example, your naughty kid); type the kid's name; set up an iCloud account (name, password, three security questions); decide whether or not to turn on **Ask To Buy** (each time your youngster tries to buy something online from Apple, you'll be asked for permission in a notification on your phone); decide whether you want the family to be able to see where the kid is at all times; and accept a bunch of legalese.

  When it's all over, the lucky kid's name appears on the Family screen.

- **If the kid already has an iCloud account and is standing right there with you in person:** Tap **Add Family Member**. Type in her name or email address. (Your child's name must already be in your Contacts; if not, go add her first. By the way, you're a terrible parent.)

  She can now enter her iCloud password on your phone to complete her setup. (That doesn't mean you'll learn what her password is; your phone stores it but hides it from you.) On the subsequent screens, you get to confirm her email address and let her turn on location sharing. In other words: The rest of the family will be able to see where she is.

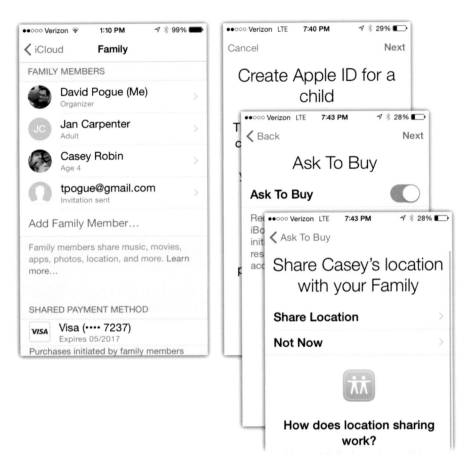

- **If the kid isn't with you at the moment:** Click Send an Invitation.

  Your little darling gets an email at that address. He must open it on his Apple gadget—the Mail app on the iPhone, or the Mail program on his Mac, for example.

  When he hits **View Invitation**, he can either enter his iCloud name and password (if he has an iCloud account), or get an Apple ID (if he doesn't). Once he accepts the invitation, he can choose a picture to represent himself; tap **Confirm** to agree to be in your family; enter his iCloud password to share the stuff he's bought from Apple; agree to Apple's lawyers' demands; and, finally, opt in to sharing his location with the rest of the family.

You can, of course, repeat this cycle to add additional family members, up to a maximum of six. Their names and ages appear on the Family screen.

From here, you can tap someone's name to perform stunts like these:

- **Delete a family member.** Man, you guys really don't get along, do you? Anyway, tap Remove.

- **Turn Ask To Buy on or off.** This option appears when you've tapped a child's name on your phone. If you decide your kid is responsible enough not to need your permission for each purchase, you can turn this option off.

NOTE: If you turn off Ask To Buy for someone after she turns 18, you can't turn it on again.

- **Turn Parent/Guardian on or off.** This option appears when you've tapped an adult's name. It gives Ask To Buy approval privileges to someone else besides you—your spouse, for example.

Once kids turn 13, by the way, Apple automatically gives them more control over their own lives. They can, for example, turn off Ask To Buy themselves, on their own phones. They can even express their disgust for you by leaving the Family Sharing group. (On her own phone, for example, your daughter can visit Settings→iCloud→Family, tap her name, and then tap Leave Family. Harsh!)

Life in Family Sharing

Once everything's set up, here's how you and your nutty kids will get along.

- **Purchases.** Whenever one of your kids (for whom you've turned on Ask To Buy) tries to buy music, videos, apps, or books from Apple—even free items—he has to ask you (next page, left). On your phone, you're notified about the purchase—and you can decline it or tap Review to read about it on its Store page. If it seems OK, you can tap Approve. You also have to enter your iCloud password, or supply your fingerprint, to prevent your kid from finding your phone and approving his own request.

  (If you don't respond within 24 hours, the request expires. Your kid has to ask again.)

  Furthermore, each of you can see and download everything that everyone else has bought. To do that, open the appropriate app: App Store, iTunes Store, or iBooks. Tap Purchased, and then tap the family member's name, to see what she's got; tap the ☁ to download any of it yourself.

TIP: Anything you buy, your kids will see. Keep that in mind when you download a book like *Sending the Unruly Child to Military School*.

However, you have two lines of defense. First, you can hide your purchases. On your computer, in iTunes (Chapter 15), click **iTunes Store**; click the relevant category (♫, ⊟, whatever). Click **Purchased**. Point to the thing you want to hide, click the ⊗, and click **Hide**. (On the phone, you can hide only one category: apps. In the App Store app, tap **Updates**, then **Purchased**, and then **My Purchases**. Swipe to the left across an app's name to reveal a **Hide** button.)

Second, remember that you can set up parental control on each kid's phone, shielding their impressionable eyes from rated-R movies and stuff. See page 618.

- **Where are you?** Open the Find My Friends app to see where your posse is right now. Or go to the Find My iPhone app (or web page; see page 530) to see where their *phones* are right now.

NOTE: If one of you needs secrecy for the afternoon (Apple sweetly gives, as an example, shopping for a gift for your spouse), open **Settings→iCloud→Share My Location**, and turn off the switch. Now you're untrackable until you turn the switch on again.

- **Photos, appointments, and reminders.** In Calendar, Photos, and Reminders, each of you will find a new category, called Family, that's auto-shared among you all. (In Photos, it's on the Shared tab.) You're all free to make and edit appointments in this calendar, to set up reminders in Reminders ("Flu shots after school!"), or to add photos or videos (or comments) to this album; everyone else will see the changes instantly.

17

Continuity: iPhone Meets Mac

Apple products have always been designed to work together. Macs, phones, tablets, watches: similar software, design, wording, philosophy. That's nice for you, of course, because you have less to learn and to troubleshoot. But it's also nice for Apple, because it keeps you in velvet handcuffs; pretty soon, you've got too much invested in its own product "ecosystem" to consider wandering over to a rival.

Apple has taken this gadget symbiosis to an astonishing new extreme. If your Mac is running Yosemite or a later Mac OS version, it can be an *accessory* to your iPhone. Suddenly the Mac can be a speakerphone, using the iPhone as a wireless antenna. Suddenly the Mac can send and receive regular text messages. Suddenly AirDrop lets you drag files back and forth, wirelessly, from phone to computer. Suddenly you can copy material on the phone, and paste it on the Mac (or vice versa).

Apple's name for this suite of symbiosis is *Continuity*. And once you've got it set up, the game changes in a big way.

Continuity Setup

For many people, all of this just works. For many others, there's a certain degree of setting up and troubleshooting. These are the primary rules:

- **You need a Mac running OS X Yosemite or later** and an iPhone running iOS 8.1 or later.

- **The Mac and the phone have to be signed into the same iCloud account.** (That's a security thing—it proves that you're the owner of both machines and therefore unlikely to pose a risk to yourself.) On the Mac, you do that in System Preferences→iCloud. On the phone, you do that in Settings→iCloud. But you should also make sure that you've entered the same iCloud address in Settings→Messages and Settings→FaceTime.

- **For some of these features, Bluetooth must be turned on.** On the Mac, you can do that in System Preferences→Bluetooth. On the phone, it's Settings→Bluetooth.

  The modern Bluetooth—called Bluetooth LE, or low energy—doesn't drain your battery the way Bluetooth once did, so it's fine to leave it on. But older Macs don't have Bluetooth LE, so most Continuity features work only on 2012 and later Macs.

All right. Setup ready? Time to experience some integration!

Mac as Speakerphone

You can make and take phone calls on your Mac. The iPhone, sitting anywhere in your house, can be the cellular module for your Mac—even if that iPhone is asleep and locked.

When a call comes in to your iPhone's number, your *Mac* plays whatever ringtone your phone is playing. And a notice appears on your Mac screen:

You can click to answer it (or decline it); your Mac's microphone and speaker become your speakerphone.

You can **place** a call the same way. Just click any phone number you find on the Mac: in Contacts, in Safari, in an email message, and so on.

To make this work, Settings→Phone→Calls on Other Devices→Allow Calls on Other Devices must be turned on for each device you want to participate in this grand experiment. The iPhone and the Mac must be on the same Wi-Fi network, too.

> **NOTE:** Actually, there's a mind-blowing exception to that statement: Continuity over **cellular**. In this scenario, your Mac and iPhone **don't** have to be on the same Wi-Fi network! Even if you left your phone at home, you can still make calls and send texts from your Mac, wherever you are in the country!
>
> This amazing feature requires participation by the cellular carrier, and so far, T-Mobile is the only company offering it. (How do you know? Open Settings→Phone→ Wi-Fi Calling; if you see an option called Allow Calls on Other Devices, you're golden.)

Once you've set things up as described, it just works. Even call-waiting works—if a second call comes in, your Mac notifies you and offers you the chance to put the first one on hold. And on the Mac, the Contacts app offers Ringtone and Texttone menus, so you can assign custom sounds that play when your **Mac** rings.

Crazy.

Texting from the Mac

You can send and receive text messages (as well as picture, audio, and video messages) on your Mac, too.

We're not talking about sending texts to other *Apple* people (with iCloud accounts). Those are called iMessages, and they're a special, Apple-only kind of message (page 174). We're talking about something much better: You can type *any* cellphone number and send a regular SMS text message to *anyone*. Or receive them when they're sent to your iPhone number.

Or you can initiate the text conversation by clicking a phone number in Contacts, Calendar, or Safari to send an SMS message. Once again, your iPhone acts as a relay station between the cellular world and your Mac.

Here's how to set it up.

First, as usual, the Mac and the phone must be on the same Wi-Fi network and signed into the same iCloud account. (Or the same cellular network, if it's T-Mobile, as already described.)

Next, on the iPhone, open Settings→Messages. Tap Text Message Forwarding. Your Mac's name appears. Turn on the switch.

Now, on the Mac, open Messages. (Its icon is probably popping out of your Dock at this moment, trying to get your attention.) When you open

To send and receive your iPhone text messages from "+1 (408) 797-7897" on this Mac, enter the code below on your iPhone now.

227724

Waiting for verification...   Cancel

Messages, a code appears. You're supposed to type it into the corresponding box on your phone:

This same code appears right now on any iPad or iPod Touch you own. They, too, will be able to send and receive texts, with your iPhone doing the relaying.

All of this is to prove, really and truly, that you're the owner of both devices. You wouldn't want some bad guy reading your text messages, would you?

That's it—your gadgets are paired. You can now use Messages to send standard text messages to *any* cellphone. You can also click and hold on a phone number wherever it appears—in Contacts, in a Spotlight search result, in Safari, in Mail—and choose Send Message from there. And when a text message comes in, a standard Mac notification bubble appears at top right.

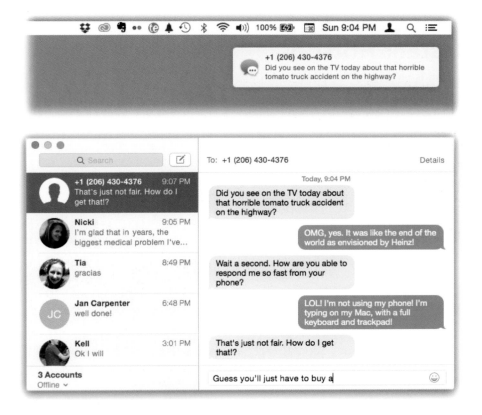

The beauty of all this is that your back-and-forths are kept in sync between the Mac and the phone. You can jump between them and continue the texting conversation. (You'll note that, as usual, the bubbles containing your utterances are green. Blue is reserved for iMessages— that is, messages to other people with iCloud accounts.)

Instant Hotspot

As you know from page 439, paying your cell carrier another $20 or so every month entitles you to use the iPhone's Personal Hotspot feature. That's where the phone itself acts as a portable Wi-Fi hotspot, so that your laptop (or any other gadgets) can get online almost anywhere.

As you also know from page 439, it's kind of a pain to get going. Each time you want your laptop to get online, you have to wake your iPhone, unlock it, open **Settings**, and turn on **Personal Hotspot**. Then you wait about 20 seconds, until the phone's name shows up in your 📶 menu.

Not with Continuity.

Now, the phone can stay in your pocket. Its name appears in your 📶 menu, ready for choosing at any time—even if the phone is asleep and locked, and even if Personal Hotspot is turned off! Handily enough, the 📶 menu also shows the phone's battery and signal status.

Once your Mac is online through your iPhone's cellular connection, it tries to save you money by suspending data-intensive jobs like full backups and software updates. And it closes down the connection when you no longer need it, to save your iPhone's battery.

As usual, this works only if the iPhone and Mac both have Bluetooth turned on and are signed into the same iCloud account.

Handoff

Handoff passes half-finished documents between the phone and the Mac, wirelessly and automatically.

For example, suppose you've been writing an email message on your iPhone (below, top). When you arrive home and sit down at the Mac, a new icon appears at the left end of the Mac's Dock (previous page, middle). When you click it, the Mac's Mail program opens, and the half-finished message is there for you to complete (bottom).

It doesn't have to be an email message, either. If you were reading a web page or a Map on your phone, then that icon on the Mac opens the same web page or map. If you were working on a Reminder; a Calendar entry; a Contacts entry; a note in Notes; or a document in Keynote, Numbers, or Pages; you can open the same in-progress item on the Mac.

And all of it works in the other direction, too. If you're working on something on the Mac, but you're called away, an icon appears on the lower-left corner of your iPhone's Lock screen that opens the same item (below, left).

TIP: There's another way to find the Handoff icon: It's in the app switcher on both devices. On the phone, for example, double-press the Home button—and notice the new strip at the bottom, identifying the document you're handing off from the Mac (below, right). On the Mac, press ⌘-Tab to open the app switcher; there, too, is the icon for the app being handed off from the phone.

Here's the setup: Once again, both gadgets must be signed into your iCloud account. Both must have Bluetooth turned on, and the Mac and phone have to be sitting within Bluetooth range of each other (about 30 feet).

On the Mac, open System Preferences→General; turn on Allow Handoff between this Mac and your iCloud devices.

On the iPhone, the on/off switch is in Settings→General→Handoff.

Now try it out. Start an email message on your iPhone. Have a look at the Dock on your Mac: There, at the left end, pops the little icon of whatever program can finish the job.

Watch for the little lower-left icon on your screens to make it work.

AirDrop

AirDrop is pretty great. As described on page 348, it lets you shoot photos, videos, maps, Contacts cards, PDF files, Word documents, and all kinds of other stuff from one iPhone to another iPhone. Wirelessly. Without having to set up names, passwords, or permissions. Without even having an Internet connection.

What page 348 didn't cover, though, was how you can use AirDrop *between* a phone and a Mac.

From iPhone to Mac

Open whatever it is you want to send to the Mac: a photo, map, website, contact...anything with a ⬆️ button.

When you tap the Share button, you see the AirDrop panel—and, after a moment, the icons of any nearby Macs show up, too. Including yours (next page, left).

If the Mac's icon *doesn't* show up, it's probably because its owner hasn't made the Mac discoverable by AirDrop.

Instruct him to open the AirDrop *window* on his Mac. (Click AirDrop in the sidebar of any Finder window.) See the small blue control at the bottom? It governs who can "see" this Mac for AirDrop purposes: No One, Contacts Only (that is, people in the Mac's address book), or Everyone.

Once that's set up right, that Mac shows up in the iPhone's AirDrop panel ("David" in the picture on the next page). Send away.

The receiving Mac displays a note like the one shown above at right.

Click **Accept** to download the incoming item to your Mac's Downloads folder (or **Decline** to reject it).

> **TIP:** If the phone and the Mac are both signed into the same iCloud account, then you don't encounter that Accept/Decline thing. The file goes directly into your Downloads folder without asking. You do get a notification on the Mac that lets you know how many files arrived, and it offers an **Open** button.
>
> Apple figures that, since you own both the phone and the Mac, the usual permission routine isn't necessary. You're probably not trying to send yourself some evil virus of death.

Universal Clipboard

Now, this is magic—and useful magic, at that. You can copy some text, a picture, or a video on your phone—and then, without any further steps, turn to your Mac and paste it. Or go the other way. Somehow, the contents of the Clipboard transfer themselves wirelessly between the two machines.

In this example, you copy something on the iPhone, in Safari (facing page, top)—and then paste it instantly in Mail on the Mac.

There's no on/off switch, no extra steps, no visible sign of this feature in Settings or System Preferences. It just works. (Provided, of course, that you've obeyed the Three Laws of Continuity Setup: The Mac and phone have to be on the same Wi-Fi network, both have to have Bluetooth turned on, and both have to be signed into the same iCloud account.)

If you don't paste within two minutes of copying, then whatever was already on the Clipboard gets restored, so you don't get confused later.

18

The Corporate iPhone

n its younger days, people thought of the iPhone as a *personal* device, meant for consumers and not for corporations. But somebody at Apple must have gotten sick of hearing, "Well, the iPhone is cool and all, but it's no BlackBerry." The iPhone now has the security and compatibility features your corporate technical overlords require. (And the BlackBerry—well...)

Even better, the iPhone can talk to Microsoft Exchange ActiveSync servers, staples of corporate computer departments that, among other things, keep smartphones wirelessly updated with the calendar, contacts, and email back at the office. (Yes, it sounds a lot like iCloud or the old MobileMe. Which is probably why Apple's MobileMe slogan was "Exchange for the rest of us.")

The Perks

This chapter is intended for you, the iPhone owner—not for the highly paid, well-trained, exceedingly friendly IT (information technology) managers at your company.

Your first task is to convince them that your iPhone is now secure and compatible enough to welcome into the company's network. Here's some information you can use:

- **Microsoft Exchange ActiveSync.** Exchange ActiveSync is the technology that keeps smartphones wirelessly synced with the data on the mother ship's computers. The iPhone works with Exchange ActiveSync, so it can remain in wireless contact with your company's Exchange servers, exactly like BlackBerry and Windows Mobile phones do.

Your email, address book, and calendar appointments are now sent wirelessly to your iPhone so it's always kept current—and they're sent in a way that those evil rival firms can't intercept. (It uses 128-bit encrypted SSL, if you must know.)

NOTE: That's the same encryption used by Outlook Web Access (OWA), which lets employees check their email, calendar, and contacts from any web browser. In other words, if your IT administrators are willing to let you access your data using OWA, they should also be willing to let you access it with the iPhone.

- **Mass setup.** These days, iPhones may wind up in corporations in two ways: They're either handed out by the company, or you bring your own. (When employees use their own phones for work, they call it BYOD: "Bring your own device.")

  Most companies set up employee iPhones using mobile device management (MDM) software. That's a program (for sale by lots of different security companies) that gives your administrators control over a huge range of corporate apps, settings, and restrictions: all Wi-Fi, network, password, email, and VPN settings; policies about what features and apps you can use, and so on; and the ability to remotely erase or lock your phone if it gets lost. Yet MDM programs don't touch the stuff that *you* install on your own. If you leave the company, your old employer can delete its own stuff, while preserving your personal stuff.

- **Security.** The iPhone can connect to wireless networks using the latest, super-secure connections (WPA Enterprise and WPA2 Enterprise), which are highly resistant to hacker attacks. And when you're using virtual private networking, as described at the end of this chapter, you can use a very secure VPN protocol called IPsec. That's what most companies use for secure, encrypted remote access to the corporate network. Juniper and Cisco VPN apps are available, too.

  Speaking of security: Whenever your phone is locked, iOS automatically encrypts all email, email attachments, calendars, contacts, notes, reminders, and the data of any other apps that are written to take advantage of this feature.

- **iOS improvements.** You can encrypt individual email messages to people in your company (and, with some effort, to people outside your company; see *http://support.apple.com/kb/HT4979*). When you're setting up a meeting, you can see your coworkers' schedules in the Calendar app. You can set up an automatic "Out of office" reply that's in force until a certain date. (It's in Settings→Mail. Tap your Exchange account's name and scroll down to Automatic Reply.) Lots more control for your IT overlords, too.

And what's in it for you? Complete synchronization of your email, address book, and calendar with what's on your PC at work. Send an email from your iPhone; find it in the Sent folder of Outlook at the office. And so on.

You can also accept invitations to meetings on your iPhone that are sent your way by coworkers; if you accept, these meetings appear on your calendar automatically, just as on your PC. You can also search the company's master address book, right from your iPhone.

The biggest perk for you, though, is just getting permission to *use* an iPhone as your company-issued phone.

Setup

Your company's IT squad can set up things on their end by consulting Apple's free setup guide: the infamous *iOS Deployment Reference*.

It's filled with handy tips, like: "Data can be symmetrically encrypted using proven methods such as AES, RC4, or 3DES. iOS devices and current Intel Mac computers also provide hardware acceleration for AES encryption and Secure Hash Algorithm 1 (SHA1) hashing, thereby maximizing app performance."

In any case, you (or they) can download the deployment guide from this site: *www.apple.com/support/iphone/business*.

Your IT pros might send you a link that downloads a *profile*—a preconfigured file that auto–sets up all your company's security and login information. It will create the Exchange account for you (and might turn off a few iPhone features, like the ability to switch off the passcode requirement).

If, on the other hand, you're supposed to set up your Exchange account yourself, then tap Settings→Mail→Add Account→Exchange. Fill in your work email address and password as they were provided to you by your company's IT person.

And that's it. Your iPhone will shortly bloom with the familiar sight of your office email stash, calendar appointments, and contacts.

Life on the Corporate Network

Once your iPhone is set up, you should be in wireless corporate heaven:

- **Email.** Your corporate email account shows up among whatever other email accounts you've set up (Chapter 14). In fact, you can have *multiple* Exchange accounts on the same phone.

  Not only is your email "pushed" to the phone (it arrives as it's sent, without your having to explicitly check for messages), but it's also synced with what you see on your computer at work. If you send, receive, delete, flag, or file any messages on your iPhone, you'll find them sent, received, deleted, flagged, or filed on your computer at the office. And vice versa.

  All the email niceties described in Chapter 14 are available to your corporate mail: opening attachments, rotating and zooming them, and so on. Your iPhone can even play back your office voicemail, presuming that your company has one of those unified messaging systems that send out WAV audio file versions of your messages via email.

  Oh—and when you're addressing an outgoing message, the iPhone's autocomplete feature consults both your built-in iPhone address book *and* the corporate directory (on the Exchange server) simultaneously.

> **TIP:** Your phone can warn you when you're addressing an email to somebody outside your company (a security risk, and something that sometimes arises from autocomplete accidents).
>
> To turn on this feature, open Settings→Mail. Scroll down; tap Mark Addresses. Type in your company's email suffix (like *yourcompany.com*). From now on, whenever you address an outgoing message to someone outside *yourcompany.com*, it appears in red in the "To:" line to catch your eye.

- **Contacts.** In the address book, you gain a new superpower: You can search your company's master name directory right from the iPhone. That's great when you need to track down, say, the art director in your Singapore branch.

  To perform this search, open the Contacts app. Tap the Groups button in the upper-left corner. On the Groups screen, your company's name appears; it may contain some group names of its own. But below these, a new entry appears that mere mortal iPhone owners never see. It might say something like Directory or Global Address Book. Tap it.

On the following screen, start typing the name of the person you're looking up; the resulting matches appear as you type. (Or type the whole name and then tap Search.)

In the list of results, tap the name you want. That person's Info screen appears so that you can tap to dial a number or compose a pread-dressed email message. (You can't send a text message to someone in the corporate phone book, however.)

- **Calendar.** Your iPhone's calendar is wirelessly kept in sync with the master calendar back at the office. If you're on the road and your minions make changes to your schedule in Outlook, you'll know about it; you'll see the change on your iPhone's calendar.

  There are some other changes to your calendar, too, as you'll find out in a moment.

TIP: Don't forget that you can save battery power, syncing time, and mental clutter by limiting how much *old* calendar stuff gets synced to your iPhone. (How often do you really look back on your calendar to see what happened more than a month ago?) Page 594 has the details.

- **Notes.** If your company uses Exchange 2010 or later, then your notes are synced with Outlook on your Mac or PC, too.

Exchange + Your Stuff

The iPhone can display calendar and contact information from multiple sources at once—your Exchange calendar/address book and your own personal data, for example.

Here's how it works: Open your iPhone calendar. Tap Calendars. Now you're looking at all the accounts your phone knows about; you might find separate headings for iCloud, Yahoo, Gmail, and so on, each with calendar categories listed under it. And one of them is your Exchange account.

You can pull off a similar stunt in Contacts, Notes, and Reminders. Whenever you're looking at your list of contacts, for example, you can tap the Groups button (top left of the screen). Here, once again, you can tap All Contacts to see a combined address book—or you can look over only your iCloud contacts, your Exchange contacts, your personal con-tacts, and so on. Or tap [group name] to view only the people in your tennis circle, book club, or whatever (if you've created groups); or [your Exchange account name] to search only the company listings.

Invitations

If you've spent much time in the world of Microsoft Outlook (that is, corporate America), then you already know about **invitations**. These are electronic invitations that coworkers send you directly from Outlook. When you get one of these invitations by email, you can click Accept, Decline, or Maybe.

If you click Accept, then the meeting gets dropped onto the proper date in your Outlook calendar, and your name gets added to the list of attendees maintained by the person who invited you. If you click Maybe, then the meeting is flagged *that* way, on both your calendar and the sender's.

Exchange meeting invitations on the iPhone show up in *four places*, just to make sure you don't miss them. You get a standard iPhone notification, a numbered "badge" on the Calendar app's icon on the Home screen, an attachment to a message in your corporate email account, and a message in the Calendar app—tap Inbox at the lower-right corner. Tapping Inbox shows the Invitations list, which summarizes all invitations you've accepted, maybe'd, or not responded to yet. Tap one to see the details (below, left).

TIP: Invitations you haven't dealt with also show up on the Calendar's List view or Day view with dotted shading (below, right). That's the iPhone's clever way of showing you just how severely your workday will be ruined if you accept this meeting.

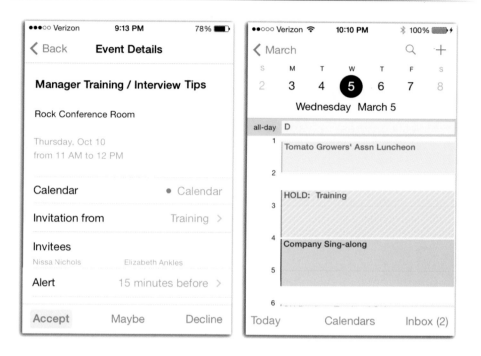

You can also *generate* invitations. When you're filling out the Info form for a new appointment, you get a field called **Invitees**. Tap there to enter the email addresses of the people you'd like to invite.

Your invitation will show up in whatever calendar programs your invitees use, and they'll never know you didn't send it from some corporate copy of Microsoft Outlook.

A Word on Troubleshooting

If you're having trouble with your Exchange syncing and can't find any steps that work, ask your Exchange administrators to make sure that ActiveSync's settings are correct on their end. You've heard the old saying that in 99 percent of computer troubleshooting, the problem lies between the keyboard and the chair? The other 1 percent of the time, it's between the *administrator's* keyboard and chair.

> **TIP:** You can access your company's SharePoint sites, too. That's a Microsoft document-collaboration feature that's also a common part of corporate online life.
>
> The iPhone's browser can access these sites; it can also open Word, Excel, PowerPoint, and PDF documents you find there. Handy indeed!

Virtual Private Networking (VPN)

The typical corporate network is guarded by a team of steely-eyed administrators for whom Job One is preventing access by unauthorized visitors. They perform this job primarily with the aid of a super-secure firewall that seals off the company's network from the Internet.

So how can you tap into the network from the road? Only one solution is both secure and cheap: the *virtual private network*, or VPN. Running a VPN lets you create a super-secure "tunnel" from your iPhone, across the Internet, and straight into your corporate network. All data passing through this tunnel is heavily encrypted. To the Internet eavesdropper, it looks like so much undecipherable gobbledygook.

VPN is, however, a corporate tool, run by corporate nerds. Your company's tech staff can tell you whether or not there's a VPN server set up for you to use.

If there is one, then you'll need to know what type of server it is. The iPhone can connect to VPN servers that speak *PPTP* (Point-to-Point Tunneling Protocol) and *L2TP/IPsec* (Layer 2 Tunneling Protocol over the IP Security Protocol), both relatives of the PPP language spoken by modems. Most corporate VPN servers work with at least one of these protocols.

The iPhone can also connect to Cisco servers, which are among the most popular systems in corporate America, and, with a special app, Juniper's Junos Pulse servers, too.

To set up your VPN connection, visit Settings→General→VPN.

Here you may see that your overlords have already set up some VPN connections; tap the one you want to use. You can also set one up yourself, by tapping Add VPN Configuration at the bottom.

Tap **Type** to specify which kind of server your company uses: IKEv2, IPsec, or L2TP (ask the network administrator). Fill in the **Server** address, the account name and password, and whatever else your system administrators tell you to fill in here.

Once everything is in place, the iPhone can connect to the corporate network and fetch your corporate mail. You don't have to do anything special on your end; everything works just as described in this chapter.

NOTE: Some networks require that you type the currently displayed password on an *RSA SecurID token*, which your administrator will provide. This James Bondish thing looks like either a credit card or a USB drive. It displays a password that changes every few seconds, making it rather difficult for hackers to learn "the" password.

VPN on Demand

If you like to access your corporate email or internal website a few times a day, having to enter your name-and-password credentials over and over again can get old fast. Fortunately, iOS offers a huge timesaving assist with **VPN on Demand**.

That is, you just open up Safari and tap the corporate bookmark; the iPhone creates the VPN channel automatically, behind the scenes, and connects.

There's nothing you have to do, or even anything you **can** do, to make this feature work; your company's network nerds have to turn it on at their end.

They'll create a **configuration profile** that you'll install on your iPhone. It includes the VPN server settings, an electronic security certificate, and a list of domains and URLs that will automatically turn on the iPhone's VPN feature.

When your iPhone goes to sleep, it terminates the VPN connection, both for security purposes and to save battery power.

> **NOTE:** Clearly, eliminating the VPN sign-in process also weakens the security the VPN was invented for in the first place. Therefore, you'd be well-advised—and probably required by your IT team—to use the iPhone's password or fingerprint feature, so some evil corporate spy (or teenage thug) can't just steal your iPhone and start snooping through the corporate servers.

19

Settings

The Settings app is like the Control Panel in Windows or System Preferences on the Mac. It houses hundreds of settings for every aspect of the iPhone and its apps.

Almost everything in the list of Settings is a doorway to another screen, where you make the actual changes.

TIP: Settings has a search box at the top! You don't need a photographic memory (or this chapter) to find which screen holds a certain setting you're looking for.

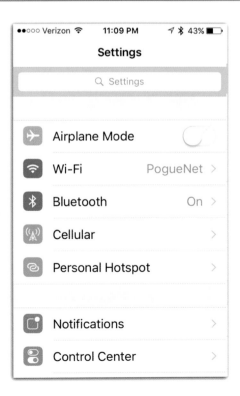

In this book, you can read about the iPhone's preference settings in the appropriate spots—wherever they're relevant. And the Control Center, of course, is designed to *eliminate* trips into Settings.

But so you'll have it all in one place, here's an item-by-item walk-through of the Settings app and its structure in iOS 10.

Three Important Settings Tricks

The Settings app is many screens deep. You might "drill down" by tapping, for example, General, then Keyboard, and then Text Replacement. It's a lot of tapping, a lot of navigation.

Fortunately, you have three kinds of shortcuts.

First, you can jump directly to a particular Settings screen—from within any app—using Siri (Chapter 5). You can say, for example, "Open Sound settings," "Open Brightness settings," "Open Notification settings," "Open Wi-Fi settings," and so on. Siri promptly takes you to the corresponding screen—no tapping required.

Second, you can jump directly to the four most frequently adjusted panels—Bluetooth, Wi-Fi, Cellular, and Battery—by *hard-pressing* the

Swipe to
go back

Settings app icon on the Home screen (6s and 7 models). The shortcut menu offers direct access to those panes.

Finally, on any model, you can **swipe to go back**. Once you've drilled down to, say, General→Keyboard→Text Replacement, you can "drill up" again by swiping across the screen to the right. (Start from the **edge** of the screen.)

Airplane Mode

As you're probably aware, you're not allowed to make cellphone calls on U.S. airplanes. According to legend (if not science), a cellphone's radio can interfere with a plane's navigation equipment.

But the iPhone does a lot more than make calls. Are you supposed to deprive yourself of all the music, videos, movies, and email that you could be using in flight, just because calling is forbidden?

Nope. Just turn on airplane mode by tapping the switch at the top of the Settings list (so the switch background turns green). The word Cellular dims there in Settings (you've turned off your cellular circuitry); but the Wi-Fi and Bluetooth switches are still available, though turned off—meaning that you're now welcome to switch them back **on**, even in airplane mode.

Now it's safe (and permitted) to use the iPhone in flight, even with Wi-Fi on, because its cellular features are turned off completely. You can't make calls, but you can do anything else in the iPhone's bag of tricks.

> **TIP:** Turning airplane mode on and off is faster if you use the Control Center (page 46) or Siri ("Turn on airplane mode"). Same for Wi-Fi, described next.

Wi-Fi

This item in Settings opens the Wi-Fi Networks screen, where you'll find three useful controls:

- **Wi-Fi On/Off.** If you don't plan to use Wi-Fi, then turning it off gets you a lot more life out of each battery charge. Tap anywhere on this On/Off switch to change its status.

> **TIP:** Turning on airplane mode automatically turns off the Wi-Fi antenna—but you can turn Wi-Fi back on. That's handy when you're on a flight with Wi-Fi on board.

- **Choose a Network.** Here's a list of all nearby Wi-Fi networks that the iPhone can "see," complete with a signal-strength indicator and a padlock icon if a password is required. An **Other** item lets you access Wi-Fi networks that are invisible and secret unless you know their names. See page 435 for details on using Wi-Fi with the iPhone.

- **Ask to Join Networks.** If this option is on, then the iPhone is continuously sniffing around to find a Wi-Fi network. If it finds one you haven't used before, a small dialog box invites you to hop onto it.

So why would you ever want to turn this feature off? To avoid getting bombarded with invitations to join Wi-Fi networks—which can happen in heavily populated areas—and to save battery power. (The phone will still hop onto hotspots it's joined in the past, and you can still view a list of available hotspots by opening **Settings→Wi-Fi**.)

Bluetooth

Here's the on/off switch for the iPhone's Bluetooth transmitter, which is required to communicate with a Bluetooth fitness band, earpiece, keyboard, or hands-free system in a car. When you turn the switch on, you're offered the chance to pair the iPhone with other Bluetooth equipment; the paired gadgets are listed here for ease of connecting and disconnecting.

 TIP: The Control Center (page 46) has a Bluetooth button. It's faster to use that than to visit Settings.

Carrier

If you see this panel at all, you're doubly lucky: First, you're enjoying a trip overseas; second, you have a choice of cellphone carriers who have roaming agreements with AT&T, Verizon, T-Mobile, or Sprint. Tap your favorite and prepare to pay some serious roaming fees.

Cellular

These days, not many cellphone plans let you use the Internet as much as you want; most have monthly limits. For example, your $50 a month might include 2 gigabytes of Internet data use.

Most of the settings on this screen are meant to help you control how much Internet data your phone uses.

- **Cellular Data.** This is the on/off switch for Internet data. If you're traveling overseas, you might want to turn this off to avoid racking up insanely high roaming charges. Your smartphone becomes a dumbphone, suitable for making calls but not for getting online. (You can still get online in Wi-Fi hotspots.)

- **Roaming.** These controls can prevent staggering international roaming fees. Enable LTE lets you turn off LTE—just for voice calls, or for both voice and data—for situations when LTE costs extra.

TIP: Every now and then, you'll be in some area where you can't connect to the Internet even though you seem to have an LTE signal; forcing your phone to the 4G or 3G network often gives you at least some connection. Turning LTE off does just that.

On AT&T or T-Mobile, you can turn off Data Roaming (when you're out of the country, you won't get slapped with outrageous Internet fees). On Verizon and Sprint, once you tap Roaming, you have separate controls for Data Roaming and Voice Roaming. Turning off the last item, International CDMA, forces the phone to use only the more common GSM networks while roaming; sometimes you get better call and data quality that way, and you may save money.

- **Personal Hotspot.** Here's the setup and On/Off screen for Personal Hotspot (page 439). Once you've turned it on, a new Personal Hotspot on/off switch appears on the main Settings screen, so you won't have to dig this deep in the future.

- **Call Time.** The statistics here break down how much time you've spent talking on the iPhone, both in the Current Period (that is, this billing month) and in the iPhone's entire Lifetime. That's right, folks: You now own a cellphone that keeps track of your minutes, to help you avoid exceeding the number you've signed up for (and therefore racking up 45-cent overage minutes).

- **Cellular Data Usage.** The phone also tracks how much Internet data you've used this month, expressed in megabytes, including email messages and web page material. These are extremely important statistics, because your iPhone plan is probably capped at, for example, 2 gigabytes a month. If you exceed your monthly maximum, then you're instantly charged $15 or $20 for another chunk of data. So keeping an eye on these statistics is a very good idea.

●●●○○ Verizon 🤙	9:13 PM	⚡ ✳ 100% 🔋
〈 Settings	**Cellular**	

Cellular Data	🔘
Enable LTE	🔘

Turn off cellular data to restrict all data to Wi-Fi, including email, web browsing, and push notifications. Using LTE loads data faster.

Roaming	Voice Only 〉

Set Up Personal Hotspot

Share your iPhone's Internet connection with your computer and iOS devices via Wi-Fi, Bluetooth, or USB.

CALL TIME

Current Period	1 Day, 0 Hours
Lifetime	1 Day, 0 Hours

●●●○○ Verizon 🤙	9:13 PM	⚡ ✳ 100% 🔋
〈 Settings	**Cellular**	

CALL TIME

Current Period	1 Day, 0 Hours
Lifetime	1 Day, 0 Hours

CELLULAR DATA USAGE

Current Period	17.0 GB
Current Period Roaming	1.7 MB

USE CELLULAR DATA FOR:

AAA 44.0 KB	⚪
Amazon 1.9 MB	🔘
American 595 KB	🔘
App Store 1.2 GB	🔘
Calendar	🔘

(The **Current Period** means so far this month; **Current Period Roaming** means overseas or in places where your cell company doesn't have service.)

Now, your cellphone company is supposed to text you as you get closer and closer to your monthly limit, too, but you can check your Internet spending at any time.

- **Use cellular data for:** This list offers individual on/off switches for every single Internet-using app on your phone. Each one is an item that could consume Internet data without your awareness. You can shut up the data hogs you really don't feel like spending megabytes on.

- **Wi-Fi Assist.** Thousands of iPhone fans know about the old Flaky Wi-Fi Trick. If the phone is struggling and struggling to load a web page or download an email message on a Wi-Fi network, it often helps to *turn off Wi-Fi*. The phone hops over to the cellular network, where it's usually got a better connection.

  That's why Apple offers Wi-Fi Assist: a feature that's supposed to do all that automatically. If the phone is having trouble with its Wi-Fi connection, it hops over to cellular data all by itself. (You'll know when that's happened because of the appearance of the cellular-network indicator on your status bar, like **4G**,or **LTE**, instead of the 🛜 Wi-Fi symbol.)

  If you're worried about this feature eating up your data allowance, you can, of course, turn Wi-Fi Assist off. Apple notes, however, that Wi-Fi Assist doesn't kick in (a) when you're data roaming, (b) for background apps (it helps only the app that's in front), or (c) if large amounts of data would be consumed. For example, it doesn't kick in for audio or video streaming or email attachments.

- **Reset Statistics** resets the Call Time and Data Usage counters to zero.

Personal Hotspot

Once you've turned this feature on (page 439) in **Cellular**, this switch appears here, too—on the main Settings screen for your convenience.

Notifications

This panel lists all the apps that think they have the right to nag for your attention. Flight-tracking programs alert you that there's an hour before takeoff. Social-networking programs ping you when someone's trying to reach you. Instant-messaging apps ding to let you know that you have a new message. It can add up to a lot of interruption.

On this panel, you can tailor, to an almost ridiculous degree, how you want to be nagged. See page 59 for a complete description.

Control Center

The Control Center is written up on page 46. There are two settings to change here. If you turn off Access on Lock Screen, then the Control Center isn't available on the phone's Lock screen. No passing prankster can change your phone's settings without your password.

And if you turn off Access Within Apps, then you won't land in the Control Center by accident when you're playing some game that involves a lot of swiping.

Do Not Disturb

This is one of iOS's most brilliant and useful features. See page 128.

General

The General pages offer a *huge*, motley assortment of settings governing the behavior of the virtual keyboard, the Spotlight search feature, and about 6 trillion other things (facing page, left).

- **About.** Here you can find out how many songs, videos, and photos your iPhone holds; how much storage your iPhone has; techie details like the iPhone's software and firmware versions, serial number, model, Wi-Fi and Bluetooth addresses; and so on. (It's kind of cool to see how many apps you've installed.)

  At the very top, you can tap the phone's name to rename it.

- **Software Update.** When Apple releases a new software update for your iPhone, you can download it directly to the phone.

  You'll know when an update is waiting for you, because you'll see a little number badge on the Settings icon, as well as on the word "General" in Settings. Tap it, and then tap Software Update, to see and install the update (facing page, right). (If no number badge is waiting, then tapping Software Update just shows you your current iOS version.)

- **Spotlight Search.** Here you can turn off iOS's Siri Suggestions screen (page 101). And you can control which kinds of things Spotlight finds when it searches your phone. Tap to turn off the kinds of data you don't want it to search: Mail, Notes, Calendar, whatever.

- **Handoff.** Handoff is for people who own both a Mac and an iPhone; it automatically passes half-finished documents between them when you come home, as described on page 551. This is the on/off switch.

- **CarPlay.** Certain car models come equipped with a technology called CarPlay, which displays a few of your iPhone's icons—Phone, Music, Maps, Messages, Music, Podcasts, and Audiobooks—on the car's dashboard touchscreen. The idea is to make them big and simple and limited to things you'll need while you're driving, to avoid distracting you. Here's where you connect your phone to your CarPlay system and, if you like, rearrange the icons on the CarPlay screen.

- **Home Button** appears only on the iPhone 7 models. The Home button on these phones, believe it or not, doesn't actually move. It doesn't actually click. Instead, a tiny speaker makes the button *feel* as though you've clicked it by producing a little twitch vibration. That helps with the iPhone 7's water resistance, of course, but it also permits features like this one: You can actually specify how *big* the phony click feels, using the settings Apple calls 1, 2, or 3 (and then try it out, right on this screen).

- **Accessibility.** These options are intended for people with visual, hearing, and motor impairments, but they might come in handy now and then for almost anyone. All these features are described in Chapter 7.

- **Storage & iCloud Usage.** This screen is proof that the iPhone is an obsessive-compulsive. You find out here that it knows everything about you, your apps, and your iPhone activity.

  The Storage section shows how much of your phone's storage space is currently used and free. Tap Manage Storage to see a list of every single app on your iPhone, along with how much space it's eating up. (Biggest apps are at the top.) Better yet, you can tap an app to see how much it and its associated documents consume—and, for apps you've installed yourself, there's a Delete App button staring you in the face.

  The idea, of course, is that if you're running out of space on your iPhone, this display makes it incredibly easy to see what the space hogs are—and delete them.

  The next section, iCloud, also reports on storage—but in this case, it shows you how much storage you're using on your iCloud account. (Remember, you get 5 gigabytes free; after that, you have to pay.) If you tap Manage Storage, you get to see how much of that space is used up by which apps. iCloud Photo Library and Backups are usually among the biggest offenders.

- **Background App Refresh.** The list that appears here identifies apps that try to access the Internet to update themselves, even when they're in the background. Since such apps can drain your battery, you have the option here to block their background updating.

  You can also turn off the master Background App Refresh switch. Now the only apps that can get online in the background are a standard limited suite (music playback and GPS, for example).

- **Restrictions.** This means "parental controls." (Apple called it "Restrictions" instead so as not to turn off potential corporate customers. Can't you just hear it? " 'Parental controls?' This thing is for *consumers?!*") Complete details appear on page 618.

- **Date & Time.** Here you can turn on 24-hour time, also known as military time, in which you see "1700" instead of "5:00 PM." (You'll see this change everywhere times appear, including at the top of the screen.)

  Set Automatically refers to the iPhone's built-in clock. If this item is turned on, then the iPhone finds out what time it is from an atomic clock out on the Internet. If not, then you have to set the clock yourself. (Turning this option off produces two more rows of controls: The Time Zone option becomes available, so you can specify your time zone, and a "number spinner" appears so you can set the clock.)

- **Keyboard.** Here you can turn off some of the very best features of the iPhone's virtual keyboard. (All these shortcuts are described in Chapter 3.)

  It's hard to imagine why you wouldn't want any of these tools working for you and saving you time and keystrokes, but here you go: **Keyboards** lets you add keyboards suited to all the different languages you speak. **Text Replacement** is where you set up auto-expanding abbreviations for longer words and phrases you type often.

  Auto-Capitalization is where the iPhone thoughtfully capitalizes the first letter of every new sentence for you. **Auto-Correction** is where the iPhone suggests spelling corrections as you type. **Check Spelling**, of course, refers to the pop-up spelling suggestions. **Enable Caps Lock** is the on/off switch for the Caps Lock feature, in which a fast double-tap on the Shift key turns on Caps Lock.

  Predictive refers to QuickType, the row of three word candidates that appears above the keyboard when you're typing. **Character Preview** is the little bubble that pops up, showing the letter, when you tap a key. The **"." Shortcut** switch turns on or off the "type two spaces to make a period" shortcut for the ends of sentences, and **Enable Dictation** is the on/off switch for the ability to dictate text. (If you never use dictation, turning this switch off hides the 🎤 button on the keyboard, giving the space bar more room to breathe.)

- **Language & Region.** The iPhone: It's not just for Americans anymore. The **iPhone Language** screen lets you choose a language for the iPhone's menus and messages. **Region Format** controls how the iPhone displays dates, times, and numbers. (For example, in the U.S., Christmas is on 12/25; in Europe, it's 25/12.) **Calendar** lets you choose which kind of calendar system you want to use: Gregorian (that is, "normal"), Japanese, or Buddhist.

- **Dictionary.** Which dictionaries (which languages) should the phone use when looking up definitions and checking your spelling?

- **iTunes Wi-Fi Sync.** You can sync your iPhone with a computer wirelessly, as long as the phone is plugged in and on Wi-Fi. Details are on page 510.

- **VPN.** See page 564 for details on virtual private networking.

- **Profile (or Device Management).** This item shows up only if your company issued you this phone. It shows what *profile* the system administrators have installed on it—the set of restrictions that govern what you're allowed to change without the company's permission.

- **Regulatory.** A bunch of legal logos you don't care about.

- **Reset.** On the all-powerful Reset screen, you'll find six ways to erase your phone.

  Reset All Settings takes all the iPhone's settings back to the way they were when it came from Apple. Your data, music, and videos remain in place, but the settings all go back to their factory settings.

  Erase All Content and Settings is the one you want when you sell your iPhone, or when you're captured by the enemy and want to make sure they will learn nothing from you or your phone.

NOTE: This feature takes awhile to complete—and that's a good thing. The iPhone doesn't just delete your data; it also overwrites the newly erased memory with gibberish to make sure the bad guys can't see any of your deleted info, even with special hacking tools.

  Reset Network Settings makes the iPhone forget all the memorized Wi-Fi networks it currently autorecognizes.

  Reset Keyboard Dictionary has to do with the iPhone's autocorrection feature, which kicks in whenever you're trying to input text. Ordinarily, every time you type something the iPhone doesn't recognize—some name or foreign word, for example—and you don't accept the iPhone's suggestion, it adds the word you typed to its dictionary so it doesn't bother you with a suggestion again the next time. If you think you've entered too many misspellings into it, you can delete from its little brain all the new "words" you've taught it.

  Reset Home Screen Layout undoes any icon moving you've done on the Home screen. It also consolidates your Home screen icons, fitting them onto as few screens as possible.

  Finally, Reset Location & Privacy refers to the "OK to use location ser-vices?" warning that appears whenever an iPhone program, like Maps or Camera, tries to figure out where you are. This button makes the iPhone forget all your responses to those permission boxes. In other words, you'll be asked for permission all over again the next time you use each of those programs.

Display & Brightness

Ordinarily, the iPhone controls its own screen brightness. An ambi-ent-light sensor hidden behind the glass at the top of the iPhone's face samples the room brightness each time you wake the phone and adjusts the screen: brighter in bright rooms, dimmer in darker ones.

When you prefer more manual control, here's what you can do:

- **Brightness slider.** Drag the handle on this slider to control the screen brightness manually, keeping in mind that more brightness means shorter battery life.

  If Auto-Brightness is turned on, then the changes you make here are relative to the iPhone's self-chosen brightness. In other words, if you goose the brightness by 20 percent, then the screen will always be 20 percent brighter than the iPhone would have chosen for itself.

TIP: The Control Center (page 46) gives you a much quicker road to the Brightness slider. And, of course, you can also tell Siri, "Make the screen brighter" (or "dimmer"). This version in Settings is just for old-timers.

- **Auto-Brightness On/Off.** Tap anywhere on this switch to disable the ambient-light sensor completely. Now the brightness of the screen is under complete manual control.

- **Night Shift.** Here's the beating heart of Night Shift, the feature that's supposed to pose less disruption to your sleepiness by dialing back blue colors in the screen near bedtime; see page 49.

  Yes, it's much quicker to use the Control Center to turn Night Shift on or off. But here's where you set up an automatic *schedule* for it—and adjust the color temperature (yellowness) of the screen when Night Shift kicks in.

- **Auto-Lock.** As you may have noticed, the iPhone locks itself (goes to sleep) after a few minutes of inactivity on your part, to save battery power and prevent accidental screen taps in your pocket.

  On the Auto-Lock screen, you can change the interval of inactivity before the auto-lock occurs (30 seconds, 1 minute, 2 minutes, and so on), or you can tap Never. In that case, the iPhone locks only when you click it to sleep.

- **Raise to Wake.** This is the on/off switch for a new iOS 10 feature (available only on the iPhone SE, 6s, or 7). it makes the phone light up when you *pick it up*—no button-pressing required. The ramifications are huge, because the Lock screen now has many more functions than it did before. There's a lot you can accomplish on the iPhone *before* you enter your password to unlock it; see Chapter 2.

- **Text Size.** As you age, small type becomes harder to read. This universal text-size slider can boost the size of text in every app on your phone.

Technically, what you're seeing is the front end for Apple's **Dynamic Type** feature. And, even more technically, not all apps work with Dynamic Type. But most of the built-in Apple apps do—Contacts, Mail, Maps, Messages, Notes, Phone, Reminders, and Safari Reader—and other software companies will follow suit.

> **TIP:** If the largest type setting here still isn't big enough, you're not out of luck. Hiding in the Accessibility panel described on page 215, there's an option called Larger Text. Tap it and then turn on Larger Accessibility Sizes to make the large end of the type-size scale twice as big. Now you can read your phone from the moon.

- **Bold Text.** If the spindly fonts of iOS are a little too light for your reading tastes, you can flip this switch on (see page 215).

- **Display Zoom.** The iPhone 6, 6s, and 7 models have bigger screens than the iPhones that came before them. The question here is: How do you want to use that extra space? If you tap View and choose Standard, then icons and controls remain the size they always were; the bigger screen fits more on a page. If you choose Zoomed, then those elements appear slightly larger, for the benefit of people who don't have bionic eyes.

Wallpaper

Wallpaper can mean either the photo on the Lock screen (what you see when you wake the iPhone up), or the background picture on your Home screen. On this panel, you can change the image used for either one.

It shows miniatures of the two places you can install wallpaper—the Lock screen and the Home screen. Each shows what you've got installed there as wallpaper at the moment.

> **TIP:** You can tap either screen miniature to open a Set screen, where you can adjust the current photo's size and positioning.

When you tap Choose a New Wallpaper, you're shown a list of photo sources you can use as backgrounds. At the top, you get three categories worth noticing.

- **Dynamic** wallpapers look like soft-focus bubbles against solid backgrounds. Once you've installed the wallpaper, these bubbles actually *move*, rising and falling on your Lock screen or Home screen behind your icons. Yes, animated wallpaper has come to the iPhone.

- **Stills** are lovely nature photographs. They don't move.

- **Live wallpapers** (iPhone 6s and 7), once installed as your Lock screen, behave like the Live Photos described on page 276: When you press the screen hard, they play as 3-second movies. (It's not immediately clear what that gains you.)

  Note that live wallpapers play back only on the Lock screen (not the Home screen).

TIP: You can install your *own* Live Photos as Lock-screen backgrounds. They, too, will play their little 3-second loops when you hard-press the Lock screen.

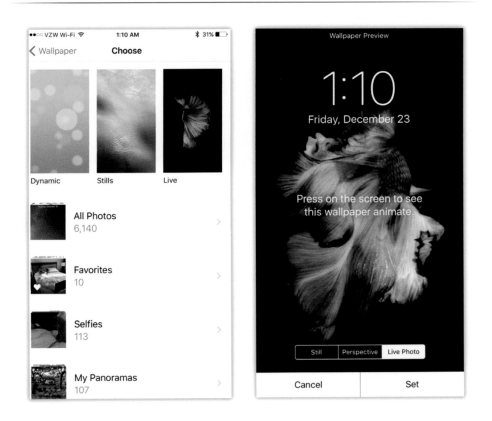

Scroll down a little, and you'll find your own photos, nestled in categories like All Photos, Favorites, Selfies, My Panoramas, and so on, as shown above at left.

All these pictures show up as thumbnail miniatures; tap one to see what it looks like at full size.

Once you've spotted a worthy wallpaper—in any of the flavors described already—tap it. You're offered a choice of two installation methods: **Still**, which is what you'd expect, and **Perspective**, which means that the photo will *shift* slightly when you tilt the phone, as though it's several inches under the glass. (If you've chosen a Live Photo, you'll see a third choice, **Live Photo**, meaning that it will "play" when it's on the Lock screen and you hard-press the glass.)

Finally, tap **Set**. Now the iPhone wants to know which of the two places you want to use this wallpaper; tap **Set Lock Screen**, **Set Home Screen**, or **Set Both** (if you want the same picture in both places).

Sounds (or Sounds & Haptics)

Here's a more traditional cellphone-settings screen: the place where you choose a ringtone sound for incoming calls.

- **Vibrate on Ring, Vibrate on Silent.** Like any self-respecting cellphone, the iPhone has a Vibrate mode—a little shudder in your pocket that might get your attention when you can't hear the ringing. There are two on/off controls for the vibration: one for when the phone is in Silent mode and one for when the ringer is on.

- **Ringer and Alerts.** The slider here controls the volume of the phone's ringing.

  Of course, it's usually faster to adjust the ring volume by pressing the up/down buttons on the left edge whenever you're not on a call or playing music or a video. But if you find that your volume buttons are getting pressed accidentally in your pocket, you can also turn off **Change with Buttons**. Now you can adjust the volume *only* with this slider, here in Settings.

- **Sounds and Vibration Patterns.** The iPhone is, of course, a cellphone—and therefore it sometimes rings. The sound it makes when it rings is up to you; by tapping **Ringtone**, you can view the iPhone's list of 25 built-in ringtones; 25 more ringtones from iOS versions past (tap **Classic** to see them); 27 "alert tones"; plus any you've added yourself. You can use any of them as a ringtone or an alert tone, no matter how it's listed.

  Tap a ring sound to hear it. After you've tapped one you like, confirm your choice by tapping **Sounds** to return to the Sounds (or **Sounds & Haptics**) screen.

NOTE: Remember, you can choose a different ringtone for each listing in your phone book (page 115).

But why stop with a ringtone? The iPhone can make all kinds of other sounds to alert you: to the arrival of a voicemail, text, or email; to the sending of an email message, tweet, or Facebook post; to Calendar or Reminders alarms; to the arrival of AirDrop files; and so on.

This is a big deal—not just because you can express your individuality through your choice of ringtones, text tones, reminder tones, and so on, but also because you can distinguish your iPhone's blips and bleeps from somebody else's in the same family or workplace.

For each of these events, tap the light-gray text that identifies the current sound for that event ("Tri-tone" or "Ding," for example). On the resulting screen, tap the different sound options to find one you like; then tap Sounds to return to the main screen.

On that Sounds screen, you can also turn on or off Lock Sounds (the sounds you get when you tap the Sleep switch) and the Keyboard Clicks that play when you type on the virtual keyboard.

Meet Haptics

If you have an iPhone 7, there's one more switch at the very bottom: **System Haptics**. *Haptics* are the tiny, click-like vibrations that Apple has scattered throughout iOS to accentuate the animations that make the iPhone fun to use.

These little bumps mark the maximum positions for things like pinch zooming, sliders, and panels that slide onto the screen (Control Center, Spotlight search, Notification Center). You'll also feel these clicks when you spin the "dials" that specify times and dates (in Calendar, Clock, and so on), when you turn a Settings switch on or off, when your icons start wiggling on the Home screen (page 44), and when you send or receive iMessage screen effects like lasers and fireworks (page 188).

Haptics are subtle but effective—but if you disagree, here's where you turn them off.

Siri

Here's the master on/off switch for Siri, and the on/off switch for the hands-free "Hey Siri" feature. Both are described in Chapter 5.

Also on this panel: a choice of languages; a choice of speaking voices (including both male and female voices—and a choice of accents, like American, British, or Australian); an option to have Siri's responses read aloud only when you're on a headset (so you don't disturb those around you); and an option to choose your own Contacts card, so Siri knows, for example, where to go when you say, "Give me directions home."

Touch ID & Passcode

Here's where you set up a password for your phone, or (if you have an iPhone 5s or later) where you teach the phone to recognize your finger-prints. Full details start on page 53.

Battery

This panel offers these goodies:

- **Low Power Mode.** See page 39.

- **Battery Percentage.** Instead of just a "filling-up-battery" fuel-gauge icon at the top of your screen, how would you like a digital percentage readout, too ("75%")?

- **Battery Usage.** Here's the readout for all your apps, showing their battery appetite over the past day or week; see page 594.

> **TIP:** Tap ⊘ to see exactly how much time you wasted using that app over the given time period—either the past 24 hours or past 7 days.

- **Usage, Standby.** These stats show you how many hours and minutes of life you've gotten from your current battery charge. (**Usage** = you using the phone. **Standby** = phone asleep.)

Privacy

By "privacy," Apple means "the ability of apps and Apple to access your data."

Many an app works better, or claims to, when it has access to your address book, calendar, photos, and so on. Generally, when you run such an app for the first time, it explicitly asks you for permission to access each kind of data. But here, on this panel, you have a central dashboard—and on/off switches—for each data type and the apps that want it.

Location Services

Suppose, for example, that you tap **Location Services**. At the top of the next screen, you'll find the master on/off switch for all Location Services. If you turn it off, then the iPhone can no longer determine where you

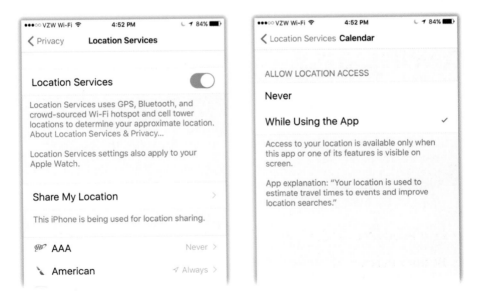

are on a map, geotag your photos, find the closest ATM, tell your friends where you're hanging out, and so on. Below this master switch, you'll find these options:

- **Share My Location.** Apple has designed plenty of ways for you to broadcast your phone's location—and, by extension, your own. For example, Find My Friends, Messages, and Family Sharing all have features that let certain other people see (with your permission) where you are right now.

  Here's the on/off switch for the whole feature. If it's off, nobody can find you right now. If Share My Location is on, then you can tap From to see every iPhone you've ever owned, so that you can specify which *one* should be transmitting its location (the one you're carrying now). The Family section lists any members of your family with whom you're sharing your location; similarly, the Friends list identifies anyone else who has permission to track you. These are handy reminders—and you can tap a name to reveal its Stop Sharing My Location button.

- **App Store, Calendar, Camera....** This screen goes on to list every single app that uses your location information, and it lets you turn off this feature on a by-app basis. You might want to do that for privacy's sake—or you might want to do that to save battery power, since the location searches sap away a little juice every time.

  Tap an app's name to see when it wants access to your location. You might see Always, Never, or While Using the App (the app can't use your location when it's in the background). On the same screen, you may see a description of why the app thinks it needs your location. Why does the Calendar need it, for example? "To estimate travel times to events."

  The little ➹ icon indicates which apps have actually *used* your location data. If it's gray, that app has checked your location in the past 24 hours; if it's purple, it's locating you right now; if it's hollow, that app is using a *geofence*—it's waiting for you to enter or leave a certain location, like home or work. The Reminders app uses the geofencing feature, for example.

- **System Services.** Here are the on/off switches for the iPhone's own features that use your location.

  For example, there's Cell Network Search (lets your phone tap into Apple's database of cellular frequencies by location, which speeds up connections); Compass Calibration (lets the Compass app know where you are, so that it can accurately tell you which way is north);

Location-Based Apple Ads (advertisements that Apple slaps at the bottom of certain apps—or, rather, their ability to self-customize based on your current location); Setting Time Zone (permits the iPhone to set its own clock when you arrive in a new time zone); and so on.

Under the Product Improvement heading, you also get Diagnostics and Usage (sends location information back to Apple, along with diagnostic information so that, for example, Apple can see where calls are being dropped); Popular Near Me (the section of the App Store that lists apps downloaded by people around your current spot); Routing & Traffic (sends anonymous speed/location data from your phone, which is how Maps knows where there are traffic tie-ups); and Improve Maps (sends Apple details of your driving, so it can improve its Maps database).

Contacts, Calendars, Reminders...

This list (on the main Privacy screen) identifies the kinds of data that your apps might wish to access; we're going way beyond location here. For example, your apps might want to access your address book or your calendar.

Tap a category—Contacts, for example—to see a list of the apps that are merrily tapping into its data. And to see the on/off switch, which you can use to block that app's access.

Twitter, Facebook

Similarly, new apps you download may sometimes want access to your Facebook and Twitter accounts. Lots of apps, for example, harness your Facebook account for the purpose of logging in or finding friends to play games with. Tap Twitter or Facebook to see which apps are using your account information.

Diagnostics & Usage

Do you give Apple permission to collect information about how you're using your phone and how well the phone is behaving each day? On this screen, you can choose Don't Send or Automatically Send. If you tap Diagnostic & Usage Data, then you can see the actual data the phone intends to send. (Hint: It's programmery gibberish.)

Share With App Developers gives the phone permission to send non-Apple app writers the details of any crashes you experience while using their apps, so that, presumably, they can get busy analyzing and fixing the bugs. Improve Activity and Improve Wheelchair Mode share your activity and (if you have an Apple Watch) wheelchair-motion data with

Apple, for similar reasons. Deciding whether to share this data all boils down to where you land on the great paranoia-to-generosity scale.

Advertising

The final Privacy option gives you a Limit Ad Tracking switch. Turning it on won't affect how many ads you see within your apps—but it will prevent advertisers from delivering ads *based on your interests*. You'll just get generic ads.

There's a Reset Advertising Identifier button here, too. You may not realize that, behind the scenes, you have an Ad Identifier number. It's "a non-permanent, non-personal device identifier" that advertisers can associate with you and your habits—the things you buy, the apps you use, and so on. That way, advertisers can insert ads into your apps that pertain to your interests—without ever knowing your name.

But suppose you've been getting a lot of ads that seem to mischaracterize your interests. Maybe you're a shepherd, and you keep seeing ads for hyperviolent games. Or maybe you're a nun, and you keep getting ads for marital aids.

In those cases, you might want to reset your Ad ID with this button, thus starting from scratch as a brand-new person about whom the advertisers know nothing.

iCloud

Here's where you enter your iCloud name and password—and where you find the on/off switches for the various kinds of data synchronization that iCloud can perform for you. Chapter 16 tells all.

iTunes & App Store

If you've indulged in a few downloads (or a few hundred) from the App Store or iTunes music store, then you may well find some settings of use here. For example, when you tap your Apple ID at the top of the panel, you get these buttons:

- **View Apple ID.** This takes you to the web, where you can look over your Apple account information, including credit card details.

- **Sign Out.** Tap when, for example, a friend wants to use her own iTunes account to buy something on your iPhone. As a gift, maybe.

- **iForgot.** If you've forgotten your Apple ID password, tap here. You'll be offered a couple of different ways of establishing your identity—and you'll be given the chance to make up a new password.

Automatic Downloads

If you have an iCloud account, then a very convenient option is available to you: automatic downloads of music, apps, and ebooks you've bought on *other* iOS gadgets. For example, if you buy a new album on your iPad, then turning on Music here means that your iPhone will download the same album automatically next time it's in a Wi-Fi hotspot.

Updates means that if you accept an updated version of an app on one of your other Apple gadgets, it will be auto-updated on this phone, too.

Those downloads are, however, big. They can eat up your cellphone's monthly data allotment right quick and send you deep into Surcharge Land. That's why the iPhone does that automatic downloading only when you're in a Wi-Fi hotspot—unless you turn on Use Cellular Data. Hope you know what you're doing.

Wallet & Apple Pay

This panel, available on the iPhone 6 and later, sets all the preferences for Apple Pay (page 536). You see any credit cards you've enrolled, plus Add Credit or Debit Card to enroll another.

Double-Click Home Button is the on/off switch for one of the ways to use Apple Pay—the method by which you can prepare the phone for payment *before* approaching the wireless cashier terminal, as described on page 537.

Allow Payments on Mac is the on/off switch for the option to use your iPhone's fingerprint reader to approve purchases you make on the web using your *Mac* (an option on sites that offer Apple Pay online). Finally, Transaction Defaults sets up the card, address, email account, and phone number you prefer to use when buying stuff online.

Mail

Here you set up your email account information, specify how often you want the iPhone to check for new messages, how you want your Mail app to look, and more. (Yes, in iOS 10, Apple finally broke up the unwieldy Mail, Contacts, Calendars settings page into three separate ones.)

Accounts

Your email accounts are listed here; this is also where you set up new ones. Page 475 covers most of the options here, but one important item is worth noting: Fetch New Data.

The beauty of "push" email is that new email appears on your phone immediately after it was sent. You get push email if you have, for example, a Yahoo Mail account, iCloud account (Chapter 16), or Microsoft Exchange account (Chapter 18).

Having an iPhone that's updated with these critical life details in real time is amazingly useful, but there are several reasons why you might want to turn off the Push feature. You'll save battery power, save money when you're traveling abroad (where every "roaming" Internet use can run up your cellular bill), and avoid the constant "new mail" jingle when you're trying to concentrate.

And what if you don't have a push email service, or if you turn it off? In that case, your iPhone can still do a pretty decent job of keeping you up to date. It can check your email every 15 minutes, every half-hour, every hour, or only on command (Manually). That's the decision you make in the Fetch New Data panel. (Keep in mind that more frequent checking means shorter battery life.)

- **Preview.** It's cool that the iPhone shows you the first few lines of text in every message. Here you can specify how *many* lines. More lines mean you can skim your inbound messages without having to open many of them; fewer lines mean more messages fit without scrolling.

- **Show To/Cc Label.** If you turn this option on, then a tiny, light-gray logo appears next to many of the messages in your inbox. The **To** logo indicates that this message was addressed directly to you; the **Cc** logo means you were merely "copied" on a message primarily intended for someone else.

  If there's no logo at all, then the message is in some other category. Maybe it came from a mailing list, or it's an email blast (a Bcc), or the message is from you, or it's a bounced message.

- **Swipe Options.** Which colorful insta-tap buttons would you like to appear when you swipe across a message in a list? See page 488 for details.

- **Flag Style.** You can flag messages to draw your own attention to them, either with the old-style flag icon—or, for visual spark, with an orange dot. Here's where you choose.

- **Ask Before Deleting.** Ordinarily, you can delete an open message quickly and easily, just by tapping the 🗑 icon. But if you'd prefer to encounter an additional confirmation step before the message disappears, then turn this option on.

- **Load Remote Images.** Spammers, the vile undercrust of lowlife society, have a trick. When they send you email that includes a picture, they don't actually paste the picture into the message. Instead, they include a "bug"—a piece of code that instructs your email program to *fetch* the missing graphic from the Internet. Why? Because that gives the spammer the ability to track who has actually opened the junk mail, making those email addresses much more valuable for reselling to other spammers.

If you turn this option off, then the iPhone does not fetch "bug" image files at all. You're not flagged as a sucker by the spammers. You'll see empty squares in the email where the images ought to be. (Graphics sent by normal people and legitimate companies are generally pasted right into the email, so they'll still show up just fine.)

- **Organize by Thread.** This is the on/off switch for the feature that clumps related back-and-forths into individual items in your Mail inbox.

- **Most Recent Message on Top.** In iOS 10, the messages in a conversation appear chronologically, oldest at the top. That's a switch from previous versions, where the *newest* message would appear at the top—but Apple thinks it makes more sense the new way. (The latest message still appears when you click the thread's name.) If you prefer the old way, then turn off this setting.

- **Complete Threads.** What if, during a particular back-and-forth, you've filed away certain messages into other folders? Should they still show up in a conversation thread? They will, if this switch is on. (The moved messages are *actually* sitting in those other folders; they just *appear* here for your convenience.) Now your conversations seamlessly combine related messages from all mailboxes.

- **Always Bcc Myself.** If this option is on, then you'll get a secret copy of any message you send. Some people use this feature to make sure their computers have records of replies sent from the phone.

- **Mark Addresses.** See the Tip on page 536.

- **Increase Quote Level.** Each time you reply to a reply, it gets indented more, so you and your correspondents can easily distinguish one reply from the next.

- **Signature.** A signature is a bit of text that gets stamped at the bottom of your outgoing messages. Here's where you can change yours.

- **Default Account.** Your iPhone can manage an unlimited number of email accounts. Here you can tap the account you want to be your *default*—the one that's used when you create a new message from another program, like a Safari link, or when you're on the All Inboxes screen of Mail.

Contacts

Contacts gets its own little set of options in Settings:

- **Sort Order, Display Order.** How do you want the names in your Contacts list sorted—by first name or by last name?

  Note that you can have them *sorted* one way but *displayed* another way. Also note that not all the combinations make sense.

- **Short Name.** When this switch is on, the Mail app may fit more email addressees' names into its narrow To box by shortening them. It may display "M. Mouse," for example, or "Mickey," or even "M.M."—whatever you select here.

- **Prefer Nicknames** is similar. It instructs Mail to display the *nicknames* for your friends (as determined in Contacts) instead of their real names.

- **My Info.** Tap here to tell the phone which card in Contacts represents *you*. Knowing who you are is useful to the phone in a number of places—for example, it's how Siri knows what you mean when you say, "Give me directions home."

- **Default Account.** Here again, the iPhone can manage multiple address books—from iCloud, Gmail, Yahoo, and so on. Tap the account you want new contacts to fall into, if you haven't specified one in advance. (This item doesn't appear unless you have multiple accounts.)

- **Contacts Found in Apps.** The iPhone does some intelligent inspection of your email. It notices when you email the same group often, or when you use the same subject line often, and proposes filling in all the recipients' addresses automatically the next time (page 499). It also examines your email in hopes of finding a matching phone number, so that Caller ID works better.

  Of course, no *person* is looking through your email—but if these features give you the privacy heebie-jeebies, you can turn them off here.

- **Import SIM Contacts.** If you came to the iPhone from another, lesser GSM phone, then your phone book may be stored on its little SIM card instead of in the phone itself. In that case, you don't have to retype all those names and numbers to bring them into your iPhone. This button can do the job for you. (The results may not be pretty. For example, some phones store all address book data in CAPITAL LETTERS.)

Calendar

Your iPhone's calendar can be updated by remote control, wirelessly, through the air, either by your company (via Exchange, Chapter 18) or by somebody at home using your computer (via iCloud, Chapter 16).

- **Time Zone Override.** Whenever you arrive in a new city, the iPhone actually learns (from the local cell towers) what time zone it's in and changes its own clock automatically.

  So here's a mind-teaser. Suppose there's a big meeting in California at 2 p.m. tomorrow—but you're in New York right now. How should that event appear on your calendar? Should it appear as 2 p.m. (that is, its local time)? Or should it appear as 5 (your East Coast time)?

  It's not an idle question, because it also affects reminders and alarms.

  Out of the box, **Time Zone Override** is turned off. The phone slides appointments around on your calendar as you travel to different time zones. If you're in California, that 2 p.m. meeting appears at 2 p.m. When you return to New York, it says 5 p.m. Handy—but dangerous if you forget what you've done.

  If you turn on the Override, though, the iPhone leaves all your appointments at the hours you record them—in the time zone you specify with the pop-up menu here. This option is great if you like to record events at the times you'll be experiencing them; they'll never slosh around as you travel. If you, a New Yorker, will travel to San Francisco next week for a 2 p.m. meeting, write it down as 2 p.m.; it will still say 2 p.m. when you land there.

- **Alternate Calendars.** If you prefer to use the Chinese, Hebrew, or Islamic calendar system, go nuts here.

- **Week Numbers.** This option makes Calendar display a little gray notation that identifies which week you're in (out of the 52 this year). It might say, for example, "W42." Because, you know, some people aren't aware enough of time racing by.

- **Show Invitee Declines.** You can invite someone to a meeting, as described on page 362. If they click Decline (they can't make it), maybe you don't need your phone to alert you. In that case, turn this switch off.

- **Sync.** If you're like most people, you refer to your calendar more often to see what events are *coming up* than to see the ones you've already lived through. Ordinarily, therefore, the iPhone saves you some syncing time and storage space by updating only relatively recent events on your iPhone calendar. It doesn't bother with events that are older than 2 weeks, or 6 months, or whatever you choose here. (Or you can turn on All Events if you want your entire life, past and future, synced each time—storage and wait time be damned.)

- **Default Alert Times.** This is where you tell the iPhone how much warning you need in advance of birthdays and events you've put on your calendar. Tailor it to your level of absent-mindedness.

- **Start Week On.** This option specifies which day of the week appears at the *left edge of the screen* in the calendar's Day and Month views. For most people, that's Sunday, or maybe Monday—but for all iOS cares, your week could start on a Thursday.

- **Default Calendar.** This option lets you answer the question: "When I add a new appointment to my calendar on the iPhone, which *calendar* (category) should it belong to?" You can choose Home, Work, Kids, or whatever category you use most often.

- **Location Suggestions.** You may have noticed that if you enter the location for a calendar appointment (page 360), iOS 10 now proposes a list of full street addresses that match what you're typing. That's to save you data entry, and also to calculate travel times. Here's the on/off switch.

- **Events Found in Apps.** As described on page 494, the iPhone mines your email for proposed calendar events. You can turn off that helpful feature here—if you're weird.

Notes

Notes can sync with various online services: iCloud, Gmail, Yahoo, and so on. Tap Accounts here to specify which ones should show up in the Notes app; tap Default Account to indicate which account you use *mainly*—the one that should contain any new note.

And now that Notes comes with ready-to-use type styles like Title, Heading, and Body, you can also use the New Notes Start With option here to choose which of those is the first line when you create a new note. If you usually start with a title for your note "card," then choose Title, for example.

Password is the command center for the new locked notes feature (page 407). You can change your password here, or create an additional one—or allow your fingerprint to unlock your locked notes.

You can take photos right from within Notes. If you turn on Save Media to Photos, then you'll also get a copy of those shots in your Photos app, just as though you'd taken them with the Camera app.

Finally: Most people use Notes with online accounts like iCloud, Gmail, Yahoo, and so on, so that their notes are always backed up and synced to their computers. But if you turn on **On My iPhone** here, then you'll have another option: Creating notes that live only on your phone, and aren't transmitted, synced, or backed up. Handy if you have deeply personal information, or you just don't trust those online services.

Reminders

Hey, it's the preference settings for the Reminders app!

- **Accounts.** The app can show you to-do lists from iCloud, Yahoo, Exchange, Gmail, and so on. Which of those accounts do you want to see?

- **Sync.** How far back to you want Reminders to look when showing you reminders? At **All** of them? Or only those up to **6 months** old? (Or **3 Months**, **1 Month**, or **2 Weeks**?) It's a question of storage and lifestyle.

- **Default List.** Suppose you've created multiple Reminder lists (Groceries, Movies to Rent, To Do, and so on). When you create a new item—for example, by telling Siri, "Remind me to fix the sink"—which list should it go on? Here's where you specify.

Phone

These settings have to do with your address book, call management, and other phone-related preferences.

- **My Number.** Here's where you can see your iPhone's own phone number. You can even edit it, if necessary (just how it appears—you're not actually changing your phone number).

- **Announce Calls.** Cool—the iPhone can speak the name or number of whoever is calling you Here, you can turn that feature on or off, or specify that you want it to happen only when you're using headphones or in the car.

- **Call Blocking & Identification.** You can block certain people's calls, texts, and FaceTime video calls.

  This isn't a telemarketer-blocking feature; you can block only people who are already in your Contacts. It's really for blocking harassing ex-lovers, jerky siblings you're not speaking to, and collection agencies. Tap **Block Contact** to view your Contacts list, where you can tap to choose the blockee. (You can also see and edit this list in the Messages and FaceTime panels of Settings.)

- **Wi-Fi Calling.** This glorious option lets you place great-sounding calls even with a crummy cellular signal, as described on page 434.

- **Calls on Other Devices.** Here's the on/off switch for Continuity, the ability to make phone calls from your Mac (page 546). In iOS 10, you can even specify *which* gadgets talk to your iPhone in this way.

- **Respond with Text.** This feature is described on page 127; here's where you can edit the canned "Can't talk right now" text messages.

- **Call Forwarding, Call Waiting** (AT&T and T-Mobile only). Here are the on/off switches for Call Forwarding and Call Waiting, which are described in Chapter 4.

- **Show My Caller ID** (AT&T and T-Mobile only). If you don't want your number to show up on the screen of the person you're calling, then turn this off.

- **Change Voicemail Password.** Yep, pretty much just what it says.

- **Dial Assist.** When this option is turned on, and when you're calling from another country, the iPhone automatically adds the proper country codes when dialing numbers in your contacts. Pretty handy, actually.

- **SIM PIN.** Your SIM card stores all your account information. SIM cards are especially desirable abroad, because in most countries, you can pop yours into any old phone and have working service. If you're worried about yours getting stolen or lost, turn this option on. You'll be asked to enter a passcode.

  Then, if some bad guy ever tries to put your SIM card into another phone, he'll be asked for the passcode. Without the passcode, the card (and the phone) won't make calls.

TIP: And if the evildoer guesses wrong three times—or if you do—then the words "PIN LOCKED" appear on the screen, and the SIM card is locked forever. You'll have to get another one from your carrier. So don't forget the password.

- **[Your carrier] Services.** This choice opens up a cheat sheet of handy numeric codes that, when dialed, play the voice of a robot providing useful information about your cellphone account. For example, *225# lets you know the latest status of your bill, *646# lets you know how many airtime minutes you've used so far this month, and so on.

Messages

These options govern text messages (SMS) and iMessages, both of which are described in Chapter 6:

- **iMessage.** This is the on/off switch for iMessages. If it's off, then your phone never sends or receives these handy, free messages—only regular text messages.

- **Show Contact Photos.** Do you want to see the tiny headshots of your conversation partners in the chat window?

- **Text Message Forwarding** is the text-message element of Continuity; it's described on page 548. You get an on/off switch for each gadget that you might want to display your phone's text messages.

- **Send Read Receipts.** If this is on, then people who send you iMessages will know when you've seen them. They'll see a tiny gray text notification beneath the iMessage bubble that contains their message. If you're creeped out by them being able to know when you're ignoring them, then turn this item off.

- **Send as SMS.** If you try to send an iMessage to somebody when there's no Internet service, what happens? If this item is on, then the message goes to that person as a regular text message, using your cell carrier's network. If it's off, then the message won't go out at all.

- **Send & Receive.** Here you can enter additional email addresses that people can use to send your phone iMessages.

  This screen also offers a Start new conversations from item that lets you indicate what you want to appear on the other guy's phone when you send a text: your phone number or email address.

- **MMS Messaging.** This is the on/off switch for picture and video messages (as opposed to text-only ones).

- **Group Messaging, Show Subject Field, Character Count.** These options are described starting on page 198.

- **Blocked.** Here's another way to build up a list of people you don't want to hear from, as described on page 199. .

- **Keep Messages.** You can specify how long you want Messages to retain a record of your exchanges: 30 days, a year, or forever.

- **Filter Unknown Senders.** This new iOS 10 feature gives you a sliver of protection from bombardment by strangers. It prevents you from getting notifications of iMessages from anyone who's not in Contacts. In fact, you'll also see two tabs in Messages—one that lists chats for people you know (and regular non-Apple text messages), and the other labeled Unknown Senders.

- **Audio Messages.** You can now shoot audio utterances to other people just as easily as you can type them. Under Expire, you can set them to autodelete after 2 minutes. Why? First, because audio files take up space on your phone. Second, because you may consider them *spoken text messages*—not *recordings* to preserve for future generations. This is also where you turn on Raise to Listen.

   The audio-texting feature lets you send and receive audio messages without looking at the screen or touching it; see page 184.

- **Low Quality Image Mode.** New in iOS 10: this way to save a huge amount of cellular data when sending photos. See page 200.

FaceTime

These options pertain to FaceTime, the video calling feature described on page 137. Here, for example, is the on/off switch for the entire feature; a place to enter your Apple ID, so people can make FaceTime calls to you; and a place to enter email addresses and a phone number, which can also be used to reach you.

The Caller ID section lets you specify how you want to be identified when you place a call to somebody else: either as a phone number or an email address.

Finally, here yet again is the Blocked option—a third way to edit the list of people you don't want to hear from.

Maps

The expanded Maps app has an expanded set of settings:

- **Preferred Transportation Type.** Do you mainly drive, walk, or take public transport? By specifying here, you save yourself a tap every time you plot directions.

- **Driving & Navigation.** Here's where you tell Maps that you want your plotted courses to avoid Tolls or Highways; turn a Compass display on or off on the map; specify the Navigation Voice Volume; and direct playback of any spoken entertainment (like podcasts or audiobooks) to Pause whenever the Maps voice is giving you an instruction.

- **Transit.** Which modes of public rides do you want Maps to show you when proposing routes? Bus, Subway, Commuter Rail, and/or Ferry?

- **Distances.** Measured in miles or kilometers, sir/madam?

- **Map Labels.** Would you like place names to appear in English—or in their native spellings?

- **Extensions.** Now that Maps *can* incorporate other apps (see page 402), which ones *should* it show you?

- **Show Parked Location.** You wouldn't turn off this cool new Maps feature, would you (page 399)?

- **Issue Reporting.** When you report a problem with Maps' still-buggy database of the world, may Apple technicians get back to you by email?

Compass

You wouldn't think that something as simple as the Compass app would need a Settings page, but here it is: an on/off switch called Use True North. (*True* north is the "top" point of the Earth's rotational axis. If you turn it off, then Compass uses *magnetic* north, the spot traditional compasses point to; it's about 11 degrees away from true north).

Safari

Here's everything you ever wanted to adjust in the web browser but didn't know how to ask.

Search

- **Search Engine.** Your choice here determines who does your searching from the search bar: Google, Bing, Yahoo, or DuckDuckGo (a limited search service famous for its refusal to collect your data or track your searches).

- **Search Engine Suggestions.** As you type into Safari's search box, it tries to save you time in two ways. First, it sprouts a list of common search requests, based on what millions of other people have sought. This list changes with each letter you type. Second, Safari may auto-

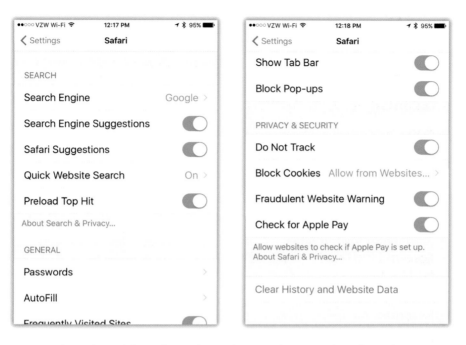

complete the address based on what you've typed so far, using suggestions from your History and bookmarks list. This switch shuts off those suggestions. (It's here primarily for the benefit of privacy hounds, who object to the fact that their search queries are processed by Apple in order to show the suggestions.)

- **Safari Suggestions.** Safari searches (Chapter 3) can find matches from the iTunes, iBooks, and App stores; from databases of local businesses, restaurants, and theaters; and from the web. Unless you turn this off.

- **Quick Website Search.** You can search *within* a site (like Amazon or Reddit or Wikipedia) using only Safari's regular search bar, as described on page 454. If, that is, this switch is on.

- **Preload Top Hit.** As you type into the search box, Safari lists websites that match. The first one is the Top Hit—and if this switch is on, Safari secretly downloads that page while you're still finishing your search. That way, if the Top Hit *is* the page you wanted, it appears almost instantly when you tap.

  But here's the thing: Safari downloads the Top Hit with *every* search—which uses up data. Which could cost you money.

General

- **Passwords, AutoFill.** Safari's AutoFill feature saves you tedious typing by filling in your passwords, name, address, and phone numbers on web forms automatically (just for the sites you want). It can even store your credit card information, which makes buying things online *much* easier and quicker.

  The AutoFill screen lists the different kinds of data that Safari can autofill for you: your contact info, website account names, and passwords. (Open the Passwords page to see the complete list of the passwords it's memorized; tap Edit to delete certain ones.) You can also see your credit cards. (Tap Saved Credit Cards to see or delete the memorized cards.)

- **Frequently Visited Sites.** As you know from page 450, when you have nothing open in Safari, it likes to offer a page full of icons representing sites you visit often. Turn off this switch if your privacy concerns outweigh the convenience of this feature.

- **Favorites.** As described on page 450, your Favorites in Safari are just ordinary bookmarks in an extraordinary folder. Here you can choose a *different* folder as the home of your Favorites.

- **Open Links.** When you tap a link with your finger, should the new page open in front of the current page—or behind it? Answer here.

- **Show Tab Bar.** A row of tab buttons appears in landscape orientation (Plus models only).

- **Block Pop-ups.** In general, you want this turned on. You really don't want pop-up ad windows ruining your surfing session. Now and again, though, pop-up windows are actually useful. When you're buying concert tickets, for example, a pop-up window might show the location of the seats. In that situation, you can turn this option off.

Privacy & Security

- **Do Not Track.** If you turn this on, then websites agree not to secretly track your activity on the web. The problem is, of course, that this program is voluntary—and the sleazy operators just ignore it.

- **Block Cookies.** You can learn all about cookies—and these options to tame them—on page 470.

- **Fraudulent Website Warning.** This option makes Safari warn you when you try to visit what it knows to be a *phishing* site. (Phishing is a common Internet scam. The bad guy builds a fake version of Amazon,

PayPal, or a bank's website—and tries to trick you into "logging in." You therefore unwittingly give up your name and password.)

- **Check for Apple Pay.** Some websites let you buy stuff with a quick touch of your fingerprint (Apple Pay)—but only if you let them offer you those controls by leaving this on.

- **Clear History and Website data.** Like any web browser, Safari keeps a list of websites you've visited recently to make it easier for you to visit them again: the History list. And like any browser, Safari therefore exposes your activities to any suspicious spouse or crackpot colleague. If you're nervous about that prospect, then tap Clear History to erase your tracks. This feature deletes all the cookies that websites have deposited on your "hard drive."

- **Use Cellular Data.** The Reading List feature (page 459) is wonderful. But because it downloads entire web pages to your phone—and then syncs them to all your other Apple gadgets—it uses a lot of data. If you fear going over your cellphone plan's monthly data allotment, then turn this off. You'll be allowed to save sites to your Reading List only when in a Wi-Fi hotspot.

- **Advanced.** Safari recognizes HTML5, a web technology that lets websites store data on your phone, for accessing even when you're not online (like your Gmail stash). In Website Data, you can see which web apps have created these databases on your phone and delete them if necessary.

  JavaScript is a programming language whose bits of code frequently liven up web pages. If you suspect some bit of code is choking Safari, though, you can turn off its ability to decode JavaScript here.

  The Web Inspector is for website programmers. You connect your phone to a Mac with a USB cable; then, in Safari on the computer, you choose Debug→iPhone→[the name of the website currently on the iPhone's screen]. You'll be able to examine errors, warnings, tips, and logs for HTML, JavaScript, and CSS—great when you're designing and debugging web pages or web apps for the iPhone.

News

Page 402 describes the News app. Here's where you indicate whether it's allowed to tailor your news to your Location, whether it can bug you with Notifications about news stories, whether it's allowed to fetch news in the Background (at some cost to battery life), and whether it can fetch new news over the Cellular Data network (at some cost to your data allowance).

And you can turn off the **Story Previews** (where the first couple of lines of each news story appear right in the app).

Music

What you see here depends on whether you've subscribed to the $10-a-month Apple Music service (Chapter 8).

- **Show Apple Music.** When this is off, the new tabs (**For You** and **New**) disappear from the Music app. Which makes sense if you're not a subscriber, since they're doing you no good.

- **Genius.** This control doesn't actually do anything, since as of iOS 10.2, the old Genius song-suggestion feature no longer exists. Oopsie!

- **iCloud Music Library** (which appears only if you use Apple Music) is described on page 235.

- **Show Star Ratings.** Turn this on if you'd like to rate the songs in your music collection from one to five stars. Note that this option doesn't appear until you've rated at least one song, either by clicking in iTunes (on your computer) or by telling Siri, "Rate this song five stars" (for example) while one of your songs is playing.

- **Cellular Data** lets you guard against having your streaming music eat up your monthly cellular data allowance. If it's off, then you can download and play back music only over Wi-Fi.

- **Downloaded Music** lets you see how much of your storage space is devoted to songs you've acquired.

- **Optimize Storage** shows up only if you're an Apple Music subscriber and you've turned on iCloud Music Library. As you download more songs from Apple Music, if your phone becomes full, this feature deletes the downloaded songs that you've played the least. (The **Minimum Storage** indicates how much music you get to keep before the autodeleting begins.) Of course, you're always welcome to listen to them over the Internet, or download them again.

- **EQ, Volume Limit, Sound Check.** See page 249.

- **Home Sharing.** Conveniently enough, you can access your iTunes music collection, upstairs on your computer, right from your iPhone, over your home Wi-Fi network. Or at least you can if both machines are signed into the same Apple ID. Here's where you enter the Apple ID that matches your iTunes setup.

TV

This is what you can adjust for the new TV app:

- **Use Cellular Data for Playback.** A safeguard against eating up your cellular data with videos. Leave off to stream videos only over Wi-Fi.

- **Playback Quality.** When you're watching videos over Wi-Fi, do you want the best possible picture, even if that uses up more data? (Yes, some people also have to worry about how much *Wi-Fi* data they use every month.) You get the same choices for cellular data.

- **Purchases and Rentals.** When you're on the road and want to buy or rent a video from Apple, do you want it in High Definition or Standard? (High Definition looks better but takes forever to download.)

- **Home Sharing.** You can also access your video collection in iTunes on your computer, as described a few paragraphs ago. Same deal here.

Photos & Camera

Here's a motley collection of photo-related settings:

- **iCloud Photo Library.** See page 323.

- **Optimize iPhone Storage, Download and Keep Originals.** See page 323.

- **Upload to My Photo Stream.** Every picture you take will be sent to all your Apple gadgets (see page 316).

- **Upload Burst Photos.** Recent iPhones can snap 10 photos a second when you hold your finger down on the shutter button. That's a lot of photos, which can fill up your iCloud storage fast. So Apple gives you the option to exclude them from the uploads.

- **iCloud Photo Sharing** is covered on page 318.

- **Summarize Photos.** In the Photos app, the Years and Collections screens generally display one tiny thumbnail for every single photo. This feature makes those displays more manageable by displaying fewer, but representative, thumbnails. (You won't see any difference unless you have a pretty huge collection of photos.)

- **Show Holiday Events.** You know the new Memories feature (page 299)? It can create auto-slideshows based on the holidays in your country, if you want. If you'd just as soon not be reminded of these stressful times, then turn this off.

- **Preserve Settings.** New in iOS 10: The Camera app can remember the last mode you selected when you last used it—Video, Photo, Panorama, or whatever—instead of always starting with Photo.

  It can also remember the last Photo Filter you used (page 275) and whether or not you had Live Photo turned on (page 276).

- **Grid** turns the "Rule of Thirds" grid (the tic-tac-toe lines) on or off on the camera's viewfinder screen.

- **Record Video.** This option, exclusive to the iPhone 6 and later, controls the frame rate and quality of the video you shoot. The first number in each option (like 720p, 1080p, or 4K) controls the *resolution* of the video (how many pixels make up each frame—and how correspondingly huge the video files are). The second, fps, controls the *frames per second*. Normal TV video is about 30 fps, so choosing 60 fps creates bigger files but smoother playback.

  A weird additional option appears here if you have an iPhone 7 Plus: Lock Camera Lens. The 7 Plus, of course, has two lenses (page 269). Under certain lighting conditions, if you zoom while recording video, a little video hiccup results as the phone switches from one lens to the other. If you turn on this option, then you'll get no such glitch, because the phone will use only one lens the whole time. (You can still zoom—but it's a digital, fake zoom, and the image will slightly degrade as you do so.)

- **Portrait Mode: Keep Normal Photo.** See page 279 for this iPhone 7 Plus option.

- **HDR: Keep Normal Photo** See the Tip on page 272.

iBooks

Why, it's every setting imaginable that pertains to the iBooks ebook reading app. They're all described starting on page 387.

Podcasts

These settings affect the Podcasts app described on page 411. They govern how often the app auto-downloads new episodes, and how many; whether it can do so using cellular data (or only Wi-Fi); and whether you want the app to autodelete podcasts you've already heard.

Game Center

For millions of people, the iPhone isn't a phone—it's a mobile game console. In fact, until iOS 10 came along, there was even an app called Game Center. It was a way to compare scores with friends and challenge buddies to games. In iOS 10, the Game Center app is gone; now you're supposed to invite players and see your place on leaderboards right inside each individual game app.

There's still this Game Center page in Settings, though. Once you've logged into it with your Apple ID, you can allow Nearby Players to invite you to multiplayer games wirelessly, and you can create or edit your Game Center Profile (your player name). And when you get good and fed up, you can Remove all Game Center Friends—the nuclear option.

Twitter, Facebook, Flickr, Vimeo

These pages let you enter your name and password just once, in this one place, for each of these popular web services—so that the iPhone and its apps can freely access those accounts without having to bother you.

●●○○○ Verizon 📶 4:21 PM ✷ 100% ▭⚡	●●○○○ Verizon 📶 4:22 PM ⬈ ✷ 100% ▬
‹ Settings **Twitter**	**Settings**
🐦 **Twitter** Twitter Inc. [INSTALL]	🖌 American ›
	👥 BSM ›
User Name @name	ⓑ Bump ›
Password Required	✏ Doodle ›
	👁 F. Melter Lite ›
Sign In	⬛ Fly Delta ›
	🐿 Hipmunk ›
Create New Account	⭐ iMovie ›
Twitter is a simple communication service made up of 140-character messages called Tweets.	📄 JotNot Pro ›
Learn More about Twitter	nest Nest ›
	NETFLIX Netflix ›

Each of these panels also offers an Install button (previous page, left), making it quick and easy to download the official Twitter, Facebook, Flickr, and Vimeo apps.

The Twitter and Facebook options offer some additional choices:

- **Twitter.** The Update Contacts button adds your friends' Twitter account names to their cards in Contacts, saving you that tedious data entry.

- **Facebook.** Tapping Settings summons some options that, by now, should be familiar: You can give it permission to know your location when you post to Facebook; you can tell the phone how to alert you when new Facebook posts arrive (Notifications); you can limit the app's updating itself in the background; and you can prevent it from using Cellular Data. You can also limit Facebook video recordings to standard definition, to avoid massive data charges.

  The Allow These Apps items let you control which built-in apps can access your Facebook account; for example, turn off Calendar if you don't want to see your Facebook friends' birthdays on your calendar.

  Finally, Update All Contacts is the powerful button that adds photos and Facebook account names to the corresponding friends' cards in your Contacts app, as described on page 114.

TV Provider

As noted on page 254, the new TV app is designed to let you watch all the shows you're paying your cable or satellite company for—on your phone. At the outset, alas, very few major cable companies are playing ball with Apple. You can sign in here if you have an account from DirecTV, Dish, or a few obscure cable companies. But if you have, say, Comcast, Time Warner, or another big one, you're probably out of luck.

App Preferences

At the bottom of the Settings screen, you see a list of apps that have installed settings screens of their own (previous page, right). For example, here's where you can edit your screen name and password for the AIM chat program, change how many days' worth of news you want the NY Times Reader to display, and so on. Each one offers an assortment of changeable preference options.

It can get to be a *very* long list.

PART FIVE

Appendixes

Appendix A
Signup & Setup

Appendix B
Troubleshooting & Maintenance

A

Signup & Setup

You gotta admit it: Opening up a new iPhone brings a certain excitement. There's a prospect of possibility, of new beginnings. Even if you intend to protect your iPhone with a case, there are those first few minutes when it's shiny, spotless, free of fingerprints or nicks—a gorgeous thing.

This chapter is all about getting started, whether that means buying and setting up a new iPhone, or upgrading an older model to the new iOS 10 software that's described in this book.

Buying a New iPhone

Each year's new iPhone model is faster, has a better camera and screen, and comes packed with more features than the previous one. Still, "new iPhone" doesn't have to mean the iPhone 7 ($650, either up front or spread out over 2 years) or 7 Plus ($770). You can still get an iPhone 6 for $550, or the SE for $400. (Thank heaven, the U.S. carriers no longer obscure the true price of the phone in 2-year contracts.) And, of course, you can get older models dirt cheap, used.

In any case, once you've chosen the model you want, you also have to choose which cellphone company you want to provide its service: AT&T, Verizon, T-Mobile, or Sprint. Each has something to offer.

Verizon has the best U.S. cellular coverage, and by far the most 4G LTE (high-speed Internet) areas. AT&T's high-speed Internet networks are faster than anyone else's. T-Mobile's plans cost the least in many ways (free texting and Internet when you're overseas; unlimited music and video without using up any of your data allowance; no 2-year contract; they'll pay off the early-termination fee if you switch from a rival carrier), but its phone network is the second smallest.

Research the coverage where you live and work. Each company's website shows a map of its coverage.

You can buy your iPhone from a phone store (Verizon, Sprint, T-Mobile, AT&T), an Apple Store, from a retail store (RadioShack, Walmart, and so on), or from the Apple website. You can buy the phone outright, or you can opt to have the price spread out in monthly payments. Or you can lease it.

All right then: Here you are in the store, or sitting down to do some ordering online. Here are some of the decisions you'll have to make:

- **Transferring your old number.** You can bring your old cellphone or home number to your new iPhone. Your friends can keep dialing your old number—but your iPhone will ring instead of the old phone.

  It usually takes under an hour for a cellphone-number transfer to take place. During that time, you can make calls on the iPhone, but you can't receive them.

NOTE: Transferring a landline number to your iPhone can take several *days*.

- **Select your monthly calling plans.** Signing up for cellphone service involves more red tape than a government contract. In essence, you have to choose *three* plans: one for voice calls, one for Internet service, and one for text messages. The variations are complicated, but a quick web search ("iPhone 7 plans compared") can help you make sense of them.

  The plan offerings change all the time, but here are some examples: For unlimited calling and texting, plus 4 gigabytes a month of Internet use, Verizon charges $70 plus fees, AT&T charges $80. T-Mobile and Sprint offer *unlimited* talk, text, and data (for $70 and $65, respectively).

  Of course, the problem with fixed data allotments is this: Who has any idea what 2 gigabytes of data is? How much of that do you eat up with email alone? How much is one YouTube video?

  As you approach your monthly limit, you'll get warnings by text message, but you can also see your data usage on your phone (see page 572). Yes, it's a pain to have to worry about data limits, but at least monitoring them is fairly easy. If you use more than your allotted amount, some carriers automatically bill a surcharge—for example, $15 for each additional gigabyte.

  All four cell companies offer unlimited free calls to other phones from the same company. All but the cheapest plans offer unlimited calls on nights and weekends.

  And all iPhone plans require an "activation fee" (ha!).

As you budget for your plan, keep in mind that, as with any cellphone, you'll also be paying taxes as high as 22 percent, depending on your state. Ouch.

Setting Up a New Phone

In the olden days, you couldn't use a new iPhone at all without hooking it up to a computer. Now, though, the setup takes place entirely on the phone's screen.

You don't need a computer to back up your phone, because iCloud backs it up. You don't need a computer to store your music and video collections, because the App Store remembers what you've bought and lets you re-download it at any time. You don't need a computer to download and install iPhone software updates, because they come straight to the phone now. You don't even need a computer to edit photos or to create mail folders; that's on the phone, too.

The first time you turn on a brand-new iPhone—or an older one that you've erased completely—the setup wizard appears. Swipe your finger where it says slide to set up. Now you're asked about 15 important questions:

- **Language; Country.** You won't get very far setting up your phone if you can't understand the instructions. So the very first step here is to tell it what language you speak. When you tap a language, you're next asked to tell the phone where in the world you live. (It proposes the country where you bought the phone. Clever, eh?)

- **Wi-Fi Networks.** Tap the name of the Wi-Fi network you want, enter the password if required, and tap Join.

  Or, if there's no Wi-Fi you can (or want to) hop onto right now, then tap Use Mobile Connection.

- **Location Services.** The iPhone knows where you are. That's how it can pinpoint you on a map, tag the photos you take with their geographic locations, find you a nearby Mexican restaurant, and so on.

  Some people are creeped out by the phone's knowing where they are, worrying that Apple, by extension, also knows where they are. So here's your chance to turn off all the iPhone's location features. Tap either **Enable Location Services** or **Disable Location Services**.

- **Touch ID.** If you have an iPhone 5s or later, you're now invited to teach it your fingerprint, for the purposes of unlocking it without having to type a password. See page 53 for more on registering fingerprints. (You can also tap **Set Up Touch ID Later**. When the time comes, you can revisit this process in **Settings→Touch ID & Passcode**.)

- **Passcode.** Whether you opted to store a fingerprint or not, you're now asked to make up a six-digit *passcode* (password) for unlocking your phone. You'll need it whenever the phone won't accept Touch ID—for example, after you've restarted the phone.

TIP: You don't have to accept iOS's proposal of a six-digit passcode. Tap **Passcode Options** to reveal more choices, like **Custom Alphanumeric Code** (any password you like, any length, any characters), **Custom Numeric Code** (any number of digits), or **4-Digit Numeric Code** (like in the old days).

- **Apps & Data.** If you've owned an iPhone before, or if you backed up this phone and then erased it, you don't have to load it up with all your apps and settings by hand. This screen offers to reload all your stuff from your most recent backup. (See chapters 15 and 16 for details on iPhone backups.)

  Tap **Restore from iCloud Backup** (if your backup was on iCloud) or **Restore from iTunes Backup** (if your backup was on your computer).

  If you've never owned an iPhone before, you can choose **Set Up as New iPhone** to start fresh.

  There's even an option here—sneaky, Apple!—called **Move Data from Android**. You download a companion app on your old Android phone (called Move to iOS). When you open it, the app (on Android) asks you to enter a number code that's offered by your iPhone at this stage. Then the Android phone asks what kinds of data you'd like copied to your iPhone: your Google account (email, calendar, and so on), web bookmarks, text messages, contacts, and photos (Camera Roll). When you hit **Next**, the transfer begins, wirelessly and automatically.

- **Apple ID.** A million features require an Apple ID—just about any transaction you make with Apple online. Buying anything from Apple, from a song to a laptop. Using iCloud (Chapter 16). Playing games against other people online. Making an appointment at an Apple Store.

  If you already have an Apple ID, tap **Sign In with Your Apple ID** and enter it here. If not, tap **Create a Free Apple ID**. You'll be asked to

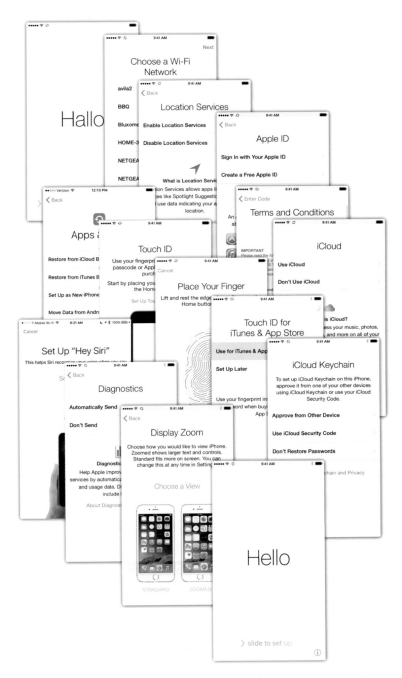

provide your name, birthday, email address (or you can create a new iCloud email address), a password of your choice, and answers to a few security questions (you'll have to get them right if you ever forget your password). You also get to decide if you'd like the honor of receiving junk email from Apple.

(You can tap **Skip This Step** if you don't want an Apple ID, at least for now. You can get one later in Settings.)

- **Terms and Conditions**. On the screen full of legalese, tap **Agree**, and then **Agree**.

- **Apple Pay.** Next up: If you have an iPhone 5s or later, you're now invited to store your credit cards, for the purpose of turning on Apple Pay. The process is described on page 536.

  If you don't want to use Apple Pay, or don't want to set it up now, hit **Next** anyway, and then hit **Set Up Later in Wallet**.

- **iCloud Keychain** is a terrific feature. It stores all your web user names and passwords—and even credit card numbers—so you don't have to memorize them and type them in over and over. It's all synchronized across all your Apple machines (iPhone, iPad, Mac, and so on).

  If you take this opportunity to set it up, you're asked what you want to use as your iCloud Security Code. That's yet another passcode, which you may need someday to recover all your passwords if you have a really lousy day and lose *all* your Apple gadgets. Fortunately, the iPhone offers to use your iPhone passcode (the one you've already set up) as your iCloud Security Code, so you don't have another code to remember.

  On the next screen, you're supposed to enter a phone number—yours or that of "someone you trust"—which Apple will use as a secondary way to verify your identity if you have to recover your iCloud Keychain without having any of your Apple gadgets available.

- **Siri.** Here's your chance to set up Siri, the greatest phone advance in 15 years. If you want to be able to use the "Hey Siri" hands-free mode (page 148), you're supposed to speak a few sample sentences so that Siri learns your voice. Tap **Set Up Siri** to do that now, or hit **Turn On Siri Later** if you don't want Siri at all, or want to do the setup later (in **Settings→Siri**).

- **Diagnostics.** Behind the scenes, your iPhone sends records back to Apple, including your location and what you're doing on your iPhone. By analyzing this data en masse, Apple can figure out where the dead spots in the cellular network are, how to fix bugs, and so on. The information is anonymous—it's not associated with you. But if the very idea seems invasive, here's your chance to prevent this data from being sent.

- **Meet the New Home Button.** On the iPhone 7 or 7 Plus, this screen appears to introduce the clickless Home button (page 7)—and to invite you to choose how hard its click feels (page 575).

- **Display Zoom.** On bigger-screened phones like the iPhone 6, 6s, and 7 models, you get this choice. It asks how you want to exploit the larger screen. If you choose Standard, you'll see more stuff (icons, menus, lines of text) per screenful than on smaller iPhones. If you choose Zoomed, then you'll see the same amount of stuff, but *bigger*. (The one exception: You may not get as many extra buttons on the widescreen keyboard described on page 78.) You can always change your mind in Settings→Display & Brightness.

- **Welcome to iPhone.** Your phone is set up. Tap Get Started to jump to the Home screen.

> **NOTE:** A new iPhone no longer asks if you want to turn on Find My iPhone. It's turned on automatically; see page 530. It also no longer asks if you want to download the free iCloud Drive app (page 351)—but you should.

Upgrading an iPhone to iOS 10

If you bought a new iPhone SE, 6s, 6s Plus, 7 or 7 Plus, great! iOS 10 (or one of its successors, like iOS 10.2) comes on it preinstalled.

But you can also upgrade an older or used iPhone to this new software in any of three ways:

- **Upgrade it wirelessly.** *Upgrading* means installing iOS 10 on top of whatever is already on your iPhone. You don't lose any data or settings.

  This is the easiest way to upgrade. You've probably already seen the little red number on your Settings app icon (see page 44), and on the word "General" inside it; the phone is trying to tell you that iOS 10 is ready to download. Tap Settings→General→Software Update to see the iOS 10 info; tap Download and Install. (You have to be on a Wi-Fi network, and it's wise to have your iPhone plugged into power.)

- **Upgrade it from iTunes.** If you wish, you can also perform the upgrade using the iTunes program on your computer. This method takes less time but, of course, requires being at your computer.

  To begin, connect your iPhone and click its icon at top left (see page 510). On the Summary tab, click Check for Update, and then click Download and Update.

- **Restore it.** This is a more dramatic step, which you should choose only if you've been having problems with your phone or if, for some other reason, you would like to start completely fresh. This step backs up the phone, erases it completely, installs iOS, and then copies your stuff back onto the phone.

Connect the phone to your computer, open iTunes, and then click Restore iPhone.

The updating or restoring process takes awhile. You'll see the iPhone restart. When it's all over, the PC-free setup process described on the previous pages begins automatically.

Software Updates

As you're probably aware, phone software like the iPhone's is a perpetual work in progress. Apple constantly fixes bugs, adds features, and makes tweaks to extend battery life and improve other services.

Updating Directly on the Phone

One day you'll be minding your own business, and you'll see a red numbered badge appear on the Settings app's icon on the phone. Open Settings→General→Software Update to read about the new update and install it. Note, though, that unless it's plugged into a power source, your phone won't install an iOS update unless its battery is at least half full.

Install Updates from Your Computer

Maybe you're not that adventurous and you'd prefer to install your software update the old-fashioned way.

No problem: Connect the iPhone to iTunes, wirelessly or not (page 510). Then click the iPhone's icon in iTunes; on the Summary pane, tap Check for Update.

Restrictions and Parental Controls

If you're issuing an iPhone to a child, or someone who acts like one, you'll be gratified to discover that iOS offers a good deal of protection. That's protection of your offspring's delicate sensibilities (it can block pornography and dirty words) and protection of your bank account (it can block purchases of music, movies, and apps without your permission).

To set this up, visit Settings→General→Restrictions. When you tap Enable Restrictions, you're asked to make up a four-digit passcode that permits only you, the all-knowing parent, to make changes to these settings. (Or you, the corporate IT administrator who's doling out iPhones to the white-collar drones.)

Once you've changed the settings described on these pages, the only way to change them again (when your kid turns 18, for example) is to return to the Restrictions page and correctly enter the passcode. That's also the only way to turn off the entire Restrictions feature (tap Disable Restrictions and correctly enter the passcode). To turn it back on, you have to make up a passcode all over again.

Once Restrictions is turned on, you can put up data blockades in a number of different categories.

••○○○ Verizon 🔆	9:57 PM	✈ ✳ 90% ⬛️
‹ General	**Restrictions**	

Disable Restrictions

ALLOW:

🧭 Safari	⬤◯
📷 Camera	⬤◯
📹 FaceTime	⬤◯
🎙 Siri & Dictation	⬤◯
📡 AirDrop	⬤◯
▶️ CarPlay	⬤◯
🎵 iTunes Store	⬤◯
📖 iBooks Store	⬤◯

••○○○ Verizon 🔆	9:57 PM	✈ ✳ 90% ⬛️
‹ General	**Restrictions**	

ALLOWED CONTENT:

Ratings For	United States >
Music, Podcasts & News	Expl... >
Movies	All >
TV Shows	All >
Books	All >
Apps	All >
Siri	All >
Websites	All >

PRIVACY:

Allow

For starters, you can turn off access to iPhone features that locked-down corporations might not want their employees—or parents might not want their children—to use, because they're considered either security holes, time drains, or places to spend your money: Safari (can't use the web at all), Camera, FaceTime, Siri & Dictation, FaceTime, AirDrop, or CarPlay

(Apple's specialized connection for certain car models, in which your iPhone's relevant icons appear on the car's dashboard screen).

A second list of options lets you block access to iTunes Store, iBooks Store, iMusic Connect, and News—and turn off the option to download Podcasts. You can stop your kid from Installing Apps or Deleting Apps, too. And you can turn off In-App Purchases so that your offspring won't be able to buy new material (game levels, book chapters, and so on) from within an app that you've already bought.

Many of these restrictions work by *removing icons altogether* from the iPhone's Home screen: Safari, iTunes, and Camera, for example. When the switch says Off, the corresponding icon has been taken off the Home screen and can't be found even by Spotlight searches.

Allowed Content

Here you can spare your children's sensitive eyes and ears by blocking inappropriate material.

Ratings are a big deal; they determine the effectiveness of the parental controls described in this section. Since every country has its own rating schemes (for movies, TV shows, games, song lyrics, and so on), you use the Ratings For control to tell the iPhone which country's rating system you want to use.

Once that's done, you can use the Music, Podcasts, News, iTunes U, Movies, TV Shows, Books, and Apps controls to specify what your kid is allowed to watch, play, read, and listen to. For example, you can tap Movies and then tap PG-13; any movies rated "higher," like R or NC-17, won't play on the iPhone now. (And if your sneaky offspring try to buy these naughty songs, movies, or TV shows wirelessly from the iTunes Store, they'll discover that the Buy button is dimmed and unavailable.)

For some categories, like Music, Podcasts & News, and Siri, you can turn off Explicit to prevent the iPhone from playing iTunes Store songs that contain naughty language, or speaking them.

Websites lets you shield impressionable young eyes from pornography online. It offers these settings:

- **All Websites.** No protection at all.

- **Limit Adult Content.** Apple will apply its own judgment in blocking dirty websites, using a blocked-site list that it has compiled.

  That doesn't mean you can't override Apple's wisdom, however. The Always Allow and Never Allow controls let you add the addresses of websites that you think should be OK (or should not be OK).

- **Specific Websites Only.** This is a "whitelist" feature. It means that the entire web is blocked except for the few sites listed here: safe bets like Disney, PBS Kids, Smithsonian Institution, and so on. You can add your own sites to this list, but the point is clear: This is the web with training wheels.

Privacy

These switches can prohibit the unauthorized user from making changes to the phone's privacy settings, which are described on page 585.

Allow Changes

These items (Accounts, Cellular Data Use, Background App Refresh, Volume Limit) are safeguards against your offspring fiddling with limits you've set.

Game Center

These controls let you stop your kid from playing multiplayer games (against strangers online), screen recording in games, or adding game-playing friends to the center.

Cases and Accessories

The iPhone has inspired a torrent of accessories. Stylish cases, speakers, docks, cables—the list goes on forever.

Just be sure you're buying something that fits your phone. For example, the Lightning connector (where the charging cable connects) on the iPhone 5 and later doesn't fit any of the charging accessories that came before it—at least not without the help of Apple's $30 adapter (or the $40 adapter that has an 8-inch cable "tail").

Accessory companies have been busy introducing Lightning-compatible gear. But for now, buyer beware—or buyer stock up on $30 adapters.

So what might you add to your iPhone?

- **Cases.** It's the iPhone Paradox: People buy the thinnest, sleekest smartphone in existence—and then bury it in a bulky carrying case. There's just something so wrong about that. On the other hand, this thing is made of glass; the instinct to protect it is understandable.

  Hundreds of cases are available. If you're worried about droppage, choose a silicone rubber case; it does a better job of protecting your phone than hard plastic cases. You can also get cases with built-in battery backups, credit card slots, and even speakers.

- **Everything else.** Speaker docks. Bluetooth speakers. Headphones and earbuds, wired and cordless. Credit card readers. Car cigarette-lighter adapters. Alarm clocks. Video-out cables. Stylish styluses. Touchscreen-compatible gloves. Tripods. Panorama stands. Kickstands. Car mounts. Activity monitors. Lenses. You Google it, you'll find it. The iPhone is, without a doubt, the most accessorized phone in the world.

B

Troubleshooting & Maintenance

The iPhone is a computer, and you know what that means: Things can go wrong. This particular computer, though, is not quite like a Mac or a PC. It runs a spin-off of the macOS operating system, but that doesn't mean you can apply the same troubleshooting techniques.

Therefore, let this appendix be your guide when things go wrong.

First Rule: Install the Updates

There's an old saying: "Never buy version 1.0 of anything." In the iPhone's case, the saying could be: "Never buy version 10.0 of anything."

The very first version (or major revision) of anything has bugs, glitches, and things the programmers didn't have time to finish the way they would have liked. The iPhone is no exception.

The beauty of this phone, though, is that Apple can send it fixes, patches, and even new features through software updates. One day you'll glance at your Home screen's Settings icon, and—bam!—there'll be a badge indicating that new iPhone software is available.

So the first rule of trouble-free iPhoning is to accept these updates when they're offered. With each new software blob, Apple removes another few dozen tiny glitches.

And sure enough: Within the first few weeks of iOS 10's existence, software updates 10.1 and 10.2 came down the pike. And more will come.

Six Ways to Reset the Phone

The iPhone runs actual programs, and as actual programs do, they actually crash. Sometimes, the program you're working in simply vanishes and you find yourself back at the Home screen. Just reopen the program and get on with your life.

If the program you're in just doesn't seem to be working right—it's frozen or acting weird, for example—then one of these resetting techniques usually clears things right up.

NOTE: Proceed down this list in order! Start with the easy ones.

- **Exit the app.** On an iPhone, you're never aware that you're launching and exiting programs. They're always just *there*, like TV channels, when you switch to them. There's no Quit command. But if a program starts acting glitchy, you can make it quit.

  To do that, double-press the Home button to bring up the app switcher. Find the "card" that represents your balky app, and then flick it upward to quit it. Try reopening it to see if the problem has gone away.

- **Turn the phone off and on again.** If it seems something more serious has gone wrong, then hold down the Sleep switch for a few seconds. When the screen says slide to power off, confirm by swiping. The iPhone shuts off completely.

  Turn it back on by pressing the Sleep switch for a second or two.

- **Force-restart the phone.** If you haven't been able to force quit the program, and you can't shut the phone off either, you might have to force a restart. To do that, hold down the Home button *and* the Sleep switch for 10 seconds.

NOTE: On the iPhone 7 and 7 Plus, hold down the *Volume Down* key (on the left edge) and the Sleep switch. (Why not the Home button, as on earlier models? Because the Home button isn't actually a moving button anymore—and when your phone is crashed and locked, it won't do anything.)

Keep holding, even if the screen goes black or you see the "power off" slider. Don't release until you see the Apple logo appear, meaning that the phone is restarting.

- **Reset the settings.** Relax. This procedure doesn't erase any of your data—only the phone's settings. From the Home screen, tap Settings→General→Reset→Reset All Settings.

- **Erase the whole phone.** From the Home screen, tap Settings→ General→Reset→Erase All Content and Settings. Now, *this* option zaps your stuff—*all* of it. Music, videos, email, settings, apps, all gone, and all overwritten with random 1's and 0's to make sure it's completely unrecoverable. Clearly, you're getting into last resorts here. Of course, you can then sync with your backup (iTunes or iCloud) to copy all that stuff back onto your iPhone.

- **Restore the phone.** If none of these steps solve the phone's glitchiness, it might be time for the nuclear option: erasing it completely, resetting both hardware and software back to a factory-fresh condition.

TIP: If you're able to sync the phone with iCloud or iTunes *first*, do it! That way, you'll have a backup of all those intangible iPhone data bits: text messages, call logs, Recents list, and so on. iTunes will put it all back onto the phone the first time you sync after the restore.

If you backed up to iTunes: Connect the phone to your computer, as described in Chapter 15. In iTunes, click the iPhone icon and then, on the Summary tab, click **Restore**.

The first order of business: iTunes offers to make a backup of your iPhone (all of its phone settings, text messages, and so on) before proceeding. Accepting this invitation is an excellent idea. Click **Back Up**.

If you backed up to iCloud: You can restore your phone this way only if your iPhone is completely wiped empty. If it's not, manually erase it using iTunes first.

During the setup screens described on page 613, tap Restore from iCloud Backup. You're shown the three most recent backups; tap the one you want. The phone goes right to work downloading your settings and account information. Then it restarts and begins to download your apps; if you're in a hurry for one particular app, tap its icon to make iCloud prioritize it. At any time, you can check the restore process's status in Settings→iCloud→Storage and Backup.

When that's all over, you can get to work downloading your music (if you're an Apple Music subscriber).

iPhone Doesn't Turn On

Usually, the problem is that the battery's dead. Just plugging it into the USB charger or your computer doesn't bring it to life immediately, either; a completely dead iPhone doesn't wake up until it's been charging for about 10 minutes. It pops on automatically when it has enough juice to do so.

If you don't think that's the trouble, try the force-restarting trick described earlier. And if even that doesn't work, read on.

The Force Restore

If your phone gets stuck starting up at the Apple logo, or it just stays black, then something more serious may have happened. Phones, like the best of us, sometimes get confused.

The solution is the drastic, but effective, force-restore process (known to techies as the Default Firmware Update mode).

Open iTunes on your computer. Connect the iPhone with its white USB cable. Now hold down the Sleep switch and Home button (Sleep switch and Volume Down key on the iPhone 7 and 7 Plus) simultaneously for 10 seconds—then release *only* the Sleep switch.

Keep the Home button (or volume key) pressed until iTunes tells you that an iPhone in Recovery mode has been detected; click OK. (If you see anything but blackness on your iPhone's screen—an Apple logo, for example—then the process didn't work. If the problem has not, in fact, gone away, then you should start again.)

iTunes tells you again that you're in Recovery mode and offers only one button: **Restore iPhone**. Click that, and then confirm by clicking **Restore & Update**. The process of reinstalling the latest, fresh copy of iOS begins.

> **TIP:** Every now and then, the cycle of backing up and restoring goes amiss. You find yourself stuck at that **Restore iPhone** button—but you don't want to wipe it empty! There's stuff on it that hasn't been backed up!
>
> In that case, download the free program called RecBoot (for Mac) or TinyUmbrella (Mac or Windows). (You can download them from this book's "Missing CD" page at *www.missingmanuals.com*.) They have one tiny purpose in life: exiting Restore mode without erasing your phone.

Once everything's running fine, you can restore all your apps and settings from the latest backup as described on page 625.

Battery Life Is Terrible

If your battery seems to drain faster after you've installed iOS 10, it might be because the Photos app is busy scanning and categorizing all your photos so that it can use its object and facial recognition.

Or maybe it's just you *using* the phone more, checking out the cool new features.

If neither of those is the problem, then consult the battery-saving tips on page 39.

Out of Space

It happens all the time. You couldn't imagine filling up 64, 128, or 256 gigabytes of storage, so you saved some money by buying an iPhone with less. And now you can't even take a video or a photo, because your phone reports that it's full. You're frozen out until you have the time and expertise to delete some less important stuff.

The biggest space hogs on your phone are video files, photo files, apps, and music files. Heck, deleting just one downloaded movie or TV show could solve your storage crunch instantly.

Fortunately, iOS makes it easy to see what's eating up your space—and to delete the fattest ones to make the most room with the least effort.

‹ Usage Storage

STORAGE

🌸	Photos & Camera	9.5 GB	›
💬	Messages	5.0 GB	›
▶▶▶	Videos	1.7 GB	›
⎺⎺	Voice Memos	1.0 GB	›
📻	Podcasts	1.0 GB	›
⭐	iMovie	1.0 GB	›
📷	JotNot Pro	802 MB	›
🧭	Safari	459 MB	›
🎆	iPhoto	314 MB	›
f	Facebook	175 MB	›

‹ Storage Videos Edit

MOVIES		1.7 GB
	Goldfinger	1.7 GB
TV SHOWS		493 MB
	LOST	493 MB ›
VIDEO PODCASTS		45.2 MB
	NYT's Circuits wit...	45.2 MB

26.6 GB available on iPhone

The key is to visit Settings→General→Storage & iCloud Usage→Manage Storage.

The list here shows what's using up your space, biggest first; by tapping the › button, you can see the details and, in most cases, make some deletions on the spot.

Delete Photos and Recorded Videos

This display shows how much space your Camera videos and photos take up, but unfortunately it doesn't let you delete them. To purge your photos, the quickest method is to hook up to iTunes, import the photos, and take advantage of the option to delete the freshly imported photos from the phone (page 520).

Turning off your Photo Stream can give you back an instant gigabyte, too (page 316).

And if solving the problem is worth a few bucks, don't forget that you can have Apple store all the full-size copies of your photos online, leaving only screen-sized versions on the phone for showing off—a sure way to ease your storage crunch. Details on page 323.

Delete "Other" Items

You know the colored graph of what's on your phone that shows up in iTunes (page 511)? Often, the biggest item here is the mysterious Other category. What is that stuff? It's caches (Internet data stored on the phone to make repeated visits faster), backups, partial downloads, and data from iOS's built-in apps—all your text messages and email, for example. Here's how you clean them out:

- **Delete the web browser cache.** The phone saves web pages into its own memory so they'll appear faster the next time you try to visit them. If you've had your iPhone awhile, those cache files can really add up. Open Settings→Safari; tap Clear History and Website Data. You may get a speed boost as a side effect.

- **Delete text messages.** In the Messages app, you can delete individual texts or entire conversations (page 179); because they frequently include photo, audio, or video files, you can reclaim a lot of space.

- **Delete email attachments.** Files downloaded with your email take up a lot of space, too. The solution is to delete the email account (Settings→Mail→[account name]; scroll down and tap Delete Account)—and then add it again.

  In the process, you'll vaporize all the attachment files and message caches that you've ever downloaded and opened on your phone. When you add the account back again, those files will still be online, ready to download—but only when you need them. (This trick works for most account types—just not for POP3 accounts.)

- **Delete voice memos, music files, and ebooks.** Audio files and ebooks eat up a lot of space, too. Consider purging the recordings, books, and songs you can do without (from within the Voice Memos, iBooks, and Music apps). You can re-download them later from the App, iTunes, or iBooks Stores—no charge—whenever you like.

- **Delete offline reading and saved web articles.** Open Safari's Reading List and delete any pages you have already read or no longer need. Do the same with saved articles in the News app.

Phone and Internet Problems

How can the phone part of the iPhone go wrong? Let us count the ways:

- **Can't make calls.** First off, do you have enough cellular signal to make a call? Check your signal-strength dots. Even if you have one or two, flakiness is par for the course, although one bar in a 3G, 4G, or LTE area is much better than one bar in a slower area. Try going outside, standing near a window, or moving to a major city (kidding).

Also, make sure airplane mode isn't turned on. Try calling somebody else to make sure the problem isn't with the number you're dialing.

If nothing else works, try the resetting techniques described starting on page 623.

- **Can't receive calls.** If calls seem to go directly to voicemail and the phone never even rings, check to make sure Do Not Disturb isn't turned on (page 128).

- **Can't get on the Internet.** If you're not in a Wi-Fi hotspot (there's no ●●○○○ at the top of the screen) and you don't have cell service (no **E**, **○**, **3G**, **4G**, or **LTE** logo at the top of the screen), well, then, you're in a "No Service" area, or the phone thinks you are. (In the latter case, try turning the phone off and then on again.)

- **Can't send text messages.** Make sure, of course, that you've signed up for a texting plan. Also, make sure you haven't turned on Show Subject Field (page 198) and forgotten to fill out the body of the message.

Warranty and Repair

The iPhone comes with a one-year warranty and 90 days of phone tech support. If you buy an AppleCare+ contract ($100), you're covered for a second year.

> **TIP:** AT&T, Sprint, T-Mobile, or Verizon tech support is free for both years of your contract. They handle questions about your iPhone's phone features.

If, during the coverage period, anything goes wrong that's not your fault, Apple will fix it free. In fact, AppleCare+ covers damage even if it *is* your fault—if you drop the phone or something—at a rate of $30 for screen damage and $100 for other damage, plus tax. Maximum: twice.

If you don't have AppleCare+, the repair fee depends on the type of phone you have but will probably set you back around $300.

You can either take the phone to an Apple Store, which is often the fastest route, or call 800-APL-CARE (800-275-2273) to arrange shipping back to Apple. In general, you'll get the fixed phone back in 3 business days.

Out-of-Warranty Repairs

Once the year or two has gone by, or if you damage your iPhone in a way that's not covered by the warranty (backing your car over it comes to mind), Apple charges $200 to repair an iPhone (it usually just replaces it).

The Battery Replacement Program

Why did Apple seal the battery inside the iPhone, anyway? Everyone knows lithium-ion batteries don't last forever. After 300 or 400 charges, the iPhone's battery begins to hold less charge (perhaps 80 percent of the original). After a certain point, the phone will need a new battery. How come you can't change it yourself, as on any normal cellphone?

Apple's answer: A user-replaceable battery takes up a lot more space inside the phone. It requires a plastic compartment that shields the guts of the phone from you and your fingers; it requires a removable door; and it needs springs or clips to hold the battery in place.

In any case, you can't change the battery yourself. If the phone is out of warranty, you must send it to Apple (or take it to an Apple Store) for an $79 battery-replacement job. (As an eco-bonus, Apple properly disposes of the old batteries, which consumers might not do on their own.)

What to Do About a Cracked Screen

Keeping your iPhone in a case may lower the chances of your dropping it or scratching it—but it can't prevent bad luck. An incredible number of iPhone screens meet an untimely end, even with cases on.

Apple will happily replace your phone's screen for $130 to $150, depending on the model. It'll do it the same day if you take the phone into an Apple Store, or you can mail it in and get a replacement in 3 to 5 days.

(If you've bought the AppleCare+ extended-warranty service, then a replacement is $50 to $100, depending on the model.)

There are plenty of other companies that can repair a cracked screen, though. The reps from *iCracked.com*, for example, send a technician to you and perform the fix on the spot.

And then there's the do-it-yourself technique. You can buy a screen-replacement kit for about $60 online, complete with the special tools you need to open the iPhone and do the job yourself. It requires care, patience, and some dexterity (Google can help you find the step-by-steps), but it's a good option if you're technically savvy.

Where to Go from Here

At this point, the iPhone is such a phenomenon that there's no shortage of resources for getting more help, news, and tips. Here are a few examples:

- **Apple's official iPhone User Guide.** Yes, there is an actual downloadable PDF user's manual for iOS 10. *help.apple.com/iphone/10*

- **Apple's official iPhone help website.** Online tips, tricks, and tutorials; troubleshooting topics; downloadable PDF help documents; and, above all, an enormous, seething treasure trove of discussion boards. *www.apple.com/support/iphone*

- **Apple's service site.** All the dates, prices, and expectations for getting your iPhone repaired. Includes details on getting a temporary replacement unit. *www.apple.com/support/iphone/service/faq*

- **iMore blog.** News, tips, tricks, all in a blog format. *www.imore.com*

- **iLounge.** Another great blog-format site. Available in an iPhone format so you can read it right on the device. *www.iLounge.com*

- **MacRumors/iPhone.** Blog-format news, accessory blurbs, help discussions; iPhone wallpaper. *www.macrumors.com/iphone*

Index

I

THE MISSING CD

There's no
CD with this book;
you just saved $5.

Instead, every single web address, practice
file, and piece of downloadable software
mentioned in this book is available at
missingmanuals.com (click the Missing
CD icon). There you'll find a tidy
list of links, organized
by chapter.

WITHDRAWN

31901060378819